Ordnance
Survey
Ireland

National Mapping Agency
www.osi.ie

Route Planner	I
M50 Map	II
Outer Orbital Route	III
Inner Orbital Route	IV
Dart, Luas and Suburban Rail Network	V
Dublin Bus Route Network	VI
Dublin City and District Maps	1-68
City Centre Maps	69-76
Town Maps	77-92

Town Maps:
77	Ashbourne	86	Dunshaughlin
79	Balbriggan	87	Kilcock
81	Blessington	88	Lusk
82	Clane	89	Rush
83	Delgany/Greystones	91	Ratoath
85	Donabate	92	Skerries

Tourist Information	93-94
Embassies	95
List of Hospitals	96
Industrial Estates and Business Parks	97-98
Street Index	99

GW00418740

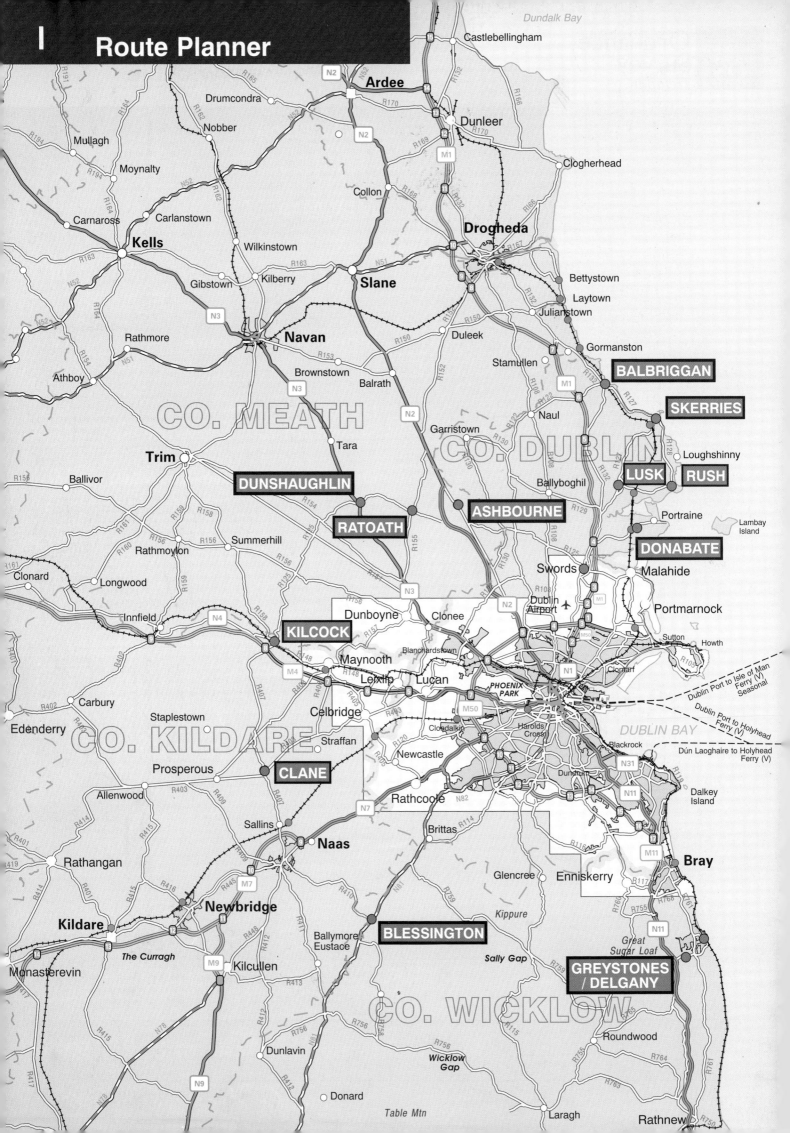

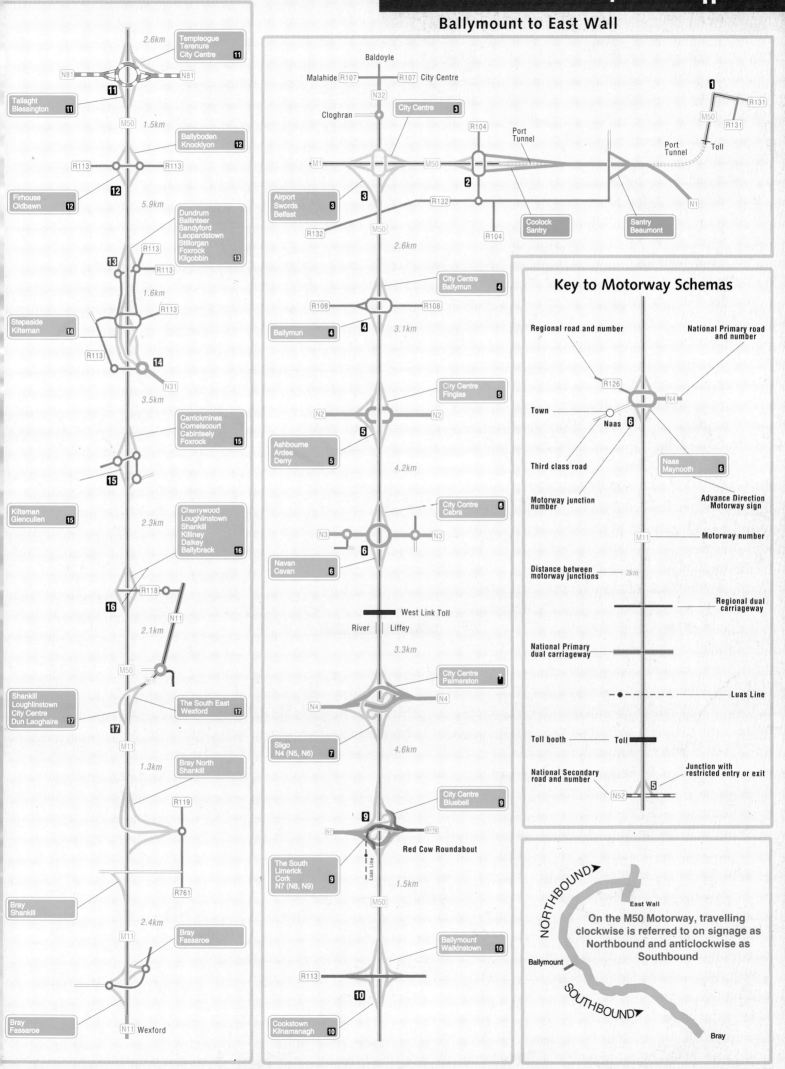

Outer Orbital Route

III

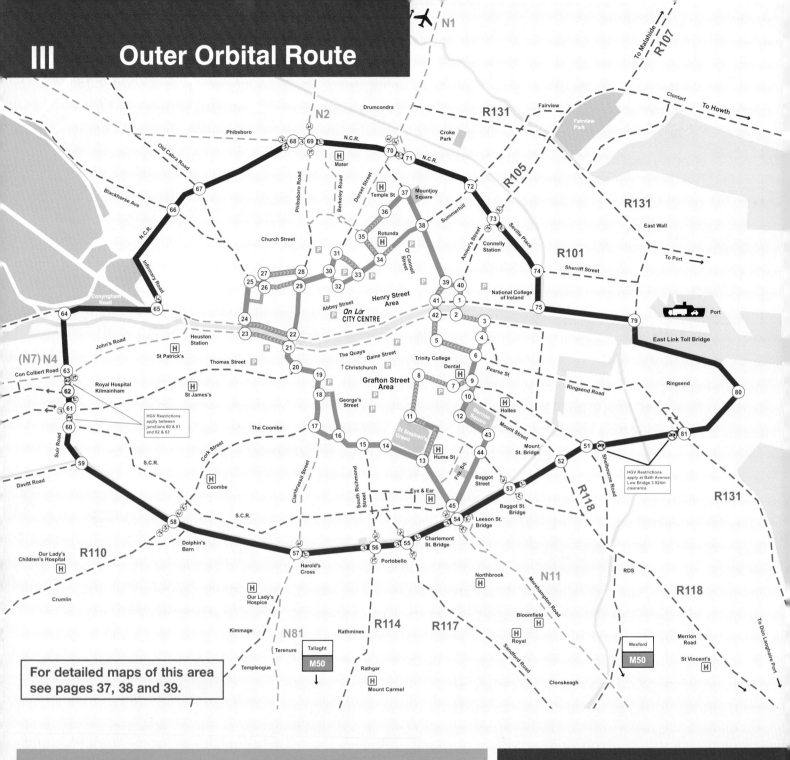

For detailed maps of this area see pages 37, 38 and 39.

INNER ORBITAL JUNCTIONS INDEX

J1 Custom House Quay / Talbot Memorial Bridge

J2 Talbot Memorial Bridge / City Quay

J3 City Quay/Lombard St. East

J4 Lombard St. East / Townsend St.

J5 Pearse St. / Tara St.

J6 Pearse St. / Westland Row

J7 Clare St./Lincoln Place

J8 Dawson St. / Nassau St.

J9 Lincoln Place / Westland Row

J10 Clare St. / Merrion Square

J11 St. Stephen's Green / Dawson St.

J12 Merrion St. Upr/Merrion Sq. Sth.

J13 St. Stephen's Green / Leeson St. Lwr.

J14 St. Stephen's Green / Harcourt St.

J15 Wexford St. / Kevin St. Lwr.

J16 Kevin St. / Bride St.

J17 Kevin St. / Patrick St.

J18 Bride Rd. / Patrick St.

J19 Christchurch Place/High St.

J20 High St. / Cornmarket

J21 Bridge St./Merchant's Quay

J22 Inns Quay / Church St.

J23 Ushers Island / Blackhall Place Bridge

J24 Ellis Quay / Blackhall Place Bridge

J25 Blackhall Place / King St.

J26 King St. / George's Lane

J27 George's Lane / Brunswick St. Nth

J28 Brunswick St. Nth. / Church St. Upr

J29 King St. / Church St.

J30 Nth. King St. / Bolton St.

J31 Bolton St. / King's Inns St.

J32 Parnell St. / Ryder's Row

J33 Parnell St. / King's Inns St.

J34 Parnell St. / Parnell Square West

J35 Parnell Square West / Granby Row

J36 Parnell Sq. Nth. / Frederick St. Nth.

J37 Gardiner St. Upr. / Mountjoy Square

J38 Summerhill / Gardiner St.

J39 Gardiner St. Lwr. / Beresford Place

J40 Amiens St./Beresford Place

J41 Eden Quay / Butt Bridge

J42 Tara St./Butt Bridge/Burgh Quay

J43 Merrion Sq. Sth. / Fitzwilliam St. Lwr

J44 Fitzwilliam St. Lwr / Baggot St. Lwr

J45 Fitzwilliam Place / Leeson St. Lwr

OUTER ORBITAL JUNCTIONS INDEX

J51 Shelbourne Rd / Haddington Rd

J52 Mount St. Lwr. / Haddington Rd

J53 Baggot St. Br. / Mespil Rd

J54 Leeson St. Br. /Grand Parade

J55 Charlemont St. Br. / Ranelagh Rd.

J56 Portobello / Rathmines Rd

J57 Harold's Cross Br. / Clanbrassil St.

J58 Dolphin's Barn / Crumlin Rd.

J59 Davitt Rd. / Suir Rd.

J60 Suir Rd. / SCR

J61 SCR / Old Kilmainham

J62 SCR / Inchicore Rd.

J63 SCR / St. John's Rd. West

J64 SCR / Conyngham Rd.

J65 Parkgate / Infirmary Rd.

J66 NCR / Blackhorse Ave.

J67 NCR / Prussia St.

J68 NCR / Cabra Rd.

J69 NCR / Phibsboro Rd.

J70 NCR / Dorset St. Lower

J71 NCR / Belvidere Road

J72 NCR / Summerhill

J73 Amiens St. / Seville Pl.

J74 Sheriff St. / Guild St.

J75 Guild St. / North Wall Quay

J79 North Wall Quay / East Link Br.

J80 Sean Moore Rd. / South Bank Rd.

J81 Sean Moore Rd. / Beach Rd.

Inner Orbital Route   IV

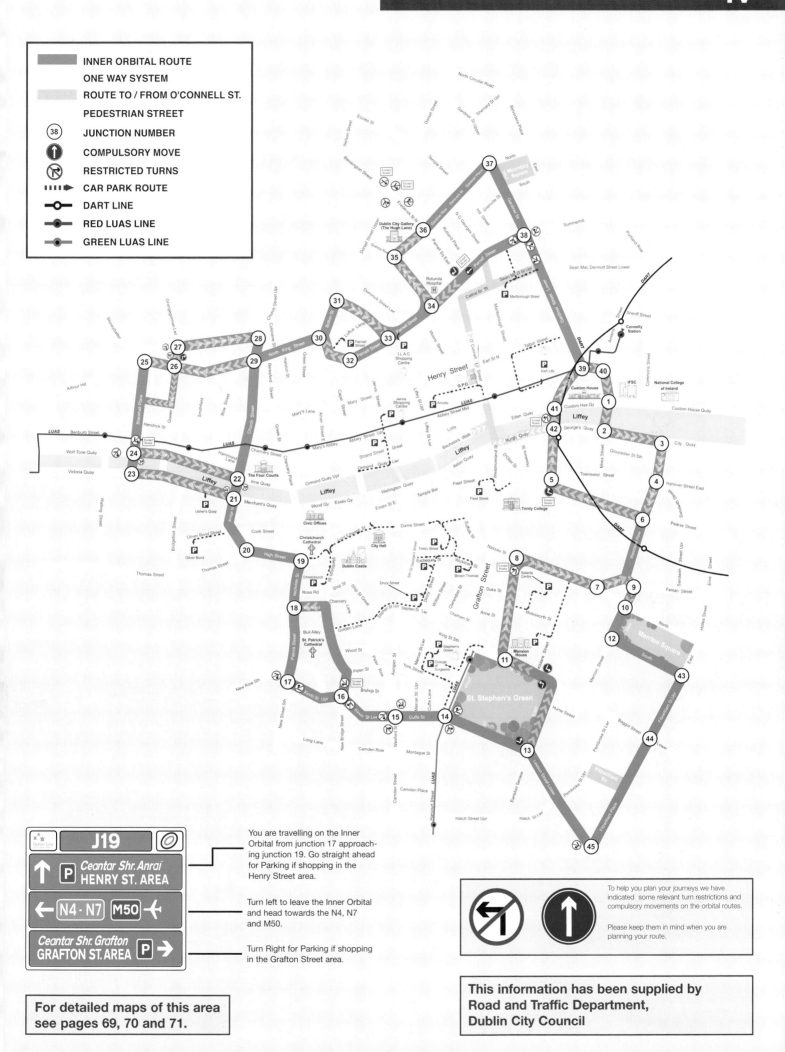

LEGEND

INNER ORBITAL ROUTE
ONE WAY SYSTEM
ROUTE TO / FROM O'CONNELL ST.
PEDESTRIAN STREET
(38) JUNCTION NUMBER
COMPULSORY MOVE
RESTRICTED TURNS
CAR PARK ROUTE
DART LINE
RED LUAS LINE
GREEN LUAS LINE

J19

P Ceantar Shr. Anraí
HENRY ST. AREA

← N4 - N7 M50 →

Ceantar Shr. Grafton P →
GRAFTON ST. AREA

You are travelling on the Inner Orbital from junction 17 approaching junction 19. Go straight ahead for Parking if shopping in the Henry Street area.

Turn left to leave the Inner Orbital and head towards the N4, N7 and M50.

Turn Right for Parking if shopping in the Grafton Street area.

For detailed maps of this area see pages 69, 70 and 71.

To help you plan your journeys we have indicated some relevant turn restrictions and compulsory movements on the orbital routes.

Please keep them in mind when you are planning your route.

This information has been supplied by **Road and Traffic Department, Dublin City Council**

V Dart, Luas and Suburban Rail Network

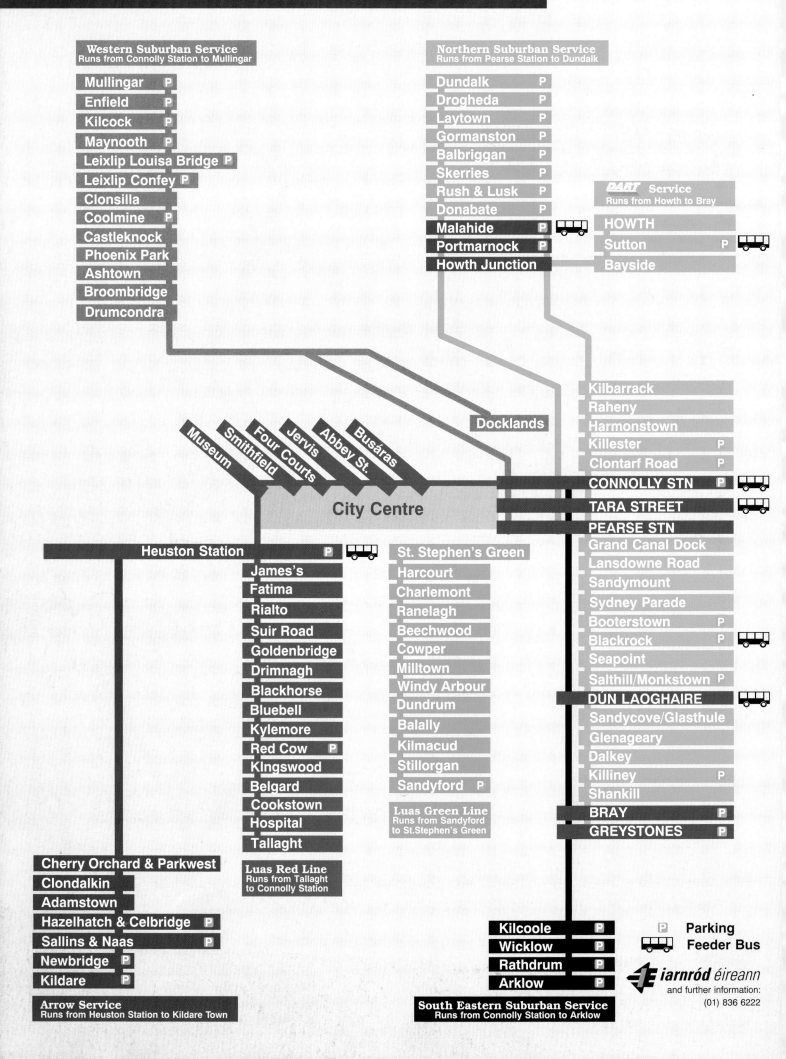

Western Suburban Service
Runs from Connolly Station to Mullingar

- Mullingar P
- Enfield P
- Kilcock P
- Maynooth P
- Leixlip Louisa Bridge P
- Leixlip Confey P
- Clonsilla
- Coolmine P
- Castleknock
- Phoenix Park
- Ashtown
- Broombridge
- Drumcondra

Northern Suburban Service
Runs from Pearse Station to Dundalk

- Dundalk P
- Drogheda P
- Laytown P
- Gormanston P
- Balbriggan P
- Skerries P
- Rush & Lusk P
- Donabate P
- Malahide P
- Portmarnock P
- Howth Junction

DART Service
Runs from Howth to Bray

- HOWTH
- Sutton P
- Bayside
- Kilbarrack
- Raheny
- Harmonstown
- Killester P
- Clontarf Road P
- CONNOLLY STN P
- TARA STREET
- PEARSE STN
- Grand Canal Dock
- Lansdowne Road
- Sandymount
- Sydney Parade
- Booterstown P
- Blackrock P
- Seapoint
- Salthill/Monkstown P
- DÚN LAOGHAIRE
- Sandycove/Glasthule
- Glenageary
- Dalkey
- Killiney P
- Shankill
- BRAY P
- GREYSTONES P

Docklands

Museum · Smithfield · Four Courts · Jervis · Abbey St. · Busáras

City Centre

Heuston Station P

Luas Red Line
Runs from Tallaght to Connolly Station

- James's
- Fatima
- Rialto
- Suir Road
- Goldenbridge
- Drimnagh
- Blackhorse
- Bluebell
- Kylemore
- Red Cow P
- Kingswood
- Belgard
- Cookstown
- Hospital
- Tallaght

St. Stephen's Green

- Harcourt
- Charlemont
- Ranelagh
- Beechwood
- Cowper
- Milltown
- Windy Arbour
- Dundrum
- Balally
- Kilmacud
- Stillorgan
- Sandyford P

Luas Green Line
Runs from Sandyford to St.Stephen's Green

- Cherry Orchard & Parkwest
- Clondalkin
- Adamstown
- Hazelhatch & Celbridge P
- Sallins & Naas P
- Newbridge P
- Kildare P

Arrow Service
Runs from Heuston Station to Kildare Town

- Kilcoole P
- Wicklow P
- Rathdrum P
- Arklow P

South Eastern Suburban Service
Runs from Connolly Station to Arklow

P Parking
🚌 Feeder Bus

iarnród éireann
and further information:
(01) 836 6222

Dublin Bus operates the bus network in the greater Dublin area. This network extends from Balbriggan in North County Dublin to Kilcoole in County Wicklow and westwards as far as Kilcock, County Kildare.

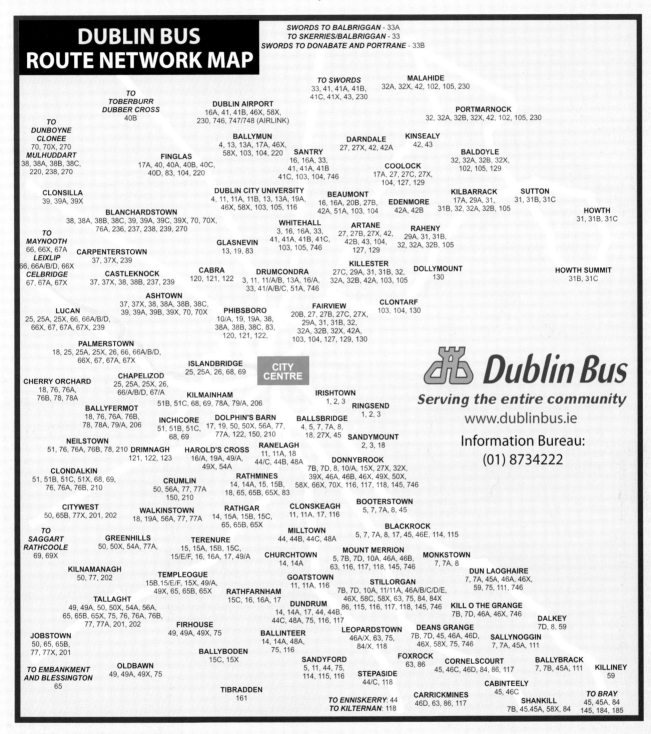

DUBLIN BUS ROUTE NETWORK MAP

SWORDS TO BALBRIGGAN - 33A
TO SKERRIES/BALBRIGGAN - 33
SWORDS TO DONABATE AND PORTRANE - 33B

TO SWORDS
33, 41, 41A, 41B, 41C, 41X, 43, 230

MALAHIDE
32A, 32X, 42, 102, 105, 230

TO TOBERBURR DUBBER CROSS
40B

DUBLIN AIRPORT
16A, 41, 41B, 46X, 58X, 230, 746, 747/748 (AIRLINK)

PORTMARNOCK
32, 32A, 32B, 32X, 42, 102, 105, 230

TO DUNBOYNE CLONEE
70, 70X, 270

MULHUDDART
38, 38A, 38B, 38C, 220, 238, 270

BALLYMUN
4, 13, 13A, 17A, 46X, 58X, 103, 104, 220

DARNDALE
27, 27X, 42, 42A

KINSEALY
42, 43

BALDOYLE
32, 32A, 32B, 32X, 102, 105, 129

FINGLAS
17A, 40, 40A, 40B, 40C, 40D, 83, 104, 220

SANTRY
16, 16A, 33, 41, 41A, 41B 41C, 103, 104, 746

COOLOCK
17A, 27, 27C, 27X, 104, 127, 129

CLONSILLA
39, 39A, 39X

DUBLIN CITY UNIVERSITY
4, 11, 11A, 11B, 13, 13A, 19A, 46X, 58X, 103, 105, 116

BEAUMONT
16, 16A, 20B, 27B, 42A, 51A, 103, 104

EDENMORE
42A, 42B

KILBARRACK
17A, 29A, 31, 31B, 32, 32A, 32B, 105

SUTTON
31, 31B, 31C

BLANCHARDSTOWN
38, 38A, 38B, 38C, 39, 39A, 39C, 39X, 70, 70X, 76A, 236, 237, 238, 239, 270

WHITEHALL
3, 16, 16A, 33, 41, 41A, 41B, 41C, 103, 105, 746

ARTANE
27, 27B, 27X, 42, 42B, 43, 104, 127, 129

RAHENY
29A, 31, 31B, 32, 32A, 32B, 105

HOWTH
31, 31B, 31C

TO MAYNOOTH
66, 66X, 67A

LEIXLIP
66, 66A/B/D, 66X

CARPENTERSTOWN
37, 37X, 239

GLASNEVIN
13, 19, 83

CELBRIDGE
67, 67A, 67X

CASTLEKNOCK
37, 37X, 38, 38B, 237, 239

CABRA
120, 121, 122

DRUMCONDRA
3, 11, 11/A/B, 13A, 16/A, 33, 41/A/B/C, 51A, 746

KILLESTER
27C, 29A, 31, 31B, 32, 32A, 32B, 42A, 103, 105

DOLLYMOUNT
130

HOWTH SUMMIT
31B, 31C

ASHTOWN
37, 37X, 38, 38A, 38B, 38C, 39, 39A, 39B, 39X, 70, 70X

LUCAN
25, 25A, 25X, 66, 66A/B/D, 66X, 67, 67A, 67X, 239

PHIBSBORO
10/A, 19, 19A, 38, 38A, 38B, 38C, 83, 120, 121, 122,

FAIRVIEW
20B, 27, 27B, 27C, 27X, 29A, 31, 31B, 32, 32A, 32B, 32X, 42A, 103, 104, 127, 129, 130

CLONTARF
103, 104, 130

PALMERSTOWN
18, 25, 25A, 25X, 26, 66, 66A/B/D, 66X, 67, 67A, 67X

ISLANDBRIDGE
25, 25A, 26, 68, 69

CITY CENTRE

CHAPELIZOD
25, 25A, 25X, 26, 66/A/B/D, 67/A

IRISHTOWN
1, 2, 3

RINGSEND
1, 2, 3

CHERRY ORCHARD
18, 76, 76A, 76B, 78, 78A

KILMAINHAM
51B, 51C, 68, 69, 78A, 79/A, 206

BALLYFERMOT
18, 76, 76A, 76B, 78, 78A, 79/A, 206

INCHICORE
51, 51B, 51C, 68, 69

DOLPHIN'S BARN
17, 19, 50, 50X, 56A, 77, 77A, 122, 150, 210

BALLSBRIDGE
4, 5, 7, 7A, 8, 18, 27X, 45

SANDYMOUNT
2, 3, 18

NEILSTOWN
51, 76, 76A, 76B, 78, 210

DRIMNAGH
121, 122, 123

HAROLD'S CROSS
16/A, 19A, 49/A, 49X, 54A

RANELAGH
11, 11A, 18, 44/C, 44B, 48A

DONNYBROOK
7B, 7D, 8, 10/A, 15X, 27X, 32X, 39X, 46A, 46B, 46X, 49X, 50X, 58X, 66X, 70X, 116, 117, 118, 145, 746

CLONDALKIN
51, 51B, 51C, 51X, 68, 69, 76, 76A, 76B, 210

CRUMLIN
50, 56A, 77, 77A, 150, 210

RATHMINES
14, 14A, 15, 15B, 18, 65, 65B, 65X, 83

CITYWEST
50, 65B, 77X, 201, 202

WALKINSTOWN
18, 19A, 56A, 77, 77A

RATHGAR
14, 15A, 15B, 15C, 65, 65B, 65X

CLONSKEAGH
11, 11A, 17, 116

BOOTERSTOWN
5, 7, 7A, 8, 45

TO SAGGART RATHCOOLE
69, 69X

GREENHILLS
50, 50X, 54A, 77A,

TERENURE
15, 15A, 15B, 15C, 15/E/F, 16, 16A, 17, 49/A

MILLTOWN
44, 44B, 44C, 48A

BLACKROCK
5, 7, 7A, 8, 17, 45, 46E, 114, 115

CHURCHTOWN
14, 14A

MOUNT MERRION
5, 7B, 7D, 10A, 46A, 46B, 63, 116, 117, 118, 145, 746

MONKSTOWN
7, 7A, 8

KILNAMANAGH
50, 77, 202

TEMPLEOGUE
15B, 15/E/F, 15X, 49/A, 49X, 65, 65B, 65X

GOATSTOWN
11, 11A, 116

STILLORGAN
7B, 7D, 10A, 11/11A, 46A/B/C/D/E, 46X, 58C, 58X, 63, 75, 84, 84X, 86, 115, 116, 117, 118, 145, 746

DUN LAOGHAIRE
7, 7A, 45A, 46A, 46X, 59, 75, 111, 746

RATHFARNHAM
15C, 16, 16A, 17

TALLAGHT
49, 49A, 50, 50X, 54A, 56A, 65, 65B, 65X, 75, 76, 76A, 76B, 77, 77A, 201, 202

DUNDRUM
14, 14A, 17, 44, 44B, 44C, 48A, 75, 116, 117

KILL O THE GRANGE
7B, 7D, 46A, 46X, 746

DALKEY
7D, 8, 59

FIRHOUSE
49, 49A, 49X, 75

BALLINTEER
14, 14A, 48A, 75, 116

LEOPARDSTOWN
46A/X, 63, 75, 84/X, 118

DEANS GRANGE
7B, 7D, 45, 46A, 46D, 46X, 58X, 75, 746

SALLYNOGGIN
7, 7A, 45A, 111

JOBSTOWN
50, 65, 65B, 77, 77X, 201

BALLYBODEN
15C, 15X

SANDYFORD
5, 11, 44, 75, 114, 115, 116

FOXROCK
63, 86

CORNELSCOURT
45, 46C, 46D, 84, 86, 117

BALLYBRACK
7, 7B, 45A, 111

KILLINEY
59

TO EMBANKMENT AND BLESSINGTON
65

OLDBAWN
49, 49A, 49X, 75

STEPASIDE
44/C, 118

CABINTEELY
45, 46C

TIBRADDEN
161

TO ENNISKERRY: 44
TO KILTERNAN: 118

CARRICKMINES
46D, 63, 86, 117

SHANKILL
7B, 45.45A, 58X, 84

TO BRAY
45, 45A, 84, 145, 184, 185

Dublin Bus
Serving the entire community
www.dublinbus.ie
Information Bureau:
(01) 8734222

Contact Information

Our Head Office is located at 59 Upper O'Connell Street, Dublin 1 and our opening hours are as follows:
Monday: 0830 – 1730hrs   Tuesday to Friday: 0900 – 1730hrs   Saturday: 0900 – 1300hrs
Please note that the Dublin Bus Head Office is closed Sundays and Bank Holidays.

Corballis Golf Links

▼18

Strand

IRISH SEA

COAST

Biscayne

ROAD

Castle
Robbswall

The
Lighthouse

Sports
Ground

ROBSWALL
WALK PATH

THE
CRESCENT

The Anchorage
The Spinnaker

THE
CRESCENT

R106

32A
32X
42N
102

105
230

MONKS
MEADOW

LIME TREE

ELMS COURT

AVENUE

32

ASHLEY RISE

CONVENT LANE

32B

142

RADLETT GRO

WHEATFIELD ROAD

WHEATFIELD

BRIAR WALK

BRACKEN DRIVE

HEATHER
GARDENS

Martello
Tower

GROVE

42N

KELVIN CLOSE

BLACKTHORN CLOSE

DEWBERRY PARK

HEATHER

WALK

STRAND

ROAD

WENDELL AVENUE

230 102 32X

1

MARTELLO COURT

WENDELL AVE

142

32B
105

CARRICKHILL

CARRICKHILL
CLOSE

PORTMARNOCK PARK

CARRICKHILL RISE

CARRICKHILL WALK

PORTMARNOCK CRESCENT

32
32A

2

PINE
CT

102
230

CARRICKHILL HTS

PARKVIEW DRIVE

RISE

BIRROW CT

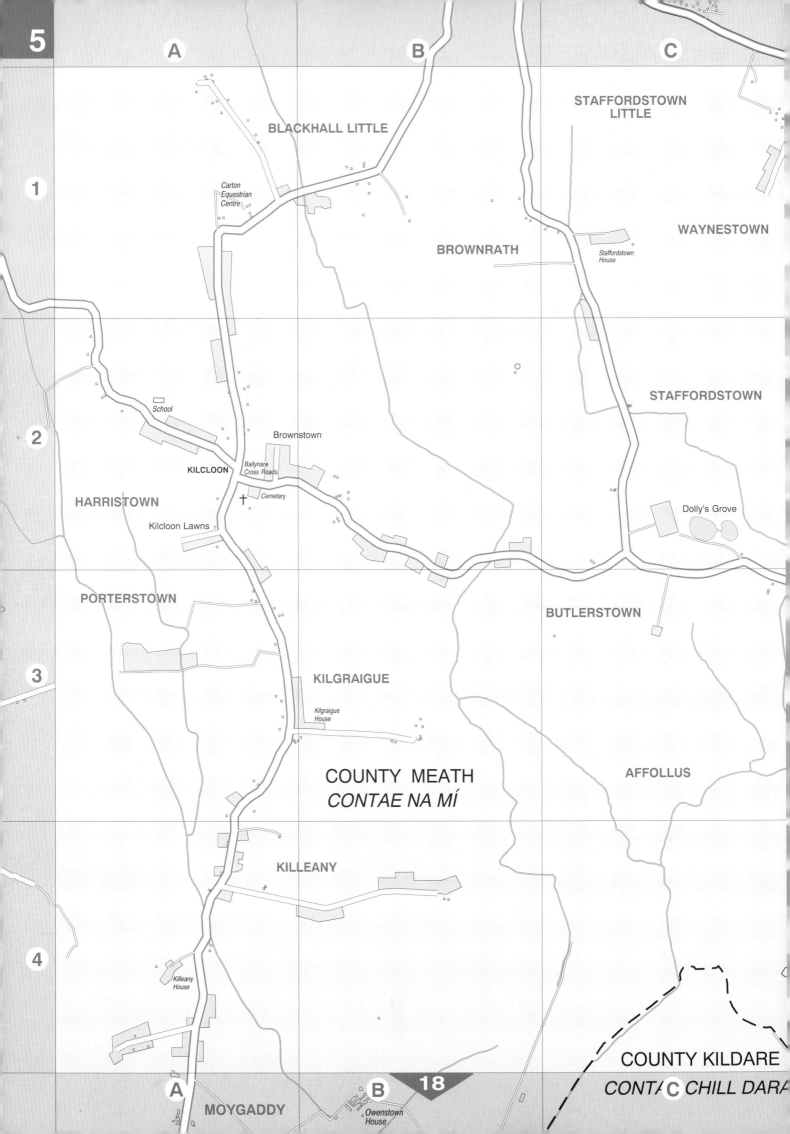

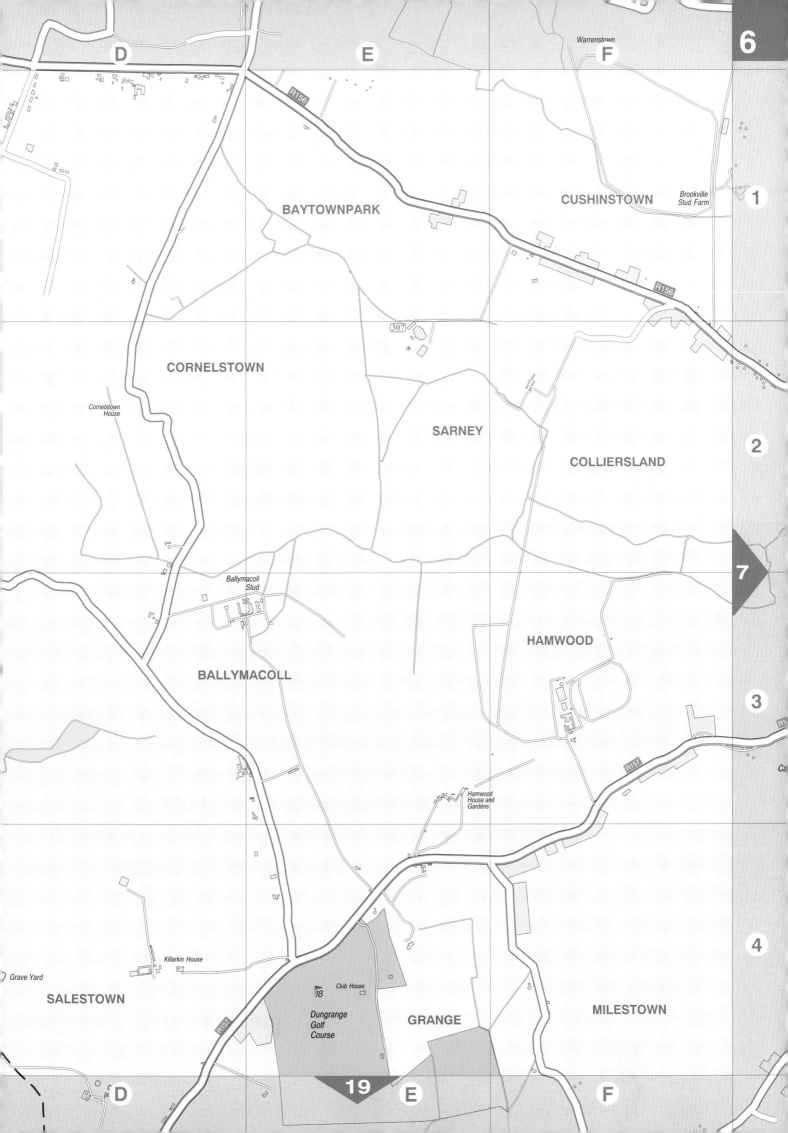

D

E

F
Warrenstown

R156

BAYTOWNPARK

CUSHINSTOWN

Brookville Stud Farm

1

R156

307

CORNELSTOWN

Cornelstown House

SARNEY

COLLIERSLAND

2

Ballymacoll Stud

7

HAMWOOD

BALLYMACOLL

3

R157

Hamwood House and Gardens

Killarkin House

Grave Yard

SALESTOWN

18

Club House

Dungrange Golf Course

GRANGE

MILESTOWN

4

R157

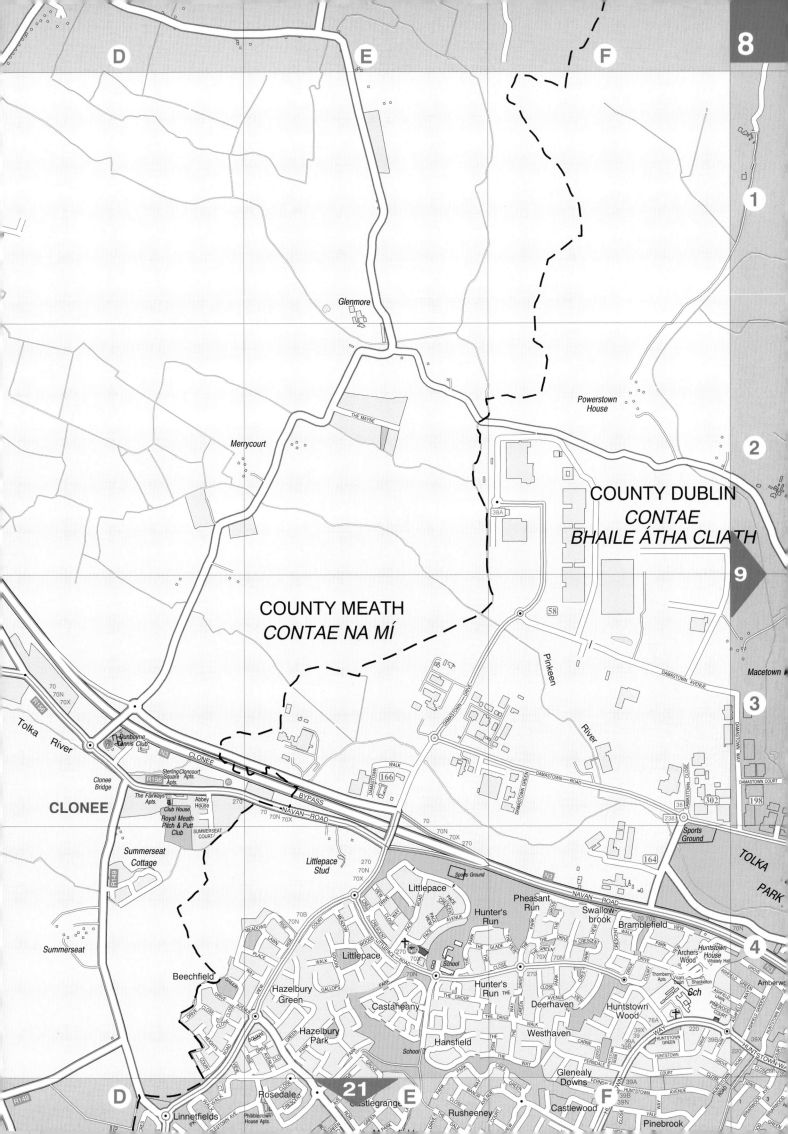

D   E   F

Broghan
New Br.

Broghan House

Pitch
and
Putt

1

Dunsoghly
Castle

Newtown

KILSHANE

Cement Works

Kilmore House

Woodlands

Kilshane
Cross

Kilshane
House

NORTH ROAD

N2

88N

2

KILSHANE AVENUE

Old Quarry

Sports
Ground

KILSHANE VIEW

KILSHANE PARK

KILSHANE DRIVE

KILSHANE ROAD

Sand &
Gravel Pit

11

N2

KILSHANE WAY

Burial
Gd

201

Cloghran House

3

202

236

238

236

13

220

38B

220

133

Electricity
Station

Kildonan House

ROSEMOUNT PARK ROAD

ROSEMOUNT PARK DRIVE

BALLYCOOLIN ROAD

40D

4

M50

CAPPAGH ROAD

CAPPOGE

Cappoge
Cottages

203

Marine

220

40D

Sp
Gr

220

D   E   F

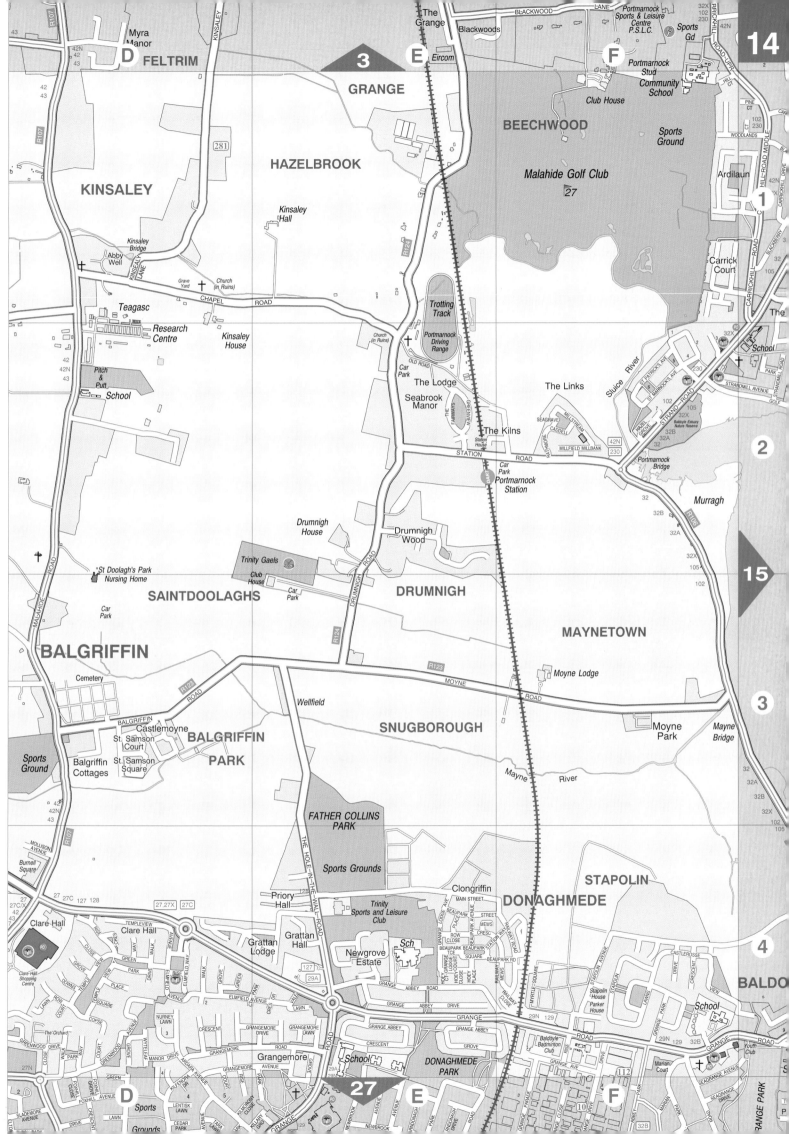

15

A

B 4 C

CARRICKHILL RISE
CARRICKHILL CLOSE
PORTMARNOCK PARK
CARRICKHILL WALK
3RD
32B
105
STRAND
CARRICKHILL CRESCENT
32
32A

PINE CT
102
230
CARRICKHILL HTS
CARRICKHILL DRIVE
BEACH PARK
BLACKBERRY LANE
BURROW CT
296

WOODLANDS
CARRICKHILL MIDDLE ROAD
HTS
RISE

1
Ardilaun
42N
32X

STRAND ROAD
R106
Grave Yard
32B

Carrick Court
105
32
32A

PORTMARNOCK

The Dunes

Pitch & Putt

Portmarnock Golf Links
▶18

Velvet Strand

32X
School
PARK
STRANDMILL ROAD

2
STRANDMILL AVENUE
5
230
GOLF LINKS ROAD

Murragh

14
105
102

3

Mayne Bridge

32
32A
32B
32X
102
105

COAST ROAD
R106

Portmarnock Golf Links
▶18

Club House

Portmarnock Point

Community Hall

4

BALDOYLE

School
VIEW
ADMIRAL PARK
32B
29N
WILLIE NOLAN ROAD
129
SHELDON LANE
COLLEGE STREET
MAIN STREET
7

Hosp

Georgian Hamlet
BROOKSTONE ROAD
Sch
31
31B
STRAND ROAD
32B
32A
29N
31

GRANGE ROAD
Youth Club
DUBLIN STREET
Grave Yard
32A
102
31

SEAGRANGE AVENUE
School
6
Nursing Home
31B

A
Turnberry
WARRENHOUSE ROAD

GRANGE PARK
TUSCANY
Parkvale
TURNBERRY SQUARE
ONBROOK AVE
PARK AVE
LAWN
29N
5

Cush Point
Club House

Sutton

B 28 29 C

The Steer

Tower

Ireland's
Eye

Carrigeen Bay

Rowan Rocks

Thulla Rocks

Thulla

Lighthouse

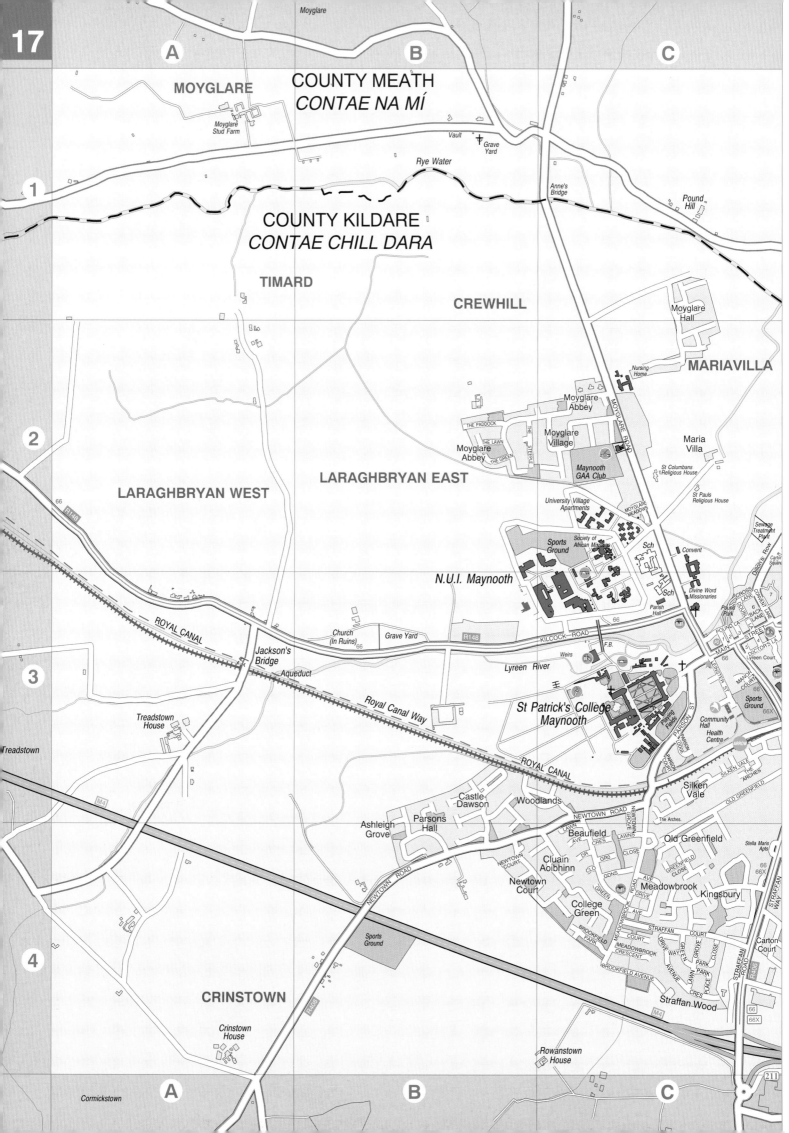

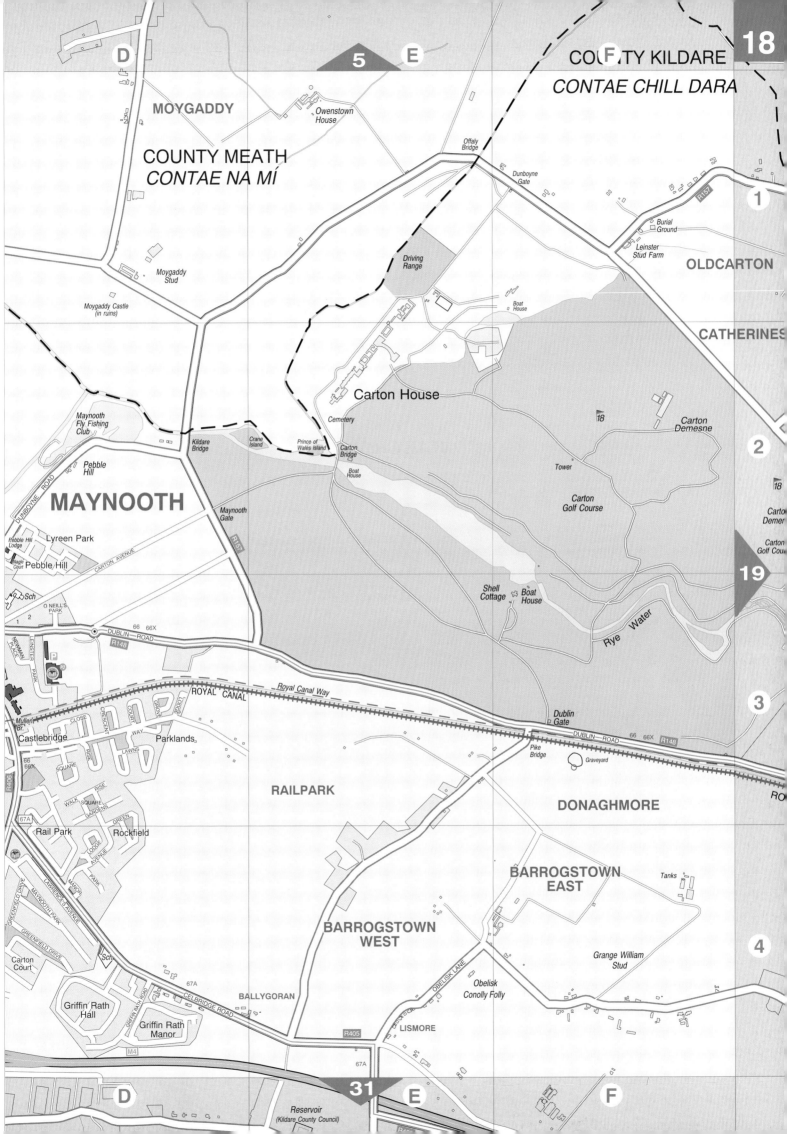

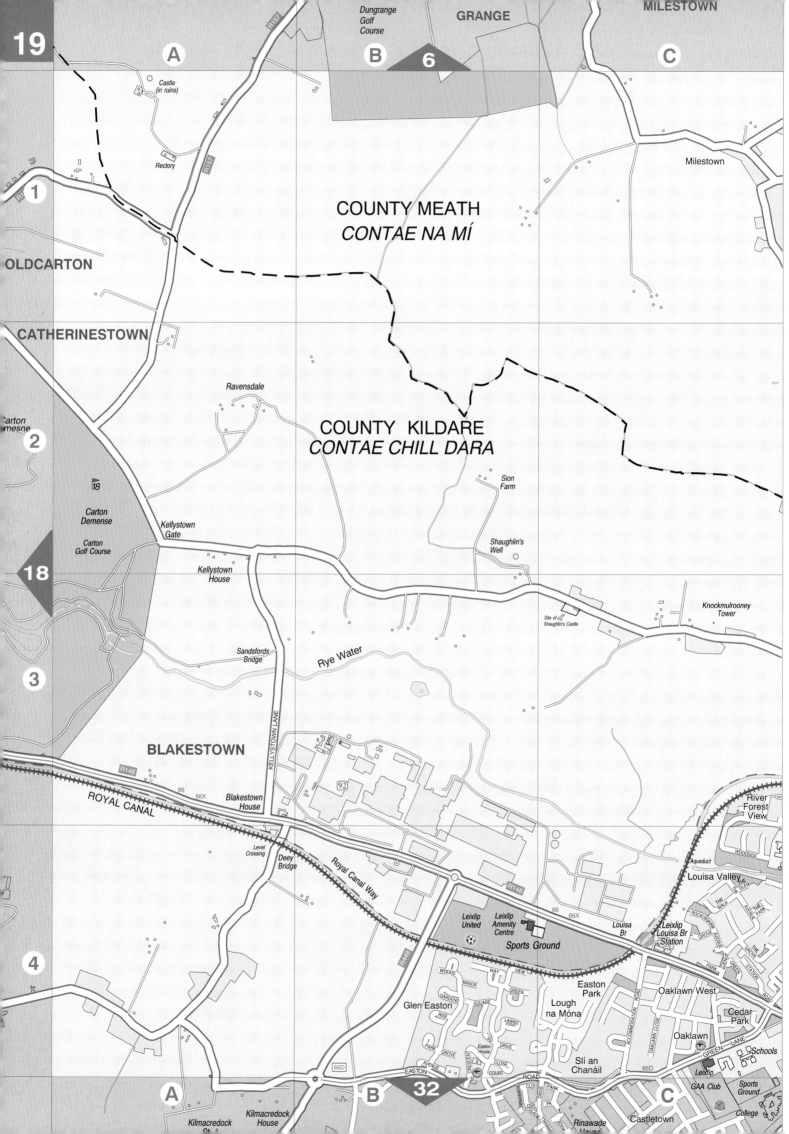

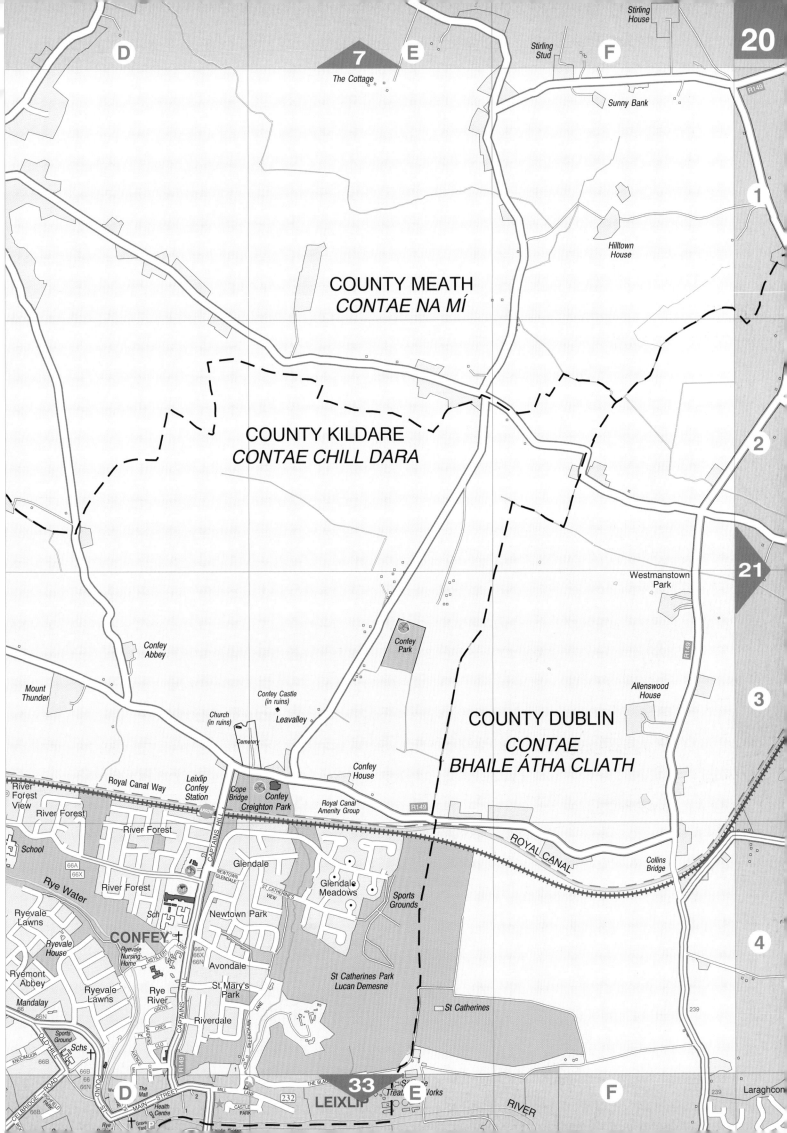

D 7 E F

1

2

21

3

4

Stirling House

Stirling Stud

Sunny Bank

The Cottage

Hilltown House

COUNTY MEATH
CONTAE NA MÍ

COUNTY KILDARE
CONTAE CHILL DARA

Westmanstown Park

Confey Abbey

Confey Park

Allenswood House

Mount Thunder

Confey Castle (in ruins)

Church (in ruins)

Leavalley

COUNTY DUBLIN
CONTAE BHAILE ÁTHA CLIATH

Cemetery

Confey House

River Forest View

Royal Canal Way

Leixlip Confey Station

Cope Bridge

Confey Creighton Park

Royal Canal Amenity Group

R149

ROYAL CANAL

River Forest

River Forest

School

Glendale

Collins Bridge

Rye Water

River Forest

66A 66X

Glendale Meadows

Sports Grounds

Ryevale Lawns

Ryevale House

Ryevale Nursing Home

Newtown Park

Ryemont Abbey

Rye River

Avondale

St Mary's Park

St Catherines Park Lucan Demesne

Mandalay

Ryevale Lawns

Riverdale

St Catherines

Sports Ground

Schs

Knockauin

R149

D 33 E F

LEIXLIP

Treatment Works

RIVER

Laraghcon

239

239

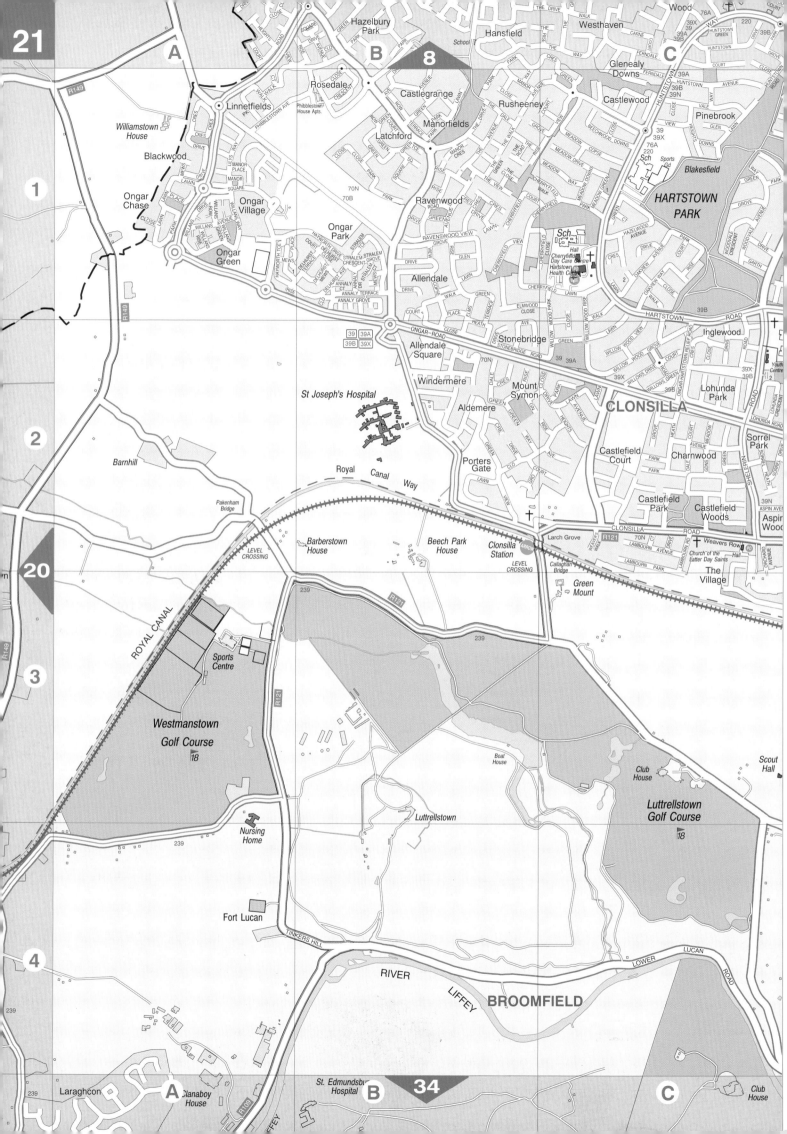

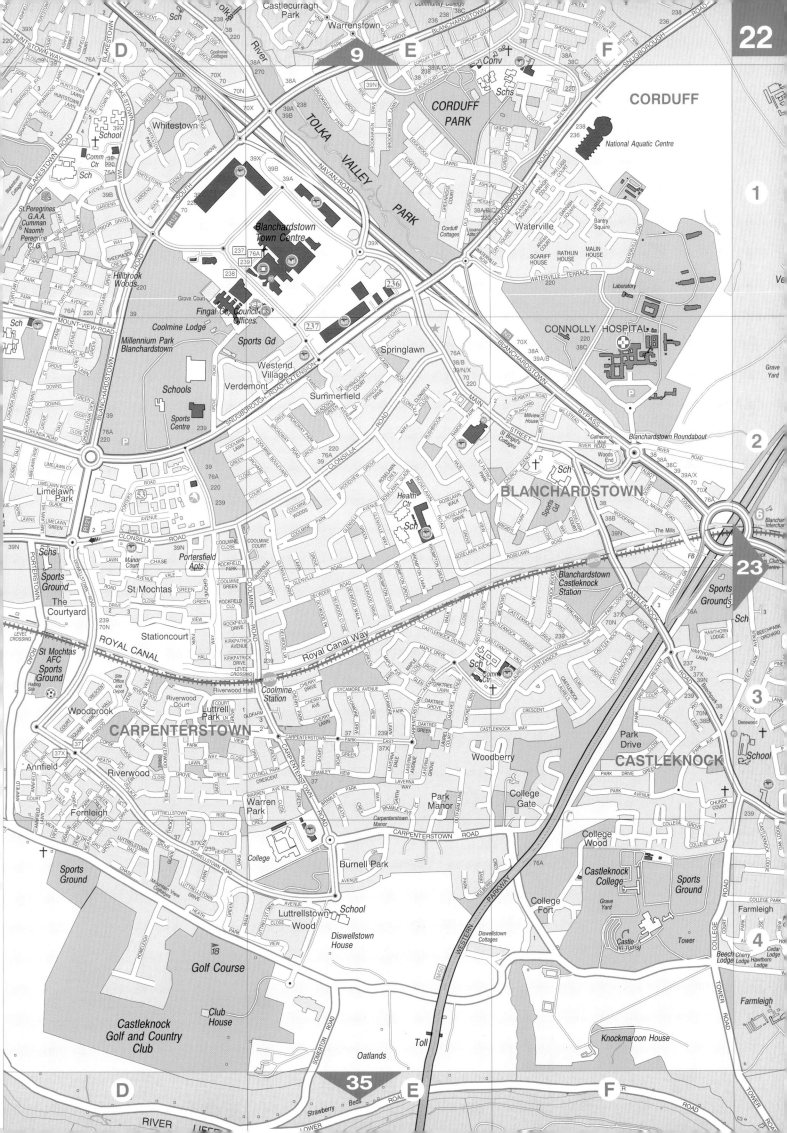

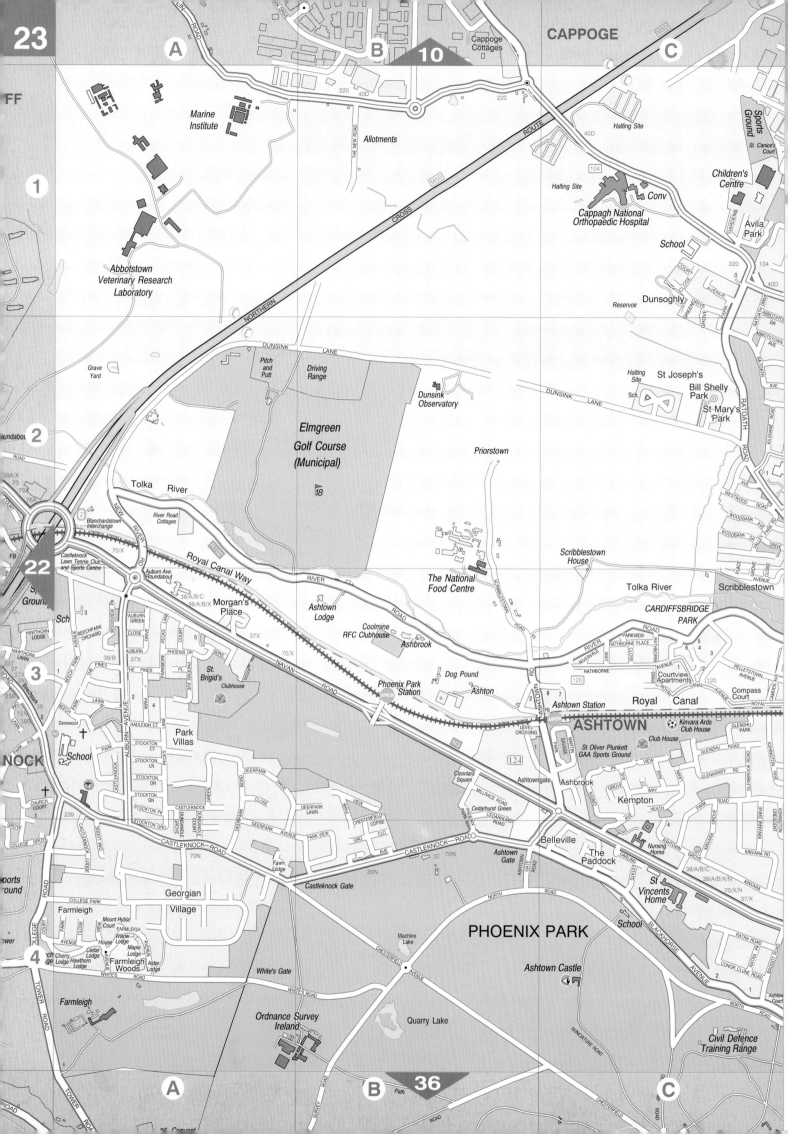

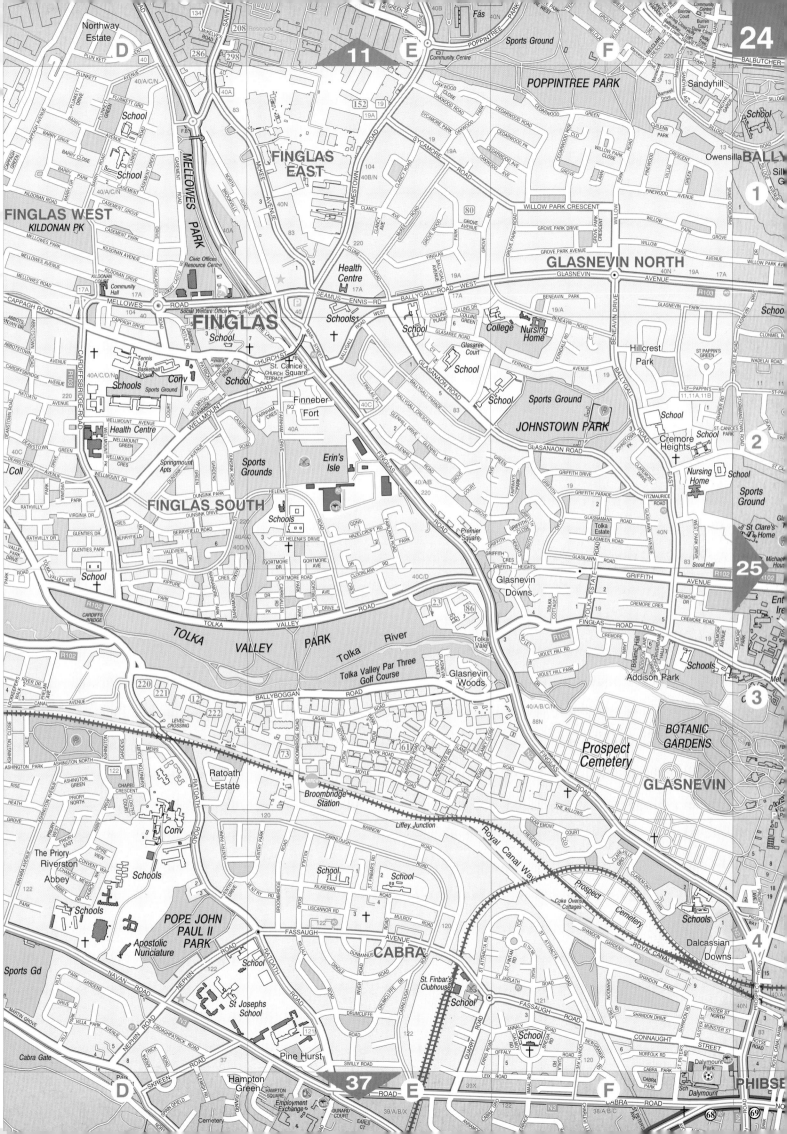

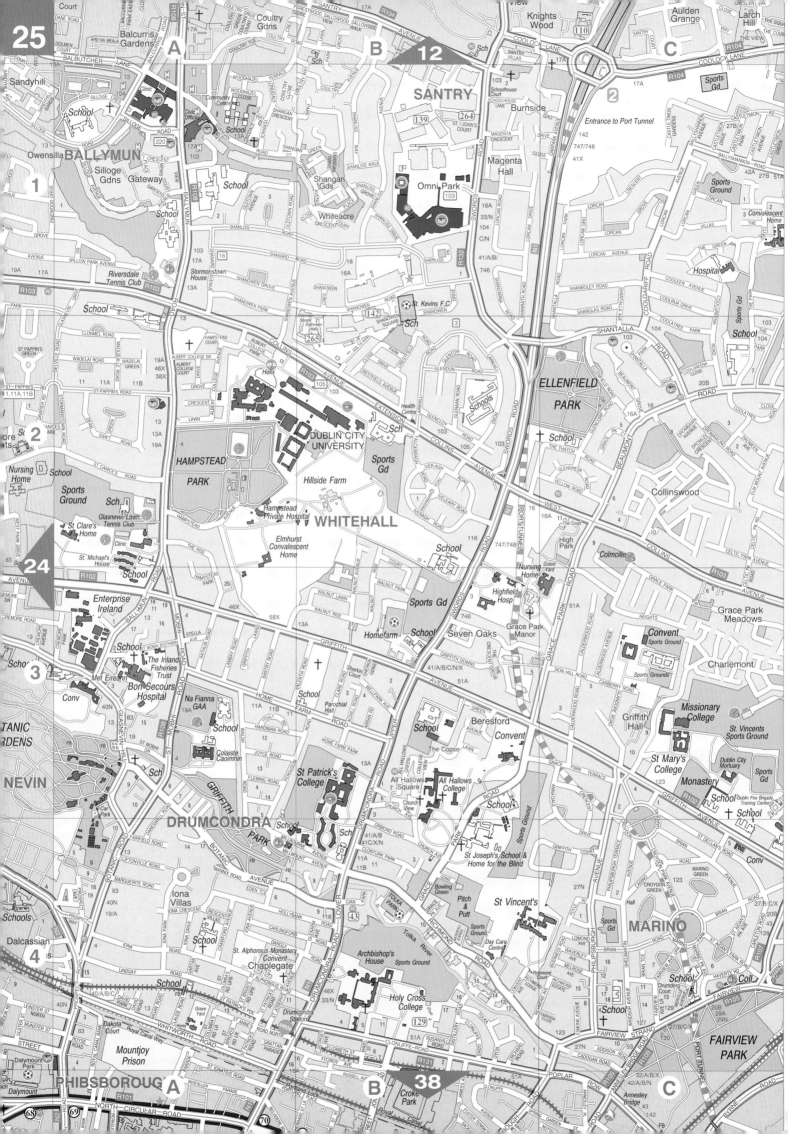

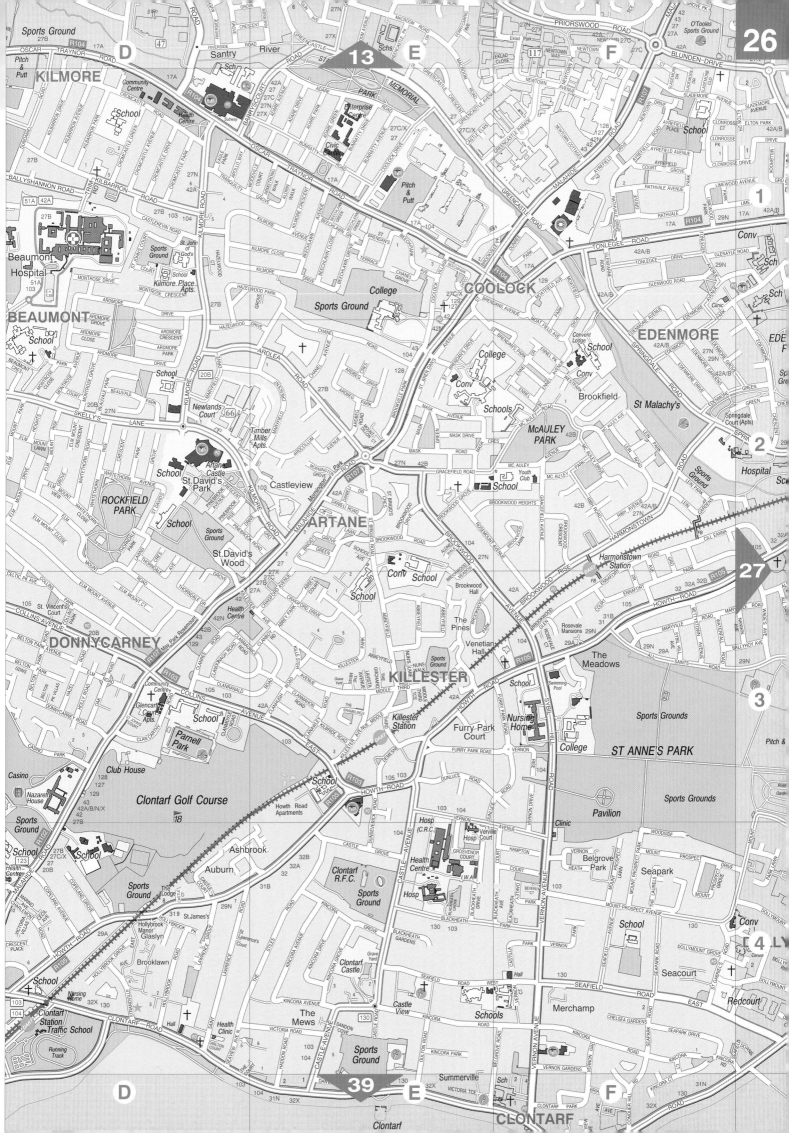

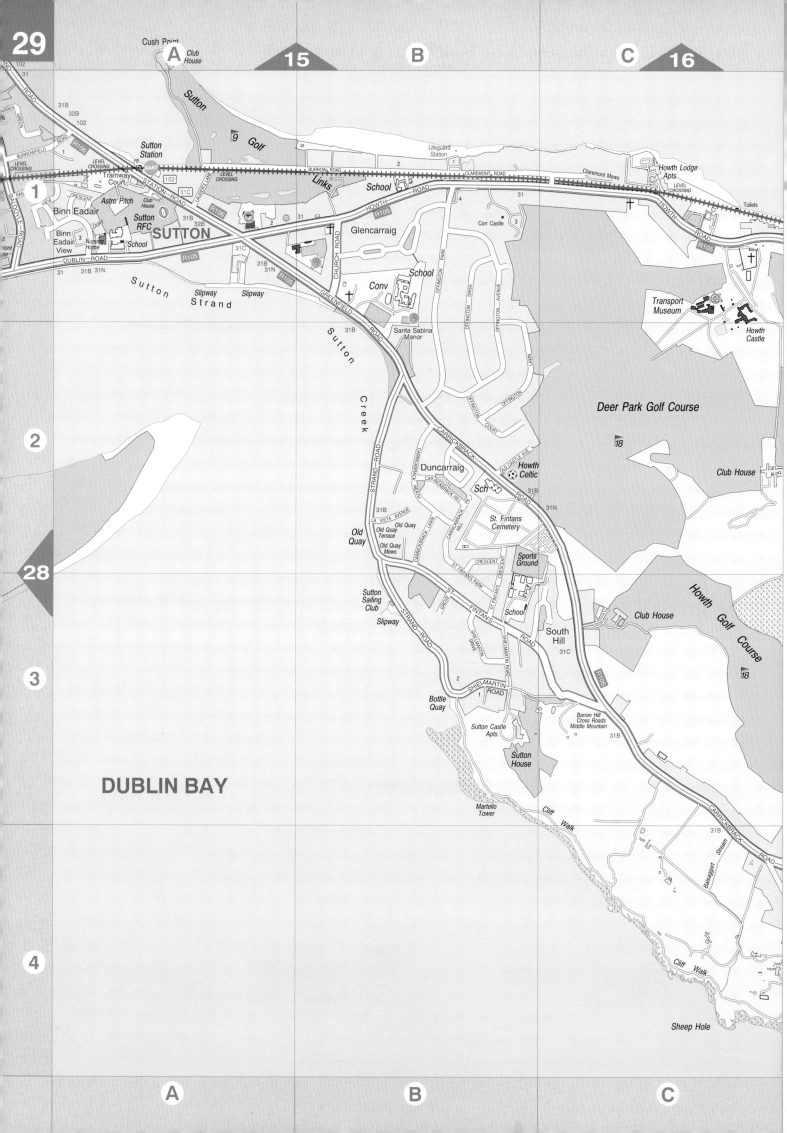

Lighthouse

Slipway

WEST PIER

HOWTH HARBOUR

Slipway

EAST PIER

Slipway
Lifeboat Station

Yacht Club

Howth Station

DART

P

Slipway

Toilets

HARBOUR ROAD

3 14 16 31
15 31C
31N

CHURCH STREET

ABBEY STREET

Tower

Asgard Apts.

Baths

Balscadden Bay

BALSCADDEN ROAD

Puck's Rocks

4
5
8
11
10

ST LAURENCE RD

EVORA PARK

Health Centre

ASGARD PARK

KILROCK ROAD

NASHVILLE PARK

P

Kilrock

Nose of Howth

GRACE O'MALLEY RD

12

6

HOWTH

31C

NASHVILLE ROAD

R105

COMMUTER LANE

Deer Park Golf Course

Sports Ground

School

1

31

16
9
12
13

MAIN STREET

Sch

ASGARD ROAD

THORMANBY

Cannon Rock

Cannon Rock Estate

Cannon Rock Cottage

ST PETER'S TERRACE

TUCKETTS LANE

Gull Cottage

BALKILL PARK

8

THORMANBY LAWNS

31

1

2

MARINERS COVE

CASANA VIEW

Casana Rock

BALGLASS RD

BALKILL PARK

DUNGRIFFAN ROAD

GREY'S LANE

WOODCLIFF HEIGHTS

3

ROAD

Cliff Walk

Green Ivy

Reservoir

Beann Éadair G.A.A. Club

Club House

Woodside

Rockstown
Thormanby Woods

Thormanby Lodge

BALKILL ROAD

WINDGATE

Ben of Howth

Loughoreen Hills
Green Hallows Quarries

The Green Hallows

Howth Hill Lodge Nursing Home

Blakeney House (Mews)

31

Piper's Gut

31C

The Gate Lodge

Fox Hole

Reservoir

NEW RD

WINDGATE RISE

31 31B

The Summit

BAILEY GREEN ROAD

Tower

Baily Green

P

Highroom Bed

Carrickbrack Reservoir (Disused)

WINDGATE ROAD

Reservoir

P

31B
31N

Lough Leven

OLD CARRICKBRACK ROAD

31N 31B

CARRICKBRACK ROAD

R105

Sisters of Charity Stella Maris

31C

THORMANBY ROAD

Gaskin's Leap

Whitewater Brook

Webb's Castle Rock

CEANCHOR ROAD

Cliff Walk

Hippy Hole

Doldrum Bay

Lion's Head

The Great Baily

Glenaveena

Helipad

The Little Baily

The Needles or Candlesticks

Baily Lighthouse

Drumleck Point

LISMORE

R405

211

Reservoir
(Kildare County Council)

R405

67A
67N

M4

MAYNOOTH ROAD

67
67X

College

Crodaun
Forest
Park

67
67A
67X

FB
FB

Ballygoran
Park

Ballygoran
Stud

Kilwogan
Manor

WOODS
CRES.
CASTLE
DRIVE
VILLAGE

Thornhill
Meadows

LAWNS
WAY
RISE
PARK
COURT

Corbally
Stud

Castle Village
Green

PLACE

CLOSE

Ashgrove

Griffin Rath
Manor

GRIFFIN

Hall

GREEN LANE

BALLYGORAN

VIEW
WALK

Thornhill
Gardens

Thornhill
Heights

School
Sports
Ground

Griffinrath
House

THE PADDOCK

THE ROAD
THE MEADOWS
THE ORCHARD

THE GREGOR
THE GLADE
THE WALK

WILLOW BROOK
PARK
WILLOWBROOK
PARK
WILLOWBROOK
GROVE

BEATTY
PARK

Oldtown Mill

WILLOWBROOK
LAWNS

Health Centre

3

THE GREEN
THE PARK

ROAD

238

Oldtown
House

Nursing Home

2
OLDTOWN
THE
HAVEN

Vanessa
Lawns

THE LAWN
THE VIEW
WOLSTAN
THE LAWN
THE DALE
THE COURT

WOLSTAN
HAVEN AVENUE
THE
GREEN
THE
PARK

Sports
Ground

Oldtown Cottages

Sch

PRIORY WAY

VANESSA CLOSE

ST PATRICKS
PARK

Pickering
Forest

PRIORY
RISE
PRIORY
CHASE
ST
RAPHAEL'S

PRIORY
CLOSE
PRIORY
VIEW
PRIORY
GREEN
PRIORY
COURT

CHURCH ROAD

Cemetery

R403

Priory Square

GRATTAN COURT

PRIORY DR.

PRIORY
WALK

St Raphael's

The
Courtyard

Oakleigh

Springfield

CLANE ROAD

Killadoon
Park

SPRINGFIELD
CLOSE

Ballymakealy
Grove

Celbridge
Abbey

Priory
Lodge

THE LAWNS

Roselawn

School

Sports
Ground

School

Ballymakealy
Lawns

THE PARK
GROVE
THE DRIVE
RIVER VIEW

Abbey
Park

NEWTOWN ROAD

THE COURT
THE LAWNS
CRES.

Temple
Manor

St. Patricks

R403

Abbeyfarm

ABBEY LANE
ABBEY GREEN
RIVER LANE
ABBEY COURT
RIVER LAWNS

Chelmsford

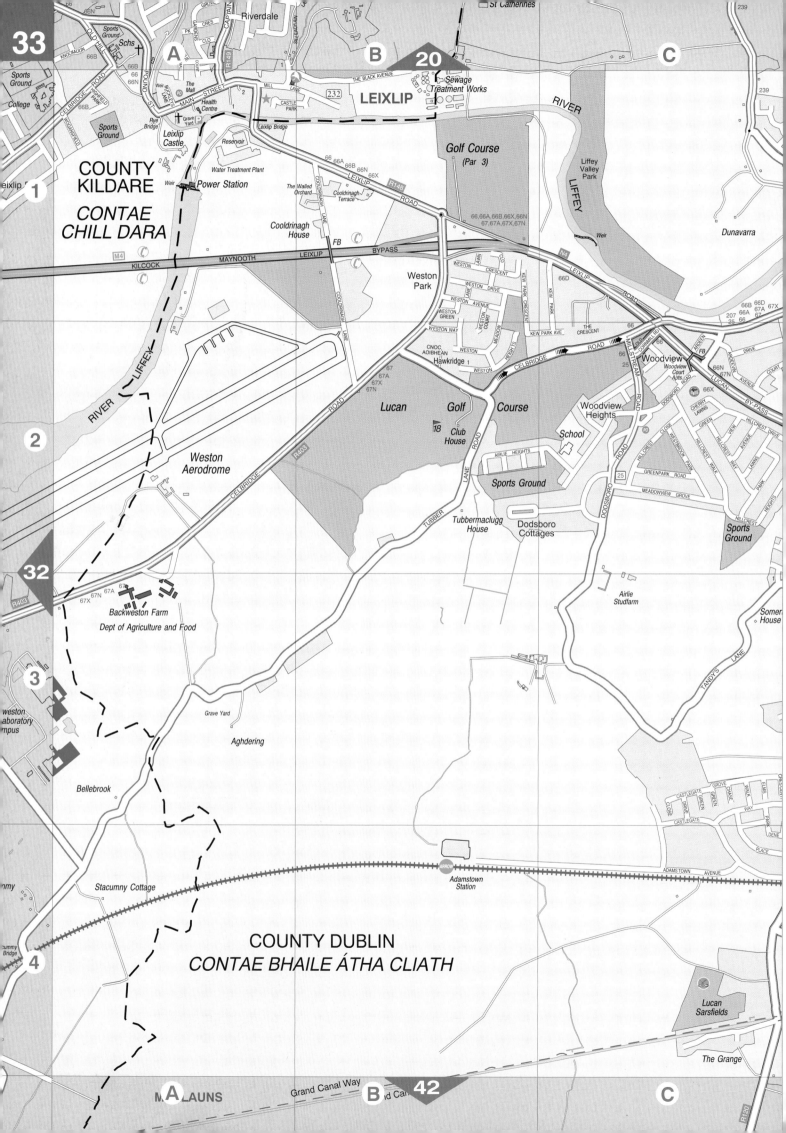

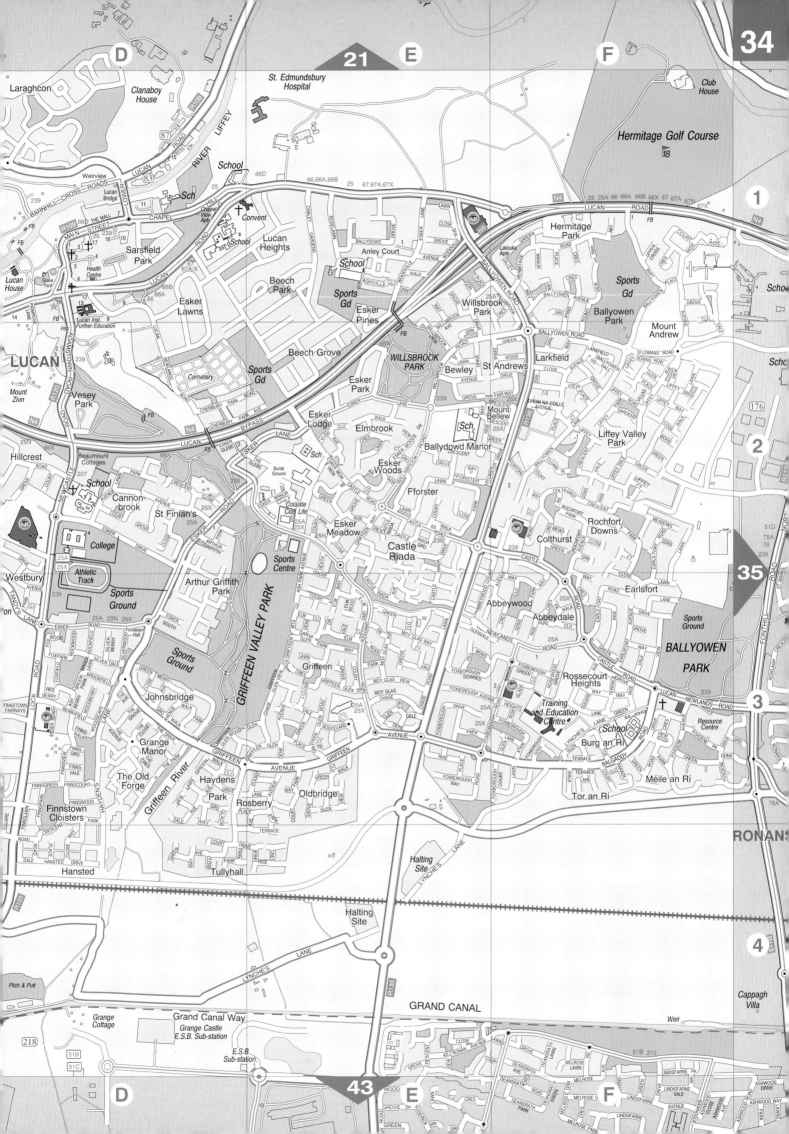

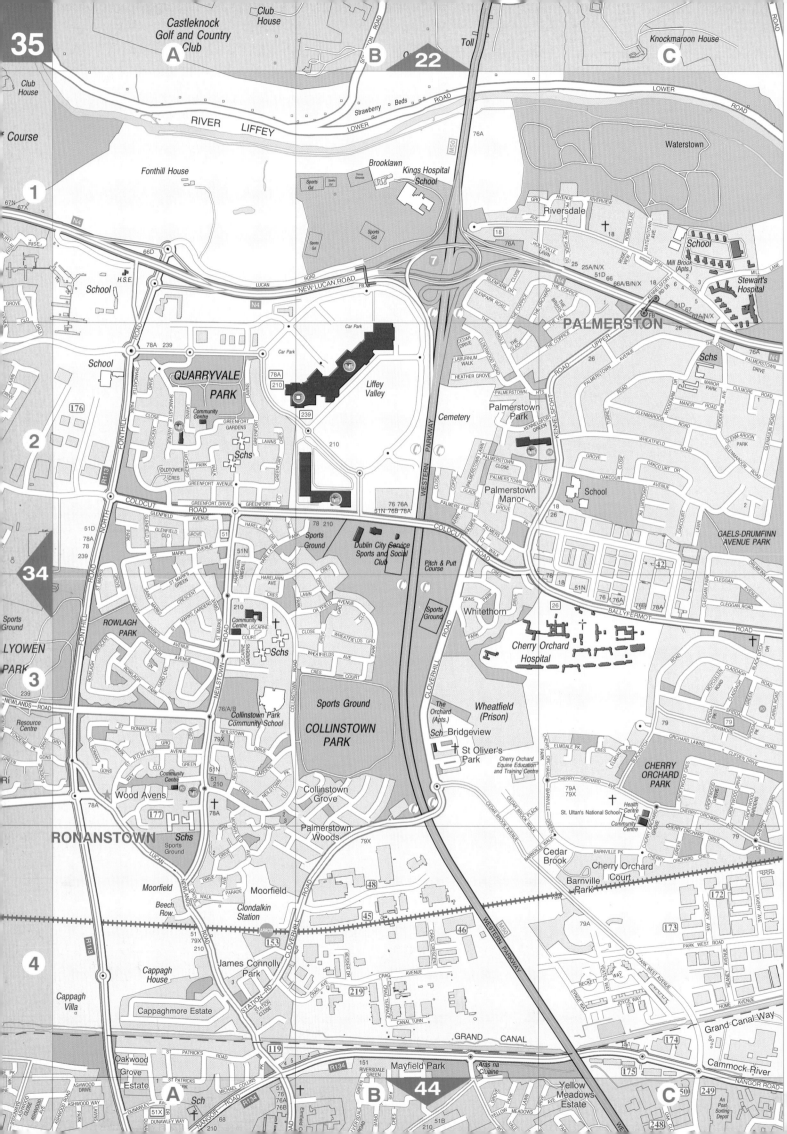

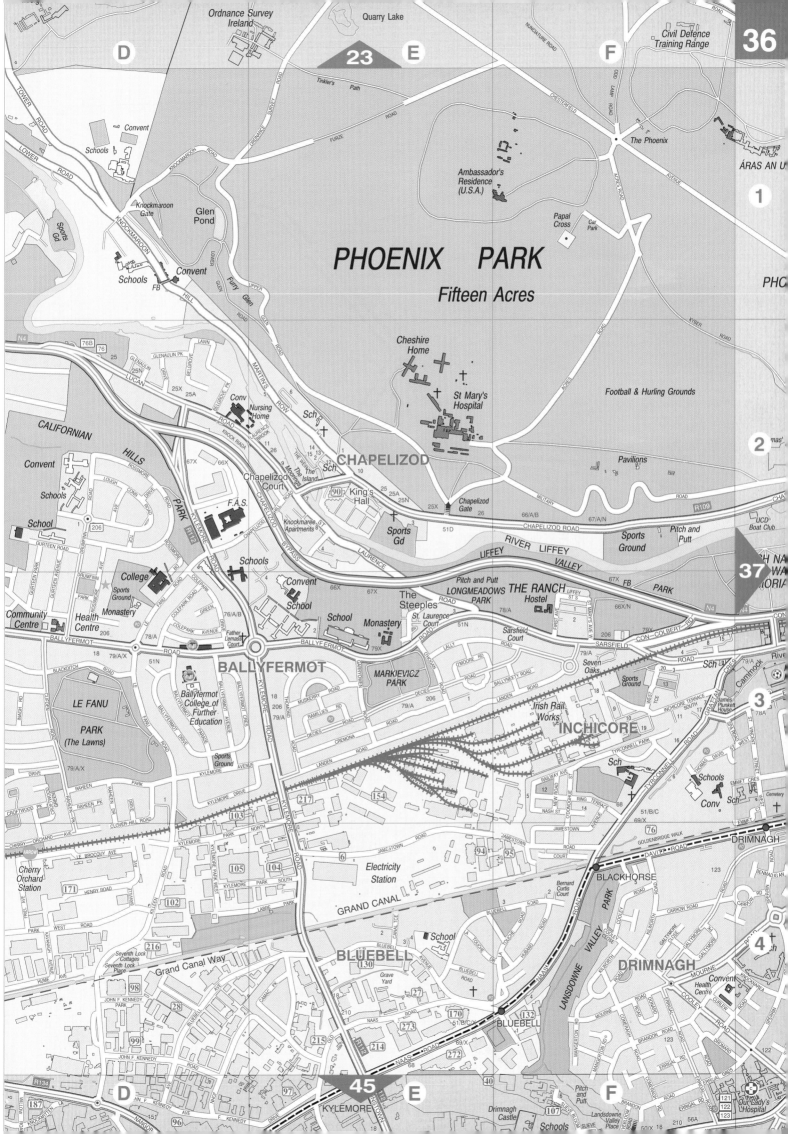

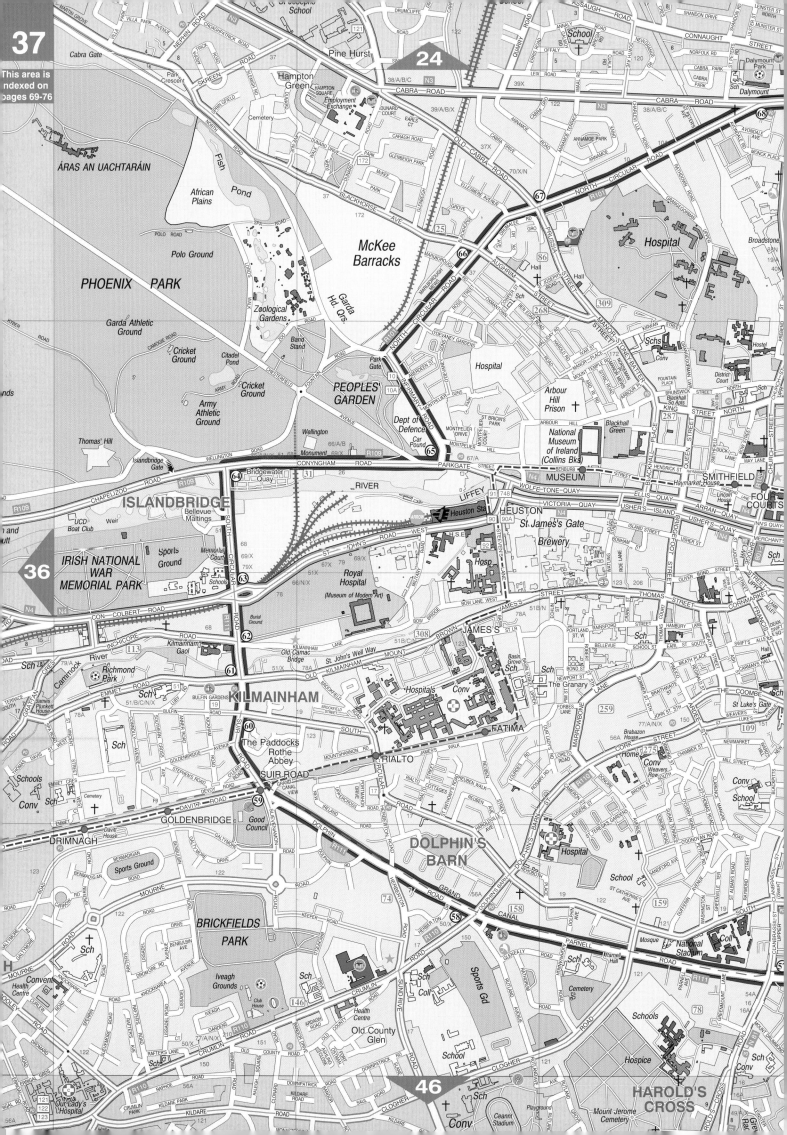

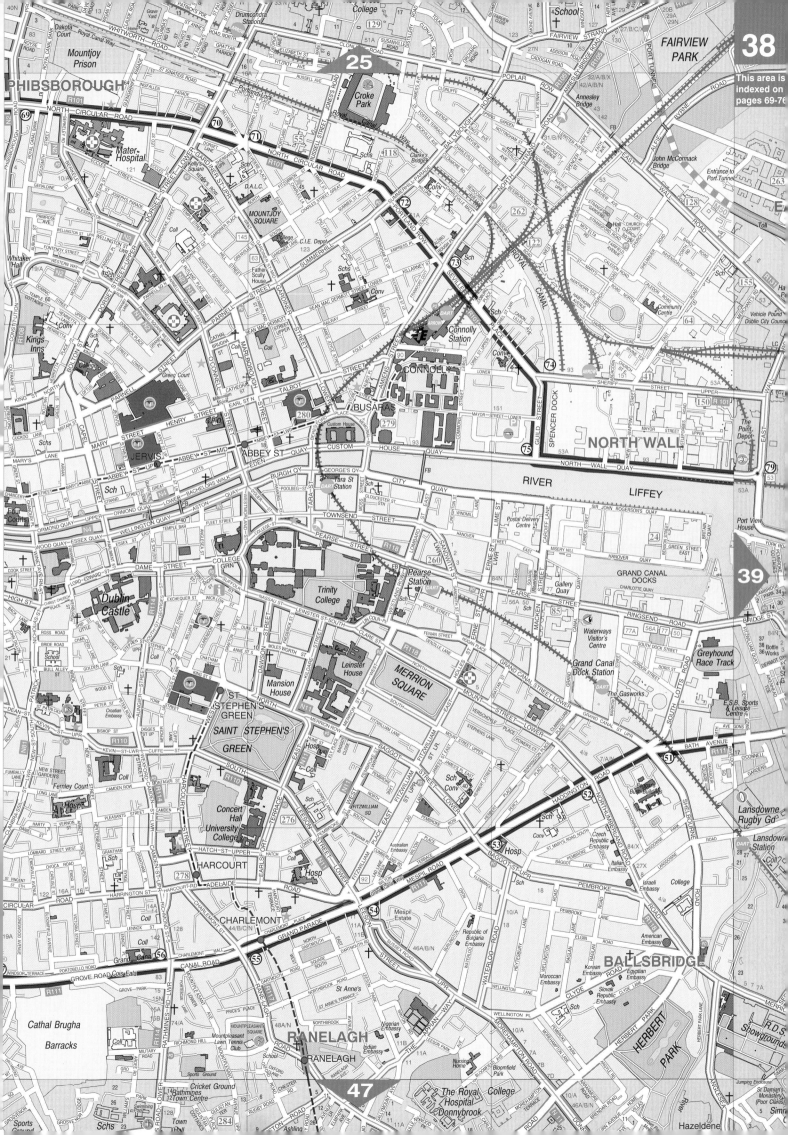

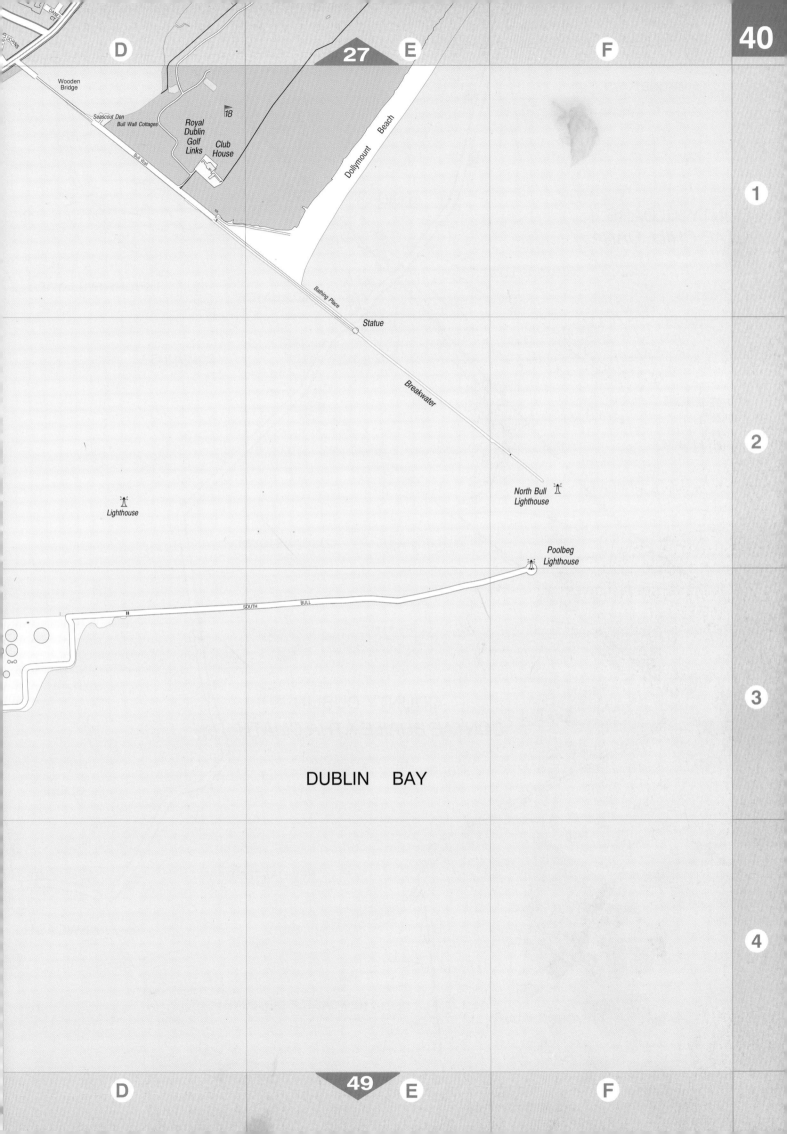

Wooden
Bridge

Seascout Den
Bull Wall Cottages

Royal
Dublin
Golf
Links

Club
House

Bull Wall

Dollymount   Beach

Bathing Place

Statue

Breakwater

North Bull
Lighthouse

Lighthouse

Poolbeg
Lighthouse

SOUTH   BULL

DUBLIN   BAY

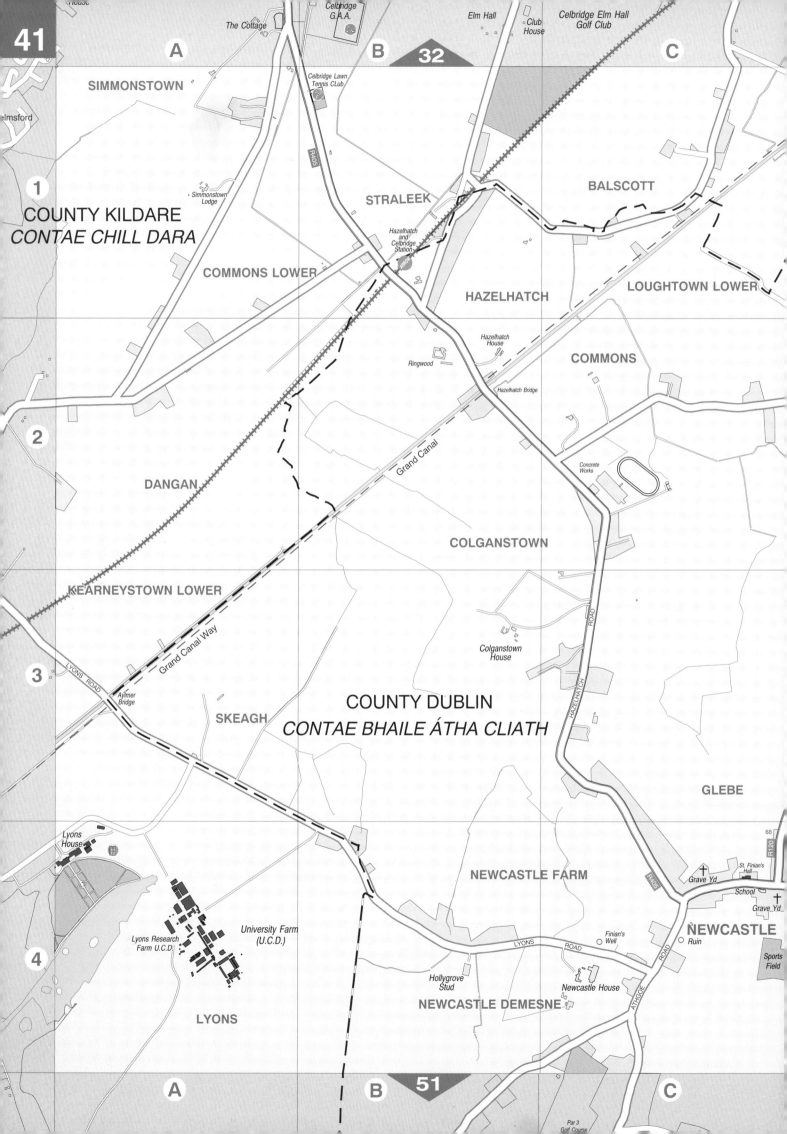

A

C

SIMMONSTOWN

Elm Hall

Club House

Celbridge Elm Hall Golf Club

The Cottage

Celbridge G.A.A.

Celbridge Lawn Tennis CLub

1

COUNTY KILDARE
CONTAE CHILL DARA

Imsford

Simmonstown Lodge

STRALEEK

Hazelhatch and Celbridge Station

BALSCOTT

COMMONS LOWER

HAZELHATCH

LOUGHTOWN LOWER

Ringwood

Hazelhatch House

COMMONS

Hazelhatch Bridge

2

Grand Canal

DANGAN

Concrete Works

COLGANSTOWN

KEARNEYSTOWN LOWER

Grand Canal Way

Colganstown House

HAZELHATCH ROAD

3

LYONS ROAD

Aylmer Bridge

SKEAGH

COUNTY DUBLIN
CONTAE BHAILE ÁTHA CLIATH

GLEBE

68

R120

St. Finian's Hall

Grave Yd

School

Grave Yd

NEWCASTLE FARM

Lyons House

R405

4

Lyons Research Farm U.C.D.

University Farm (U.C.D.)

Finian's Well

NEWCASTLE

LYONS ROAD

ROAD

ROAD

Ruin

Sports Field

Hollygrove Stud

NEWCASTLE DEMESNE

Newcastle House

ATHGOE

LYONS

A

C

Par 3 Golf Course

The Grange

MULLAUNS

Grand Canal Way
Grand Canal

CLUTTERLAND

BROWNSTOWN

Rock Road
Mansion

R120

LOUGHTOWN UPPER

88

Newcastle Golf Centre
and Driving Range

Par 3
Golf Course

Grave
Yard

Relickam
Well

68
R134

MILLTOWN

PEAMOUNT ROAD

Peamount
Hospital

PEAMOUNT

68

Nurses
Home

HYNESTOWN

Griffeen River

Castle
Bagot

Peamount
Hospital
Farm

68

KEELOGES

KILMACTALWAY

ROAD

Blundelstown
House

68

WESTMANSTOWN

Westmanstown
House

BLUNDELSTOWN

R120
PEAMOUNT

CORNERPARK

St Finians

Club
House

GRANTS HILL
COLLEGE ROAD

JORDANSTOWN

GRANTS PLACE

Castlelyon

Peamount Utd.

AYLMER ROAD

GRANTS CRESCENTS

GRANTS ROAD

Aylmer
Heath

GRANTS RISE

68

AYLMER
AVE

GRANTS WAY

COLLEGE ROAD

MAIN STREET

JORDANSTOWN AVENUE

The Rise

COMMONS
LITTLE

GRANTS AVENUE

JORDANSTOWN ROAD

ORCHARD GROVE

JORDANSTOWN DRIVE

Common
Little

GRANTS ROAD

235

Parsons
Court

Newcastle
Manor

GRANTS COURT

GRANTS DRIVE

COLLEGE ROAD

Strangford
Drive

GRANTS PARK

Newcastle
Lyons

R120

GRANTS VIEW

GRANTS LANE

THE SQUARE

GREENOGE

Ballinakelly
Village

GRANTS ROW

Ballynakelly

Newcastle
Grave Yard

COLLEGELAND

313

RATHCREEDAN

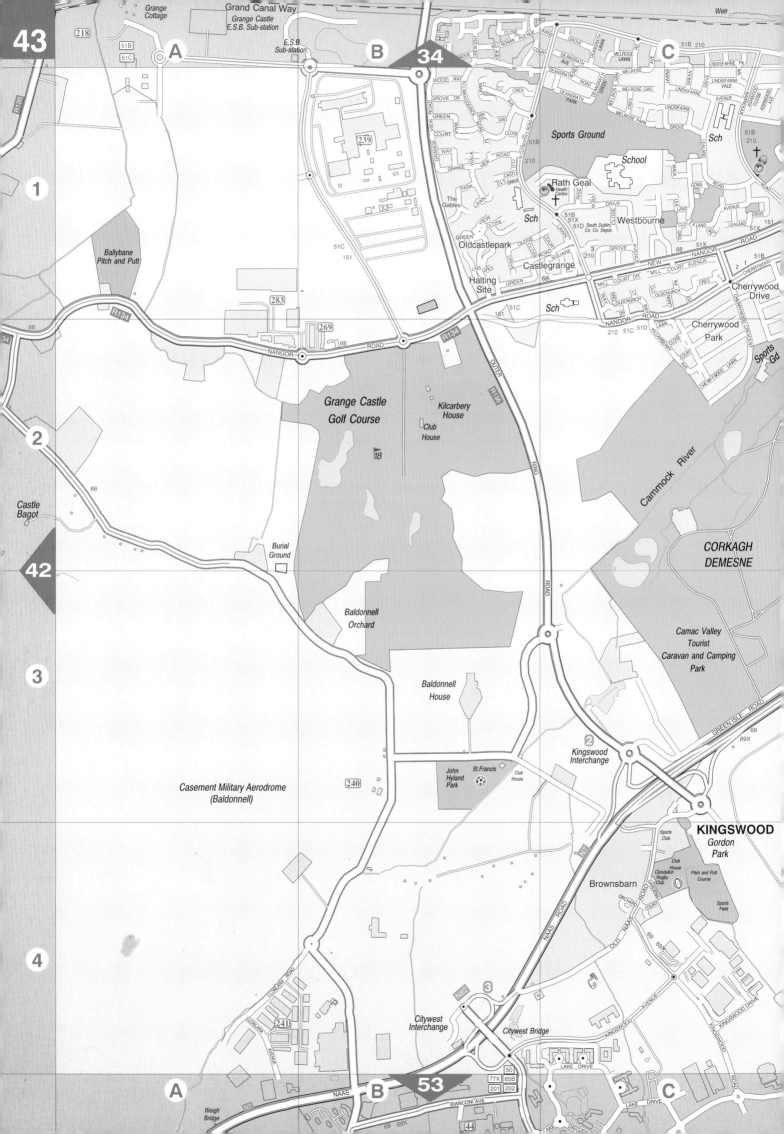

218

51B
51C

A

Grange Cottage

Grand Canal Way
Grange Castle
E.S.B. Sub-station

E.S.B.
Sub-station.

B

Weir

WOOD WAY
GROVE DR
GREEN COURT
GRANGE VIEW ROAD

KILMAHUDDRICK ROAD
ST. CUTHBERTS ROAD

239

CRESCENT
CLOSE
VIEW
LAWNS
GROVE
DEANSRATH AVE
DEANSRATH LAWN
MELROSE
AVE

KILCRONAN AVENUE
COURT

LAWN
CRES
GRN
CLOSE
PL
GRANGE VIEW CLOSE
WALK
GRO
WALK
VIEW
ROAD
GRANGE
PARK

DEANSRATH
ROAD
DEANSRATH GRN
DEANSRATH PARK
MELROSE
MELROSE GRO
MELROSE PARK
GROVE

LINDISFARNE PK
LINDISFARNE VALE
LINDISFARNE
AVENUE

51B 210

C

Sch

51B
210

Sports Ground

School

H

Sch

Rath Geal
Health Centre

CASTLE OLD DRIVE
RISE
VIEW
DRIVE

51B
51X
51D

The Gables

GREEN
VIEW
CLOSE
LAWN

GRANGE VIEW COURT

South Dublin
Co. Co. Depot

Oldcastlepark

Castlegrange

LNS GRO
GREEN
SQUARE

Halting
Site

Sch

MILL COURT DR
MILL COURT AVENUE
CRES

GRO
CT
OLDCHURCH
OLDCHURCH WAY
WAY
DR

NEW
3
210

GROVE AVENUE

68

NANGOR

51X

Westbourne

LEALAND ROAD
CLO
LEA
LAND

GRO
CK

LEALAND AVENUE
151
51X

51B

1
2
CHERRYWOOD

Cherrywood
Drive

Cherrywood
Park

CHERRYWOOD CRESCENT
CHERRYWOOD DRIVE

KILCARBERY CLOSE
COURT
AVE
LAWN

CHERRYWOOD LAWN

Sports
Gd

51C
151

51C
151

283

269

68

R134

NANGOR

ROAD

R134

210
51C
51D

NANGOR
ROAD

OUTER

R136

RING

ROAD

Grange Castle
Golf Course

Kilcarbery
House

Club
House

18

Cammock River

**CORKAGH
DEMESNE**

68

Castle
Bagot

Burial
Ground

Baldonnell
Orchard

Baldonnell
House

Camac Valley
Tourist
Caravan and Camping
Park

GREEN ISLE ROAD

69
69X

3

Casement Military Aerodrome
(Baldonnell)

240

John
Hyland
Park

St.Francis

Club
House

2

Kingswood
Interchange

N7

Sports
Club

KINGSWOOD

Gordon
Park

Club
House
Clondalkin
Rugby Club

Pitch and Putt
Course

Sports
Field

Brownsbarn

NAAS ROAD

ORCHARD
COURT

KINGSWOOD GREENS ROAD

OLD NAAS ROAD
69X
69

BAINGOOD CLOSE
ASHWOOD CLOSE

KINGSWOOD AVENUE

KINGSWOOD DRIVE

4

N82

3

Citywest
Interchange

Citywest Bridge

CLONLARA ROAD

CLONLARA AVENUE

241

NAAS

N7

Weigh
Bridge

69 69X

BIANCONI AVE

50
77X 65B
201 202

44

LAKE DRIVE

LAKE
DRIVE

A

B

C

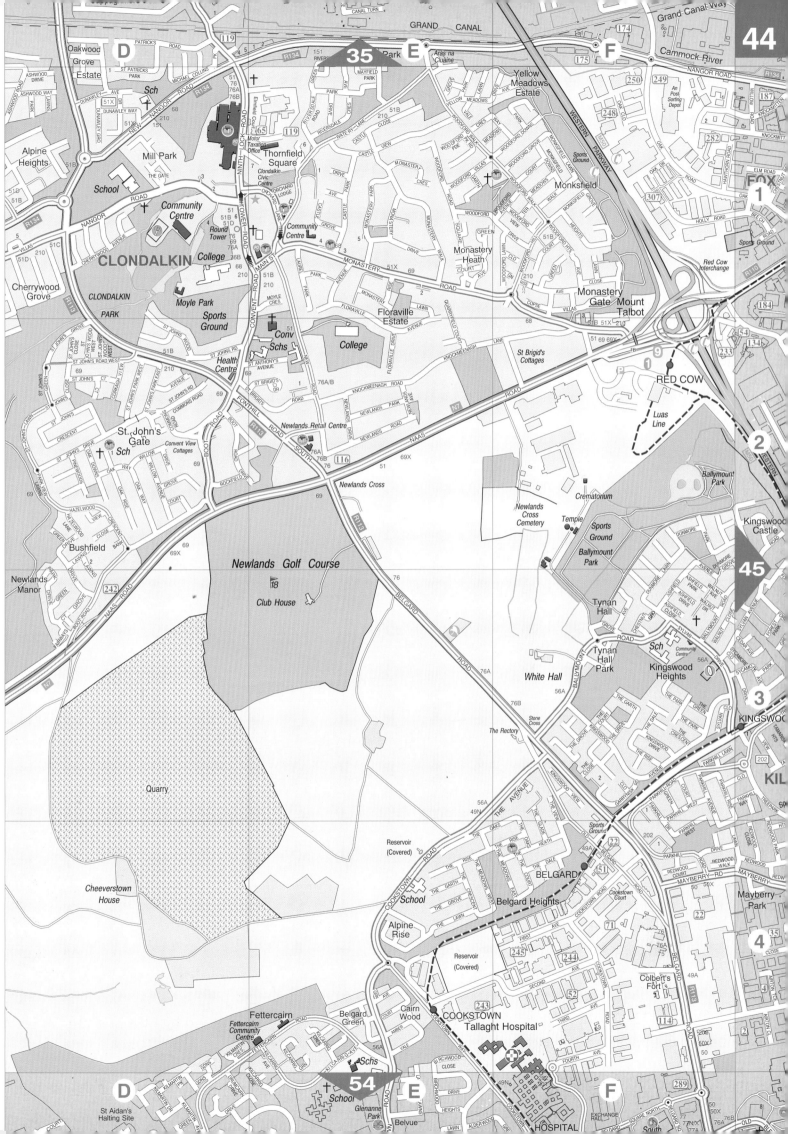

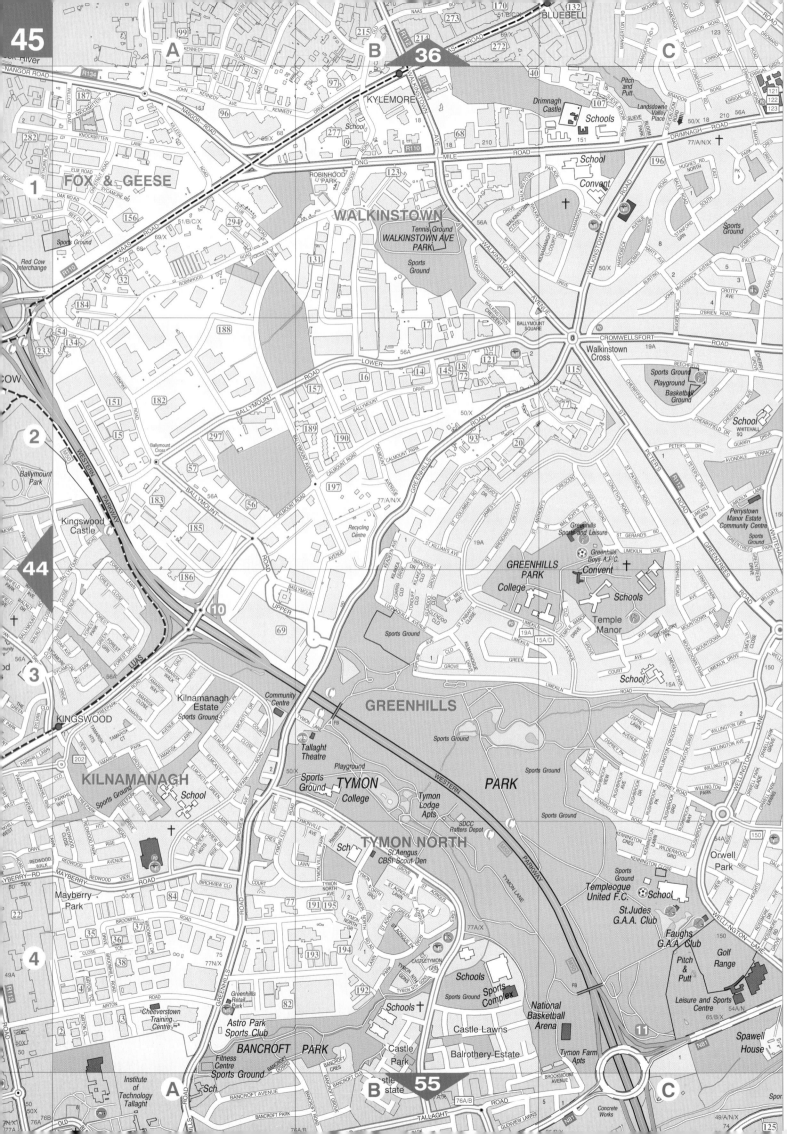

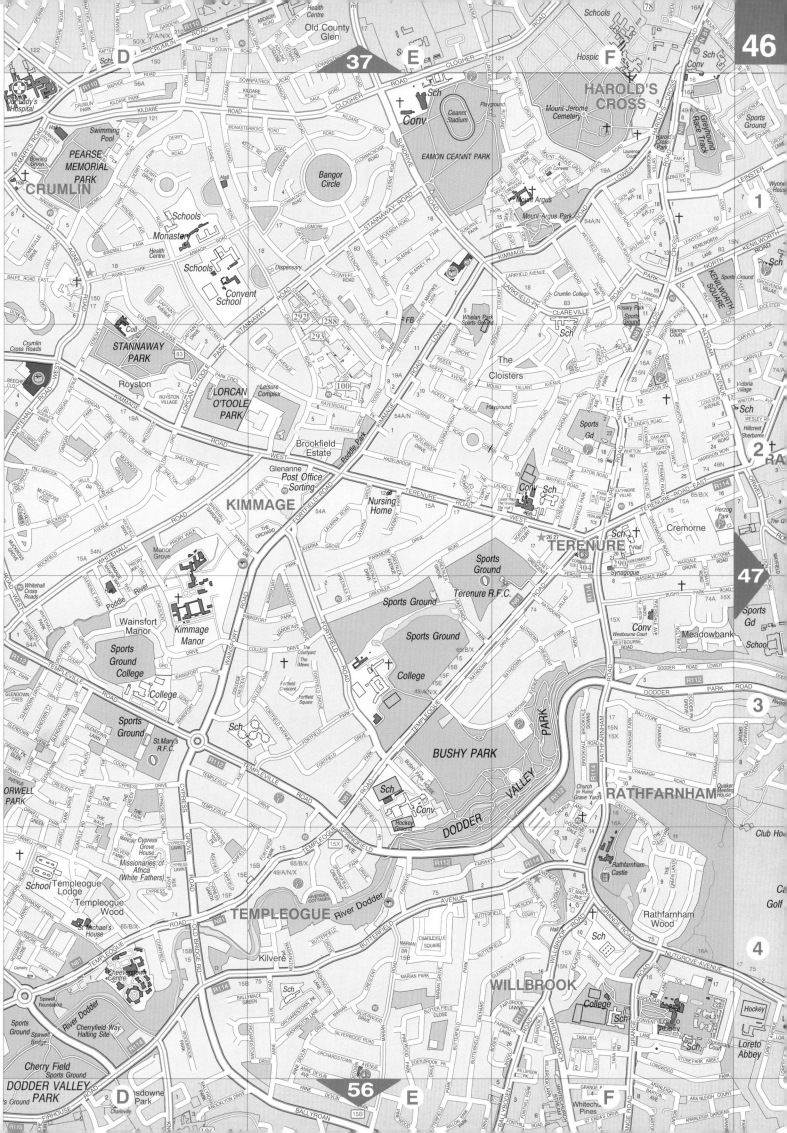

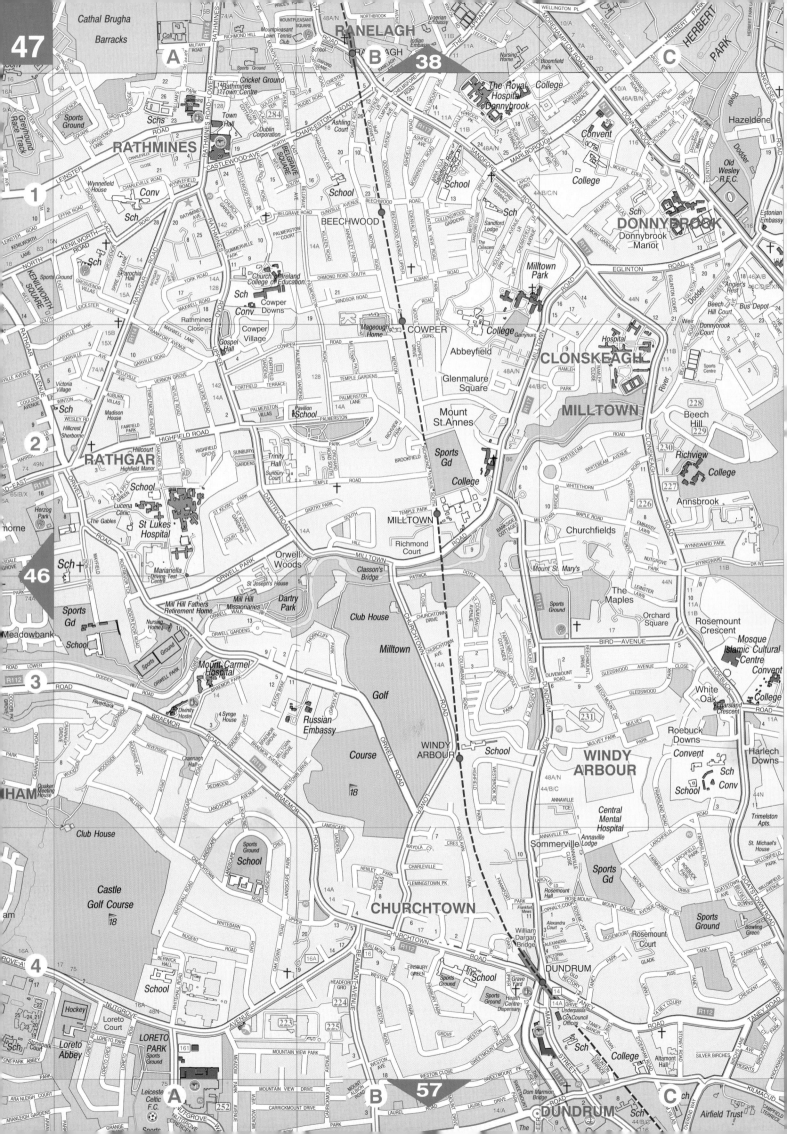

Lighthouse

Lighthouse

Harbour

EAST PIER

Car Ferry Terminal

Yacht Club

7B	746
45A	46A
46X	59
75	111

Car Ferry Terminal

Band Stand

HARBOUR ROAD

CROFTON ROAD

Dún Laoghaire Station

Yacht Club

Yacht Club

Geographical Pointer
Toilets

QUEEN'S ROAD

Harbour View
Harbour Square

Dun-Laoghaire/Rathdown
Co. Council

Town Hall

Hosp

Sch.

EBLANA AVE.

MARINE RD.

MORAN PARK

Maritime Museum

DÚN LAOGHAIRE

Sch

Sch

DOMINICK ST.

Health Centre

GEORGE'S STREET LOWER

GEORGE'S STREET UPPER

Baths

PARK ROAD

PEOPLE'S PARK

WINDSOR TCE.

Scotsman's Bay

Forty Foot
Bathing Place

Nursing Home

Sandycove/Glasthule Station

SUMMERHILL ROAD

Harbour

Tower

Baths

SANDYCOVE POINT

SANDYCOVE AVE. EAST

MARINE PARADE

NEWTOWNSMITH

F.H.B. Nursing Home

Children's Home

Clarinda Manor

Sch

EDEN RD UPR

Coll Schs

GLASTHULE ROAD

SANDYCOVE ROAD

SANDYCOVE AVE. WEST

Bullock Harbour

BREFFNI

R119

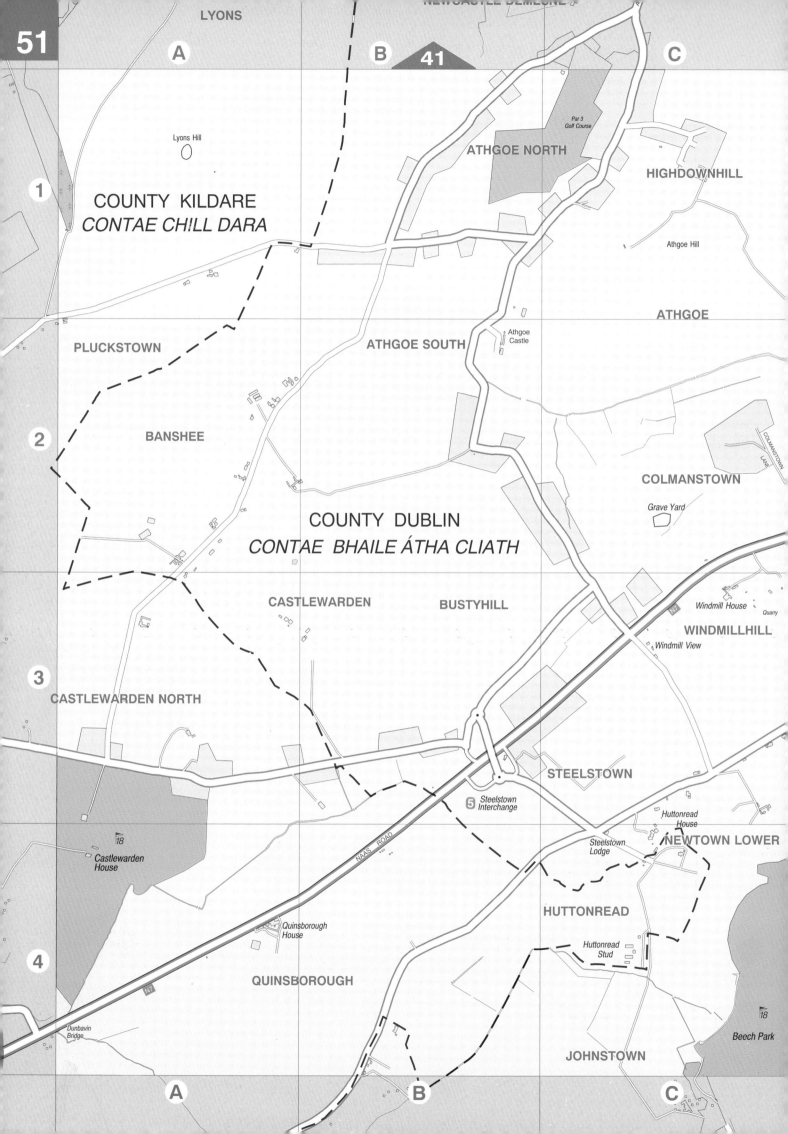

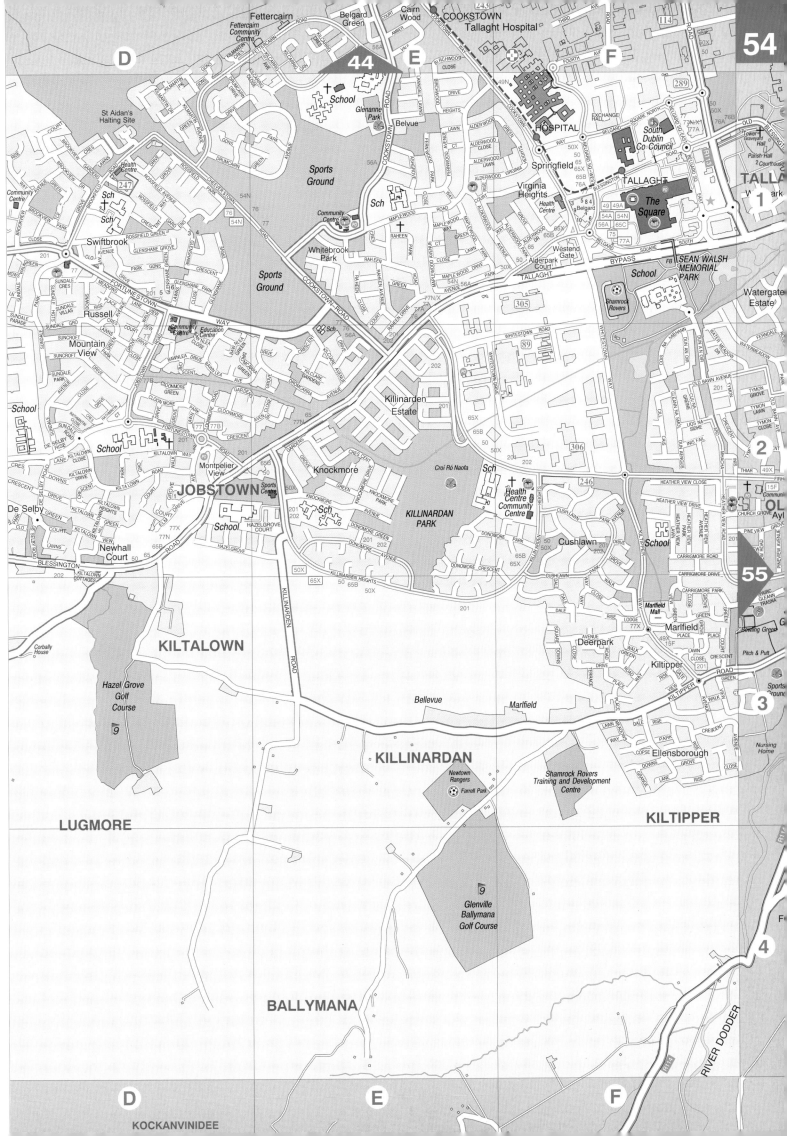

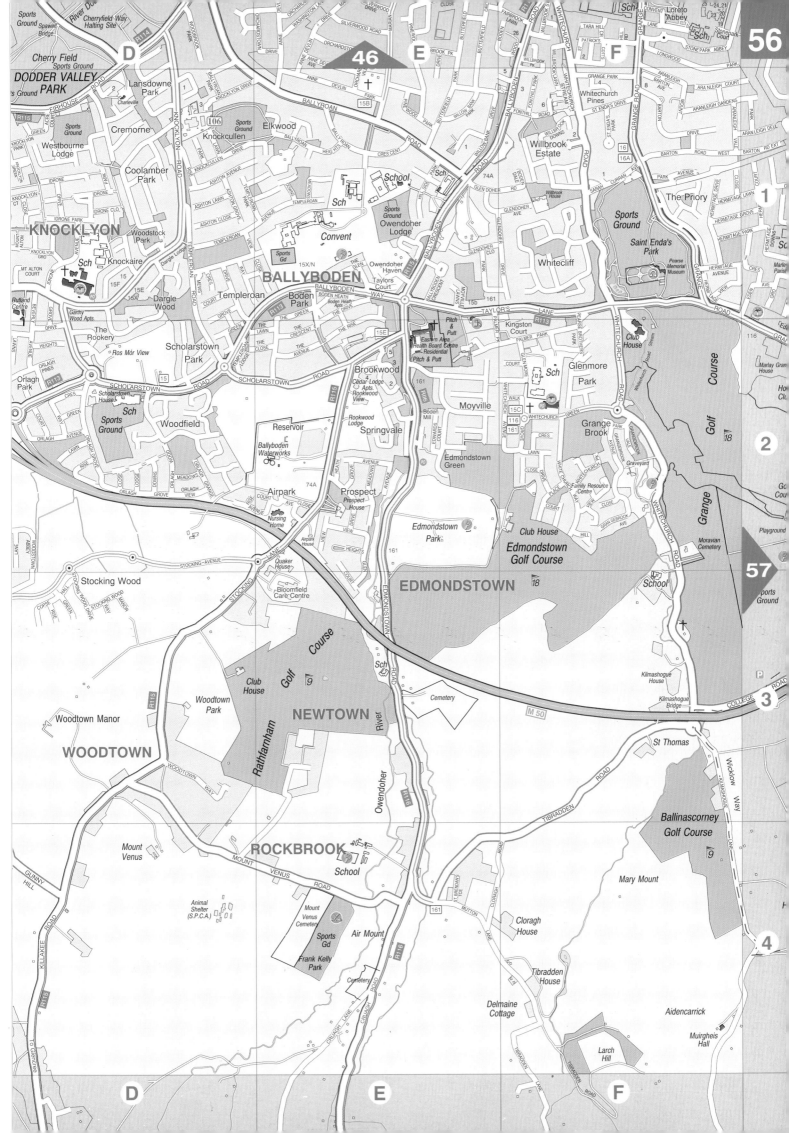

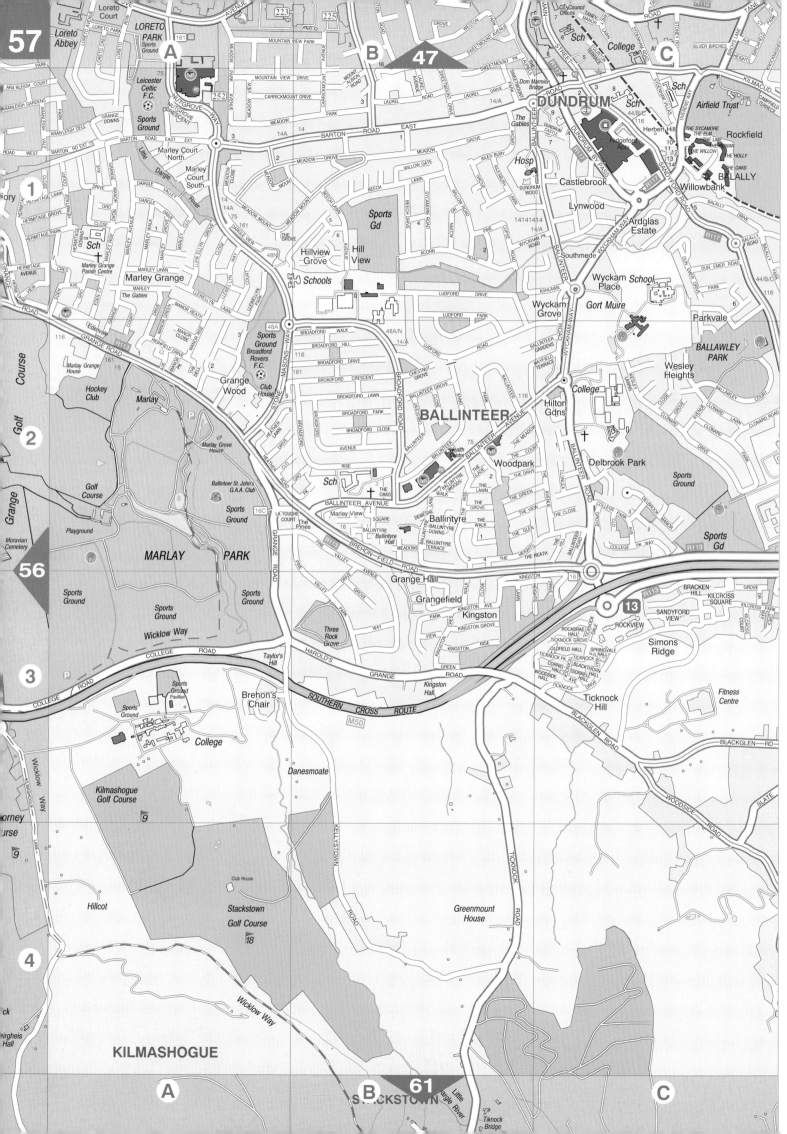

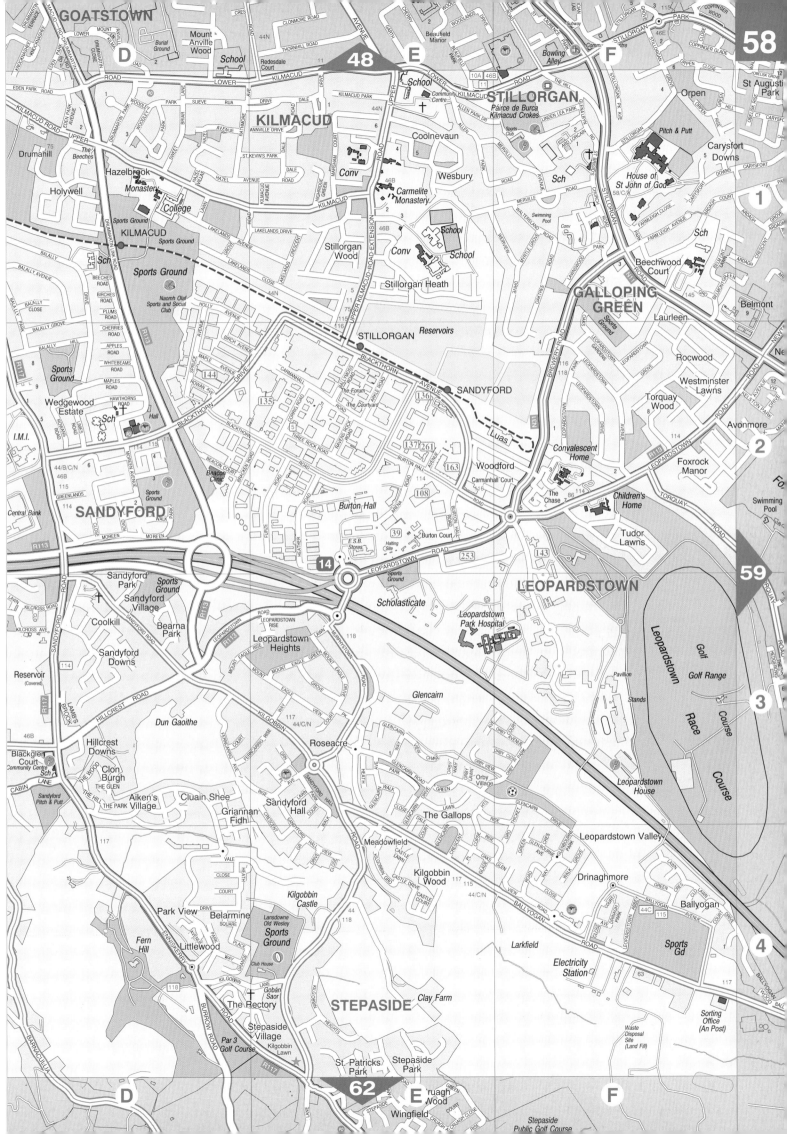

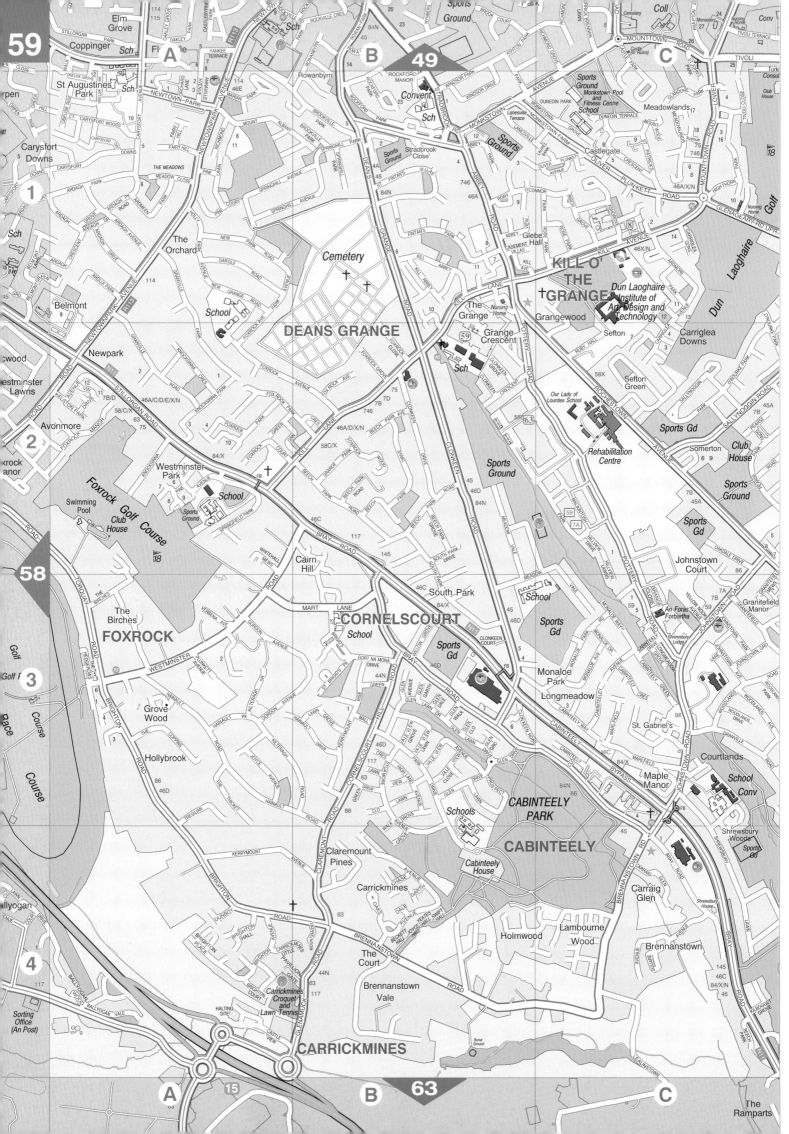

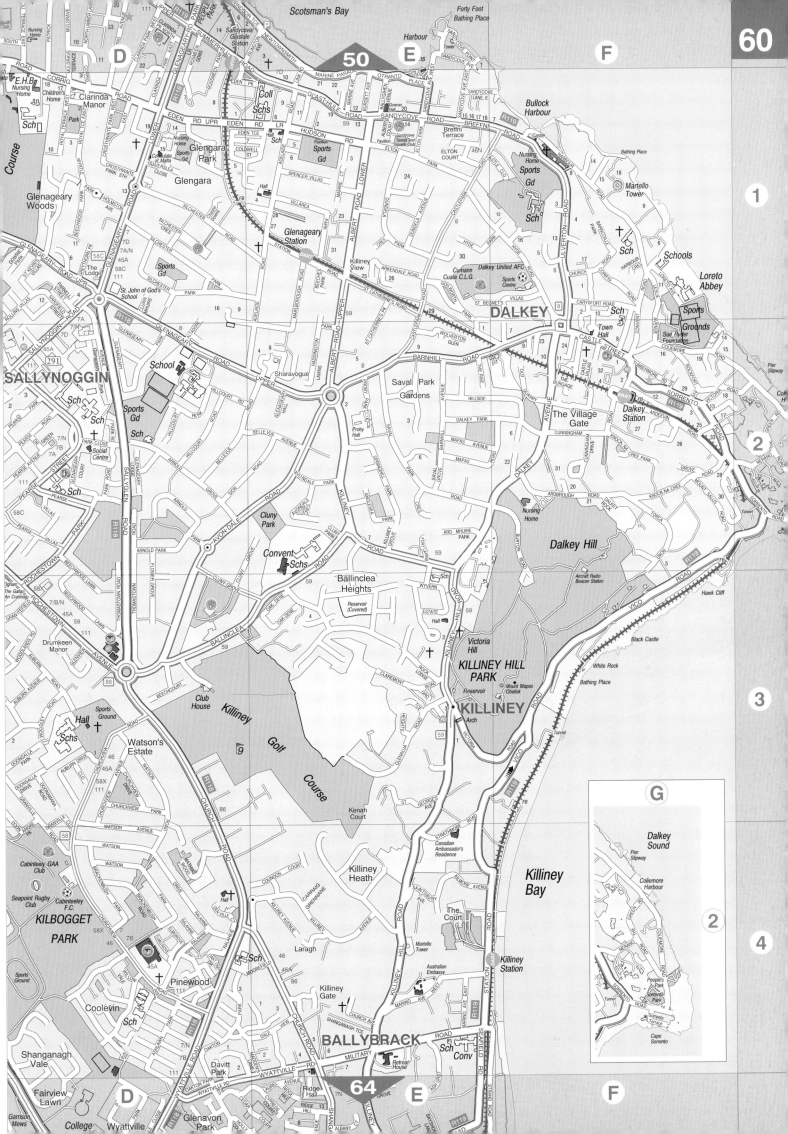

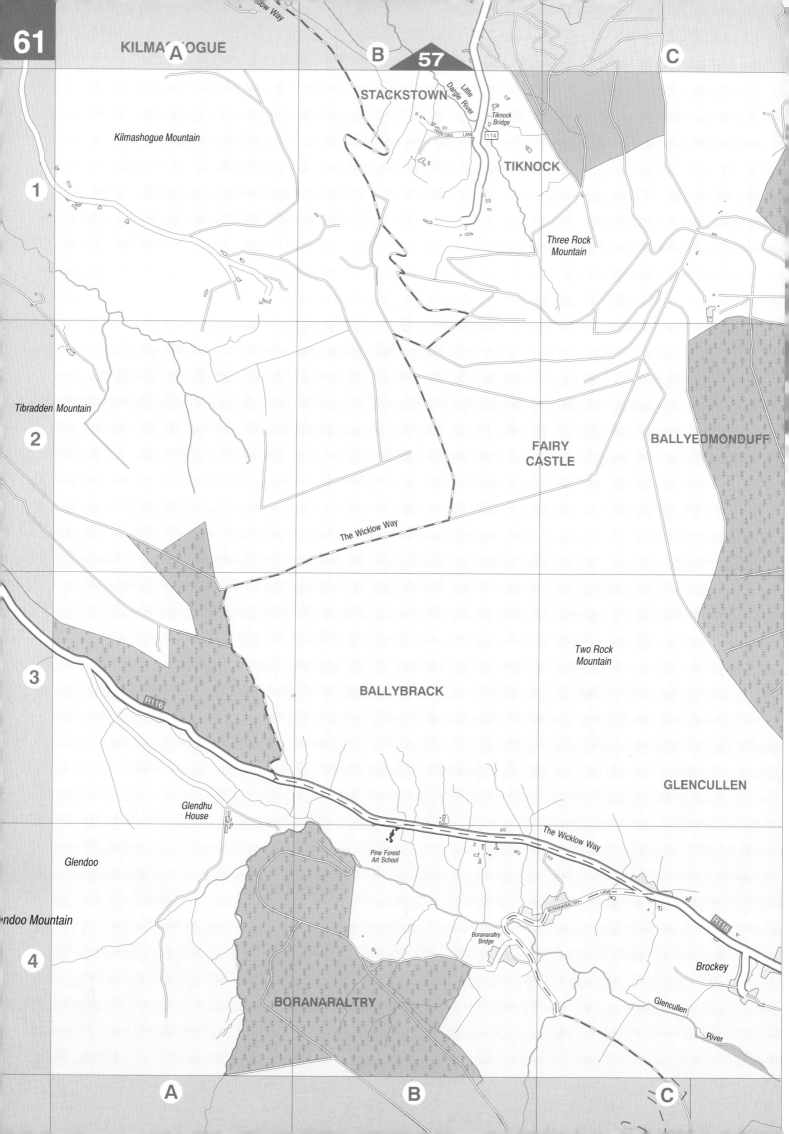

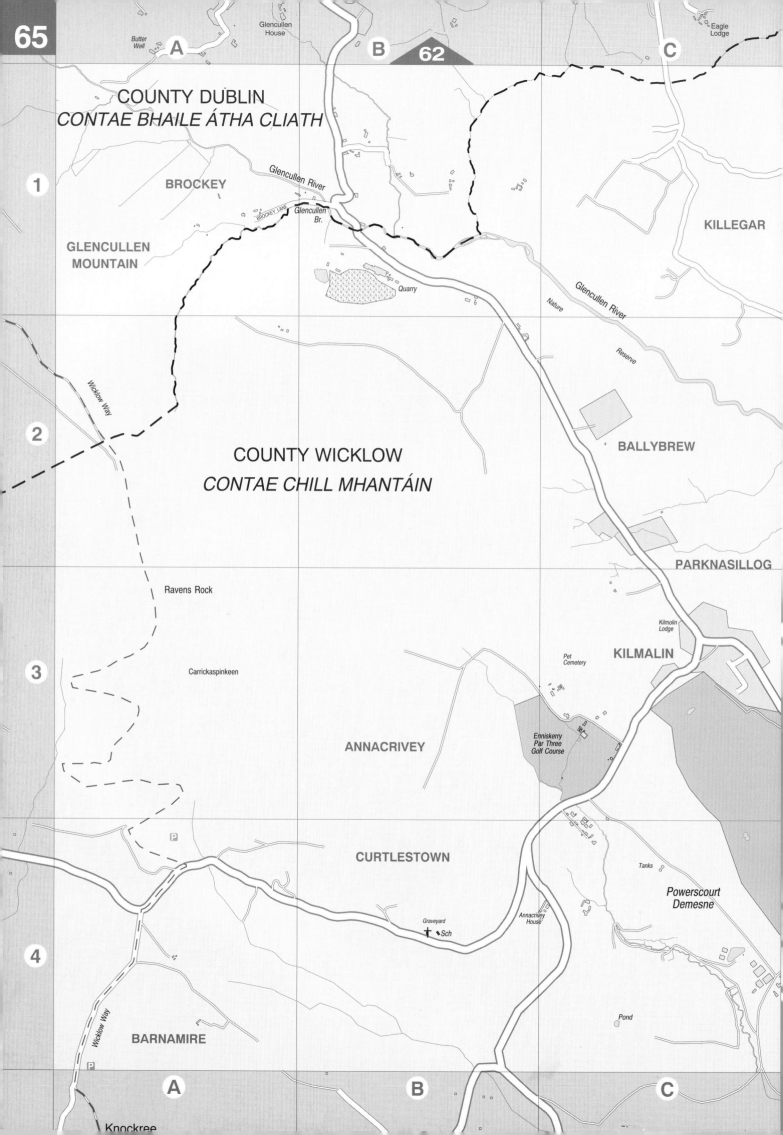

62

A

Butter
Well

Glencullen
House

B

Eagle
Lodge

C

COUNTY DUBLIN
CONTAE BHAILE ÁTHA CLIATH

1

BROCKEY

Glencullen River

KILLEGAR

BROCKEY LANE

Glencullen
Br.

GLENCULLEN
MOUNTAIN

Quarry

Glencullen River

Nature

Reserve

Wicklow Way

2

COUNTY WICKLOW
CONTAE CHILL MHANTÁIN

BALLYBREW

PARKNASILLOG

Ravens Rock

Kilmolin
Lodge

KILMALIN

3

Carrickaspinkeen

Pet
Cemetery

ANNACRIVEY

Enniskerry
Par Three
Golf Course

P

CURTLESTOWN

Tanks

*Powerscourt
Demesne*

Graveyard

Annacrivey
House

✝ ♦Sch

64

Pond

Wicklow Way

BARNAMIRE

P

A

Knockree

B

C

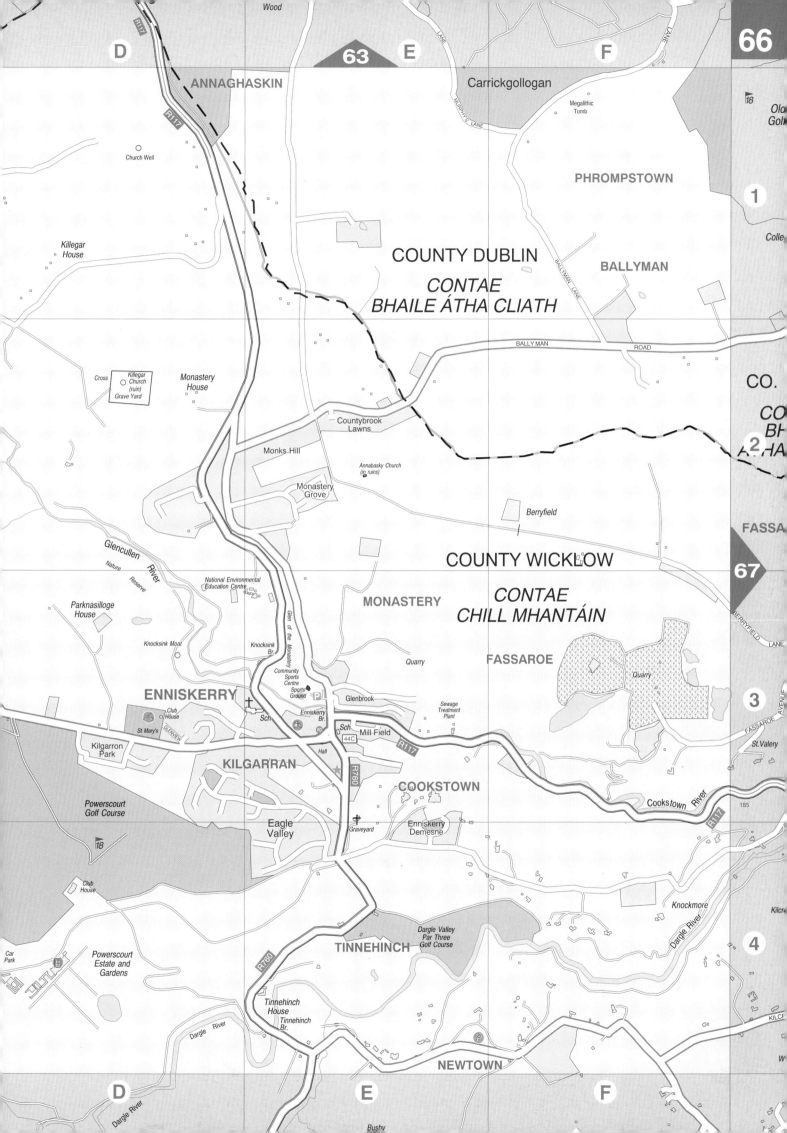

D   E   F

1

2

3

4

BRAY

Esplanade

21
16
*National
Sea Life
Aquarium*
75

ALBERT AVE

STRAND ESPLANADE

14

SIDMONTON

17-18

STRAND ROAD

2
45
VICTORIA AVE

MEATH

13

3

MARON

CONVENT AVENUE

Hall

19

R768

23

20

45

SIDMONTON PK

4

5

EDENHAM MEWS

6

PUTLAND

ROAD

NEWCOURT ROAD

*Fontenoy
Terrace*

2

EDWARD RD

3

RAHEEN PARK

CUALA ROAD

CAMADERRY RD

Naylor's Cove

CUALA GROVE

NEWCOURT ROAD

AVENUE

1

Golf Course

*Raheenacluig Church
(in Ruins)*

NEWCOURT ROAD

*Briar
Wood*

4/N

NEWCOURT

R761

Tunnel

*Bray
Head*

84/X/N
184

Golf Course

COUNTY WICKLOW

*CONTAE
CHILL MHANTÁIN*

Tunnel

Tunnel
Tunnel

D   E   F

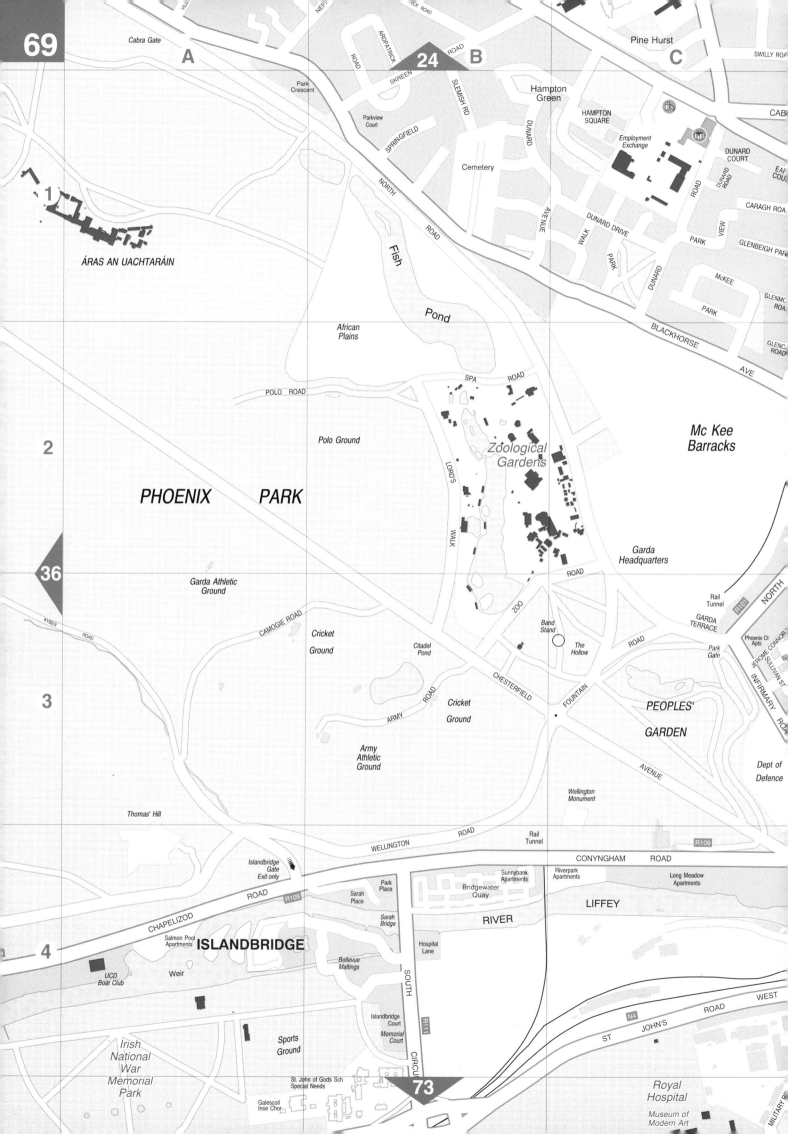

A

B

C

Cabra Gate

Pine Hurst

SWILLY ROAD

VILLA

NEF

RICK ROAD

ROAD

ARDPATRICK

ROAD

CAB

Park Crescent

SKREEN

SLEMISH RD

Hampton Green

HAMPTON SQUARE

Parkview Court

SPRINGFIELD

Employment Exchange

DUNARD COURT

Cemetery

DUNARD

EAR COU

NORTH

AVENUE

DUNARD DRIVE

WALK

DUNARD ROAD

CARAGH ROA

ROAD

Fish

PARK

DUNARD

PARK

VIEW

GLENBEIGH PAR

GLENMO ROA

Pond

McKEE PARK

GLENC ROA

African Plains

1

ÁRAS AN UACHTARÁIN

SPA   ROAD

BLACKHORSE

AVE

POLO   ROAD

Polo Ground

Zoological Gardens

Mc Kee Barracks

LORD'S

2

PHOENIX   PARK

WALK

Garda Headquarters

Rail Tunnel

R101

NORTH

GARDA TERRACE

36

Garda Athletic Ground

ZOO

Phoenix Ct Apts

KYBER   ROAD

CAMOGIE ROAD

Cricket Ground

Citadel Pond

Band Stand

The Hollow

ROAD

Park Gate

JEROME CONNOR

INFIRMARY RO

SULLIVAN ST

ARMY

ROAD

CHESTERFIELD

FOUNTAIN

3

Cricket Ground

PEOPLES'

Army Athletic Ground

GARDEN

Thomas' Hill

Wellington Monument

AVENUE

Dept of Defence

WELLINGTON   ROAD

Rail Tunnel

CONYNGHAM   ROAD

R109

Islandbridge Gate Exit only

Sunnybank Apartments

Riverpark Apartments

Long Meadow Apartments

CHAPELIZOD

ROAD   R109

Park Place

Bridgewater Quay

LIFFEY

Sarah Place

Salmon Pool Apartments

Sarah Bridge

RIVER

ISLANDBRIDGE

Hospital Lane

SOUTH

4

UCD Boat Club

Weir

Bellevue Maltings

R111

Islandbridge Court

N4

ROAD

WEST

Memorial Court

ST JOHN'S

Irish National War Memorial Park

Sports Ground

CIRCU

Royal Hospital

St. John of Gods Sch Special Needs

MILITARY

Galescoil Inse Chor

Museum of Modern Art

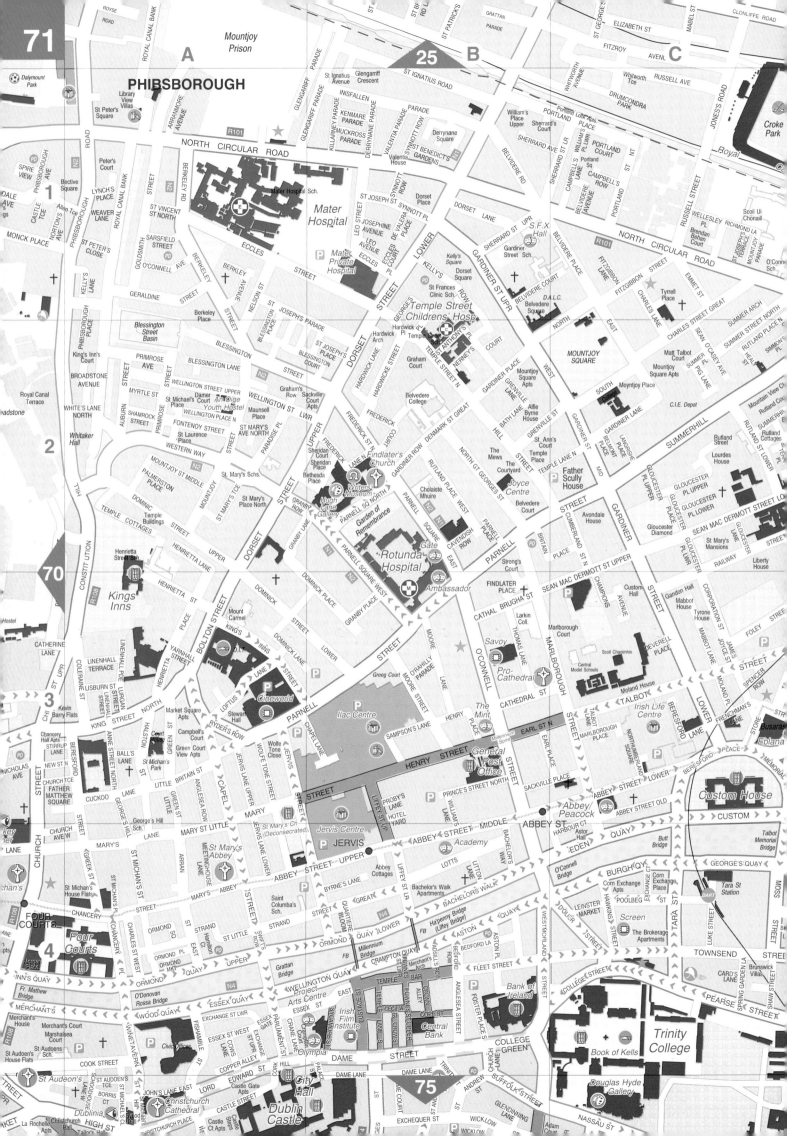

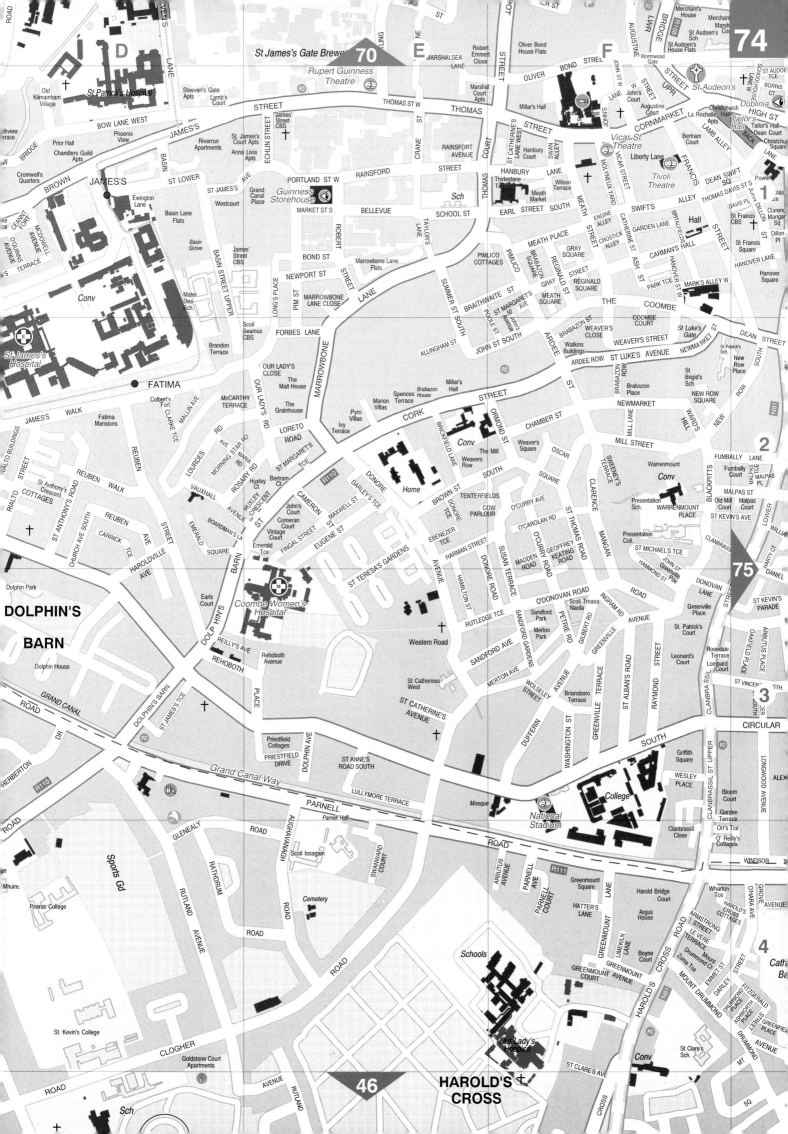

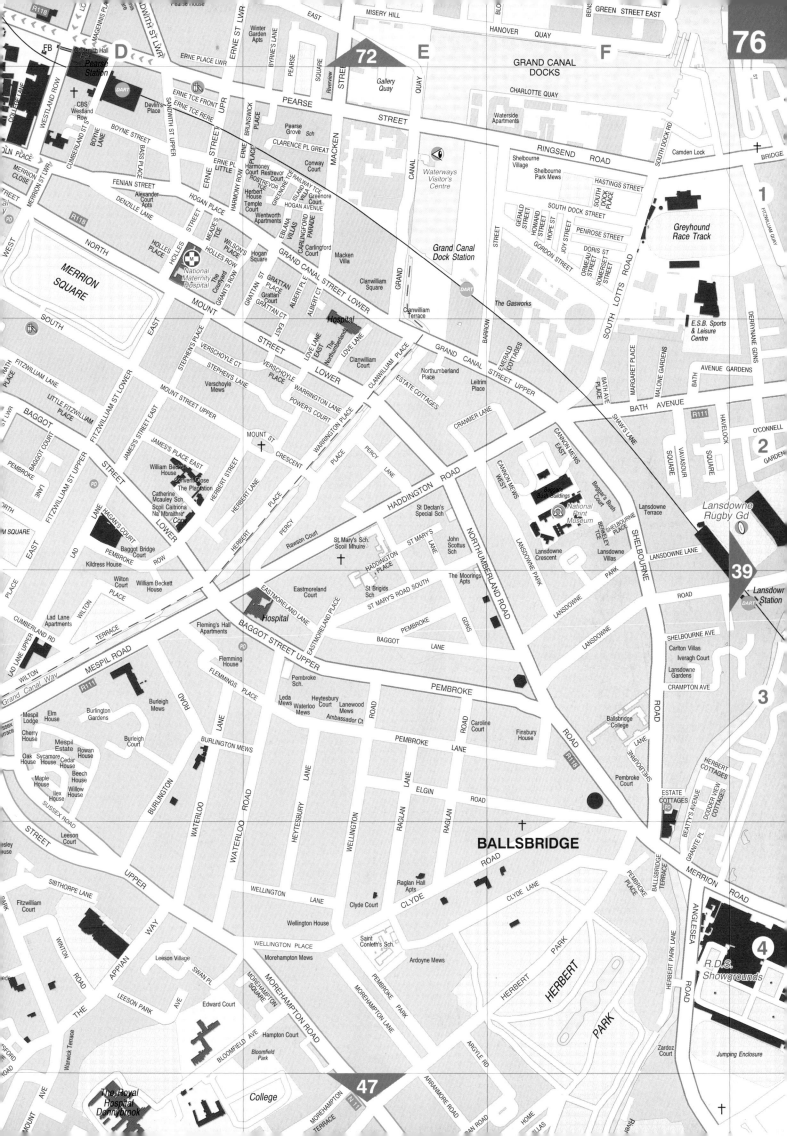

ASHBOURNE

LEGEND

Symbol	Description
M1	MOTORWAY
N9	NATIONAL PRIMARY ROAD
N81	NATIONAL SECONDARY ROAD
R683	REGIONAL ROAD
	MAIN ROADS/STREETS
	OTHER ROADS/STREETS
	NARROW / STREET PRIVATE ROADS
	ROAD UNDER CONSTRUCTION
	PEDESTRIAN STREETS
	BUILT UP AREA
	GREEN AREA
	WOODED AREA
	COMMERCIAL / INDUSTRIAL
	HOSPITAL / SCHOOL
	WATER
✚	HOSPITAL
	FIRE STATION
★	GARDA
P	PARKING
PO	POST OFFICE
†	CHURCH
▪	MONUMENT / STATUE
	LIGHTHOUSE
	ONE WAY STREETS
	MAINLINE RAIL STATION
	ART GALLERY
	SAMPLE LANDMARK BUILDING
	CINEMA
	GAELIC GROUND
	LIBRARY
	MUSEUM
	RUGBY GROUND
i	TOURIST OFFICE
	SHOPPING COMPLEX
	SCHOOL / COLLEGE
	SOCCER GROUND
	THEATRE
	VISITOR CENTRE
⚑	GOLF COURSE
♠	CAMPING SITE
	CARAVAN SITE
	RAIL LINE

L C
(Level Crossing)

1

2

3

A

B

To Slane

To Slane

R135

N2

Monument

Ashbourne Industrial Park

Rath Cross Roads

Ashbourne Retail Park

Rath Cross Business Park

Rath Lodge

BALLYBIN ROAD

Ashbourne Industrial Park

Westfield Green

Tudor Grove

Tudor Close

Tudor Crescent

TUDOR GROVE

Westfield View

BRINDLEY PARK GN

Saint Johns Wood Court

Brindley Park Square

Brindley Park Crescent

Saint Johns Wood Park

KILDERRY HALL

Ashbourne Business Park

Brindley Park

St Johns Wood Drive

CLUAIN RI

Health Centre

Cookstown Bridge

Killegland Park

KILLEGLAND

WESTBOURNE VIEW

WESTVIEW

To Finglas

Factory

To Ratoath

R125

Factory

A

B

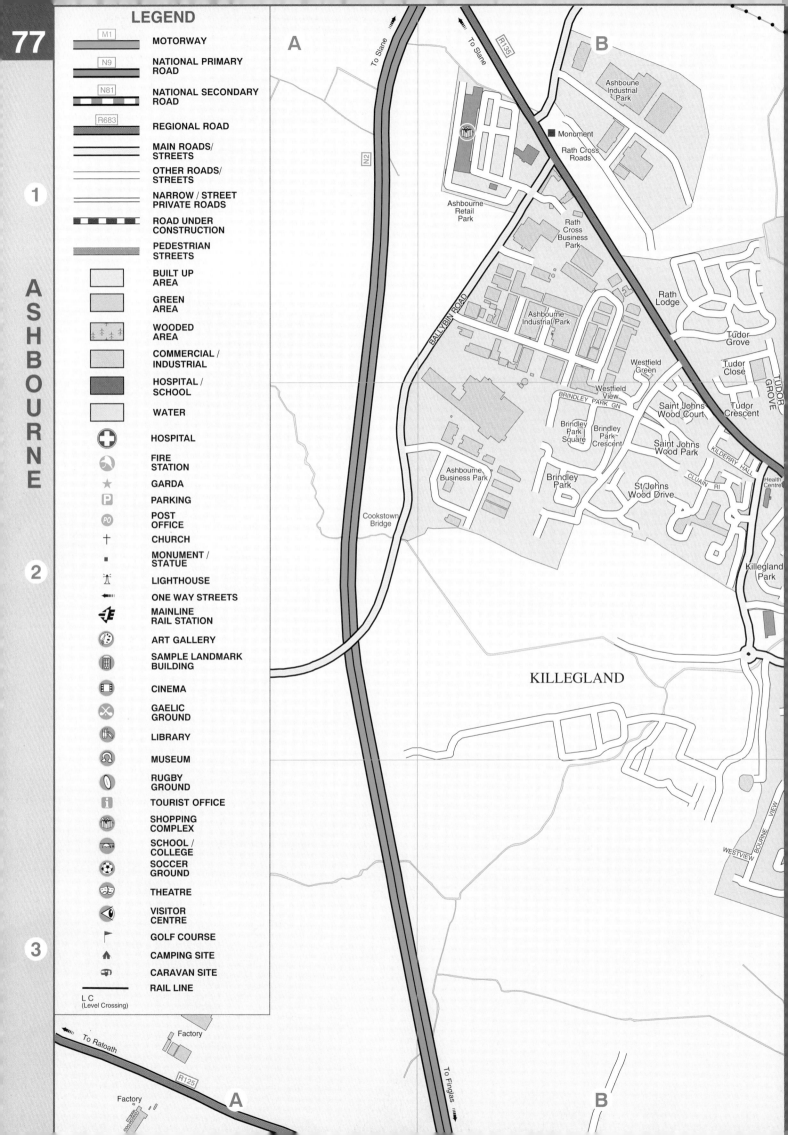

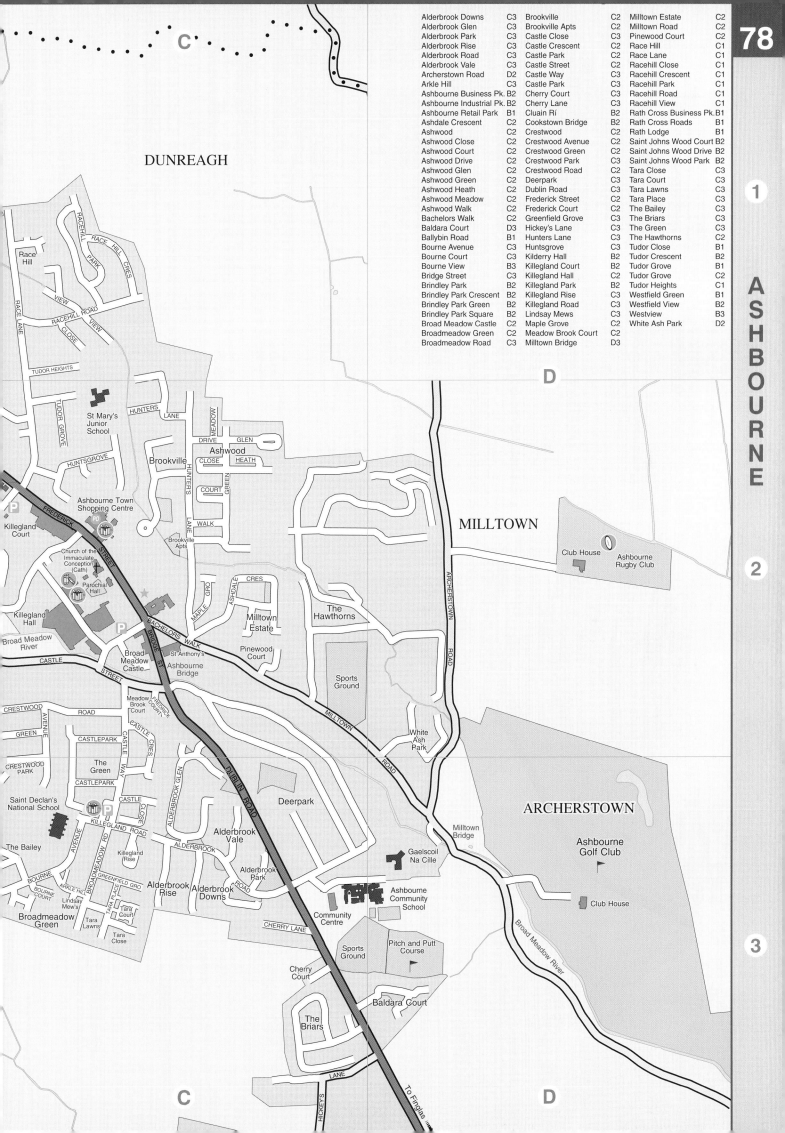

Street	Grid	Street	Grid	Street	Grid
Alderbrook Downs	C3	Brookville	C2	Milltown Estate	C2
Alderbrook Glen	C3	Brookville Apts	C2	Milltown Road	C2
Alderbrook Park	C3	Castle Close	C3	Pinewood Court	C2
Alderbrook Rise	C3	Castle Crescent	C2	Race Hill	C1
Alderbrook Road	C3	Castle Park	C2	Race Lane	C1
Alderbrook Vale	C3	Castle Street	C2	Racehill Close	C1
Archerstown Road	D2	Castle Way	C3	Racehill Crescent	C1
Arkle Hill	C3	Castle Park	C3	Racehill Park	C1
Ashbourne Business Pk.	B2	Cherry Court	C3	Racehill Road	C1
Ashbourne Industrial Pk.	B2	Cherry Lane	C3	Racehill View	C1
Ashbourne Retail Park	B1	Cluain Rí	B2	Rath Cross Business Pk.	B1
Ashdale Crescent	C2	Cookstown Bridge	B2	Rath Cross Roads	B1
Ashwood	C2	Crestwood	C2	Rath Lodge	B1
Ashwood Close	C2	Crestwood Avenue	C2	Saint Johns Wood Court	B2
Ashwood Court	C2	Crestwood Green	C2	Saint Johns Wood Drive	B2
Ashwood Drive	C2	Crestwood Park	C3	Saint Johns Wood Park	B2
Ashwood Glen	C2	Crestwood Road	C2	Tara Close	C3
Ashwood Green	C2	Deerpark	C3	Tara Court	C3
Ashwood Heath	C2	Dublin Road	C3	Tara Lawns	C3
Ashwood Meadow	C2	Frederick Street	C2	Tara Place	C3
Ashwood Walk	C2	Frederick Court	C2	The Bailey	C3
Bachelors Walk	C2	Greenfield Grove	C3	The Briars	C3
Baldara Court	D3	Hickey's Lane	C3	The Green	C3
Ballybin Road	B1	Hunters Lane	C3	The Hawthorns	C2
Bourne Avenue	C3	Huntsgrove	C3	Tudor Close	B1
Bourne Court	C3	Kilderry Hall	B2	Tudor Crescent	B2
Bourne View	B3	Killegland Court	B2	Tudor Grove	B1
Bridge Street	C3	Killegland Hall	C2	Tudor Grove	C2
Brindley Park	B2	Killegland Park	B2	Tudor Heights	C1
Brindley Park Crescent	B2	Killegland Rise	C3	Westfield Green	B1
Brindley Park Green	B2	Killegland Road	C3	Westfield View	B2
Brindley Park Square	B2	Lindsay Mews	C3	Westview	B3
Broad Meadow Castle	C2	Maple Grove	C2	White Ash Park	D2
Broadmeadow Green	C2	Meadow Brook Court	C2		
Broadmeadow Road	C3	Milltown Bridge	D3		

BALBRIGGAN

A

B

BREMORE

FLEMINGTOWN

1

To Drogheda

Dublin/Belfast Railway

R132

Cardy Rock

COURT

WALK

CLOSE

AVE

SQUARE

CRES

Sports Ground

HAMLET CLO

DRIVE

CLOSE

AVE

RISE

VIEW

CLO

DRIVE

Mount Rochford

O'Dwyers GAA Club

Club House

ROAD

Castle

St Molaga's Church (in Ruins)

Sports Ground

FLEMINGTON LANE

COURT

AVE

RISE

New Haven

Dún Saithne

PARK

RISE

Clonuske

GN

HAMLET LANE

DROGHEDA

Saint Molaga's National School

BATHS ROAD

Lambeecher

BELLSFIELD COURT

CLO RD

BAY

Flemington Park

New Haven Bay

Trimleston

BREGA

Chieftain's

Bremore Castle

RISE

DRIVE

GREEN

RISE

BREMORE CT

BREMORE DRIVE

COVETOWN

Oakleigh

DROGHEDA

Hastings

Hamlet Avenue

Barons Hall Rise

Lane Mews

HAMLET SQ.

HAMLET LANE

CLOSE

ROAD

Ashfield

WAY

CLOSE

TEMPLE VILLE

Chapel Gate

Brecan Close

Brackenwood

Castlemill

Barons Hall Park

DRIVE

Hampton Woods

ROAD

CHAPEL GROVE

Balbriggan Community College

Bremore Pastures

Barons Hall Grove

ROAD

CRES

DRIVE

MOYLARAGH

CRESCENT

Moylaragh Park

CHAPEL CLOSE

CHAPEL AVENUE

Balbriggan Educate Together National School

AVENUE

GROVE

GATE

CHAPEL

PINE RIDGE

CHAPEL

Martello

MEWS

MOYLARAGH LANE

Moylaragh

GROVE

MOYLARAGH WALK

COURT

MOYLARAGH

Westbrook

RISE

CLOSE

DRIVE

Saint Peter and Paul's Junior School

FULLAM

MOYLARAGH GDNS

RISE

WAY

CLOSE

GREEN PARK

HEIGHTS

GREEN LN

LAWN

GREEN

AVENUE

PROSPECT

FULLAM TCE

2

CRESCENT

St. Peter and Paul's Cemetery

TARA COURT

RISE

CLONARD

TARA COVE

Balbriggan Business Park

R122

CLONARD ROAD

CLOGHEDER

HARRY REYNOLDS ROAD

Fingal Bay Business Park

CLONARD or FOLKSTOWN GREAT

Stephenstown Business Park

To M1 and Naul

STEPHENSTOWN

Halting Site

3

FOLKSTOWN LITTLE

A

B

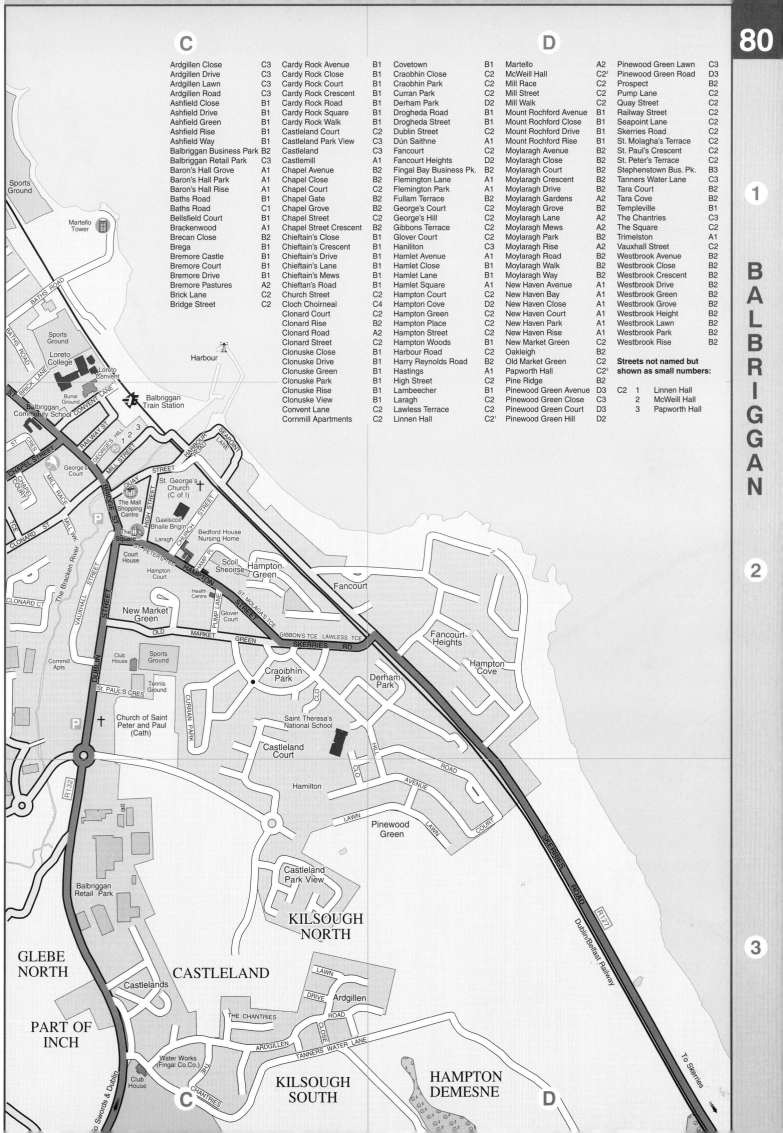

1

2

3

Ardgillen Close	C3	Cardy Rock Avenue	B1	Covetown	B1
Ardgillen Drive	C3	Cardy Rock Close	B1	Craobhin Close	C2
Ardgillen Lawn	C3	Cardy Rock Court	B1	Craobhin Park	C2
Ardgillen Road	C3	Cardy Rock Crescent	B1	Curran Park	C2
Ashfield Close	B1	Cardy Rock Road	B1	Derham Park	D2
Ashfield Drive	B1	Cardy Rock Square	B1	Drogheda Road	B1
Ashfield Green	B1	Cardy Rock Walk	B1	Drogheda Street	B1
Ashfield Rise	B1	Castleland Court	C2	Dublin Street	C2
Ashfield Way	B1	Castleland Park View	C3	Dún Saithne	A1
Balbriggan Business Park	B2	Castleland	C3	Fancourt	C2
Balbriggan Retail Park	C3	Castlemill	A1	Fancourt Heights	D2
Baron's Hall Grove	A1	Chapel Avenue	B2	Fingal Bay Business Pk.	B2
Baron's Hall Park	A1	Chapel Close	B2	Flemington Lane	A1
Baron's Hall Rise	A1	Chapel Court	C2	Flemington Park	A1
Baths Road	B1	Chapel Gate	B2	Fullam Terrace	B2
Baths Road	C1	Chapel Grove	B2	George's Court	C2
Bellsfield Court	B1	Chapel Street	C2	George's Hill	C2
Brackenwood	A1	Chapel Street Crescent	B2	Gibbons Terrace	C2
Brecan Close	B2	Chieftain's Close	B1	Glover Court	C2
Brega	B1	Chieftain's Crescent	B1	Haniliton	C3
Bremore Castle	B1	Chieftain's Drive	B1	Hamlet Avenue	A1
Bremore Court	B1	Chieftain's Lane	B1	Hamlet Close	B1
Bremore Drive	B1	Chieftain's Mews	B1	Hamlet Lane	B1
Bremore Pastures	A2	Chieftain's Road	B1	Hamlet Square	A1
Brick Lane	C2	Church Street	C2	Hampton Court	C2
Bridge Street	C2	Cloch Choirneal	C4	Hampton Cove	D2
		Clonard Court	C2	Hampton Green	C2
		Clonard Rise	B2	Hampton Place	C2
		Clonard Road	A2	Hampton Street	C2
		Clonard Street	C2	Hampton Woods	B1
		Clonuske Close	B1	Harbour Road	C2
		Clonuske Drive	B1	Harry Reynolds Road	B2
		Clonuske Green	B1	Hastings	A1
		Clonuske Park	B1	High Street	C2
		Clonuske Rise	B1	Lambeecher	B1
		Clonuske View	B1	Laragh	C2
		Convent Lane	C2	Lawless Terrace	C2
		Cornmill Apartments	C2	Linnen Hall	C2¹

Martello	A2	Pinewood Green Lawn	C3
McWeill Hall	C2²	Pinewood Green Road	D3
Mill Race	C2	Prospect	B2
Mill Street	C2	Pump Lane	C2
Mill Walk	C2	Quay Street	C2
Mount Rochford Avenue	B1	Railway Street	C2
Mount Rochford Close	B1	Seapoint Lane	C2
Mount Rochford Drive	B1	Skerries Road	C2
Mount Rochford Rise	B1	St. Molagha's Terrace	C2
Moylaragh Avenue	B2	St. Paul's Crescent	C2
Moylaragh Close	B2	St. Peter's Terrace	C2
Moylaragh Court	B2	Stephenstown Bus. Pk.	B3
Moylaragh Crescent	B2	Tanners Water Lane	C3
Moylaragh Drive	B2	Tara Court	B2
Moylaragh Gardens	A2	Tara Cove	B2
Moylaragh Grove	C2	Templeville	B1
Moylaragh Lane	A2	The Chantries	C3
Moylaragh Mews	A2	The Square	C2
Moylaragh Park	B2	Trimelston	A1
Moylaragh Rise	A2	Vauxhall Street	C2
Moylaragh Road	B2	Westbrook Avenue	B2
Moylaragh Walk	B2	Westbrook Close	B2
Moylaragh Way	B2	Westbrook Crescent	B2
New Haven Avenue	A1	Westbrook Drive	B2
New Haven Bay	A1	Westbrook Green	B2
New Haven Close	A1	Westbrook Grove	B2
New Haven Court	A1	Westbrook Height	B2
New Haven Park	A1	Westbrook Lawn	B2
New Haven Rise	A1	Westbrook Park	B2
New Market Green	C2	Westbrook Rise	B2
Oakleigh	B2		
Old Market Green	C2	
Papworth Hall	C2³	
Pine Ridge	B2	
Pinewood Green Avenue	D3	
Pinewood Green Close	C3	
Pinewood Green Court	D3	
Pinewood Green Hill	D2	

Streets not named but shown as small numbers:

C2	1	Linnen Hall	
	2	McWeill Hall	
	3	Papworth Hall	

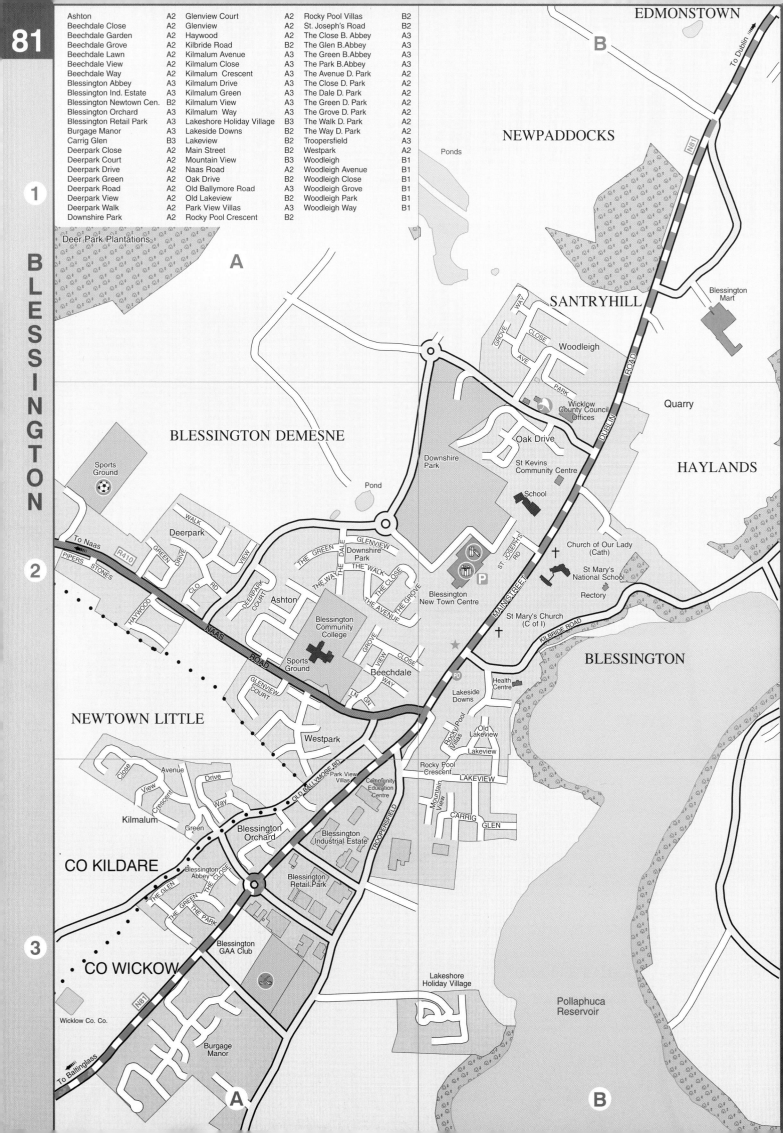

Ashton	A2	Glenview Court	A2	Rocky Pool Villas	B2
Beechdale Close	A2	Glenview	A2	St. Joseph's Road	B2
Beechdale Garden	A2	Haywood	A2	The Close B. Abbey	A3
Beechdale Grove	A2	Kilbride Road	B2	The Glen B.Abbey	A3
Beechdale Lawn	A2	Kilmalum Avenue	A3	The Green B.Abbey	A3
Beechdale View	A2	Kilmalum Close	A3	The Park B.Abbey	A3
Beechdale Way	A2	Kilmalum Crescent	A3	The Avenue D. Park	A2
Blessington Abbey	A3	Kilmalum Drive	A3	The Close D. Park	A2
Blessington Ind. Estate	A3	Kilmalum Green	A3	The Dale D. Park	A2
Blessington Newtown Cen.	B2	Kilmalum View	A3	The Green D. Park	A2
Blessington Orchard	A3	Kilmalum Way	A3	The Grove D. Park	A2
Blessington Retail Park	A3	Lakeshore Holiday Village	B3	The Walk D. Park	A2
Burgage Manor	A3	Lakeside Downs	B2	The Way D. Park	A2
Carrig Glen	B3	Lakeview	B2	Troopersfield	A3
Deerpark Close	A2	Main Street	B2	Westpark	A2
Deerpark Court	A2	Mountain View	B3	Woodleigh	B1
Deerpark Drive	A2	Naas Road	A2	Woodleigh Avenue	B1
Deerpark Green	A2	Oak Drive	B2	Woodleigh Close	B1
Deerpark Road	A2	Old Ballymore Road	A3	Woodleigh Grove	B1
Deerpark View	A2	Old Lakeview	B2	Woodleigh Park	B1
Deerpark Walk	A2	Park View Villas	A3	Woodleigh Way	B1
Downshire Park	A2	Rocky Pool Crescent	B2		

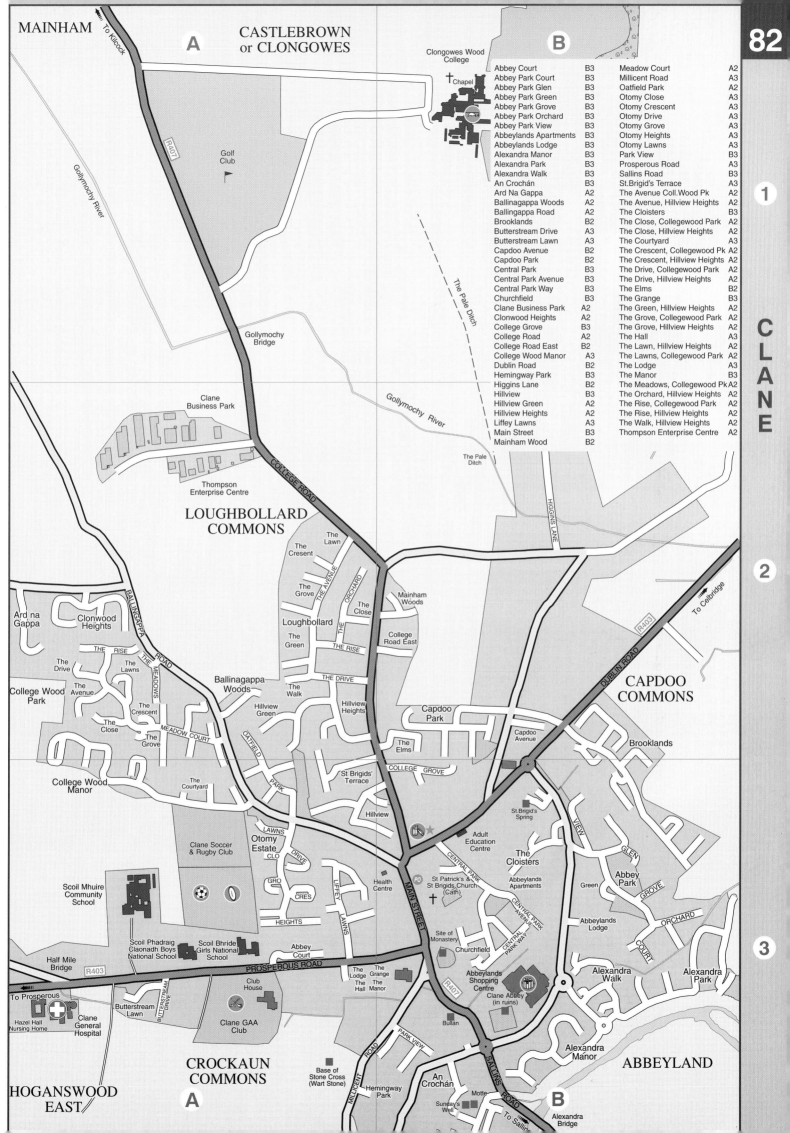

82

CLANE

DELGANY

GREYSTONES

INSET FOR PAGE 84

KINDLESTOWN UPPER

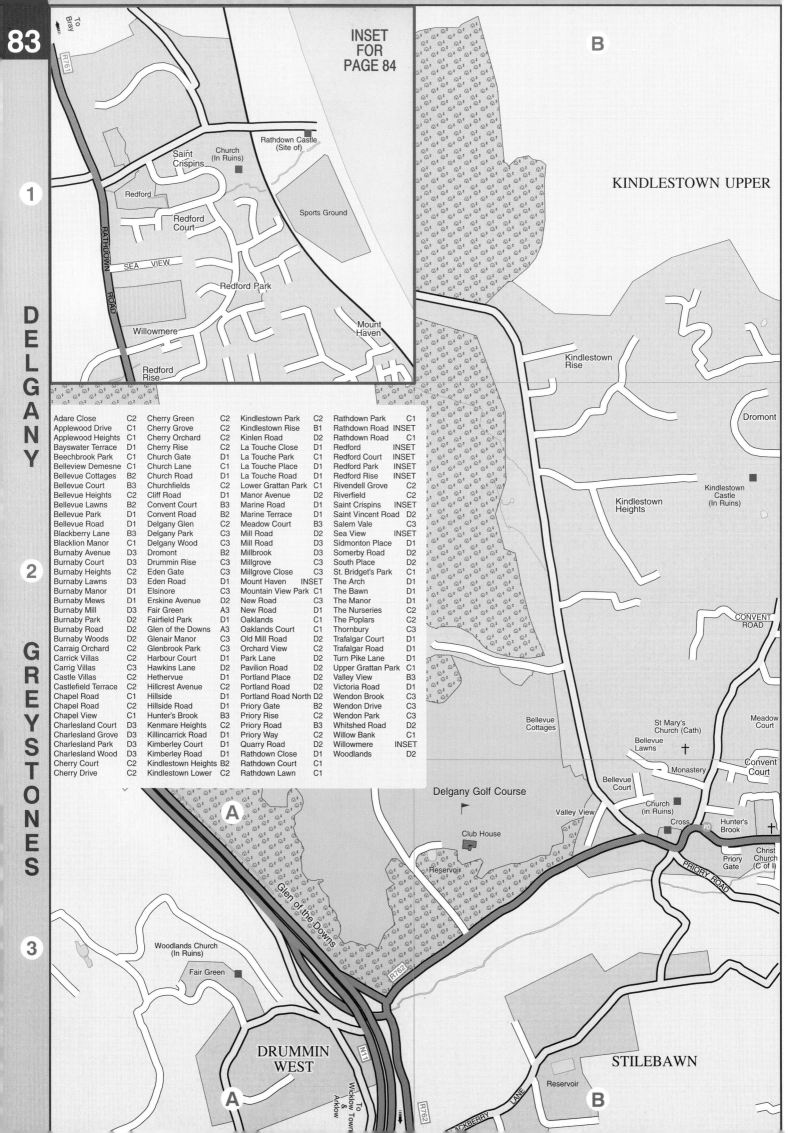

To Bray

R761

Rathdown Castle (Site of)

Saint Crispins

Church (In Ruins)

Redford

Redford Court

Sports Ground

SEA VIEW

RATHDOWN ROAD

Redford Park

Willowmere

Mount Haven

Redford Rise

Kindlestown Rise

Dromont

Kindlestown Castle (In Ruins)

Kindlestown Heights

CONVENT ROAD

Bellevue Cottages

St Mary's Church (Cath)

Meadow Court

Bellevue Lawns

Convent Court

Monastery

Bellevue Court

Delgany Golf Course

Valley View

Church (in Ruins)

Cross

PO

Hunter's Brook

Club House

Christ Church (C of I)

Priory Gate

PRIORY ROAD

Reservoir

Glen of the Downs

Woodlands Church (In Ruins)

Fair Green

R762

DRUMMIN WEST

N11

To Wicklow Town & Arklow

STILEBAWN

Reservoir

LANE

R762

BLACKBERRY LANE

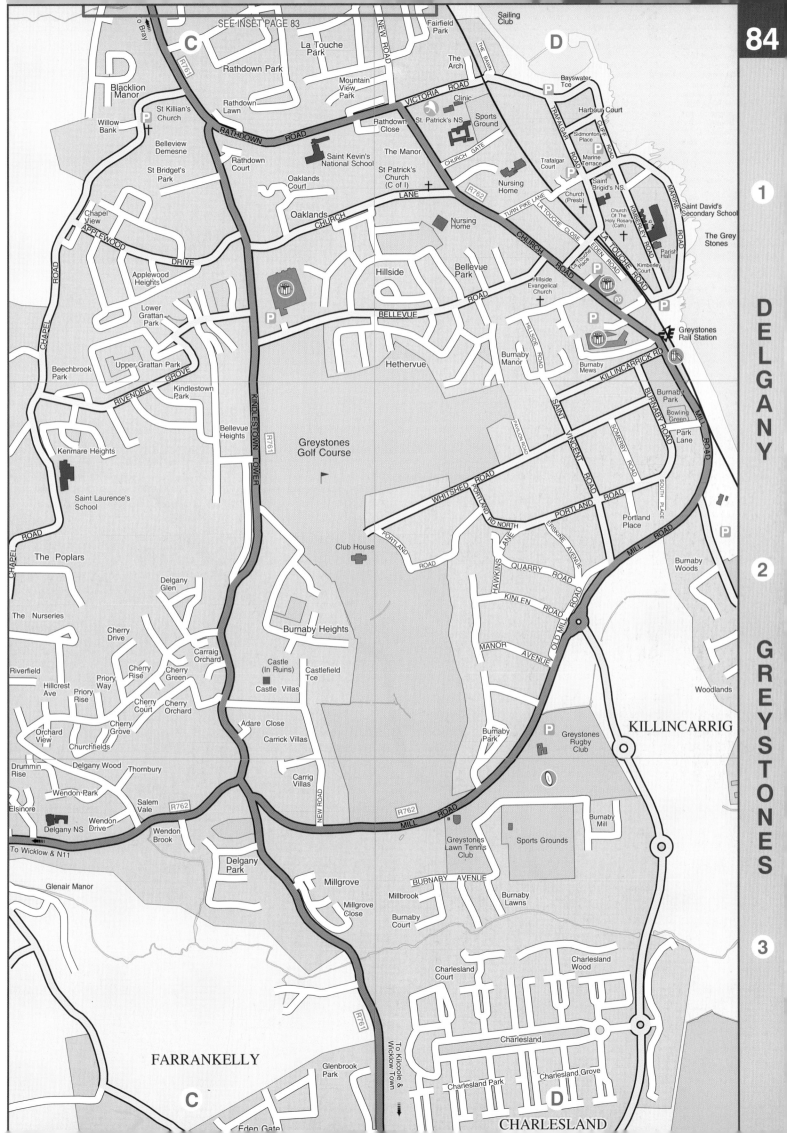

SEE INSET PAGE 83

C
D

Sailing Club

Fairfield Park

Blacklion Manor

Rathdown Park

La Touche Park

The Arch

Bayswater Tce

NEW ROAD

Mountain View Park

St Killian's Church

VICTORIA ROAD

Clinic

Harbour Court

Willow Bank

Rathdown Lawn

Sports Ground

St. Patrick's NS

Sidmonton Place

Belleview Demesne

RATHDOWN ROAD

Rathdown Close

CHURCH GATE

Trafalgar Court

Marine Terrace

St Bridget's Park

Rathdown Court

The Manor

R762

Nursing Home

Church (Presb)

Saint Brigid's NS

Chapel View

Oaklands Court

St Patrick's Church (C of I)

LANE

Saint Brigid's NS

Church Of The Holy Rosary (Cath)

Saint David's Secondary School

APPLEWOOD

Oaklands

CHURCH

Nursing Home

La Touche Place

KIMBERLEY ROAD

Parish Hall

The Grey Stones

DRIVE

Applewood Heights

Hillside

Bellevue Park

Hillside Evangelical Church

EDEN ROAD

Kimberley Court

CHAPEL ROAD

Lower Grattan Park

Road

BELLEVUE

CHURCH ROAD

PO

Greystones Rail Station

Beechbrook Park

Upper Grattan Park

Hethervue

Burnaby Manor

HILLSIDE ROAD

Burnaby Mews

KILLINCARRICK RD

RIVENDELL

GROVE

Kindlestown Park

Burnaby Park

Bowling Green

Burnaby Road

Bellevue Heights

SAINT VINCENT ROAD

SOMERBY ROAD

Park Lane

MILL ROAD

Kenmare Heights

R761

Greystones Golf Course

WHITSHED ROAD

PORTLAND RD NORTH

PORTLAND ROAD

Portland Place

SOUTH PLACE

Saint Laurence's School

KINDLESTOWN LOWER

ERSKINE AVENUE

Burnaby Woods

The Poplars

Club House

PORTLAND ROAD

HAWKINS LANE

QUARRY ROAD

P

Delgany Glen

Burnaby Heights

KINLEN ROAD

OLD MILL ROAD

Burnaby Woods

The Nurseries

Cherry Drive

Carraig Orchard

MANOR AVENUE

Woodlands

Riverfield

Cherry Rise

Cherry Green

Castle (In Ruins)

Castlefield Tce

KILLINCARRIG

Hillcrest Ave

Priory Way

Priory Rise

Cherry Court

Cherry Orchard

Castle Villas

Adare Close

Burnaby Park

Greystones Rugby Club

Orchard View

Cherry Grove

Carrick Villas

Churchfields

Delgany Wood

Thornbury

Drummin Rise

Wendon Park

Salem Vale

R762

Carrig Villas

NEW ROAD

MILL ROAD

R762

Greystones Lawn Tennis Club

Sports Grounds

Burnaby Mill

Elsinore

Delgany NS

Wendon Drive

Wendon Brook

Burnaby Lawns

To Wicklow & N11

Delgany Park

Millgrove

Millbrook

Burnaby Court

BURNABY AVENUE

Glenair Manor

Millgrove Close

R761

To Kilcoole & Wicklow Town

Glenbrook Park

Charlesland Court

Charlesland Wood

Charlesland Grove

FARRANKELLY

Eden Gate

Glenbrook Park

Charlesland

Charlesland Park

C
D

CHARLESLAND

DONABATE

B

Rogerstown Estuary

Raheen Point

Dublin/Belfast Railway

Club House

BEAVERSTOWN

Windmill (in Ruins)

RAHILLION

Beaverbrook

Beaverstown Golf Club

Beaverstown Orchard

Orchard Close

Cois Inbhir

Carrs Mill

St. Patrick's Girls National School

Eden Grove

Lambourne Park

St. Patrick's Boys National School

GREEN

LAWNS

AVE

CRES

DRIVE

BEAVERSTOWN ROAD

Somerton

BALLISK COMMON

The Priory

Beverton

GROVE

CLOSE

DRIVE

RISE

CRES

WAY

Turvey

GREEN

DRIVE

CLO

WALK

AVENUE

Hazelwood

Donabate Community Centre

Educate Together Primary School

PORTRANE ROAD UPPER

Willowbrook

PRIORY WOOD

BALLALEASE NORTH

Court

WOODS

PARK

CRES

PARK

The Links

PORTRAINE ROAD

TURVEY AVENUE

GROVE

TURVEY WALK

Ballisk Court

Baltra Hall

R126

MAIN STREET

FAIRWAYS

Donabate Shopping Centre

St. Patrick's Church (Cath)

THE SPIRES

BALLISK

St Patricks Park

St. Patricks (C of I)

Donabate Rail Station

PO

St Patricks Terrace

ST. MARY'S TERRACE

BALLYMASTONE

NEWBRIDGE AVE

CHAPEL VIEW

Station Court

THE STRAND

Prospect Hill

R126

To M1

DONABATE

BALLALEASE SOUTH

CORBALLIS

Dublin/Belfast Railway

A

B

1

2

3

A

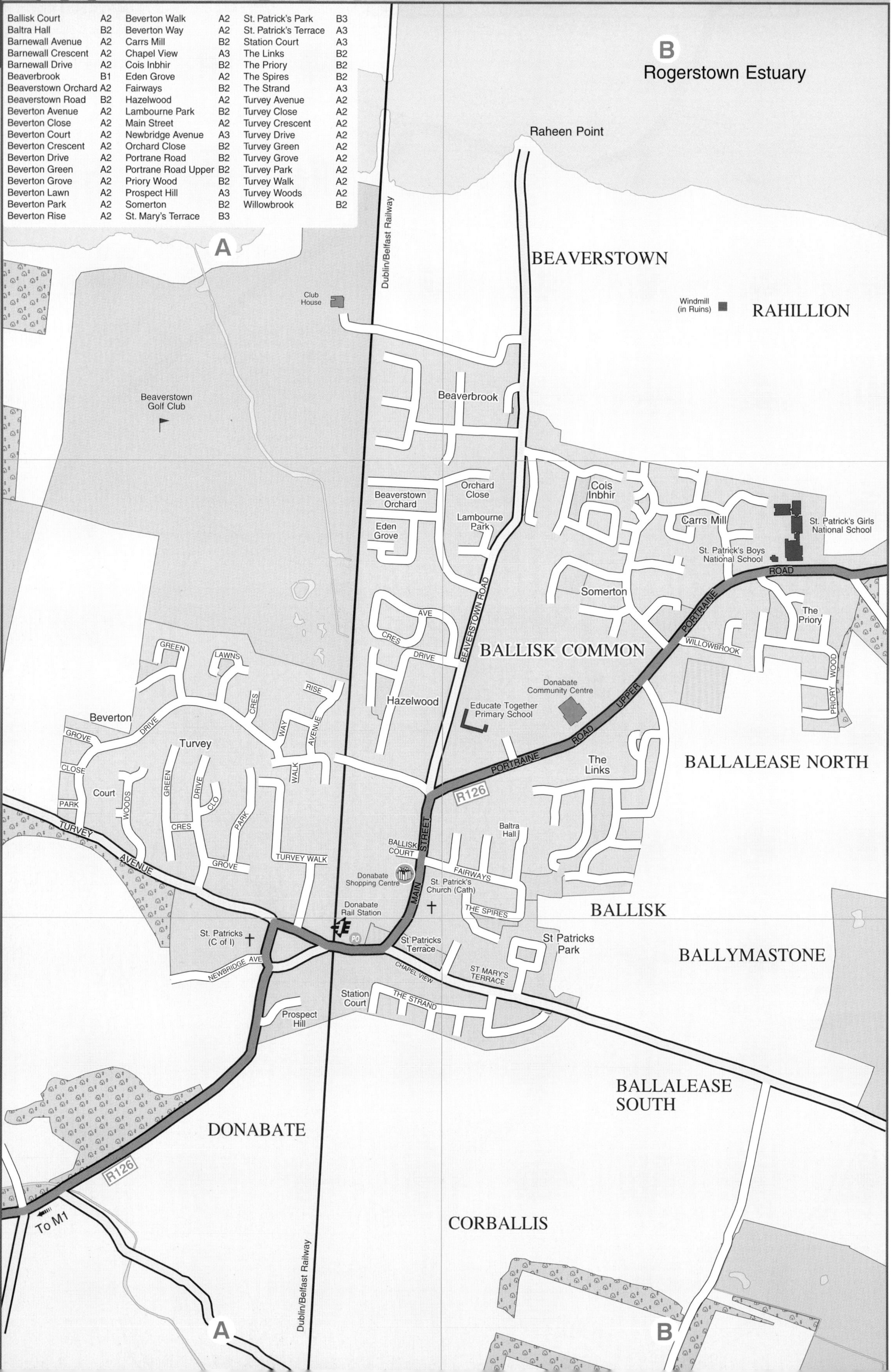

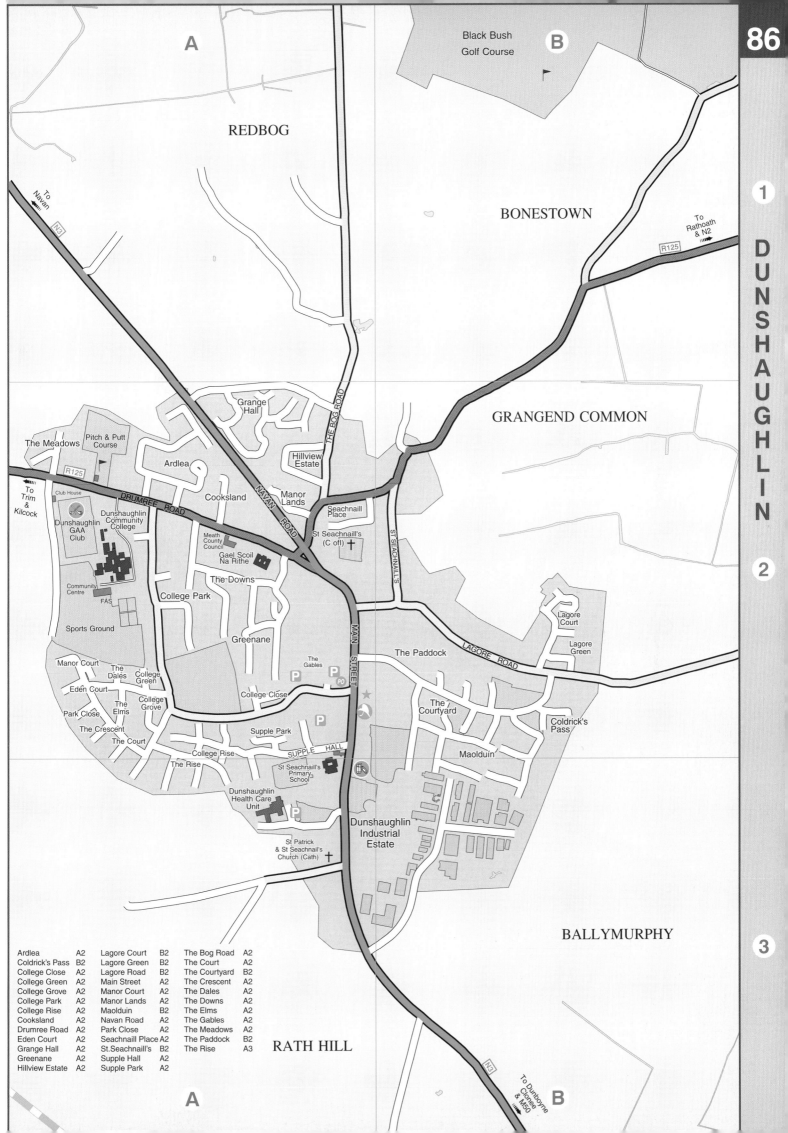

DUNSHAUGHLIN

A

B

1

2

3

REDBOG

Black Bush
Golf Course

BONESTOWN

To Navan
N3

To Rathoath
& N2
R125

GRANGEND COMMON

Grange
Hall

The Meadows

Pitch & Putt
Course

Ardlea

Hillview
Estate

R125

Club House

Drumree Road

Cooksland

Manor
Lands

To Trim
& Kilcock

Dunshaughlin
GAA Club

Dunshaughlin
Community
College

NAVAN ROAD

Seachnaill
Place

St Seachnaill's
(C of I)

ST SEACHNAILL'S

Community
Centre

FÁS

Meath
County
Council

Gael Scoil
Na Rithe

The Downs

College Park

Sports Ground

Greenane

Manor Court

The
Dales

College
Green

The Gables

P

P
PO

MAIN STREET

The Paddock

Lagore
Court

Lagore
Green

LAGORE ROAD

Eden Court

The
Elms

College
Grove

College Close

P

Park Close

The Crescent

The Court

College Rise

Supple Park

The Rise

SUPPLE HALL

St Seachnaill's
Primary
School

Dunshaughlin
Health Care
Unit

P

St Patrick
& St Seachnail's
Church (Cath)

The
Courtyard

Maolduin

Coldrick's
Pass

Dunshaughlin
Industrial
Estate

BALLYMURPHY

RATH HILL

To Dunboyne
Clonee & M50
N3

A

B

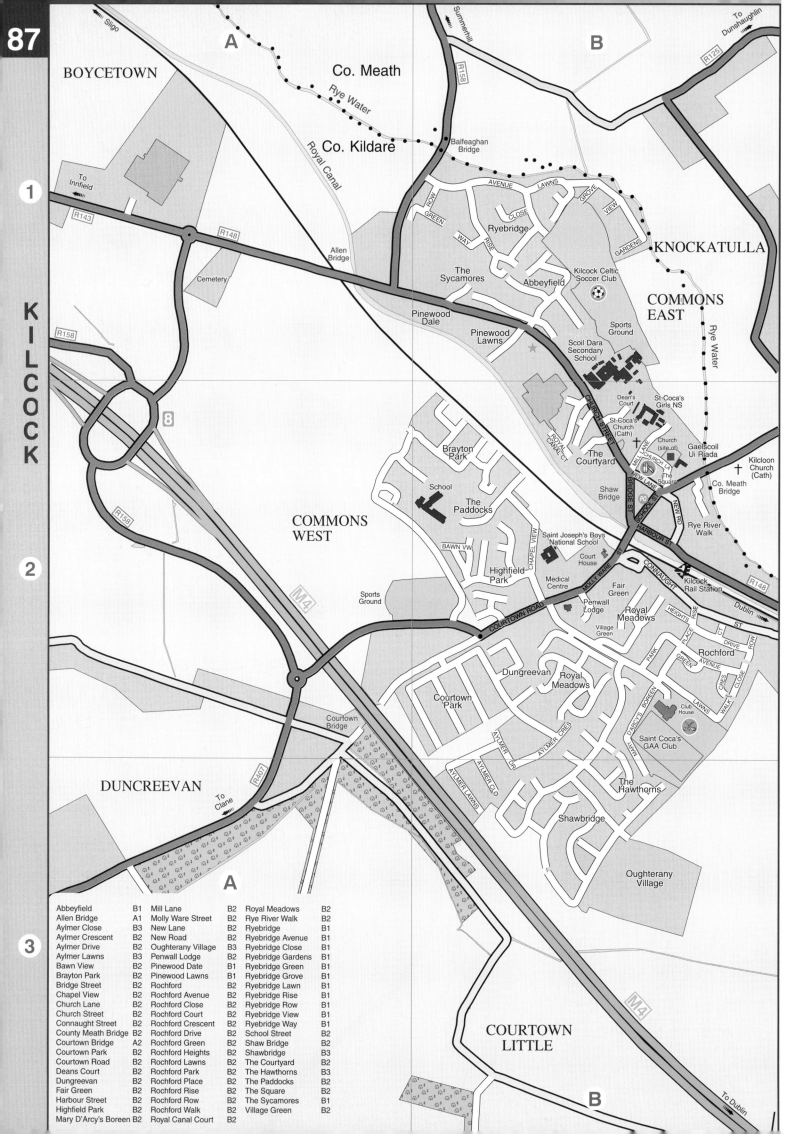

KILCOCK

BOYCETOWN

Co. Meath

Rye Water

Co. Kildare

Royal Canal

To Innfield

Sligo

Summerhill

To Dunshaughlin

R125

R158

R143

R148

Allen Bridge

Cemetery

Balfeaghan Bridge

AVENUE

LAWNS

ROW

GREEN

CLOSE

GROVE

VIEW

WAY

RISE

GARDENS

Ryebridge

The Sycamores

Abbeyfield

Kilcock Celtic Soccer Club

KNOCKATULLA

COMMONS EAST

Sports Ground

Pinewood Dale

Pinewood Lawns

Scoil Dara Secondary School

Rye Water

CHURCH STREET

ROYAL CANAL CT

Dean's Court

St Coca's Girls NS

St Coca's Church (Cath)

Church (site of)

Gaelscoil Ui Riada

Kilcloon Church (Cath)

Co. Meath Bridge

Brayton Park

School

The Paddocks

The Courtyard

MILL LANE

CHURCH LA

NEW LANE

BRIDGE ST

SCHOOL ST

The Square

Shaw Bridge

PO

NEW RD

Rye River Walk

COMMONS WEST

CHAPEL VIEW

BAWN VW

Highfield Park

Saint Joseph's Boys National School

Court House

Medical Centre

Penwall Lodge

MOLLY WARE ST

CONNAUGHT

Fair Green

Royal Meadows

HEIGHTS

RISE

Dublin

Kilcock Rail Station

R148

Sports Ground

COURTOWN ROAD

Village Green

Dungreevan

Royal Meadows

PARK

PLACE

AVENUE

GREEN

CRES

CT

WALK

CLOSE

DRIVE

ROW

Rochford

8

R158

R158

M4

Courtown Bridge

R407

To Clane

DUNCREEVAN

Courtown Park

AYLMER DR

AYLMER CLO

AYLMER LAWNS

AYLMER CRES

MARY D'ARCY'S BOREEN

Club House

Saint Coca's GAA Club

The Hawthorns

Shawbridge

Oughterany Village

M4

COURTOWN LITTLE

To Dublin

A

B

A

B

1

2

3

Abbeyfield	B1	Mill Lane	B2	Royal Meadows	B2
Allen Bridge	A1	Molly Ware Street	B2	Rye River Walk	B2
Aylmer Close	B3	New Lane	B2	Ryebridge	B1
Aylmer Crescent	B2	New Road	B2	Ryebridge Avenue	B1
Aylmer Drive	B2	Oughterany Village	B3	Ryebridge Close	B1
Aylmer Lawns	B3	Penwall Lodge	B2	Ryebridge Gardens	B1
Bawn View	B2	Pinewood Date	B1	Ryebridge Green	B1
Brayton Park	B2	Pinewood Lawns	B1	Ryebridge Grove	B1
Bridge Street	B2	Rochford	B2	Ryebridge Lawn	B1
Chapel View	B2	Rochford Avenue	B2	Ryebridge Rise	B1
Church Lane	B2	Rochford Close	B2	Ryebridge Row	B1
Church Street	B2	Rochford Court	B2	Ryebridge View	B1
Connaught Street	B2	Rochford Crescent	B2	Ryebridge Way	B1
County Meath Bridge	B2	Rochford Drive	B2	School Street	B2
Courtown Bridge	A2	Rochford Green	B2	Shaw Bridge	B2
Courtown Park	B2	Rochford Heights	B2	Shawbridge	B3
Courtown Road	B2	Rochford Lawns	B2	The Courtyard	B2
Deans Court	B2	Rochford Park	B2	The Hawthorns	B3
Dungreevan	B2	Rochford Place	B2	The Paddocks	B2
Fair Green	B2	Rochford Rise	B2	The Square	B2
Harbour Street	B2	Rochford Row	B2	The Sycamores	B1
Highfield Park	B2	Rochford Walk	B2	Village Green	B2
Mary D'Arcy's Boreen	B2	Royal Canal Court	B2		

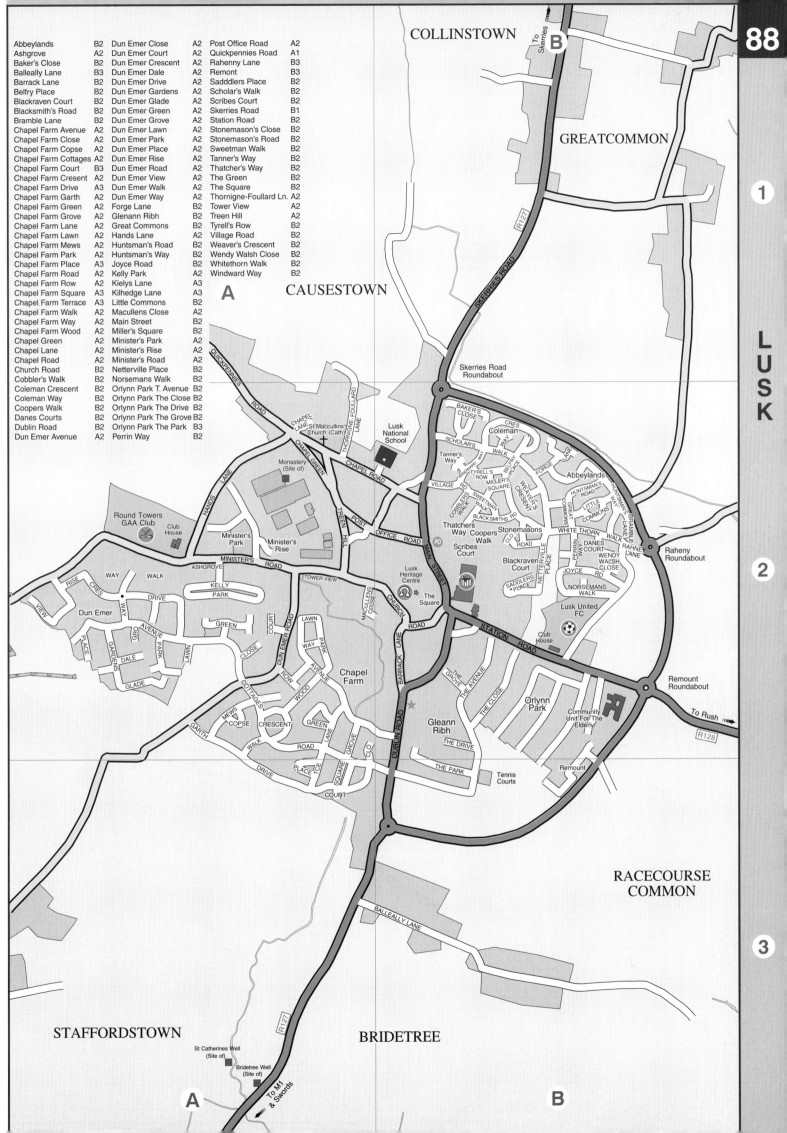

LUSK

Abbeylands	B2	Dun Emer Close	A2	Post Office Road	A2
Ashgrove	A2	Dun Emer Court	A2	Quickpennies Road	A1
Baker's Close	B2	Dun Emer Crescent	A2	Rahenny Lane	B3
Balleally Lane	B3	Dun Emer Dale	A2	Remont	B3
Barrack Lane	B2	Dun Emer Drive	A2	Sadddlers Place	B2
Belfry Place	B2	Dun Emer Gardens	A2	Scholar's Walk	B2
Blackraven Court	B2	Dun Emer Glade	A2	Scribes Court	B2
Blacksmith's Road	B2	Dun Emer Green	A2	Skerries Road	B1
Bramble Lane	B2	Dun Emer Grove	A2	Station Road	B2
Chapel Farm Avenue	A2	Dun Emer Lawn	A2	Stonemason's Close	B2
Chapel Farm Close	A2	Dun Emer Park	A2	Stonemason's Road	B2
Chapel Farm Copse	A2	Dun Emer Place	A2	Sweetman Walk	B2
Chapel Farm Cottages	A2	Dun Emer Rise	A2	Tanner's Way	B2
Chapel Farm Court	B3	Dun Emer Road	A2	Thatcher's Way	B2
Chapel Farm Cresent	A2	Dun Emer View	A2	The Green	B2
Chapel Farm Drive	A3	Dun Emer Walk	A2	The Square	B2
Chapel Farm Garth	A2	Dun Emer Way	A2	Thornigne-Foullard Ln.	A2
Chapel Farm Green	A2	Forge Lane	B2	Tower View	A2
Chapel Farm Grove	A2	Glenann Ribh	B2	Treen Hill	A2
Chapel Farm Lane	A2	Great Commons	B2	Tyrell's Row	A2
Chapel Farm Lawn	A2	Hands Lane	A2	Village Road	B2
Chapel Farm Mews	A2	Huntsman's Road	B2	Weaver's Crescent	B2
Chapel Farm Park	A2	Huntsman's Way	B2	Wendy Walsh Close	B2
Chapel Farm Place	A3	Joyce Road	B2	Whitethorn Walk	B2
Chapel Farm Road	A2	Kelly Park	A2	Windward Way	B2
Chapel Farm Row	A2	Kielys Lane	A3		
Chapel Farm Square	A3	Kilhedge Lane	A3		
Chapel Farm Terrace	A3	Little Commons	B2		
Chapel Farm Walk	A2	Macullens Close	B2		
Chapel Farm Way	A2	Main Street	B2		
Chapel Farm Wood	A2	Miller's Square	B2		
Chapel Green	A2	Minister's Park	A2		
Chapel Lane	A2	Minister's Rise	A2		
Chapel Road	A2	Minister's Road	A2		
Church Road	B2	Netterville Place	B2		
Cobbler's Walk	B2	Norsemans Walk	B2		
Coleman Crescent	B2	Orlynn Park T. Avenue	B2		
Coleman Way	B2	Orlynn Park The Close	B2		
Coopers Walk	B2	Orlynn Park The Drive	B2		
Danes Courts	B2	Orlynn Park The Grove	B2		
Dublin Road	B2	Orlynn Park The Park	B3		
Dun Emer Avenue	A2	Perrin Way	B2		

RUSH

An Tearmann	B3	Eden Terrace	C2	Melbourne Gardens	C3	St Catherines Drive	C1
Barrack Lane	C2	Farran's Lane	C2	Mill Bank	B2	St Catherines Green	C1
Bawn Road	C2	Finistere	D2	Mill Bank Court	B2	St Catherines Grove	C1
Bayview Villas	C2	Golden Ridge	C2	Old Barrack Road	D3	St Catherines Lawn	C1
Bollum Lane	C2	Golf Road	B3	Old Haystown	B2	St Catherines Park	C1
Brookfield Park	C2	Hand Park	D2	Old Road	B2	St Catherines View	C1
Brookfield	B2	Hands Lane	C3	Old Road Court	B2	St Catherines Way	C1
Brookside Gardens	B2	Harbour Road	D2	Old Road Grove	B2	St. Joseph's Road	C3
Carthy's Lane	A3	Haystown	B2	Palmer Court	C1	St. Maur's Park	C2
Ceol na Mara	C2	Haystown Road	B2	Palmer Road	C1	Sundrive Road	B3
Channel Road	A3	Healy's Lane	C2	Park Road	C2	Sundrive Road	C3
Chapel Green	B2	Kenure Crescent	C2	Quay Road	D2	Sunlock Court	C2
Clifflands	C1	Kenure Lawns	C1	Ravenswell	C1	Sunset Court	C2
Clifflands Court	C1	Kenure Park	C2	Rogerstown Court	B3	Tayleurs Point	D3
Clifflands Rise	C1	Kilbush Lane	C2	Rogerstown Park	B3	The Cairn	C1
Cois Tra	C2	Kilbush View	C2	Sandy Lane	C3	The Forge	D2
Congress Gardens	C3	Knockabawn	D2	Sandy Road	C2	The Mall	C2
Convent Lane	C3	Lady Cove	C1	Seafield Court	D2	Thorn Chase	C1
Cooper's Bank	C2	Lambay View	C1	Skerries Road	C2	Thornleigh	C2
Cooper's Lane	C2	Linkside	INSET	South Shore Road	C3	Tower Street	D2
Coopersfield	C2	Linn Ban	B2	South Strand	C3	Upper Main Street	C3
Crescent Road	B3	Linn Beag	B2	Spout Road	A3	Whitestown Road	A3
Daly's Lane	B3	Linn Cuin	B2	St Catherines Avenue	C1	Woodbury	C2
Doctor's Lane	B2	Linn Dubh	B2	St Catherines Close	C1	Woodland Park	C2
Echlin Court	C2	Lower Main Street	C2	St Catherines Crescent	C1	Woodvale Road	C1

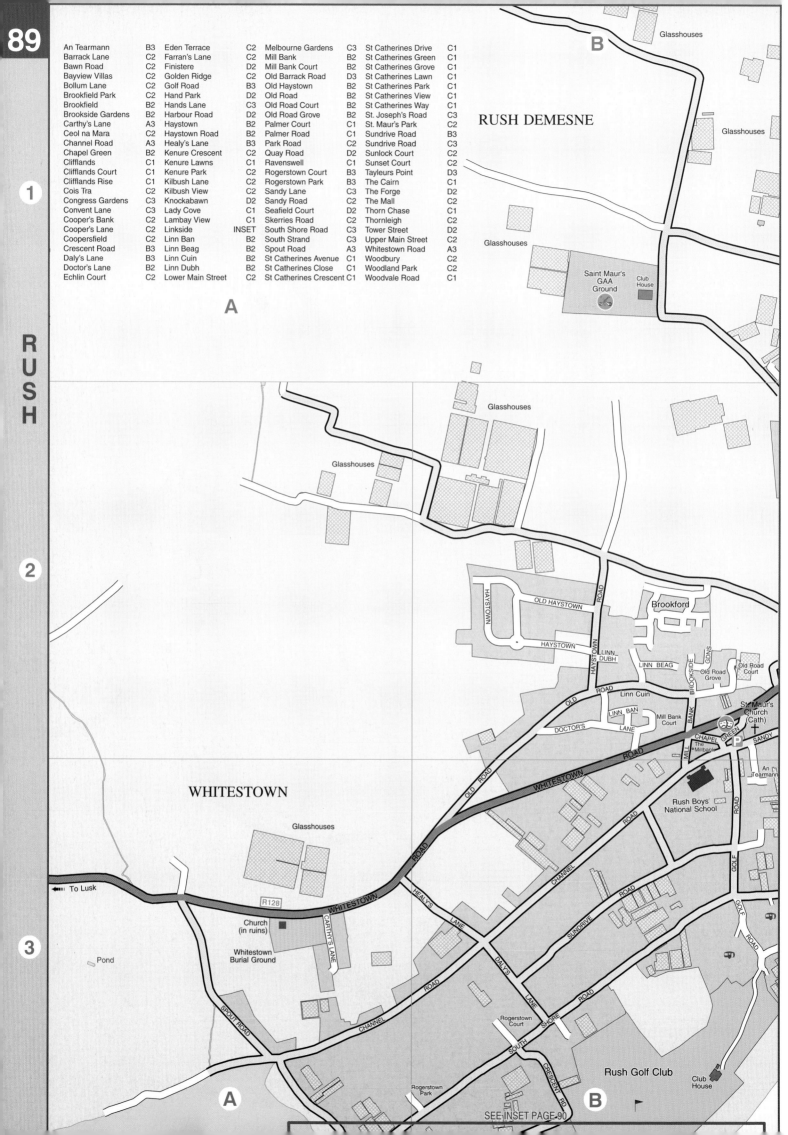

1

RATOATH

2

3

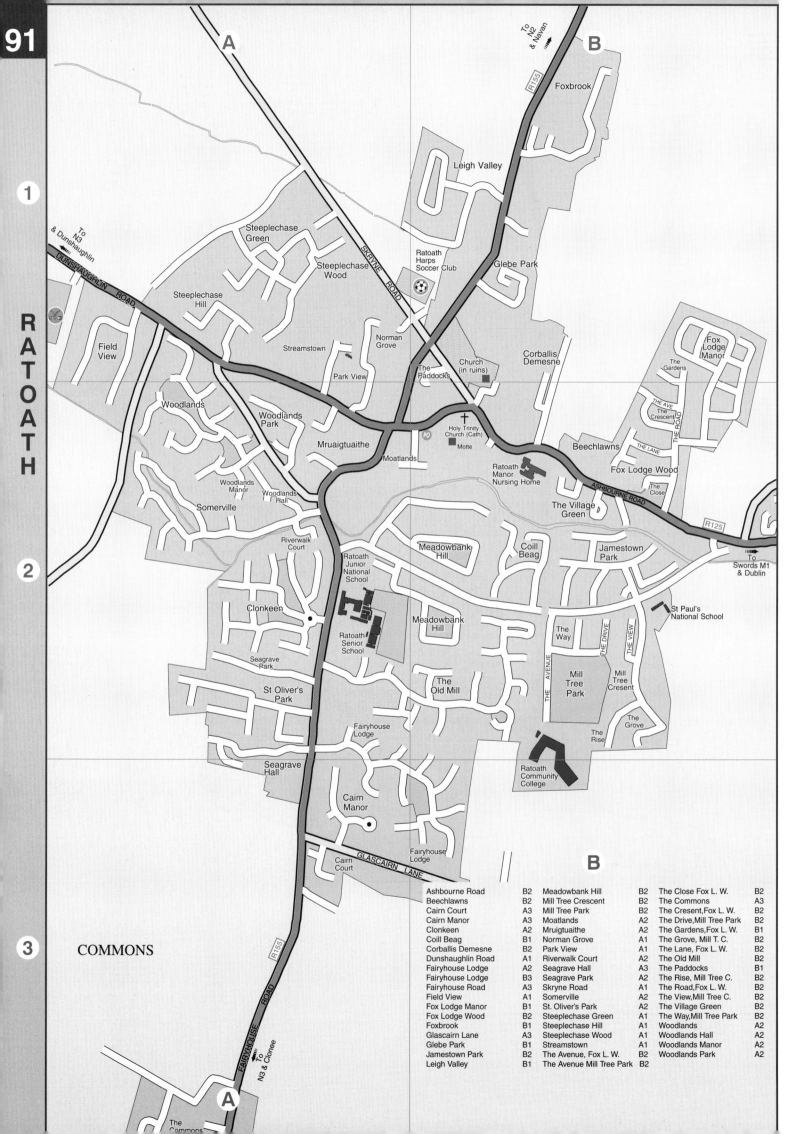

COMMONS

To N3 & Dunshaughlin

DUNSHAUGHLIN ROAD

Field View

Woodlands

Somerville

Woodlands Manor

Woodlands Hall

Steeplechase Hill

Steeplechase Green

Steeplechase Wood

Streamstown

Woodlands Park

Mruaigtuaithe

Park View

SKRYNE ROAD

Norman Grove

The Paddocks

Church (in ruins)

Ratoath Harps Soccer Club

Moatlands

Holy Trinity Church (Cath)

PO

Motte

Meadowbank Hill

Coill Beag

Riverwalk Court

Ratoath Junior National School

Clonkeen

Ratoath Senior School

Seagrave Park

St Oliver's Park

Meadowbank Hill

The Old Mill

Fairyhouse Lodge

Seagrave Hall

Cairn Manor

Fairyhouse Lodge

Cairn Court

GLASCAIRN LANE

FAIRYHOUSE ROAD

R155

To N3 & Clonee

Ratoath Community College

Ratoath Manor Nursing Home

The Village Green

Jamestown Park

The Way

THE AVENUE

THE DRIVE

THE VIEW

Mill Tree Park

Mill Tree Cresent

The Rise

The Grove

St Paul's National School

ASHBOURNE ROAD

Corballis Demesne

Beechlawns

Fox Lodge Wood

The Close

R125

Fox Lodge Manor

The Gardens

THE AVE

The Crescent

THE ROAD

THE LANE

To Swords M1 & Dublin

To N2 & Navan

R155

B

Foxbrook

Leigh Valley

Glebe Park

A

The Commons

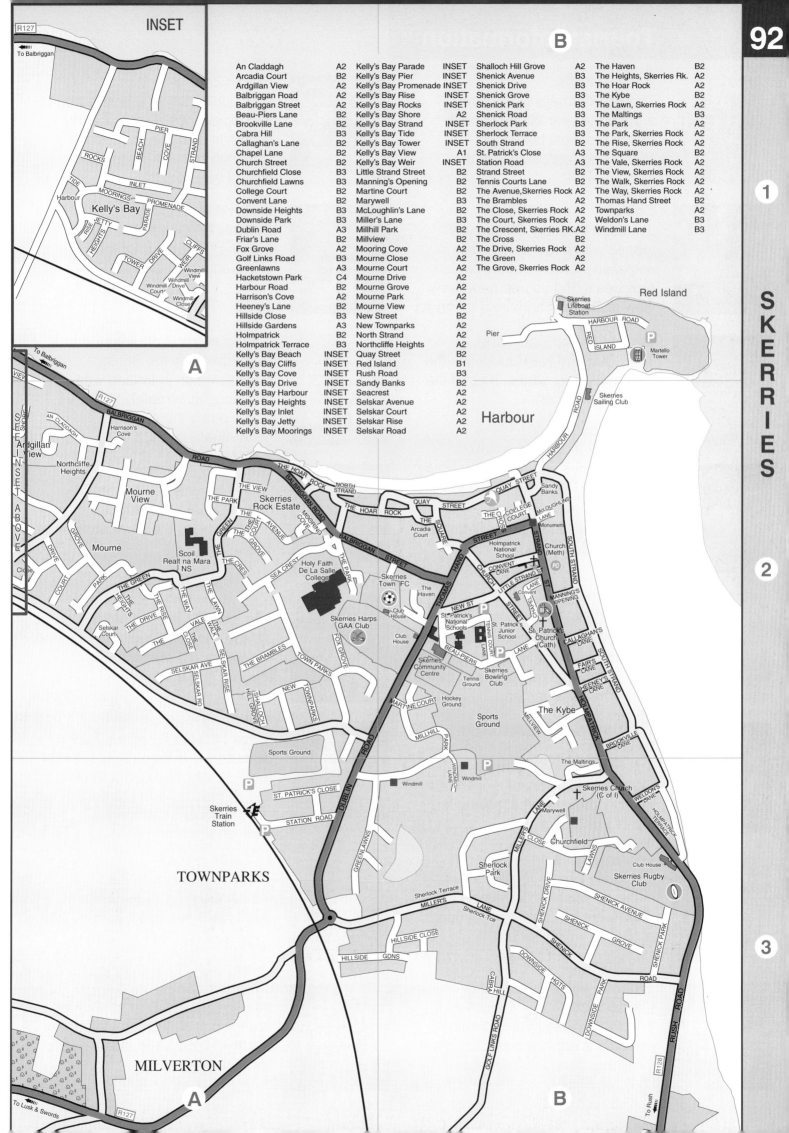

INSET

An Claddagh	A2	Kelly's Bay Parade	INSET	Shalloch Hill Grove	A2	The Haven	B2
Arcadia Court	B2	Kelly's Bay Pier	INSET	Shenick Avenue	B3	The Heights, Skerries Rk.	A2
Ardgillan View	A2	Kelly's Bay Promenade	INSET	Shenick Drive	B3	The Hoar Rock	A2
Balbriggan Road	A2	Kelly's Bay Rise	INSET	Shenick Grove	B3	The Kybe	B2
Balbriggan Street	A2	Kelly's Bay Rocks	INSET	Shenick Park	B3	The Lawn, Skerries Rock	A2
Beau-Piers Lane	B2	Kelly's Bay Shore	A2	Shenick Road	B3	The Maltings	B3
Brookville Lane	B2	Kelly's Bay Strand	INSET	Sherlock Park	B3	The Park	A2
Cabra Hill	B3	Kelly's Bay Tide	INSET	Sherlock Terrace	B3	The Park, Skerries Rock	A2
Callaghan's Lane	B2	Kelly's Bay Tower	INSET	St. Patrick's Close	A3	The Rise, Skerries Rock	A2
Chapel Lane	B2	Kelly's Bay View	A1	Station Road	A3	The Square	B2
Church Street	B2	Kelly's Bay Weir	INSET	Strand Street	B2	The Vale, Skerries Rock	A2
Churchfield Close	B3	Little Strand Street	B2	Tennis Courts Lane	B2	The View, Skerries Rock	A2
Churchfield Lawns	B3	Manning's Opening	B2	The Avenue, Skerries Rock	A2	The Walk, Skerries Rock	A2
College Court	B2	Martine Court	B2	The Brambles	A2	The Way, Skerries Rock	A2
Convent Lane	B2	Marywell	B3	The Close, Skerries Rock	A2	Thomas Hand Street	B2
Downside Heights	B3	McLoughlin's Lane	B2	The Court, Skerries Rock	A2	Townparks	A2
Downside Park	B3	Miller's Lane	B3	The Crescent, Skerries RK.	A2	Weldon's Lane	B3
Dublin Road	A3	Millhill Park	B2	The Cross	B2	Windmill Lane	B3
Friar's Lane	B2	Millview	B2	The Drive, Skerries Rock	A2		
Fox Grove	A2	Mooring Cove	A2	The Green	A2		
Golf Links Road	B3	Mourne Close	A2	The Grove, Skerries Rock	A2		
Greenlawns	A3	Mourne Court	A2				
Hacketstown Park	C4	Mourne Drive	A2				
Harbour Road	B2	Mourne Grove	A2				
Harrison's Cove	A2	Mourne Park	A2				
Heeney's Lane	B2	Mourne View	A2				
Hillside Close	B3	New Street	B2				
Hillside Gardens	A3	New Townparks	A2				
Holmpatrick	B2	North Strand	A2				
Holmpatrick Terrace	B3	Northcliffe Heights	A2				
Kelly's Bay Beach	INSET	Quay Street	B2				
Kelly's Bay Cliffs	INSET	Red Island	B1				
Kelly's Bay Cove	INSET	Rush Road	B3				
Kelly's Bay Drive	INSET	Sandy Banks	B2				
Kelly's Bay Harbour	INSET	Seacrest	A2				
Kelly's Bay Heights	INSET	Selskar Avenue	A2				
Kelly's Bay Inlet	INSET	Selskar Court	A2				
Kelly's Bay Jetty	INSET	Selskar Rise	A2				
Kelly's Bay Moorings	INSET	Selskar Road	A2				

Book of Kells
The Book of Kells was written around the year 800 AD and is one of the most beautifully illuminated manuscripts in the world.   **71 C4**

Chimney Viewing Tower
Jameson Distillery Chimney is topped with a two-tiered glass enclosed viewing platform which provides a 360 degree panoramic view of Dublin city.   **70 F4**

Christ Church Cathedral
The Cathedral was founded in the year c.1030 by Sitriuc, King of the Dublin Norsemen.

75 A1

Croke Park Experience
A must for anyone interested in the history and development of Ireland's national games of hurling and gaelic football.   **71 C1**

Dublin Castle
Dublin Castle is the heart of historic Dublin. In fact the city gets its name from the Black Pool, Dubh Linn which was on the site of the present Castle garden.   **75 A1**

The Hugh Lane Dublin City Gallery
The Hugh Lane Dublin City Gallery, is a gallery of modern art and it is the municipal gallery for the city of Dublin.   **71 B2**

Dublin City Hall
The Story of the Capital Exhibition in the atmospheric vaults of Dublin City Hall is an exciting multimedia exhibition which traces the evolution of Dublin city.   **75 A1**

Dublinia and the Medieval Viking World
The Dublinia and Viking World exhibitions are amongst Dublin's most popular visitor attractions.

75 A1

Dublin Zoo
Visit Dublin Zoo for a unique, fun, wild experience close to the city centre! In doing so, you are contributing directly to the continued care of the animals.   **69 B2**

General Post Office
Dublin's GPO is a landmark building, situated prominently in the middle of O'Connell Street.

71 B3

Government Buildings
Undertaken by the British administration in Ireland was available immediately to be occupied by the new Irish government in 1922.   **71 C3**

Guinness Storehouse
Located in the heart of the St James's Gate Brewery, this has been home to the black stuff since 1759.

74 E1

Irish Museum of Modern Art
The Irish Museum of Modern Art is Ireland's leading institution for the collection and presentation of modern and contemporary art.   **73 C1**

Kilmainham Gaol
Kilmainham Gaol gives the visitor a dramatic and realistic insight into what is was like to have been confined in one of these forbidding bastions of punishment and correction between 1796 and 1924.   **73 B1**

Mansion House
The Mansion House is the residence of the Lord Mayor of Dublin and has been since 1715.

75 C1

Marsh's Library
Marsh's Library, built in 1701 by Archbishop Narcissus Marsh (1638 - 1713) is the oldest public library in Ireland.

75 A2

Molly Malone Statue
The Molly Malone statue is located at the end of Grafton Street Molly Malone was a semi historical/legendary figure commerated in song. **75 B1**

National Botanic Gardens
The Gardens contain many attractive features including an arboretum, sensory garden, rock garden large pond and extensive herbaceous borders. **24 F3**

National Gallery of Ireland
The National Gallery of Ireland was established by an Act of Parliament in 1854 and first opened its doors to the public in January 1864. **75 C1**

National Library of Ireland
Established in 1877, National Library's holdings of books, and manuscripts, comprise a comprehensive collection of Irish documentary heritage. **75 C1**

National Museum of Ireland - Archaeology
The Museum first opened its doors in 1890 and since then it has been filling in the blanks for us through its extensive archeological collections. **75 C1**

National Museum of Ireland Decorative Arts & History
Formerly Collins Barracks has been completely renovated and now charts Ireland's progress through the ages. **70 E4**

National Museum of Ireland - Natural History
This zoological museum encompasses outstanding examples of wildlife from Ireland and the far corners of the globe. **75 C1**

Phoenix Park
One of the largest and most magnificent city parks in Europe. an exhibition on the history and wildlife of the Phoenix Park is on display in the Visitor Centre. **69 A2**

St. Mary's Pro Cathedral
Dublin has not possessed a Catholic cathedral since the Reformation, St. Mary's Pro Cathedral has served as the 'mother-church' of Dublin. **71 B3**

Saint Patrick's Cathedral
Saint Patrick's Cathedral has contributed much to Irish life throughout its long history (it was founded in 1191). **75 A1**

St Stephen's Green
Probably Ireland's best known Victorian Public Park is a sanctuary from the bustle of the city streets. **75 B2**

Smithfield
Smithfield village has been developed into a sophisticated residential, commercial and cultural district, a village within the city. **70 F4**

The Spire
The Spire of Dublin, a 120 metre high landmark in the heart of Dublin City, was unveiled in 2002. **71 B3**

Trinity College
Trinity College is the oldest college in Ireland. Founded in 1592 by Queen Elizabeth I. **71 C4**

Malahide Castle
Set on 250 acres of parkland. The castle was the home of the Talbot family from 1185 to 1973. The house contains period furniture and Irish portrait paintings. **3 B3**

Dublin Tourism located in the restored former church of St. Andrew in Suffolk Street is the official tourist board for Dublin. For further tourist interest information visit http://www.visitdublin.com **71 C4**

Apostolic Nunciature
183 Navan Road
Dublin 7
Tel: 838 0577   24 D4

Argentine Embassy
15 Ailesbury Drive
Dublin 4
Tel: 269 1546   48 D1

Australian Embassy
7th Floor,
Fitzwilton House
Wilton Terrace, Dublin 2
Tel: 664 5300   38 E4

Austrian Embassy
15 Ailesbury Court Apts.
93 Ailesbury Road
Dublin 4
Tel: 269 4577   48 D1

Belgian Embassy
2 Shrewsbury Road
Dublin 4
Tel: 269 2082   48 D1

**Embassy of the
Federative Republic
of Brazil**
HSB House
Fifth Floor
41-54 Harcourt House,
Dublin 2.
Tel: 475 6000   38 D4

British Embassy
29 Merrion Road
Dublin 4
Tel: 205 3700   48 D1

Bulgarian Embassy
22 Burlington Road
Dublin 4
Tel: 660 3293   38 E4

Canadian Embassy
7/8 Wilton Place.
Dublin 2
Tel: 234 4001   38 E4

Chilean Embassy
44 Wellington Road
Ballsbridge
Dublin 4
Tel: 667 5094   38 F4

**Embassy of the
People's Republic
of China**
40 Ailesbury Road
Ballsbridge, Dublin 4
Tel: 260 1119   48 D1

**Embassy of the
Republic of Croatia**
Adelaide Chambers
Peter Street
Dublin 8
Tel: 476 7181   38 D3

**Embassy of the
Republic of Cuba**
2 Adelaide Court,
Adelaide Road,
Dublin 2
Tel: 475 0899   38 D4

**Embassy of
Republic of Cyprus**
71 Lower Leeson Street
Dublin 2
Tel: 676 3060   38 E3

**Embassy of
Czech Republic**
57 Northumberland Road
Dublin 4
Tel: 668 1135   38 F4

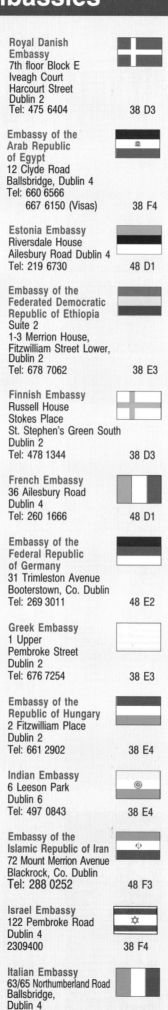

**Royal Danish
Embassy**
7th floor Block E
Iveagh Court
Harcourt Street
Dublin 2
Tel: 475 6404   38 D3

**Embassy of the
Arab Republic
of Egypt**
12 Clyde Road
Ballsbridge, Dublin 4
Tel: 660 6566
     667 6150 (Visas)   38 F4

Estonia Embassy
Riversdale House
Ailesbury Road Dublin 4
Tel: 219 6730   48 D1

**Embassy of the
Federated Democratic
Republic of Ethiopia**
Suite 2
1-3 Merrion House,
Fitzwilliam Street Lower,
Dublin 2
Tel: 678 7062   38 E3

Finnish Embassy
Russell House
Stokes Place
St. Stephen's Green South
Dublin 2
Tel: 478 1344   38 D3

French Embassy
36 Ailesbury Road
Dublin 4
Tel: 260 1666   48 D1

**Embassy of the
Federal Republic
of Germany**
31 Trimleston Avenue
Booterstown, Co. Dublin
Tel: 269 3011   48 E2

Greek Embassy
1 Upper
Pembroke Street
Dublin 2
Tel: 676 7254   38 E3

**Embassy of the
Republic of Hungary**
2 Fitzwilliam Place
Dublin 2
Tel: 661 2902   38 E4

Indian Embassy
6 Leeson Park
Dublin 6
Tel: 497 0843   38 E4

**Embassy of the
Islamic Republic of Iran**
72 Mount Merrion Avenue
Blackrock, Co. Dublin
Tel: 288 0252   48 F3

Israel Embassy
122 Pembroke Road
Dublin 4
2309400   38 F4

Italian Embassy
63/65 Northumberland Road
Ballsbridge,
Dublin 4
Tel: 660 1744   38 F4

Japanese Embassy
Nutley Building
Merrion Centre
Nutley Lane, Dublin 4
Tel: 202 8300   48 E1

**Embassy of the
Republic of Kenya**
11 Elgin Road
Ballsbridge, Dublin 4
Tel: 613 6380 / 668 3506   38 F4

**Embassy of the
Republic of Korea**
15 Clyde Road
Ballsbridge, Dublin 4
Tel: 660 8800   38 F4

**Embassy of the
Republic of Latvia**
92 St Stephen's Green
Dublin 2
Tel: 428 3320   38 E4

Embassy of Lesotho
2 Clanwilliam Square,
Grand Canal Quay,
Dublin 2.
Tel: 676 2233   38 F3[41]

**Embassy of the
Republic of Lithuania**
90 Merrion Road,
Ballsbridge,
Dublin 4.
Tel: 668 8292   48 E1

Embassy of Malaysia
Level 3A-5A
Shelbourne House
Shelbourne Road
Ballsbridge
Dublin 4.
Tel: 667 7280   38 F3

Maltese Embassy
17 Earlsfort Terrace
Dublin 4
Tel: 6762340   38 E4

Mexican Embassy
19 Raglan Road
Dublin 4
Tel: 667 3105   38 F4

**Embassy of the
Kingdom of Morocco**
39 Raglan Road
Dublin 4
Tel: 667 0020   38 F4

Netherlands Embassy
160 Merrion Road
Dublin 4
Tel: 269 3444   48 D1

**Embassy of the Federal
Republic of Nigeria**
56 Leeson Park
Dublin 6
Tel: 660 4366   38 E4

**Royal Norwegian
Embassy**
Hainault House
34 Molesworth Street,
Dublin 2
Tel: 662 1800   38 E3

**Embassy of the Islamic
Republic of Pakistan**
Ailesbury Villa
Ailesbury Road
Ballsbridge
Dublin 4
Tel: 261 3032   48 D1

**Embassy of the
Republic of Poland**
5 Ailesbury Road
Dublin 4
Tel: 283 0855   48 D1

Portuguese Embassy
15 Leeson Park
Dublin 2
Tel: 412 7040   38 E4

Embassy of Romania
26 Waterloo Road
Dublin 4
Tel: 668 1085   48 D1

**Embassy of the
Russian Federation**
184/186 Orwell Road
Rathgar, Dublin 14
Tel: 492 2048(Embassy)
492 3492 (Consular Section)   47 B3

**Embassy of the
Slovak Republic**
20 Clyde Road
Dublin 4
Tel: 660 0012 / 660 0008   38 F4

**Embassy of the
Republic of Slovenia**
Morrison Chambers
2nd Floor,
32 Nassau Street
Dublin 2
Tel: 670 5240   38 E3

**Embassy of
South Africa**
Alexandra House,
Earlsfort Centre,
Earlsfort Terrace, Dublin 2
Tel: 661 5553   38 E3

Spanish Embassy
17A Merlyn Park
Dublin 4
Tel: 269 1640   48 E1

Swedish Embassy
3rd floor Block E
Iveagh Court
Harcourt Street
Dublin 2
Tel: 474 4400   38 D4

Swiss Embassy
6 Ailesbury Road
Ballsbridge
Dublin 4
Tel: 218 6382   48 D1

**Embassy of the
Republic of Turkey**
11 Clyde Road
Ballsbridge, Dublin 4
Tel: 668 5240   38 F4

Embassy of Ukraine
16 Elgin Road,
Ballsbridge,
Dublin 4.
Tel: 668 5189   38 F4

**Embassy of the
United States of America**
42 Elgin Road
Ballsbridge, Dublin 4
Tel: 668 8777   38 F4

**For further information contact:
Dept of Foreign Affairs,
80 St. Stephen's Green, Dublin 2.
Tel: 478 0822 / www.foreignaffairs.gov.ie**

Adelaide & Meath (A&E)
Hospital & The National
Childrens Hospital
Tallaght
Dublin 24
Tel: 01-414 2000   **54 F1**

Beaumont Hospital (A&E)
Beaumont Road
Beaumont Dublin 9
Tel: 01-809 3000   **26 D1**

Cherry Orchard Hospital
Ballyfermot
Dublin 10.
Tel: 01-620 6000   **35 C3**

Cheeverstown House
Kilvare
Templeogue
Dublin 12 Tel:
01-490 4681   **46 D4**

City Of Dublin
Skin & Cancer Hospital
Hume St.
Dublin
Tel: 01-676 6935   **38 E3**

Connolly Hospital (A&E)
Blanchardstown
Dublin 15.
Tel: 01-646 5000   **22 F2**

Dublin Dental
School & Hospital
Lincon Place
Dublin 2
Tel: 01-612 7200   **38 E3**

National Orthopaedic
Hospital
Cappagh
Finglas
Dublin 11
Tel: 01-814 0400   **23 C1**

National Rehabilitation
Hospital
Dun Laoghaire
Co.Dublin
Tel: 01-235 5000   **59 C2**

Orthopaedic Hospital
Of Ireland
Castle Ave.
Clontarf
Dublin 3.
Tel: 01-833 2521   **26 E4**

Peamount Hospital
Newcastle
Co. Dublin
Tel: 01-628 0685   **42 E2**

Royal Hospital
Donnybrook
off Morehampton Rd.
Dublin 4
Tel: 01-497 2844   **47 B1**

Royal Victoria
Eye & Ear Hospital
Adelaide Road
Dublin 2.
Tel: 01-664 4600   **38 E4**

St. Bricins Military Hospital
Infirmary Road
Dublin
Tel: 01-677 6112   **37 B2**

St.Columcilles Hospital (A&E)
Loughlinstown
Co . Dublin
Tel: 01-282 5800   **64 D2**

St. James's Hospital (A&E)
James's St.
Dublin 8.
Tel: 01-410 3100   **37 B3**

St. Joseph's Hospital
Clonsilla
Dublin 15
Tel: 01-821 7177   **21 B2**

St. Joseph's Hospital
Springdale Road
Raheny
Dublin 5
Tel: 01 877 4900   **27 A2**

St. Luke's Hospital
Highfield Road.
Rathgar
Dublin 6.
Tel: 01-406 5314   **47 A2**

St. Mary's Hospital
Phoenix Park
Dublin 20
Tel: 01-625 0300   **36 E2**

St. Michael's Hospital (A&E)
Lower George's St.
Dun Laoghaire
Co. Dublin.
Tel: 01-280 6901   **50 D4**

St. Vincent's Hospital (A&E)
Elm Park
Dublin 4.
Tel: 01-277 4000   **48 E1**

Stewart's Hospital
Palmerston
Dublin
Tel: 01-626 4444   **35 C1**

The Mater Hospital (A&E)
Eccles St.
Dublin 7.
Tel: 01-803 2000   **38 D1**

MATERNITY HOSPITALS

Coombe Women's Hospital
Dolphin's Barn
Dublin 8
Tel: 01-408 5200   **37 C4**

National Maternity Hospital
Holles Street
Dublin 2.
Tel: 01-637 3100   **38 E3**

Rotunda Hospital
Parnell St.
Dublin 1
Tel: 01-873 0700   **38 D1**

CHILDRENS HOSPITALS

Childrens University
Hospital (A&E)
Temple Street
Dublin 1
Tel: 01-878 4200   **38 D1**

National Childrens
Hospital
Tallaght
Dublin 24
Tel: 01-414 2000   **54 F1**

Our Lady's Hospital
for Sick Children (A&E)
Crumlin
Dublin 12
Tel: 01-409 6100   **46 D1**

PSYCHIATRIC HOSPITALS

Central Mental Hospital
Dundrum
Dublin 14
Tel: 01-298 9266   **47 C3**

St. Brendan's Hospital
Rathdown Road
Dublin 7
Tel: 01-869 3000   **37 C1**

St. Ita's Hospital
Portrane
Donabate
Co. Dublin
Tel: 01-843 6337

St. John of God Hospital
Stillorgan
Co. Dublin
Tel: 01-288 1781   **58 F1**

St. Vincent's Hospital
Richmond Road
Fairview
Dublin 3
Tel: 01-837 5101   **25 B4**

St. Patrick's Hospital
James's St.
Dublin 8
Tel: 01-249 3200   **37 B3**

PRIVATE HOSPITALS

Beacon Hospital
Sandyford
Dublin 18
Tel: 01-293 6600   **58 D2**

Blackrock Clinic
Rock Road
Blackrock
Co. Dublin
Tel: 01-283 2222   **48 F3**

Bon Secours Hospital
Glasnevin
Dublin 9
Tel: 01-837 5111   **25 A3**

Hermitage Medical Clinic
Old Lucan Road
Dublin 20.
Tel: 01-645 9000   **35 A1**

Clane General Hospital
Prosperous Road
Clane
Co. Kildare
Tel: 045-982 300   **82 A3**

Name	Page	Grid/Ref.	No.
Abbey Business Park	14	F4	112
Advance Business Park	12	F3	179
Aerodrome Business Park	52	F1	60
Airport Business Park	13	A1	213
Airport Industrial Campus	12	E4	1
Airside Business Park	2	D3	266
Airside Retail Park	1	C3	295
Airton Business Park	45	A4	2
Airton Business Park	45	A4	3
Airton Business Park	45	A4	4
Airton Coporate Park	45	A4	38
Airways Industrial Estate	12	F4	5
Allied Industrial Estate	36	E4	6
Alltech Technology Park	6	E2	307
Ardee Court	67	B2	7
Ashgrove Industrial Estate	59	C1	8
Aughrim Lane Ind Est	37	C1	268
Avonbeg Enterprise Centre	55	A1	85
Avonbeg Ind Est	45	B1	277
Avondale	49	A4	167
Baldonnel Business Park	43	A4	241
Baldoyle Ind Est	27	C1	10
Balfe Road Ind Est	45	C1	196
Balheary Ind Park	2	D1	11
Ballyboggan Ind Est	24	D3	12
Ballycoolin Business Park	10	D4	13
Ballymount Business Centre	45	B2	14
Ballymount Court Business Centre	45	B2	72
Ballymount Cross Ind. Est.	45	A2	15
Ballymount Ind Est	45	B2	16
Ballymount Road Ind. Est.	45	B2	17
Ballymount Trading Centre	45	B2	18
Ballymun Ind Est	12	D4	19
Barbeque Poultry Business Park	64	E3	300
Base Enterprise Centre	9	A4	301
Beech Hill Office Campus	47	C2	228
Beechlawn Industrial Complex	45	B2	20
Beechwood Close Ind Est	67	C4	21
Belfield Office Park	47	C2	229
Belgard Ind Est	44	F4	22
Bellevue Industrial Park	24	E3	86
Benson Street Enterprise Centre	38	F2	24
Blackhorse Ind Est	37	B1	25
Blackrock Business Park	49	A3	169
Blanchardstown Corporate Park	9	C3	165
Blanchardstown Ind Park	9	C4	26
Bluebell Business Centre	36	E4	273
Bluebell Business Park	36	E4	27
Bluebell Ind Est	36	D4	28
Bow Bridge Business Centre	37	B3	308
Bracetown Business Park	7	C1	29
Bray Business Park	67	C4	255
Bray Ind Est	67	C4	30
Bridges Ind Est	45	A1	32
Bridgewater Business Centre	37	B2	31
Brookfield Enterprise Centre	54	D1	247
Broombridge Ind Est	24	E3	33
Broomfield Business Park	3	B4	271
Broomhill Bus Pk Close	45	A4	35
Broomhill Bus Pk Drive	45	A4	36
Broomhill Bus Pk Road	45	A4	37
Broomhill Business Park	45	A4	84
Burton Hall Campus	58	E2	39
Butterly Business Park	26	D2	66
Calmount Business Park	45	B2	197
Carrigalea Ind Est	45	B1	40
Cashel Business Centre	46	E2	293
Castleforbes Business Park	38	F2	41
Cedar Ind Park	67	B4	258
Celbridge Ind Est	31	C3	238
Central Park Business Park	58	E2	253
Century Business Park	11	B4	206
Chapelizod Ind Est	36	E2	90
Charlestown Centre	11	A4	160
Cherry Orchard Ind Est	35	C2	42
Cherrywood Business Park	64	D1	251
Churchtown Business Park	47	B4	225
Cian Park Ind Est	25	B4	43
City Junction Business Park	13	C4	212
City Link Business Park	36	E4	215
City West Business Campus	53	B1	44
Clondalkin Business Centre	35	B4	46
Clondalkin Commercial Park	35	B4	45
Clondalkin Enterprise Centre	35	A3	177
Clonshaugh Business & Technology Park	13	A4	311
Clonshaugh Ind Est	13	A4	47
Clonskeagh House Office Park	47	C2	226
Clonskeagh Square Office Park	47	C2	227
Cloverhill Ind Est	35	B4	48
College Business & Technology Park	9	C4	200
Collinstown Cross Ind Est	12	F2	49
Collinstown Ind Est	12	F3	50
Collinstown Ind Park (Intel)	19	B3	92
Concord Ind Est, Naas Road	36	E4	272
Cookstown Business Centre	44	F4	245
Cookstown Enterprise Park	44	F4	51
Cookstown Ind Est	44	F4	52
Cookstown Ind Est The Extension	44	E4	243
Cookstown Square	44	F4	244
Coolmine Industrial Est	22	D2	53
Courtyard Business Park	43	B2	269
Crag Avenue Ind Centre	35	B4	219
Cranford Centre, Stillorgan	48	D2	274
Croke Park Ind Est	38	E1	55
Crosbie Business Centre	38	F1	262
Crossbeg Ind Est	45	A2	56
Crosslands Business Park	45	A2	297
Crosslands Ind Park	45	A2	57
Cruiserath Business Park	9	C3	199
Crumlin Business Park	46	E1	292
Damastown Ind Est	8	F3	58
Damastown Ind Park	8	F3	302
Damastown Technology Park	8	E3	166
Dartmouth House Ind Centre	36	E3	217
Deansgrange Business Park	59	B2	59
Docklands Innovation Park	39	A1	155
(The)Donnelly Centre Cork Street	37	C3	275
Dublin Ind Est / Glasnevin/Broombridge	24	E3	61
Dun Laoghaire Ind Est	59	B2	63
Dunboyne Ind Est	7	B2	62
Dundrum Business Park	47	C3	231
Earlscourt Industrial Estate	47	B4	224
Earlsfort Centre	38	E3	276
East Point Business Park	39	A1	263
East Road Ind Est	38	F1	64
Elmfield Ind Est	44	E1	65
Fashion City	45	A3	69
Feltrim Industrial Park	2	E3	67
Finches Industrial Park	45	B1	68
Finglas Business Centre	11	B4	140
Finglas Business Park	24	E3	23
Finglas Business Park	9	C3	210
Fonthill Retail Park	35	A2	176
Frank Fahey Centre	45	B1	9
Furry Park Ind Est, Santry	12	E3	181
Gaywood Ind Est	9	B3	70
Glasnevin Business Centre	24	D3	220
Glasnevin Business Park	24	D3	221
Glen Abbey Complex	44	F4	71
Glen Ind Est	24	E3	73
Glenageary Office Park	60	D2	291
Glenview Ind Est	37	B4	74
Glenville Ind Est	48	E3	75
Goldenbridge Ind Est	36	F4	76
Grange Castle Business Park	34	D4	218
Grange Castle International Business Park	43	B1	239
Great Keppel Business Centre	15	A1	296
Green Isle Business Park	44	D3	242
Greenhills Business Centre	45	B4	193
Greenhills Business Park	45	B4	192
Greenhills Centre	45	B4	191
Greenhills Ind Est	45	A4	77
Greenmount Ind Est	37	C4	78
Greenogue Business Park	42	E4	235

Name	Page	Grid/ Ref.	No.
Grove Ind Est Dubber Cross	11	B3	79
Grove Ind Est, Finglas	24	E1	80
Harbour Ind Est	67	C1	81
(The) Harcourt Centre,	38	D4	278
Hewlett Packard Ind Park	32	F2	234
Hibernian Industrial Estate	45	A4	82
Hillcrest Industrial Estate	45	B2	93
Hills Ind Est	34	D1	83
Hollywood Business Park	9	C3	303
Horizon Logistics	11	B2	204
Howth Junction Business Park	27	B1	270
I.D.A.Tallaght Business Park	54	F2	89
Industrial Yarns Complex	67	C1	91
International Financial Services Centre (IFSC)	38	E2	279
Irish Life Centre	38	E2	280
J.F.K. Ave	45	A1	96
J.F.K. Drive	45	B1	97
J.F.K. Park	36	D4	98
J.F.K. Road	36	D4	99
Jamestown Business Park	11	A4	208
Jamestown Ind Centre	36	F4	95
Jamestown Ind Estate	36	E4	94
Jamestown Little Ind Estate	11	A4	298
KCR Ind Est	46	E2	100
Kilbarrack Ind Est	27	B1	101
Kilcarberry Ind Park	43	A1	283
Kileen Ind Park	36	D4	216
Killarney Road Business Park	67	B3	257
Killinardin Enterprise Park	54	F2	246
Kinsealy Business Park	14	D1	281
Knockmitten Business Park	44	F1	282
Kylemore Ind Est	36	D4	102
Kylemore Park North	36	D3	103
Kylemore Park South	36	E4	104
Kylemore Park West	36	D4	105
Landys Ind Est	56	D1	106
Lansdown Valley	45	C1	107
Leopardstown Office Park	58	E2	261
Leopardstown Retail Park	58	E2	108
Liberties Craft & Small Industries Centre	37	C3	109
(The)Liffey Trust Enterprise Centre	38	F2	150
Lilmar Ind Est	12	F4	110
Loughlinstown Ind Est	64	D1	111
(The)Maltings Business Park	37	C3	259
Manor Street Business Park	37	C1	309
Maynooth Business Campus	17	C4	211
Merrywell Business Park	45	A2	188
Merrywell Ind Est	45	A2	182
Metropolitan Ind Est	37	A3	113
Mill Lane Business Park	33	B1	232
Millbank Business Park	34	D1	87
Millenium Business Park	10	E3	202

Name	Page	Grid/ Ref.	No.
Monarch Ind Est	44	F4	114
Montone Business Park	44	F1	248
Mount Pleasant Ind Est	47	A1	284
Mulcahy Keane Est	45	C2	115
Mygan Industrial Estate	11	B4	207
Naas Road Business Park	36	E4	132
Naas Road Ind Park	36	F4	170
Nangor Road Business Centre	35	C4	174
Newcastle Business Centre	42	E1	88
Newcourt Business Park	11	A2	205
Newlands Business Centre	44	E2	116
Newtown Ind Est	13	C4	117
North Park Business & Office Park	11	A4	209
North Richmond Ind Est	38	E1	118
North Ring Business Park	12	F3	180
Northern Cross Business Park	11	A4	285
Northwest Business Park	10	D3	201
Nutgrove Enterprise Park	57	A1	252
Nutgrove Office Park	47	A4	223
Oak Road Business Park	44	F1	250
Oakfield Ind Est	35	A4	119
Old Court Ind Est	67	B4	120
Old Sawmills Ind Est	45	B2	121
Ossory Ind Est	38	F1	122
Palmgrove Ind Est	25	B2	265
Park West Business Park	35	C4	173
Park West Enterprise Centre	35	C4	172
Park West Ind Park	36	D4	171
Parkmore Ind Est	45	B1	123
Parkway Business Centre	45	A2	183
Phoenix Ind Est	23	B3	124
Pineview Ind Est	55	C1	125
Pinewood Close Ind Est	67	C4	126
Plato Business Park	9	A3	198
Poppintree Ind Est	11	B4	127
Port Tunnel Business Park	13	A4	310
Portside Business Centre	38	F1	128
Red Cow Business Park	45	A1	184
(The)Red Cow Interchange Est	44	F2	233
Richmond Road Ind Est	25	B4	129
Richview Park	47	C2	230
Riversdale Ind Est	36	E4	130
Riverview Business Centre	35	C4	175
Robinhood Business Park	45	A1	294
Robinhood Ind Est	45	B1	131
Rock Enterprise Centre	43	B3	240
Rosemount Business Park	10	D4	133
Royal Liver Retail Park	36	E4	214
Sandyford Business Centre	58	E2	137
Sandyford Ind Est	58	E2	135
Sandyford Office Park	58	E2	136
Sandyford Park	58	E2	163
Santry Avenue Ind Est	12	E4	138

Name	Page	Grid/ Ref.	No.
Santry Hall Ind Est	25	B1	139
Shankhill Business Centre	64	E2	141
Shanowen Ind Est, Santry	25	B1	142
Sitecast Ind Est	45	B4	194
Solus Retail Park, Bray	67	C1	254
South City Business Park	54	F2	306
South City Executive Park	46	E1	288
South County Business Park	58	F2	143
Southern Cross Business Park	67	B4	256
S.P.A.D.E. Unemployment Enterprise Centre	37	C2	287
(The)Square Industrial Complex	54	F1	289
St. Joans Ind Est	45	A2	134
St. John's Court Office Park	25	B1	264
St. Margaret's Business Park	11	A4	286
St. Anthony's Business Park	45	A2	54
Stadium Ind Est	10	E4	203
Stillorgan Ind Park	58	D2	144
Sunbury Ind Est	45	B2	145
Sunshine Ind Est	37	A4/B4	146
Swanward Business Centre	45	A2	185
Swiftbrook Ind Est	53	A2	147
Swords Business Campus	2	D1	267
Swords Business Park	2	E1	148
Tallaght Enterprise Centre	55	A1	149
Taurus Business Park	45	B4	195
Terenure Business Park	46	F2	290
Terenure Enterprise Centre	46	F2	304
Tolka Ind Park	24	D3	34
Tolka Valley Business Park	24	D3	222
Turnpike Ind Est see Ballymount Cross	45	A2	151
Unidare/Jamestown Business Park	24	E1	152
Weatherwell Ind Est	35	A4	153
West Pier Business Campus	49	C4	168
Westend Retail Park	22	E2	237
Western Business Park	44	F1	249
Western Ind Est	45	A1	156
Western Office Park	22	E1	236
Western Parkway Business Centre, Ballymount Road	45	B2	157
Western Parkway Business Park	45	B2	190
Westgate Business Park	45	A3	186
Westland Square Business Park	38	E2	260
Westlink Ind Est	36	E3	154
Westpoint Buisness Park	8	F4	164
Westway Centre	45	B2	189
White Heather Ind Est	37	B4	158
White Swan Business Park	37	C4	159
Whitestown Ind Est	54	F1	305
Willow Business Park	45	A1	187
Woodford Business Park	12	F3	178
Woodlawn Ind Est	12	F3	162

Due to the limitations imposed by scale it has not been possible to include all street names on the maps. Unnamed streets have been given small numbers which appear after their grid reference in this index. A list of such streets, by grid reference, is given on page 140.

Streets not named or indicated by number on map pages are prefixed by * and are given their approximate location and grid reference.

STREET NAME	PAGE/GRID REFERENCE

A

STREET NAME	PAGE/GRID REFERENCE
1 Branch Road North	39 A2
1 Branch Road South	39 A2
2 Branch Road North	39 B2
2 Branch Road North Extension	39 B1
2 Branch Road South	39 A2
3 Branch Road Sth.	39 A2
4 Branch Road South	39 B2
A.W. Pugin House	46 F4 [19]
Abberley	64 E1
Abberley Square Apts.	54 F1 [2]
Abbey Cottages	71 B4
Abbey Court (Celbridge)	31 C4
Abbey Court (Killester)	26 E3
Abbey Court (Monkstown)	59 B1 [7]
Abbey Drive	24 D4
Abbey Green	31 C4
Abbey House	8 D3
Abbey Lane	31 C4
Abbey Park (Baldoyle)	27 C1
Abbey Park (Kill o' the Grange)	59 B1
Abbey Park (Killester)	26 E3
Abbey Road	59 B1
Abbey Street (Howth)	30 D1
Abbey Street Lower	71 C3
Abbey Street Middle	71 B4
Abbey Street Old	71 C3
Abbey Street Upper	71 B4
Abbey Terrace	30 D1 [11]
Abbey View	59 B1
Abbeydale	34 F3
Abbeydale Close	34 F3
Abbeydale Crescent	34 F3
Abbeydale Gardens	34 F3
Abbeydale Park	34 F3
Abbeydale Rise	34 F3
Abbeydale Walk	34 F3
Abbeyfarm	31 C4
Abbeyfield	26 E3
Abbeyfield (Clonskeagh)	47 B2
Abbeyfield (Killester)	26 E3
Abbeylea Avenue	1 C1
Abbeylea Close	1 C1
Abbeylea Drive	1 C1
Abbeylea Green	1 C1
Abbeyvale Avenue	1 B1
Abbeyvale Close	1 B1
Abbeyvale Court	1 B1
Abbeyvale Crescent	1 B1
Abbeyvale Drive	1 B2
Abbeyvale Green	1 B2
Abbeyvale Grove	1 B1
Abbeyvale Lawn	1 B1
Abbeyvale Place	1 B1
Abbeyvale Rise	1 B1
Abbeyvale View	1 B2
Abbeyvale Way	1 B2
Abbeywood	34 F3
Abbeywood Avenue	34 F3
Abbeywood Close	34 F3
Abbeywood Court	34 E3
Abbeywood Crescent	34 F3
Abbeywood Park	34 F3
Abbeywood Way	34 F3
Abbots Hill	3 C3
Abbotstown Avenue	23 C2
Abbotstown Drive	23 C1
Abbotstown Drive	24 D2
Abbotstown Road	24 D2
Abby Well	14 D1
Abercorn Road	72 E3
Abercorn Square	36 F3 [19]
Abercorn Terrace	36 F3 [10]
Aberdeen Street	70 D3
Abington	2 F3
Accommodation Road	19 C4
Achill Road (Drumcondra)	25 B3
Achill Road (Loughlinstown)	64 E1
Acorn Drive	57 B1
Acorn Road	57 B1
Acres Road	36 F2
Acres Road	36 F2
Adair	39 A4 [14]

STREET NAME	PAGE/GRID REFERENCE
*Adair Lane (off Aston Place)	71 B4
*Adair Terrace (on St Joseph's Parade)	71 A1
Adam Court (off Grafton Street)	75 B1
Adams Town Court	34 D2 [2]
Adamstown Avenue	33 C4
Adamstown Road	34 D2
Adare Avenue	26 E1
Adare Drive	26 E1
Adare Green	26 E1
Adare Park	26 E1
Adare Road	26 E1
Addison Avenue	24 F3 [8]
Addison Drive	24 F3
Addison Hall	24 F3 [6]
Addison Lane	24 F3
Addison Park	24 F3
Addison Place	25 A3 [9]
Addison Road	25 C4
Adelaide Court	75 B3
Adelaide Mews	48 E1
Adelaide Road (Bray)	67 C2
Adelaide Road (Dun Laoghaire)	60 E1
Adelaide Road (Leeson Street)	75 B3
Adelaide Street	50 D4
Adelaide Terrace (Dun Laoghaire)	60 E1 [28]
Adelaide Terrace (off Brookfield Road)	73 C2
Adelaide Villas (Bray)	67 C2
Adelaide Villas (Dun Laoghaire)	60 E1 [27]
Admiral Court	15 A4 [9]
Admiral Park	15 A4
Adrian Avenue	46 F1
Aengus Hall (Belgard Square)	54 F1 [3]
Affollus	5 C3
Aideen Avenue	46 E2
Aideen Drive	46 E2
Aideen Place	46 E2
Aikenhead Terrace	39 A3
Aiken's Village	58 D3
Ailesbury	25 B1 [1]
Ailesbury Close	48 D1 [4]
Ailesbury Drive	48 D1
Ailesbury Gardens	48 E1
Ailesbury Grove (Donnybrook)	48 D1
Ailesbury Grove (Dundrum)	57 B1
Ailesbury Lane (off Ailesbury Road)	48 D1
Ailesbury Lawn	57 B1
Ailesbury Mews	48 E1
Ailesbury Park	48 E1
Ailesbury Road	48 D1
Ailesbury Wood	48 D1
Airfield Court	48 D2
Airfield Drive	47 B4 [13]
Airfield Park	48 D2
Airfield Road	46 F2
Airlie Heights	33 B2
Airpark Avenue	56 E2
Airpark Close	56 E2
Airpark Court	56 E2
Airpark House	56 E2
Airpark Rise	56 E2
Airside	2 D3
Airton Close	45 A4
Airton Road	45 A4
*Airton Terrace (off Greenhills Rd)	45 A4
Albany Avenue	49 B4
Albany Court	64 E1
Albany Road	47 B1
Albert Avenue	68 D2
Albert College Avenue	25 A2
Albert College Court	25 A2
Albert College Crescent	25 A2
Albert College Drive	25 A2
Albert College Grove	25 A2
Albert College Lawn	25 A2
Albert College Park	25 A2
Albert Court (Grand Canal St. Lower)	76 E1
Albert Court (off Grand Canal St)	76 E1
Albert Court (Sandycove Road)	60 E1
Albert Park	60 E1 [3]

STREET NAME	PAGE/GRID REFERENCE
Albert Place East	76 E1
Albert Place West	75 B3
Albert Road Lower	60 E1
Albert Road Upper	60 E2
Albert Terrace (Charlemont Street)	75 B3
Albert Terrace (Dún Laoghaire)	50 D4 [27]
Albert Walk	67 C2
Aldborough House	72 D2
Aldborough Parade	72 D2
Aldborough Place	72 D2
Aldborough Square (off Aldborough Place)	72 D2
Aldemere	21 B2
Alden Drive	27 C1
Alden Park	27 C1
Alden Road	27 C1
Alder Court	4 D4 [1]
Alder Lodge	23 A4
Alderpark Court	54 F1
Alderwood Avenue	54 E1
Alderwood Close	54 E1
Alderwood Court	54 E1
Alderwood Drive	54 F1
Alderwood Green	54 E1
Alderwood Grove	54 F1
Alderwood Lawn	54 E1
Alderwood Park	54 F1
Alderwood Rise	54 E1
Alderwood Way	54 F1
Aldrin Walk	26 E1
Alen Hall (Belgard Square)	54 F1 [4]
Alensgrove	32 F2
Alexander Court Apts.	76 D1
Alexander Terrace (Bray)	67 C2 [43]
Alexander Terrace (North Wall)	72 F3
Alexandra Court	47 C4
Alexandra Quay	39 A2 [2]
Alexandra Quay	39 A2
Alexandra Road	39 A2
Alexandra Road Extension	39 C2
Alexandra Terrace (Dundrum)	47 C4
Alexandra Terrace (Portobello)	75 A3
Alexandra Terrace (Terenure)	46 F2
Alexandra Villas	47 C4 [3]
Alfie Byrne House	71 B2
Alfie Byrne Road	72 F1
All Hallows Green	25 B3
All Hallows Lane	25 B3 [7]
All Hallows Square	25 B3
All Saint's Close	27 A3
All Saints Drive	27 A3
All Saints Park	27 A3
All Saints Road	26 F3
Allen Park Drive	58 E1
Allen Park Road	58 E1
Allen Terrace (off Avondale Avenue)	70 F1
Allendale Close	21 B2
Allendale Copse	21 B1
Allendale Court	21 B1
Allendale Drive	21 B1
Allendale Elms	21 B1
Allendale Glen	21 B1
Allendale Green	21 B1
Allendale Grove	21 B1
Allendale Heath	21 B1
Allendale Lawn	21 B1
Allendale Place	21 B1
Allendale Rise	21 B1
Allendale Square	21 B2
Allendale Terrace	21 B1
Allendale View	21 B1
Allendale Walk	21 B1
Allenton Avenue	55 A3
Allenton Crescent	55 A2 [3]
Allenton Drive	55 A3
Allenton Gardens	55 A3
Allenton Green	55 A3
Allenton Lawns	55 A2
Allenton Park	55 A2
Allenton Road	55 B3
Allenton Way	55 A3
Allies River Road	67 A1
Allingham Street	74 E2
Alma Park	49 C4 [30]

STREET NAME	PAGE/GRID REFERENCE
Alma Place	49 C4 [14]
Alma Road	49 B4
Alma Terrace	47 A1 [13]
Almeida Avenue	73 C1
Almeida Terrace	73 C2
Alone Walk	26 E2
Alpine Heights	44 D1
Alpine Rise	44 E4
Altadore	60 D2
Altamont Hall	47 C4
Alverno	39 B1 [1]
Ambassador Court	76 E3
Amber Vale	44 E4
Amberwood	9 A4
Amiens Street	72 D3
An Crannog	60 D3
Anastasia Lane	60 F2 [3]
Anglers Rest	47 C1
Anglesea Avenue	49 A3
Anglesea House	39 A4 [40]
Anglesea Lane	50 D4 [20]
Anglesea Park	60 E2
Anglesea Road	47 C1
Anglesea Row	71 A3
Anglesea Street	71 B4
Anley Court	34 E1
Ann Devlin Avenue	46 E4
Ann Devlin Drive	46 E4
Ann Devlin Park	56 E1
Ann Devlin Road	46 E4
Anna Livia Apts.	74 E1
Anna Villa	47 B1
Annabeg	60 D4 [1]
Annacrivey	65 B3
Annadale	47 B4 [16]
Annadale Avenue	25 C4 [1]
Annadale Crescent	25 C3
Annadale Drive	25 C3
Annagh Court	22 F1
Annaghaskin	66 D1
Annaly Close	21 B1
Annaly Court	21 B1
Annaly Drive	21 B1
Annaly Grove	21 B1
Annaly Road	24 F4
Annaly Terrace	21 B1
Annamoe Drive	70 E1
Annamoe Parade	70 E1
Annamoe Park	70 E1
Annamoe Road	70 D1
Annamoe Terrace	70 E1
Annaville Avenue	59 A1
Annaville Close	47 C4
Annaville Grove	47 C3 [1]
Annaville Lodge	47 C4
Annaville Park	47 C4
Annaville Terrace	47 C3
Anne Street North	71 A3
Anne Street South	75 B1
Anner Road	73 B2
Anne's Bridge	17 C1
Anne's Lane	75 B1
Annesley Avenue	72 E1
Annesley Bridge	72 E1
Annesley Bridge Road	72 E1
Annesley Close	72 E1
Annesley Park	47 B1
Annesley Place	72 E1
Annfield	22 D3
Annfield Court	22 D3
Annfield Crescent	22 D3
Annfield Drive	22 D3
Annfield Lawn	22 D4
Annsbrook	47 C2
Annville Drive	58 E1
Apollo Way	26 D1
*Appian Close (on Leeson Park)	76 D4
Apples Road	58 D2
Applewood Avenue East	1 Inset
Applewood Birch	1 Inset
Applewood Crescent	1 Inset
Applewood Drive	1 Inset
Applewood Main Street	1 Inset
Applewood Mews	1 Inset
Applewood Place	1 Inset
Applewood Square	1 Inset

STREET NAME	PAGE/GRID REFERENCE
Aranleigh Court	56 F1
Aranleigh Dell	57 A1
Aranleigh Gardens	56 F1
Aranleigh Mount	56 F1
Aranleigh Park	57 A1
Aranleigh Vale	56 F1
Arás na Cluaine	35 B4
Aravon Court	68 D2
Arbour Hill	70 E3
Arbour Place	70 E3
Arbour Terrace	70 D3
Arbutus Avenue	74 F4
Arbutus Grove	67 B1 [4]
Arbutus Place	75 A3
Archers Wood	8 F4
Archers Wood	8 F4
Ard Lorcain	58 F1
Ard Lorcain Villas	58 F1 [2]
Ard Mhacha	54 F2
Ard Mhuire Park	60 E2
Ard Mor Avenue	53 C1
Ard Mor Close	53 C1
Ard Mor Court	53 C1
Ard Mor Crescent	53 C1
Ard Mor Dale	53 C1
Ard Mor Drive	53 C1
Ard Mor Green	53 C1
Ard Mor Lawn	53 C1
Ard Mor Park	53 C1
Ard Mor Walk	53 C1
Ard na Glaise	48 F4
Ard Na Gréine	47 A3 [11]
Ard Na Gréine (Ballymorris)	67 B4
Ard na Mara	3 A3
Ard na Meala	12 D4
Ard Ri Road	70 E3
Ard Righ Place	70 E3
Ardagh Avenue	59 A1
Ardagh Close	59 A1 [6]
Ardagh Court	58 F1
Ardagh Crescent	59 A1
Ardagh Drive	59 A1
Ardagh Grove	59 A1
Ardagh Park	59 A1
Ardagh Park Road	59 A1
Ardagh Road	73 C4
Ardara Avenue	14 D4
Ardbeg Crescent	26 E2
Ardbeg Drive	26 E2
Ardbeg Park	26 E2
Ardbeg Road	26 E2
Ardbrugh Close	60 F2 [31]
Ardbrugh Road	60 F2
Ardbrugh Villas	60 F2 [21]
Ardcian Park	1 C1
Ardcollum Avenue	26 E2
Ardee Grove	75 B4
Ardee Road	75 B4
Ardee Row	74 F2
Ardee Street (Bray)	67 B2
Ardee Street (The Coombe)	74 F2
Ardeen	33 C2
Ardeevin Avenue	33 C2
Ardeevin Court	33 C2
Ardeevin Drive	33 C2
Ardeevin Road	60 F2
*Ardeevin Terrace (off Ardeevin Road)	60 F2
Ardenza Park	49 B3 [3]
Ardenza Terrace	49 B3 [1]
Ardglas Estate	57 C1
Ardilaun	14 F1
Ardilaun Road	72 D1
*Ardilaun Square (off Sackville Avenue)	72 D1
Ardlea Downs	48 D4
Ardlea Road	26 E2
Ardlui Park	59 A1
Ardmeen Park	59 A1
Ardmore Avenue	70 D1
Ardmore Close	26 D2
Ardmore Crescent (Artane)	26 D2
Ardmore Crescent (Bray)	67 B2
Ardmore Drive	26 D1
Ardmore Grove	26 D1
Ardmore Lawn	67 B3
Ardmore Park (Artane)	26 D2
Ardmore Park (Bray)	67 B2
Ardmore Park (Kill o' the Grange)	59 C1
Ardmore Wood	67 B3
Ardoyne Mews	76 E4
Ardpatrick Road	24 D4
Ardtona Avenue	47 B4 [6]
Arena Road	58 E2
Argus House	74 F4
Argyle House Apts.	39 A4 [37]
Argyle Road	76 E4
Argyle Square	47 C1 [25]
Arkendale Court	60 E1 [26]
Arkendale Road	60 E1
Arkendale Woods	60 E1 [25]
Arkle Road	58 E2
Arkle Square	58 F2 [6]
Arklow Street	70 D2
Armagh Road	46 D1
Armstrong Street	74 F4
Armstrong Street (off Harold's Cross Road)	74 F4
Armstrong Walk	26 E1
Army Road	69 B3
Arnold Grove	60 D2
Arnold Park	60 D2
Arnott Street	75 A2
Arran Avenue	64 E1
Arran Close	64 E1
Arran Court	22 F1
Arran Drive	64 E1
Arran Green	67 C2
Arran Quay	70 F4
Arran Quay Apts.	70 F4
Arran Quay Terrace (Arran Quay)	70 F4
Arran Road	25 B3
Arran Square Apts.	70 F4
Arran Street East	71 A4
Arran Street West	70 F4
Arranmore Avenue	71 A1
Arranmore Road	47 C1
Artane	26 E2
Artane Cottages Lower	26 E2 [2]
Artane Cottages Upper	26 E2 [3]
Arthur Griffith Court	34 D2 [1]
Arthur Griffith Park	34 D3
Arundel	49 B4 [19]
Asdill's Row (off Temple Bar)	71 B4
Asgard Apts.	30 D1
Asgard Park	30 D2
Asgard Road	30 D2
Asgard Road	72 E4
*Ash Grove (Meath Street)	74 F1
Ash Park Avenue	34 E3
Ash Park Court	34 E3
Ash Park Grove	34 E2
Ash Park Heath	34 E2
Ash Street	74 F1
Ashberry	34 D3
Ashbrook (Ashtown)	23 C3
Ashbrook (Bray)	67 C2
Ashbrook (Clontarf)	26 D4
*Ashbrook Terrace (Ranelagh)	47 B1
*Ashbrook Villas (Ranelagh)	47 B1
Ashbury Park	67 C2
Ashcroft	27 A2
Ashcroft Court	22 D1 [5]
Ashcroft Grove	22 D1 [6]
Ashdale Avenue	46 F2
Ashdale Close	2 E3
Ashdale Gardens	46 F2
Ashdale Park	46 F2 [1]
Ashdale Road (Swords)	2 E3
Ashdale Road (Terenure)	46 F2
Ashe Court	2 E2
Ashfield	46 D4
Ashfield Avenue (Clondalkin)	44 F3
Ashfield Avenue (Ranelagh)	47 B1
Ashfield Close (Clondalkin)	44 F3
Ashfield Court (Ballymorris)	67 B4
Ashfield Court (Mulhuddart)	9 A4
Ashfield Drive	44 F3
Ashfield Gardens	9 A4
Ashfield Green	8 F4
Ashfield Grove	9 A4
Ashfield Lawn	8 F4
Ashfield Park (Booterstown)	48 E2
Ashfield Park (Clondalkin)	44 F3
Ashfield Park (Huntstown Way)	9 A4 [2]
Ashfield Park (Terenure)	46 F2
Ashfield Road (Ranelagh)	47 B1
Ashfield Way	8 A4
Ashford Cottages	70 D2
Ashford Place	70 D2
Ashford Street	70 D2
Ashgrove (Baskin Lane)	13 C1
Ashgrove (Celbridge)	31 C2
Ashgrove (Kill o' the Grange)	59 C1
Ashgrove (Tallaght)	54 E1
Ashgrove Court	57 C1 [8]
Ashgrove Terrace	57 C1 [2]
Ashington Avenue	24 D3
Ashington Close	24 D3
Ashington Court	24 D3
Ashington Crescent	23 C3
Ashington Dale	24 D3
Ashington Gardens	24 D3
Ashington Green	24 D3
Ashington Grove	24 D3
Ashington Heath	24 D3
Ashington Mews	24 D3
Ashington North	24 D3
Ashington Park	24 D3
Ashington Rise	23 C3
Ashlawn	57 C1
Ashlawn Court	67 B2
Ashlawn Park	60 D4
Ashleigh Court	22 F3 [3]
Ashleigh Green	22 F3
Ashleigh Grove (Blanchardstown)	22 F3
Ashleigh Grove (Maynooth)	17 B4
Ashleigh Lawn	3 B3
Ashley Avenue	2 D2
Ashley Drive	2 D2
Ashley Grove	2 D2
Ashley Heights	67 B2 [4]
Ashley Rise	4 D4
Ashling Close	73 C4
Ashling Court	47 B1
Ashling Heights	22 E1
Ashmount	9 A4 [1]
Ashmount Court	73 B1
Ashton Avenue	1 Inset
Ashton Avenue	56 D1
Ashton Close	1 Inset
Ashton Close	56 D1
Ashton Court	1 Inset
Ashton Drive	1 Inset
Ashton Green	1 Inset
Ashton Grove	1 Inset
Ashton Grove	56 D1
Ashton Lawn	56 D1
Ashton Lawns	1 Inset
Ashton Park	49 B4
Ashton Rise	1 Inset
Ashton Wood	67 A3
Ashtown	23 C3
Ashtown Court	23 C4
Ashtown Gate (Phoenix Park)	23 B4
Ashtown Gate Road	23 B4
Ashtown Grove	23 C4
Ashtown Lodge	23 C4 [4]
Ashtown Road	23 B3
Ashtowngate	23 C3
Ashurst	60 E4
Ashurst (Ballybrack)	64 E1
Ashurst (Mount Merrion)	48 E4 [3]
Ashville Close	34 E1
Ashwood Avenue	43 C1
Ashwood Close	43 C1
Ashwood Drive	44 D1
Ashwood Lawns	44 D1
Ashwood Park	44 D1
Ashwood Road	44 D1
Ashwood Way	44 D1
Ashworth Place (off Mount Drumond Avenue)	75 A4
Aspen Drive	2 E3
Aspen Park (Kill O'The Grange)	59 C1 [11]
Aspen Park (Kinsealy Court)	2 E3
Aspen Road	2 E3
Aspen Wood	22 D2
Aspin Avenue	21 C2
Aspin Lawns	22 D2
Assumpta Park	64 E3
Aston Place	71 B4
Aston Quay	71 B4
Astor Hall	71 C4
Athgoe	51 C1
Athgoe Drive	64 E2 [4]
Athgoe North	51 B1
Athgoe Road (Newcastle)	41 C4
Athgoe Road (Shankill)	64 E2
Athgoe South	51 B2
Atlumney Villas	75 B4
Atmospheric Road	60 E1 [29]
Aubrey Grove	64 E3
Aubrey Park	64 E3
Auburn	26 D4
Auburn Avenue (Cabinteely)	60 D3
Auburn Avenue (Castleknock)	23 A3
Auburn Avenue (Donnybrook)	47 C1
Auburn Avenue Roundabout	23 A3
Auburn Close (Cabinteely)	60 D3
Auburn Close (Castleknock)	23 A3
Auburn Drive (Cabinteely)	60 D3
Auburn Drive (Castleknock)	23 A3
Auburn Green	23 A3
Auburn Grove	3 A3
Auburn Road (Cabinteely)	60 D3 [1]
Auburn Road (Cabinteely)	60 D3
Auburn Road (Donnybrook)	47 C1 [11]
Auburn Street	71 A2
Auburn Terrace (Old Kilmainham)	73 C1
Auburn Villas (Bray)	67 B2 [1]
Auburn Villas (Rathgar)	47 A2
Auburn Walk	70 D2
Aughavannagh Road	74 E4
Aughrim Court	70 E3
Aughrim Lane	70 E2
Aughrim Place	70 D2
Aughrim Street	70 D2
Aughrim Villas	70 D2
Augustine Court (St Margaret's Tce)	74 F1
Augustine Villas	67 C2 [30]
Aulden Grange	12 F4
Aungier Lane	75 B2
Aungier Place	75 B2
Aungier Street	75 B1
Austin's Cottages	72 E1
Avalon	59 A3 [3]
Avalon Apts.	29 B1 [2]
Ave Maria Road	74 D2
Avenue Road	75 A3
Avila Apts	59 A1 [10]
Avila Park	23 C1
Avila Park Gardens	23 C1
Avoca Apartments	32 D3
Avoca Avenue (Dun Laoghaire)	67 C3
Avoca Avenue (Stillorgan)	48 F4
Avoca Court	48 F4
Avoca Hall	49 A4 [10]
Avoca Park	48 F4
Avoca Place	49 A3
Avoca Road	48 F4
Avoca Terrace	48 F4
Avoca Wood	48 F4
Avonbeg Court	55 A1 [3]
Avonbeg Drive	55 A1
Avonbeg Gardens	55 B1
Avonbeg Park	55 A1
Avonbeg Road	55 B1
Avondale	20 D4
Avondale Avenue	70 F1
Avondale Court (Blackrock)	49 A4
Avondale Court (Dalkey)	60 E1 [31]
Avondale Crescent	60 E2
Avondale House	71 C2
Avondale Lawn	49 A4
Avondale Mews	39 A4 [55]
Avondale Park (Blackrock)	49 A4 [1]
Avondale Park (Dalkey)	60 E2
Avondale Park (Dun Laoghaire)	67 B3

STREET NAME	PAGE/GRID REFERENCE		STREET NAME	PAGE/GRID REFERENCE		STREET NAME	PAGE/GRID REFERENCE		STREET NAME	PAGE/GRID REFERENCE	
Avondale Park (Raheny)	27	A2	Ballentree Grove	9	B3	Ballymacartle	13	C1	Bankside Cottages	47	B2
Avondale Road (Dalkey)	60	D2	Ballentree Lodge Apts.	9	B2	Ballymace Green	46	E4	Bann Road	24	E3
Avondale Road (Phibsborough)	70	F1	Ballentree Villa	9	B3	Ballymacoll	6	D3	Bannaville	75	B4
Avondale Square	7	B2 [2]	Ballinakelly Village	42	D4	Ballymadrough Road	2	F1	Bannow Road	24	E4
Avondale Terrace	45	C2	Ballinclea Heights	60	E3	Ballymakealy Grove	31	C4	Banshee	51	A2
Avonmore	59	A2	Ballinclea Road	60	D3	Ballymakealy Lawns	31	C4	Bantry Road	25	A3
Avonmore Avenue	55	B1 [5]	Ballinteer	57	B2	Ballyman	66	F1	Bantry Square	22	F1
Avonmore Close	55	B1	Ballinteer Avenue	57	B2	Ballyman Lane	63	C4	Banville Avenue	36	D4
Avonmore Drive	55	B1	Ballinteer Close	57	B2	Ballyman Lane	66	F1	Barberstown Lane	1	A4
Avonmore Grove	55	B1	Ballinteer Court	57	B2 [2]	Ballyman Road	66	F2	Barclay Court	49	A3
Avonmore Park	55	B1	Ballinteer Crescent	57	B2	Ballymana	54	E4	Bargy Road	72	F2
Avonmore Road	55	B1	Ballinteer Drive	57	B2	Ballymanagin Lane	35	A4 [1]	Barnacoille Park	60	F1
Aylesbury	55	A2	Ballinteer Gardens	57	C2	Ballymorris	67	B4 [2]	Barnamire	65	A4
Aylmer Ave	42	D4	Ballinteer Grove	57	B2	Ballymorris	67	B4	Barnamore Crescent	24	D3
Aylmer Heath	42	D4	Ballinteer Park	57	B2	Ballymoss Parade	58	F2 [5]	Barnamore Grove	24	D3
Aylmer Road	42	D4	Ballinteer Road	57	C1	Ballymoss Road	58	E2	Barnamore Park	24	D3
Ayrefield Avenue	26	F1	Ballinteer Road (Delbrook Park)	57	C2	Ballymount Avenue	45	B2	Barnaslingan Lane	63	A3
Ayrefield Court	26	F1	Ballintrane Wood	1	C2	Ballymount Cottages	45	B2 [2]	Barneville Green	35	C3
Ayrefield Drive	26	F1	Ballintyre Demesne	57	B2	Ballymount Drive	45	B2	Barneville Walk	35	C4
Ayrefield Grove	26	F1	Ballintyre Downs	57	B2	Ballymount Road	44	F3	Barnhall	32	F1
Ayrefield Park	26	F1 [2]	Ballintyre Lane	57	B2	Ballymount Road Lower	45	B2	Barnhall Drive	32	F1
Ayrefield Place	26	F1	Ballintyre Meadows	57	B2	Ballymount Road Upper	45	A2	Barnhill Avenue	60	E2
Ayrefield Road	26	F1	Ballintyre Square	57	B2	Ballymount Square	45	B2	Barnhill Cross Road	34	D1
Ayward Green	24	D2	Ballintyre Terrace	57	B2	Ballymun	25	A1	Barnhill Grove	60	F2 [7]
			Ballintyre Walk	57	B2	Ballymun Main Street	12	D4	Barnhill Lawn	60	E2 [1]
B			Ballintyre Woods	57	B2	Ballymun Road	12	D4	Barnhill Park	60	E2 [3]
			Ball's Lane	71	A3	Ballymun Road	25	A1	Barnhill Road	60	E2
Bachelor's Walk	71	B4	Ballsbridge	76	F4	Ballymun Road	25	A3	*Barnhill Villas	60	F2
Bachelors Walk Apartments.	71	B4	Ballsbridge Avenue	39	A4 [26]	Ballynakelly	42	D4	(on Barnhill Road)		
Bachelors Way	71	B4	Ballsbridge Court	39	A4 [39]	Ballyneety Road	36	F3	Barnville Park	35	C4
Back Lane (Baldoyle)	15	A4 [3]	Ballsbridge Gardens	39	A4 [25]	Ballynoe Court	67	B3 [1]	Barnwell Drive	24	F1
Back Lane (High Street)	75	A1	Ballsbridge Park	39	A4 [23]	Ballyogan Avenue	58	F4	Baroma	46	E2 [10]
Back Lane (Maynooth)	17	C3	Ballsbridge Terrace	76	F4	Ballyogan Close	58	F4	Barrack Bridge	3	C2
*Back Lane (off Sandwith St Upr)	76	D1	Ballsbridge Wood	39	A4 [27]	Ballyogan Court	58	F4	Barrack Court	52	F2
Back Road	3	B4	Ballybetagh	62	F4	Ballyogan Crescent	58	F4	*Barrack Lane	39	A3
Baggot Bridge Court	76	D2	Ballybetagh Road	62	E4	Ballyogan Drive	58	F4	(off Irishtown Road)		
Baggot Close	75	C2	Ballyboden	56	E1	Ballyogan Estate	58	F4	Barrett Street	49	C4 [2]
Baggot Court	76	D2	Ballyboden Crescent	56	E1	Ballyogan Green	58	F4	Barrogstown East	18	F4
Baggot Lane	76	E3	Ballyboden Road	56	E1	Ballyogan Lawn	58	F4	Barrogstown West	18	E4
Baggot Rath House	39	A3 [48]	Ballyboden Way	56	E1	Ballyogan Park	58	F4 [1]	Barron Place	25	A3 [4]
Baggot Road	23	C4	Ballyboggan Road	24	E3	Ballyogan Road	58	F4	Barrow Road	24	E3
Baggot Street Lower	76	D2	Ballybough Avenue	72	D1	Ballyogen Vale	59	A4	Barrow Street	76	F1
Baggot Street Upper	76	E3	Ballybough Court	72	D1	Ballyogen Wood	59	A4	Barry Avenue	24	D1
Baggot Terrace	23	C4 [1]	*Ballybough Lane	72	D1	Ballyolaf Manor	57	C1 [6]	Barry Close (off Barry Drive)	24	D1
Baggotrath Place	76	D2	(King's Avenue)			Ballyoulster Park	32	E3	Barry Drive	24	D1
Bailey Green	30	E3	Ballybough Road	72	D1	Ballyowen Avenue	34	F1	Barry Green	24	D1
Bailey Green Road	30	E3	Ballybrack	60	E4	Ballyowen Court	34	F1	Barry Park	24	D1
Bailey View	60	F1 [15]	Ballybrack	61	B3	Ballyowen Crescent	34	F1	Barry Road	24	D1
Bailey's Row	72	D2	(Two Rock Mountain)			Ballyowen Drive	34	F1	Barry's Park	2	D2
Balally Avenue	58	D1	Ballybrew	65	C2	Ballyowen Green	34	F1	Barryscourt Road	26	E1
Balally Close	58	D1	Ballybride	64	D3	Ballyowen Grove	34	F1	Barton Avenue	56	F1
Balally Drive	58	D1	Ballybride Road	64	D3	Ballyowen Hall	34	F2	Barton Court	57	A1 [3]
Balally Grove	58	D2	Ballycoolin Road	10	D4	Ballyowen Lane	34	F2	Barton Drive	56	F1
Balally Hill	58	D2	Ballycorus	63	B3	Ballyowen Lawn	34	F1	Barton Road East	57	B1
Balally Park	58	D1	Ballycorus Road	62	F2	Ballyowen Road	34	F1	Barton Road East Extension	57	A1
Balally Road	57	C1	Ballycorus Road	63	A2	Ballyowen Square	34	F2	Barton Road Extension	57	A1
Balally Terrace	58	D2 [1]	Ballycullen Avenue	55	B2	Ballyowen View	34	F1	Barton Road West	56	F1
Balbutcher Drive	11	C4	Ballycullen Drive	55	B2	Ballyowen Way	34	F1	Bartra Rock Apts.	60	F1 [18]
Balbutcher Lane	11	C4	Ballycullen Road	55	C1	Ballyroan Court	56	D1 [3]	Basin Grove	74	D1
Balbutcher Lane Lower	11	C4	Ballydowd Grove	34	E1	Ballyroan Crescent	56	E1	Basin Lane Flats	74	D1
Balbutcher Way	11	C4	Ballydowd Manor	34	E2	Ballyroan Heights	56	E1	Basin Street Lower	74	D1
Balcurris Close	12	D4	Ballyedmonduff	61	C2	Ballyroan Park	56	D1	Basin Street Upper	74	D1
Balcurris Gardens	12	D4	Ballyedmonduff	62	E1	Ballyroan Road	56	E1	*Basin View	74	D1
Balcurris Park East	12	D4	Ballyedmonduff Road	62	D1	Ballyshannon Avenue	25	C1	(off Basin Street Upper)		
Balcurris Road	12	D4	Ballyfermot	36	D3	Ballyshannon Road	26	D1	Baskin Cottages	13	C1
Baldoyle	15	A4	Ballyfermot Avenue	36	D3	Ballytore Road	46	F3	Baskin Lane	13	B1
Baldoyle Road	28	D1	Ballyfermot Crescent	36	D3	Ballywaltrim Cottages	67	B4 [1]	Bass Place	76	D1
Balfe Avenue	45	C1	Ballyfermot Drive	36	D3	Ballywaltrim Heights	67	B3	Bath Avenue (Malahide)	3	C2
Balfe Road	45	C1	Ballyfermot Parade	36	D3	Ballywaltrim Lane	67	A4	Bath Avenue (Sandymount)	76	F2
Balfe Road East	46	D1	Ballyfermot Road	35	C3	Ballywaltrim Road	67	B4	Bath Avenue Gardens	76	F2
Balfe Street	75	B1	Ballyfermot Road	36	E3	Ballywilliam Close	67	B4	Bath Avenue Place	76	F2
Balgaddy Road	34	F3	Ballyfermot Road	36	D3	Balnagowan	47	B2 [4]	Bath Lane	71	B2
Balglass Road	30	D2	(Cherry Orchard)			Balrothery Cottages	55	C1 [5]	Bath Place	49	A3 [8]
Balgriffin	14	D3	Ballygall Avenue	24	E1	Balrothery Estate	45	B4	Bath Street	39	A3
Balgriffin Cottages	14	D3	Ballygall Crescent	24	E2	Balscadden Road	30	E1	Bawnlea Avenue	54	D2
Balgriffin Park	14	D3	Ballygall Parade	24	E2	Balscott	41	C1	Bawnlea Close	54	D2
Balgriffin Road	14	D3	Ballygall Place	24	E2 [1]	Bancroft Avenue	55	A1	Bawnlea Crescent	54	D2
Balheary Road	2	D1	Ballygall Road	24	E2	Bancroft Close	55	B1	Bawnlea Drive	54	D2
Balkill Park	30	D2	Ballygall Road East	24	F2	Bancroft Crescent	45	B4	Bawnlea Green	54	D2
Balkill Road	30	D2	Ballygall Road West	24	E1	Bancroft Downs	45	A4	Bawnogue Cottages	43	C1 [1]
Ballawley Court	57	C2	Ballygihen Avenue	60	E1	Bancroft Grove	55	B1	Bawnogue Road	43	C1
Ballentree	9	B2	Ballygihen Villas	60	E1 [20]	Bancroft Park	55	A1	Bawnville Avenue	55	A2
Ballentree Avenue	9	B2	Ballygoran	18	E4	Bancroft Road	55	B1	Bawnville Close	55	A2
Ballentree Close	9	B2	Ballygoran Court	31	C2	Bangor Circle	46	E1	Bawnville Drive	55	B2
Ballentree Crescent	9	B2	Ballygoran View	31	C2	Bangor Drive	73	C4	Bawnville Park	55	B2
Ballentree Drive	9	B2	Ballyhoy Avenue	27	A3	Bangor Road	46	E1	Bawnville Road	55	A2

STREET NAME	PAGE/GRID REFERENCE
Baymount Park	27 A4
Bayshore Lane	64 E1
Bayside Boulevard North	27 C1
Bayside Boulevard South	27 C1
Bayside Crescent	27 C1 [1]
Bayside Park	27 C1
Bayside Square East	27 C1
Bayside Square North	27 C1
Bayside Square South	27 C1
Bayside Square West	27 C1
Bayside Walk	27 C1
Bayswater Terrace	60 F1 [7]
Baytownpark	6 E1
Bayview (Bray)	67 C2 [51]
Bayview (Loughlinstown)	64 E1
*Bayview (On Seapoint Road)	67 C2
Bayview Avenue	72 D1
Bayview Close	64 E1
Bayview Court	64 E1
Bayview Crescent	64 E1
Bayview Drive	64 E1
Bayview Glade	64 E1 [12]
Bayview Glen	64 E1
Bayview Green	64 E1
Bayview Grove	64 E1
Bayview Lawn	64 E1
Bayview Rise	64 E1
Beach Avenue	39 A3
Beach Drive	39 A3
Beach Park	15 A1
Beach Road	39 A3
Beach View	27 C2
Beacon Court	58 D2
*Beacon Hill (off Nerano Road)	60 F2
Beaconsfield Court	73 A1
Bealing	9 B2
Bealing Avenue	9 B2
Bealing Close	9 B3
Bealing Crescent	9 B2
Bealing Grove	9 B2
Bealing Mews	9 B2
Bealing View	9 B2
Bealing Walk	9 B2
Bealing Wood	9 B3
Bearna Park	58 D3
Beatty Grove	32 D2
Beatty Park	32 D3
Beatty's Avenue	76 F3
Beaucourt	25 B3 [4]
Beaufield	17 C4
Beaufield Ave	17 C4
Beaufield Close	17 C4
Beaufield Crescent	17 C4
Beaufield Drive	17 C4
Beaufield Gardens	17 C4
Beaufield Green	17 C4
Beaufield Grove	17 C4
Beaufield Lawn	17 C4
Beaufield Manor	48 E4
Beaufield Mews	48 E4 [2]
Beaufield Park	48 E4
Beaufort	60 E1 [19]
Beaufort Court	46 F4 [10]
Beaufort Downs	46 F4
Beaufort Villas	46 F4 [3]
Beaumont	26 D1
Beaumont Avenue	47 B4
Beaumont Close	47 B4 [3]
Beaumont Cottages	34 D2
Beaumont Court	25 C1 [2]
Beaumont Crescent	26 D2
Beaumont Drive	47 B4
Beaumont Gardens	48 F4
Beaumont Grove	25 C2
Beaumont Hall	25 C2 [7]
Beaumont House	46 F2 [25]
Beaumont Road	25 C2
Beaumont Wood	25 C1 [3]
Beaumont Wood	25 C2
Beaupark Downs	49 B4 [15]
Beaupark Avenue	14 D4
Beaupark Close	14 D4
Beaupark Cresc	14 D4
Beaupark Mews	14 D4
Beaupark Place	14 D4
Beaupark Road	14 D4

STREET NAME	PAGE/GRID REFERENCE
Beaupark Row	14 D4
Beaupark Street	14 D4
Beaupark Tce	14 D4
Beauvale Park	26 D2
Beaver Close	72 D2
Beaver Row	47 C1
Beaver Street	72 D2
Beckett Hall	59 B4
Beckett Way	35 C4
Bective Square	70 F1
Bedford Court	46 E1 [5]
Bedford Lane (off Aston Quay)	71 B4
Bedford Row (off Aston Quay)	71 B4
Beech Drive	57 B1
Beech Grove (Blackrock)	48 F2
Beech Grove (Lucan)	34 E2
Beech Hill	47 C2
Beech Hill Avenue	47 C2
Beech Hill Court	47 C1
Beech Hill Crescent	47 C2 [3]
Beech Hill Drive	47 C2
Beech Hill Road	47 C2
Beech Hill Terrace	47 C2 [4]
Beech Hill Villas	47 C2 [2]
Beech House	76 D3
Beech House (Swords)	1 Inset
Beech Lawn	57 B1
Beech Lodge	23 A4
Beech Park (Cabinteely)	59 C4
Beech Park (Castleknock)	22 F3
Beech Park (Lucan)	34 E1
Beech Park Avenue (Castleknock)	23 A3
Beech Park Avenue (Deans Grange)	59 B2
Beech Park Crescent	23 A3 [1]
Beech Park Drive	59 B2
Beech Park Grove	59 B2
Beech Park Lawn	23 A3
Beech Park Road	59 B2
Beech Road	64 E3
Beech Road (Bray)	67 B1
Beech Road (Fox & Geese)	45 A1
Beech Row (Nangor Road)	44 D1 [3]
Beech Row (Newlands Road)	35 A4
Beech Walk	56 E2 [4]
Beechbrook Grove	14 D4 [4]
Beechcourt	60 D3
Beechdale	7 B3
Beechdale Avenue	55 B3
Beechdale Close	55 B3 [6]
Beechdale Court	55 B3
Beechdale Crescent	55 B3
Beechdale Lawn	55 B3
Beechdale Mews	47 B1 [19]
Beechdale Park	55 B3
Beechdale Place	55 C3
Beechdale Road	55 C3
Beechdale Way	55 B3
Beeches Park	60 E1
Beeches Road	58 D1
Beechfield	8 D4
Beechfield Avenue (Clonee)	8 D4
Beechfield Avenue (Walkinstown)	45 C2
Beechfield Close (Clonee)	8 D4
Beechfield Close (Walkinstown)	46 D2
Beechfield Court	8 D4
Beechfield Drive	8 D4
Beechfield Green	8 D4
Beechfield Haven	64 E2 [3]
Beechfield Heights	8 D4
Beechfield Lawn	8 E4
Beechfield Manor	64 E2
Beechfield Meadows	8 E4
Beechfield Mews	46 D2 [4]
Beechfield Place	8 E4
Beechfield Rise	8 E4
Beechfield Road (Clonee)	8 D4
Beechfield Road (Walkinstown)	45 C2
Beechfield View	8 E4
Beechfield Way	8 E4
Beechlawn	48 F3
Beechlawn Avenue (Ballinteer)	57 B1
Beechlawn Avenue (Coolock)	26 E1
Beechlawn Close	26 E1

STREET NAME	PAGE/GRID REFERENCE
Beechlawn Green	26 E1
Beechlawn Grove	26 E1
Beechlawn Manor	46 F2 [20]
Beechlawn Mews	46 F2 [21]
Beechmount Drive (Windy Arbour)	47 C3
Beechpark Avenue	26 E1
Beechpark Close	23 A3 [3]
Beechpark Court	26 E1
Beechpark Orchard	23 A3
Beechurst	67 B2
Beechview	56 E2 [1]
Beechwood	14 F1
Beechwood Avenue Lower	47 B1
Beechwood Avenue Upper	47 B1
Beechwood Close (Boghall Road)	67 C4
Beechwood Close (Hartstown)	21 C1
Beechwood Court	58 F1
Beechwood Downs	21 C1
Beechwood Grove	60 D1 [11]
Beechwood House	64 E2 [10]
Beechwood Lawn	60 D2
Beechwood Lawns	52 F2
Beechwood Park (Dun Laoghaire)	60 D1
Beechwood Park (Rathmines)	47 B1 [7]
Beechwood Road	47 B1
Beggar's Bush Buildings	76 F2
Beggars Bush Court	76 F2
Belarmine	58 D4
Belarmine Avenue	58 D4
Belarmine Close	58 D4
Belarmine Court	58 D4
Belarmine Drive	58 D4
Belarmine Grange	58 D4
Belarmine Heath	58 D4
Belarmine Park	58 D4
Belarmine Place	58 D4
Belarmine Square	58 D4
Belarmine Vale	58 D4
Belarmine Way	58 D4
Belcamp Avenue	13 B4
Belcamp Crescent	13 B4
Belcamp Gardens	13 B4
Belcamp Green	13 B4
Belcamp Grove	13 B4
Belcamp Lane	13 C4
Belcamp Park	13 A3
Belclare Avenue	11 C4
Belclare Crescent	11 C4
Belclare Drive	11 C4
Belclare Green	11 C4
Belclare Grove	11 C4
Belclare Lawns	11 C4
Belclare Park	11 C4
Belclare Terrace	11 C4
Belclare View	11 C4
Belclare Way	11 C4
Belfield Close	47 C3 [8]
Belfield Court	48 D2
Belfield Downs	47 C4
Belfield Park Apts.	48 E3
Belfry Avenue	53 C2
Belfry Close	53 C2
Belfry Court	53 C2
Belfry Crescent	53 C2
Belfry Dale	53 C2
Belfry Downs	53 C2
Belfry Drive	53 C2
Belfry Gardens	53 C2
Belfry Green	53 C2
Belfry Hall	53 C2
Belfry Lawn	53 C2
Belfry Lodge	53 C2
Belfry Manor	53 C2
Belfry Meadows	53 C2
Belfry Park	53 C2
Belfry Place	53 C2
Belfry Rise	53 C2
Belfry Road	53 C2
Belfry Square	53 C2
Belfry Terrace	53 C2
Belfry Walk	53 C2
Belfry Way	53 C2
Belgard Close	44 F3 [2]

STREET NAME	PAGE/GRID REFERENCE
Belgard Green	44 E4
Belgard Heights	44 F4
Belgard Road	44 E3
Belgard Square	54 F1
Belgard Square East	54 F1
Belgard Square North	54 F1
Belgard Square South	54 F1
Belgard Square West	54 F1
Belgrave Avenue	47 B1
Belgrave Place (Monkstown)	49 B4 [10]
Belgrave Place (Rathmines)	47 A1 [15]
Belgrave Road (Monkstown)	49 B4
Belgrave Road (Rathmines)	47 A1
Belgrave Square (Monkstown)	49 B4
Belgrave Square (Rathmines)	47 A1
Belgrave Square East (Monkstown)	49 B4
Belgrave Square East (Rathmines)	47 A1
Belgrave Square North (Monkstown)	49 B4
Belgrave Square North (Rathmines)	47 A1
Belgrave Square South (Monkstown)	49 B4
Belgrave Square South (Rathmines)	47 A1
Belgrave Square West (Monkstown)	49 B4
Belgrave Square West (Rathmines)	47 A1
Belgrave Terrace (Bray)	68 D2 [10]
Belgrave Terrace (Monkstown)	49 B4 [11]
Belgrave Villas (Bray)	68 D2 [9]
Belgrave Villas (Rathmines)	47 B1 [16]
Belgree	9 B2
Belgree Avenue	9 B2
Belgree Close	9 B2
Belgree Court	9 B2
Belgree Drive	9 B2
Belgree Green	9 B2
Belgree Grove	9 B2
Belgree Heights	9 B2
Belgree Lawns	9 B2
Belgree Rise	9 B2
Belgree Square	9 B2
Belgree Walk	9 B2
Belgree Woods	9 B2
Belgrove Lawn	36 D2
Belgrove Park (Chapelizod)	36 D2
Belgrove Park (Vernon Avenue)	26 F4
Belgrove Road	26 F4
*Bella Avenue (off Bella St)	72 D2
Bella Place (off Bella St)	72 D2
Bella Street	71 C2
Belleview Maltings	69 B4
Belleville	23 C4
Belleville Avenue	47 A2
Bellevue	74 E1
Bellevue Ave (Merrion)	48 E2
Bellevue Avenue (Dalkey)	60 E2
Bellevue Copse	48 E2
Bellevue Cottages	24 F3 [4]
Bellevue Court	48 E2 [2]
Bellevue Park	48 E2
Bellevue Park Avenue	48 E2
Bellevue Road	60 D2
Bellman's Walk	72 E3
Bell's Lane	1 C2
Bell's Lane	75 C2
Belmont (Irishtown)	67 C4
Belmont (Stillorgan)	59 A1
Belmont Avenue	47 C1
*Belmont Court (off Belmont Ave)	47 C1
Belmont Gardens	47 C1
Belmont Green	58 F1
Belmont Grove	58 F1
Belmont Lawn	58 F1
Belmont Park (Donnybrook)	47 C1 [3]
Belmont Park (Raheny)	27 A2
Belmont Place (off Gardiner St Middle)	71 C2
Belmont Square	27 A2
*Belmont Terrace (off Stillorgan Road)	58 F1

STREET NAME	PAGE/GRID REFERENCE		STREET NAME	PAGE/GRID REFERENCE		STREET NAME	PAGE/GRID REFERENCE		STREET NAME	PAGE/GRID REFERENCE	
Belmont Villas	47	C1	Bewley Avenue	34	E2	Blackthorn Hall	57	C3	Booterstown	48	E2
Belmount Court	25	C4 18	Bewley Drive	34	E2	Blackthorn Hill Avenue	52	E2	Booterstown Avenue	48	F3
Belton Park Avenue	26	D3	Bewley Grove	34	E2	Blackthorn Hill Close	52	E2	*Booterstown Grove	48	F2
Belton Park Gardens	26	D3	Bewley Lawn	34	E2	Blackthorn Hill Crescent	52	E2	(off Booterstown Avenue)		
Belton Park Road	26	D3	Bianconi Ave	53	B1	Blackthorn Hill Drive	52	E2	Booterstown Park	48	F3
Belton Park Villas	26	D3	Big Lane	32	D3	Blackthorn Hill View	52	E2	Boranaraltry	61	B4
Belton Terrace	67	C2 44	Bigger Road	45	C2	Blackthorn Road	58	D2	Boranaraltry Bridge	61	B4
Belvedere Court	71	B2	Bill Shelly Park	23	C2	Blackwater Road	24	E3	Boranaraltry Lane	61	C4
Belvedere Square	71	B1	Binn Eadair	29	A1	Blackwood Close	21	A1	Boroimhe Alder	1	C3
Belvidere Avenue	71	C1	Binn Eadair Court	29	A1	Blackwood Crescent	21	A1	Boroimhe Ash	1	C3
Belvidere Court	71	B1	Binn Eadair Crescent	29	A1	Blackwood Drive	21	A1	Boroimhe Aspen	1	C3
Belvidere Place	71	C1	Binn Eadair View	29	A1	Blackwood Lane	3	C4	Boroimhe Beech	1	C3
Belvidere Road	71	B1	Birch Avenue	58	D2	Blackwood Lawn	21	A1	Boroimhe Birches	1	C3
Ben Edar Road	70	D2	Birch Dale (Foxrock)	59	A2 9	Blackwood Mews	21	A1	Boroimhe Blackthorn	1	C3
Ben Inagh Park	49	A3 3	Birch Dale (Kill O'The Grange)	59	C1 12	Blackwood Park	21	A1	Boroimhe Cedars	1	C3
Ben Of Howth	30	D3	Birch Grove	59	C1	Blackwood Place	21	A1	Boroimhe Cherry	1	C3
Benbulbin Avenue	73	B3	Birchdale Close	2	E3	Blackwoods	3	B4	Boroimhe Elms	1	C3
Benbulbin Road	73	B3	Birchdale Drive	2	E3	Blakeney House	2	E2	Boroimhe Hawthorns	1	C3
Benburb Street	70	E3	Birchdale Park	2	F3	Blakeney House (Mews)	30	E3	Boroimhe Hazel	1	C3
Beneavin Court	24	F2	Birchdale Road	2	E3	Blake's Court	22	D1 7	Boroimhe Laurels	1	C3
Beneavin Drive	24	F2	Birches Road	58	D1	Blakes Villas	70	F2	Boroimhe Maples	1	C3
Beneavin Park	24	F1	Birchfield Avenue	47	C4	(on Grangegorman Lower)			Boroimhe Oaks	1	C3
Beneavin Road	24	F2	Birchfield Court	47	C4	Blakesfield	21	C1	Boroimhe Pines	1	C3
Bengal Terrace	24	F4 4	Birchfield Heights	47	C4	Blakestown Cottages	22	D1	Boroimhe Poplars	1	C3
Benmadigan Road	73	A3	Birchfield Lawn	47	C4	Blakestown Drive	22	D1	Boroimhe Rowan	1	B3
Benson Street	72	F4	Birchfield Park	47	C4	Blakestown Road	9	A4	Boroimhe Willows	1	C3
Bentley Avenue	67	C4 3	Birch's Lane	47	C4	Blakestown Road	22	D1	Botanic Avenue	25	A4
Bentley Park	67	C4	Birchview Avenue	45	A4	Blakestown Way	22	D1	Botanic Hall	24	F3
Bentley Road	67	C4	Birchview Close	45	A4	Blanchardstown	22	F2	Botanic Hall	24	F3 7
Bentley Villas	49	C4 17	Birchview Court	45	A4	Blanchardstown ByPass	22	F2	Botanic Mews	25	A4 18
Beresford	25	B3	Birchview Drive	45	A4	Blanchardstown Interchange	23	A2	Botanic Park	25	A4 14
Beresford Avenue	25	B3	Birchview Heights	45	A4	Blanchardstown Road North	9	B4	Botanic Road	25	A4
Beresford Green	25	B3	Birchview Lawn	45	A4	Blanchardstown Road South	22	D2	Botanic Square	25	A4 17
Beresford Lane	71	C3	Birchview Rise	45	A4	Blanchardstown Roundabout	22	F2	Botanic Villas	25	A4 10
Beresford Lawn	25	B3	Birchwood Close	44	E4	Blarney Park	46	E1	Bottle Works	39	A3
Beresford Place	71	C3	Birchwood Drive	54	E1	Blasket Square	22	F1	Boulevard Mount Eustace	9	B2
Beresford Street	71	A3	Birchwood Heights	54	E1	Blessington Court	71	A2	Boundary Road	39	A1
Berkeley Avenue	71	A1	Bird Avenue	47	C3	Blessington Lane	71	A2	Bow Bridge	74	D1
Berkeley Place	71	A1	Biscayne	3	C3	Blessington Place	71	A2	Bow Bridge Court (Bow Bridge)	74	D1
Berkeley Road	71	A1	Bishop Street	75	A2	(off St Joseph's Parade)			*Bow Bridge Place	74	D1
Berkeley Street	71	A1	Bishops Lane	62	F2	Blessington Road	53	C2	Bow Lane East	75	B1
Berkeley Terrace	76	F2	Bishop's Orchard	9	B2	Blessington Street	71	A2	Bow Lane West	74	D1
Bernard Curtis Court	36	F4	Bishop's Orchard Boulevard	9	B2	Blizzard Apts.	2	F3 1	Bow Street	70	F4
Bernard Curtis House	36	F4 2	Bishop's Orchard House Apts.	9	B2	Blood Stoney Road	72	F4	Bowbridge House	74	D1
Berryfield	34	D3	Bishop's Square	75	A2	Bloom Court	74	F3	(Mount Brown)		
Berryfield Crescent	24	D2	Bissett's Loft Apts.	3	B2	Bloomfield Avenue	76	D4	Boyne Court	74	F4
Berryfield Drive	24	D2	Bissett's Strand	3	B2	(Donnybrook)			Boyne Lane	76	D1
Berryfield Lane	67	A3	Black Street	69	C3	Bloomfield Avenue (Portobello)	75	A3	Boyne Road	24	E3
Berryfield Lane	67	A3	Blackberry Lane (Portmarnock)	15	A1	Bloomfield Cottages	75	A3	Boyne Street	76	D1
Berryfield Road	24	D2	Blackberry Lane (Rathmines)	75	B4	Bloomfield Park (Ballsbridge)	76	E4	Brabazon Cottages	67	C2 16
Berrys Court	73	A2	Blackberry Rise	15	A1	Bloomfield Park (Rathmines)	75	A3	Brabazon House	74	E2
Bertram Court	74	E2	Blackburn Square	46	F4 15	Bluebell	36	E4	Brabazon Place	74	F2
Berwick Avenue	1	B2	Blackcourt Road	22	E1	Bluebell Avenue	36	E4	Brabazon Row	74	F2
Berwick Court	1	B1	Blackditch Drive	35	C3	Bluebell Road	36	E4	Brabazon Square	74	F1
Berwick Crescent	1	B1	Blackditch Road	35	C3	Blundelstown	42	E3	Brabazon Street	74	F2
Berwick Drive	1	B1	Blackditch Road	36	D3	Blunden Drive	13	C4	Bracken Drive	4	D4
Berwick Grove	1	B1	Blackglen Court	58	D3	Blythe Avenue	72	E3	Bracken Hill	57	C3
Berwick Hall	47	A4	Blackglen Road	57	C3	Boardman's Lane	74	D2	Bracken Road	58	D2
Berwick Lawn	1	B1	Blackhall Court	70	E3	(off Cork Street)			Brackenbush Park	60	D4
Berwick Place	1	B1	Blackhall Green	70	E3	Boden Dale	56	F1	Brackenbush Road	60	D4
Berwick Rise	1	B2	Blackhall Little	5	B1	Boden Heath	56	E1	Bracken's Lane	71	C4
Berwick View	1	B1	Blackhall Parade	70	F3	Boden Heath Apts.	56	E1	Brackenstown Avenue	1	C2
Berwick Walk	1	B2	(Blackhall Street)			Boden Mill	56	E2	Brackenstown Road	1	C2
Berwick Way	1	B1	Blackhall Place	70	E4	Boden Park	56	E1	Braeburn Terrace	1	Inset
Berystede	75	C4	Blackhall Place Apts.	70	E3	Boden Wood	46	F4	Braemor Avenue	47	A3
Bessborough Avenue	72	E1	Blackhall Street	70	F4	Boeing Road	12	F4	Braemor Drive	47	A3
Bessborough Court	75	B4	Blackhall View	70	E3	Boghall Road	67	B4	Braemor Grove	47	A3
Bessborough Parade	75	B4	Blackhall Walk	70	F4	Boghall Road (off Vevay road)	67	C4	Braemor Park	47	A3
Besser Drive	35	B4	Blackheath Avenue	26	F4	Bohammer	13	C2	Braemor Road	47	A3
Bethany House	39	B4 4	Blackheath Court	26	F4	Boherboy	53	B2	Braithwaite Street	74	E1
Bethesda Place	71	B2	Blackheath Drive	26	E4	Boherboy Road	53	B2	Bramblefield	8	F4
Bettyglen	27	B2	Blackheath Gardens	26	E4	Bohernabreena Road	55	A3	Bramblefield Court	8	F4
Bettysford	44	E1 3	Blackheath Grove	26	E4	Bolbrook Avenue	55	B1 3	Bramblefield Crescent	8	F4
Bettystown Avenue	26	F3	Blackheath Park	26	E4	Bolbrook Close	55	B1 4	Bramblefield Drive	8	F4
Beverly Avenue	56	D1	Blackhorse Avenue	23	C4	Bolbrook Drive	55	B1 1	Bramblefield Park	8	F4
Beverly Court	26	F4	Blackhorse Avenue	69	C2	Bolbrook Grove	55	B1	Bramblefield View	8	F4
Beverly Crescent	55	C2	Blackhorse Grove	70	D2	Bolbrook Park	55	B1	Bramblefield Walk	8	F4
Beverly Downs	55	C2	Blackpitts	74	F2	Bolbrook Villas	55	B1	Bramley Avenue	22	E3
Beverly Drive	56	D2	Blackrock	49	A3	Bolton Green	1	A2	Bramley Court	22	E3
Beverly Green	55	C2	Blackthorn Avenue	58	E2	Bolton Street	71	A3	Bramley Crescent	22	E3
Beverly Grove	56	D1	Blackthorn Close (Portmarnock)	4	D4	Bond Drive	39	A1	Bramley Garth	22	E3
Beverly Heights	56	D2	Blackthorn Close (Sandyford)	58	D2 7	Bond Road	39	A1	Bramley Green	22	E3
Beverly Lawns	56	D2	Blackthorn Court	58	D2 4	Bond Street	74	E1	Bramley Grove	22	E3
Beverly Park	55	C1	Blackthorn Drive	58	D2	Bonham Street	70	E4	Bramley Heath	22	E3
Beverly Rise	55	C2	Blackthorn Green	58	D2 6	Boolavogue Road	72	F2	Bramley Park	22	E3
Bewley	34	E2	Blackthorn Grove	58	D2 3	Boot Road	44	D2	Bramley Road	22	E3

STREET NAME	PAGE/GRID REFERENCE
Bramley View	22 E3
Bramley Walk	22 E3
Bramley Way	22 E3
Brandon Road	36 F4
Brandon Road	45 C1
*Brandon Terrace	74 D2
Bray	68 D1
Bray Commons	67 B2
Bray Head Terrace	67 C3 [20]
Bray Road	59 B2
Bray Road	59 C4
Bray Southern Cross Road	67 B4
Breakwater Road North	39 B2
Breakwater Road South	39 B2
Breffini Terrace	60 E1
Breffni Gardens	15 A4 [5]
Breffni Road	60 E1
Bregia Road	24 F4
Brehon Field Road	57 B2
Brehon's Chair	57 A3
Bremen Avenue	39 A3
Bremen Grove	39 A3
Bremen Road	39 A3
Brendan Behan Court	71 C1
Brendan Road	47 C1
Brennans Parade	68 D2 [14]
Brennans Terrace	68 D2 [4]
Brennanstown Avenue	59 C4
Brennanstown Road	59 B4
Brennanstown Square	59 C4
Brennanstown Vale	59 B4
Brewery Road	58 F2
Brian Avenue	25 C4
Brian Boru Avenue	39 C1
Brian Boru Street	39 C1
Brian Road	25 C4
Brian Terrace	25 C4
Briansboro Terrace	74 F3
Briar Walk	4 D4
Briar Wood	68 D3
Briarfield Grove	27 B1
Briarfield Road	27 B2
Briarfield Villas	27 B1 [5]
Briarly Court	47 B4 [4]
Briarsfield Walk	27 B1 [4]
Briarwood Avenue	22 D1
Briarwood Close	9 A4
Briarwood Gardens	22 D1
Briarwood Green	22 D1
Briarwood Lawn	22 D1
Briarwood Park	22 D1 [1]
Briarwood Road	22 D1 [3]
Brickfield	67 B3
Brickfield Drive	73 C3
Brickfield Lane	74 E2
Brickfield Lane	67 B3 [8]
Bride Close	75 A1
Bride Road	75 A1
Bride Street	75 A1
Brides Glen	63 C2
Brides Glen Avenue	1 Inset
Brides Glen Park	1 C1
Bride's Glen Park	1 Inset
Bridge Street (Ringsend)	39 A3
Bridge Street (Swords)	2 D2
Bridge Street Lower	70 F4
*Bridge Street Upper	74 F1
Bridgefoot Street	70 F4
Bridgeview	35 B3
Bridgewater Quay	69 B4
Bridon	62 F1
Brighton Avenue (Carrickmines)	59 A4
Brighton Avenue (Clontarf)	26 D4 [1]
Brighton Avenue (Monkstown)	49 B4
Brighton Avenue (Rathgar)	46 F2
Brighton Cottages	59 A3 [1]
Brighton Court	59 A4
Brighton Gardens	46 F2
Brighton Green	46 F2 [13]
Brighton Hall	59 A4
Brighton Lane	49 B4 [22]
Brighton Lodge	59 A3 [4]
Brighton Place	59 A4
Brighton Road (Foxrock)	59 A3
Brighton Road (Terenure)	46 F2
Brighton Square	46 F2
Brighton Terrace (Dun Laoghaire)	60 E1 [13]
Brighton Terrace (Monkstown)	49 B4 [9]
Brighton Vale	49 B3
Britain Place	71 B2
Britain Quay	72 F4
Broadfield Avenue	52 E2
Broadfield Close	52 E2
Broadfield Court	52 E2
Broadfield Heath	52 E2
Broadfield Manor	52 E2
Broadfield Meadows	52 E2
Broadfield Park	52 E2
Broadford Avenue	57 B2
Broadford Close	57 B2
Broadford Crescent	57 B2
Broadford Drive	57 B2
Broadford Hill	57 B2
Broadford Lawn	57 B2
Broadford Park	57 B2
Broadford Rise	57 B2
Broadford Road	57 B2
Broadford Walk	57 B2
Broadmeadow	1 C1
Broadmeadow Mews	3 B2 [7]
Broadstone	70 F2
Broadstone Avenue (off Royal Canal Bank)	71 A2
*Broadstone Place (off Royal Canal Bank)	71 A2
Broadway Drive	22 E2
Broadway Grove	22 E2
Broadway Park	22 E2
Broadway Road	22 E2
Brockey	61 C4
Brockey	65 A1
Brockey Lane	65 A1
Brodin Row	70 D3
Brompton Court	22 E3
Brompton Green	22 E2
Brompton Grove	22 E3
Brompton Lawn	22 E2
Brook Court	49 B4
Brook House	25 B4 [14]
Brook Wood	67 B2
Brookdale	55 A2
Brookdale Avenue	1 B3
Brookdale Close	1 B2
Brookdale Court	1 B3
Brookdale Drive	1 B2
Brookdale Green	1 B2
Brookdale Grove	1 B2
Brookdale Lawns	1 B2
Brookdale Park	1 B2
Brookdale Road	1 B2
Brookdale Walk	1 B2
Brookdale Way	1 B2
Brookdene	64 E2
Brookfield (Blackrock)	48 F3
Brookfield (Coolock)	26 F2
Brookfield (Donnybrook)	47 C1 [19]
Brookfield (Lucan)	34 D3
Brookfield (Milltown)	47 B2
Brookfield Avenue (Blackrock)	49 A4
Brookfield Avenue (Bray)	68 D3 [4]
Brookfield Avenue (Maynooth)	17 C4
Brookfield Court (Blackrock)	49 A4 [12]
Brookfield Court (Kimmage)	46 E2 [6]
Brookfield Court (Tallaght)	54 D1 [1]
Brookfield Estate	46 E2
Brookfield Green	46 E2 [5]
Brookfield Grove	49 A4 [11]
Brookfield Park	17 C4
Brookfield Place	49 A4
Brookfield Road (Kilmainham)	73 C1
Brookfield Road (Tallaght)	54 D1
Brookfield Street	73 C2
Brookfield Terrace	49 A4
Brookhaven Drive	22 E1
Brookhaven Grove	22 E1
Brookhaven Lawn	22 E1
Brookhaven Park	22 E1
Brookhaven Rise	22 E1
Brooklands	48 E1
Brooklawn	35 B1
Brooklawn (Blackrock)	48 F3
Brooklawn (Clontarf)	26 D4
Brooklawn (Lucan)	34 D3
Brooklawn Avenue	49 B4 [12]
Brooklawn Wood	49 B4 [13]
Brookmount Avenue	55 C1
Brookmount Court	46 E4 [2]
Brookmount Lawns	55 C1 [1]
Brookpark	34 D3
Brookstone Lane	15 A4 [6]
Brookstone Road	15 A4
Brookvale	34 D1 [8]
Brookvale Downs	46 F3
Brookvale Road (Donnybrook)	47 C1 [8]
Brookvale Road (Rathfarnham)	46 F3
Brookview Avenue	54 D1
Brookview Close	54 D1
Brookview Court	54 D1
Brookview Crescent	54 D1
Brookview Drive	54 D1
Brookview Gardens	54 D1
Brookview Green	54 D1
Brookview Grove	54 D1
Brookview Lawns	54 D1
Brookview Park	54 D1
Brookview Rise	54 D1
Brookview Terrace	54 D1
Brookview Way	54 D1
Brookville	24 D1
Brookville Crescent	26 E1 [2]
Brookville Park (Artane)	26 E2
Brookville Park (Coolock)	26 E1
Brookville Park (Dean's Grange)	59 B1
Brookwood	56 E2
Brookwood Abbey	26 E2 [4]
Brookwood Avenue	26 E2
Brookwood Crescent	26 F2
Brookwood Drive	26 E2
Brookwood Glen	26 F3
Brookwood Grove	26 E2
Brookwood Hall	26 E3
Brookwood Heights	26 F2
Brookwood Lawn	26 F2
Brookwood Meadow	26 E2
Brookwood Park	26 E3
Brookwood Rise	26 F3
Brookwood Road	26 E2
Broombridge Road	24 E4
Broomfield	21 B4
Broomfield (Malahide)	3 B4
Broomfield Court	64 E2
Broomfield Mews	3 B4
Broomhill Close	45 A4
Broomhill Drive	45 A4
Broomhill Road	45 A4
Broomhill Terrace (Off Broomhill Road)	45 A4
Brown Street North	70 F3
Brown Street South	74 E2
Brownrath	5 B1
Brownsbarn	43 C4
Brownsbarn Court	43 C4
Brownsbarn Garden	43 C4
Brownsbarn Orchard	43 C4
Brownstown	42 D1
Brownstown (Kilcloon)	5 A2
Bruce's Terrace	67 B2 [29]
Brug Chroimlinn	46 D1 [6]
Brunswick Place	76 E1
Brunswick Street North	70 F3
Brunswick Villas (Pearse Street)	71 C4
Brusna Cottages	49 A3 [12]
Buckingham St Lower	72 D2
Buckingham St Upper	72 D2
Buckingham Village	71 C2
Buckleys Lane	33 A1
Bulfin Court	73 A2
Bulfin Gardens	73 B1
Bulfin Road	73 A2
Bull Alley Street	75 A1
Bull Lane (Off Main Street)	67 C2 [59]
Bull Wall	40 D1
Bull Wall Cottages	40 D1
Bullock Steps	60 F1 [8]
Bunbury Gate Avenue	1 Inset
Bunbury Gate Crescent	1 Inset
Bunratty Avenue	26 E1
Bunratty Drive	26 E1
Bunratty Road	26 E1
Bunting Road	45 C1
Burdett Avenue	60 E1
Burg an Rí Glen	34 F3
Burg an Rí Terrace	34 F3
Burgage	13 C3
Burgess Lane	70 F4
Burgh Quay	71 C4
Burke Place	74 D1
Burke Place (off Mount Brown)	74 D1
Burleigh Court	76 D3
Burleigh Mews	76 D3
Burlington Gardens	76 D3
Burlington Mews	76 D3
Burlington Road	76 D3
Burmah Close	60 F2 [22]
Burnell Park Avenue	22 E4
Burnell Park Green	22 E4
Burnell Square	14 D4
Burnside	25 B1
Burren Court	11 C4
Burris Court (off High Street)	75 A1
Burrow Court (Poppintree)	11 C4
Burrow Court (Portmarnock)	15 A1
Burrow Road (Stepaside)	58 D4
Burrow Road (Stepaside)	62 D1
Burrow Road (Sutton)	29 B1
Burrowfield Road	28 D1
Burton Court	58 E2
Burton Hall Avenue	58 E2
Burton Hall Road	58 E2
Burton Road	60 F2
Bushfield Avenue	47 B1 [8]
Bushfield Drive	44 D2
Bushfield Green	44 D2
Bushfield Grove	44 D3
Bushfield Lawns	44 D2
Bushfield Place	47 B1 [17]
Bushfield Square	25 C4 [15]
Bushfield Terrace	47 B1
Bushy Park Gardens	46 F3
Bushy Park House	46 E3
Bushy Park Road	46 F3
Bustyhill	51 B3
Butlerstown	5 C3
Butt Bridge	71 C4
Buttercup Close	13 C4
Buttercup Drive	13 C4
Buttercup Park	13 C4
Buttercup Square	13 C4
Buttercup Terrace	13 C4
Butterfield Avenue	46 E4
Butterfield Close	46 E4
Butterfield Court	46 F4
Butterfield Crescent	46 E4
Butterfield Drive	46 E4
Butterfield Grove	46 E4
Butterfield Meadow	46 E4 [1]
Butterfield Orchard	46 E4
Butterfield Park	46 E4
*Byrne's Cottages (Francis Street)	74 E2
Byrne's Lane (Jervis St)	71 B4
Byrnes Lane (Pearse Sq West)	72 E4
Byrne's Terrace	47 C2 [12]

C

STREET NAME	PAGE/GRID REFERENCE
Cabinteely	59 C4
Cabinteely Avenue	59 C3
Cabinteely Bypass	59 C3
Cabinteely Close	59 C3
Cabinteely Court	59 C3 [2]
Cabinteely Crescent	59 C3
Cabinteely Drive	59 C3
Cabinteely Green	59 C3
Cabinteely Park	59 C3 [3]
Cabinteely Way	59 C3
Cabra	24 E4
Cabra Drive	70 D1
Cabra Grove	70 D1
Cabra Park	24 F4
Cabra Road	70 D1
Caddell	14 F2
Cadogan Road	25 C4
Cairn Brook	63 A1

STREET NAME	PAGE/GRID REFERENCE
Cairn Brook Hall	63 A1
Cairn Brook Manor	63 A1
Cairn Brook View	63 A1
Cairn Brook Way	63 A1
Cairn Court	12 D4
Cairn Hill	59 B2
Cairnfort	62 E1
Cairnwood Avenue	44 E4
Cairnwood Court	44 E4
Cairnwood Green	44 E4
Calderwood Avenue	25 C3
Calderwood Grove	25 C3 [3]
Calderwood Road	25 C3
Caledon Court	72 F2
Caledon Road	72 F2
Callaghan Bridge	21 C2
Callary Road	48 D3
Calmount Avenue	45 B2
Calmount Park	45 B2
Calmount Road	45 B2
Camac Close	73 A1
Camac Court	73 A1
Camac Park	36 E4
Camaderry Road	68 D3
Camberley Elms	47 B4 [20]
Camberley Oaks	47 B4 [19]
Cambridge Avenue	39 A3 [7]
Cambridge Court	39 A3 [24]
Cambridge Park	39 A3
Cambridge Road (Rathmines)	47 A1
Cambridge Road (Ringsend)	39 A3
*Cambridge Square (off Thorncastle St.)	39 A3
Cambridge Street	39 A3 [1]
Cambridge Terrace (Dun Laoghaire)	49 C4 [24]
Cambridge Terrace (Ranelagh)	75 C4
Cambridge Villas	47 A1 [16]
Camden Avenue	23 C3
Camden Buildings	75 B2
Camden Court	75 B3
Camden Lock	76 F1
Camden Market	75 B3
Camden Place	75 B2
Camden Row	75 A2
Camden Street Lower	75 B2
Camden Street Upper	75 B3
Camden Villas	75 B2
Cameron Square	73 C1
Cameron Street	74 E2
Cammock Apts.	73 C1
Camogie Road	69 A3
Campbell Court	30 D2 [16]
Campbell's Court	71 A3
Campbell's Lane (off Belvidere Ave)	71 C1
Campbell's Row (off Portland Street N)	71 C1
Campfield Terrace	57 C1
Campshire Hall	72 D4
Campshire Mews	72 D4
Canal Road	75 B4
Canal Terrace	36 E4
Canal Turn	35 B4
Cannon Mews	39 A4 [29]
Cannon Mews East	76 F2
Cannon Mews West	76 F2
Cannon Place	39 A4 [30]
Cannon Rock Estate	30 E2
Cannon Rock View	30 E2 [1]
Cannonbrook	34 D2
Cannonbrook Avenue	34 D2
Cannonbrook Court	34 D2
Cannonbrook Lawn	34 D2
Cannonbrook Park	34 D2
Canon Lillis Avenue	72 E2
Canon Mooney Gardens	39 A3 [15]
Capel Street	71 A3
Cappagh Avenue	24 D1
Cappagh Drive	24 D2
Cappagh Green	24 D1
Cappagh Road	10 E4
Cappagh Road	24 D1
Cappaghmore Estate	35 A4
Cappoge	10 F4
Cappoge Cottages	10 E4
Captain's Avenue	46 D1
Captain's Drive	46 D2
Captain's Hill	20 D4
Captain's Road	46 D2
Cara Park	13 B3
Caragh Court	25 C4 [12]
Caragh Road	69 C1
Carberry Road	25 C3
Carbury Place	49 A3 [20]
Carbury Terrace	72 F3
Cardiff Castle Road	24 D2
Cardiff Lane	72 E4
Cardiffs Bridge	24 D3
Cardiffsbridge Avenue	24 D2
Cardiffsbridge Grove	24 D1 [1]
Cardiffsbridge Road	24 D2
Card's Lane (Pearse St)	71 C4
Carleton Road	25 C4
Carlingford Court	76 E1
Carlingford Parade	76 E1
Carlingford Road	25 A4
Carlisle Avenue	47 B1
Carlisle Court	46 F2 [23]
Carlisle Street	75 A3
Carlisle Terrace (Dún Laoghaire)	60 D1 [17]
Carlisle Terrace (Malahide)	3 B3
*Carlisle Terrace (Off N C Rd)	70 F1
*Carlisle Terrace (On Seymour Road)	67 C2
*Carlisle Terrace (on Tivoli Road)	60 D1
Carlton Court (Clontarf)	26 D4
Carlton Court (Swords)	2 D2
Carlton Terrace	67 C2 [41]
Carlton Villas (Ballsbridge)	76 F3
Carlton Villas (Clontarf)	67 C2 [42]
Carmanhall Court	58 E2
Carmanhall Road	58 E2
Carman's Hall	74 F1
Carna Road	35 C3
Carndonagh Drive	27 B1
Carndonagh Lawn	27 B1
Carndonagh Park	27 B1
Carndonagh Road	27 B1
Carne Court	8 F4
Carnegie Court	2 D1
Carnew Street	70 D2
Carnlough Road	24 E4
Caroline Court	76 E3
Caroline Row	39 A3 [16]
Caroline Row	39 A3 [35]
Carpenterstown	22 D3
Carpenterstown Avenue	22 E3
Carpenterstown Manor	22 E3
Carpenterstown Park East	22 E3
Carpenterstown Road	22 E4
Carraig Close	11 C4
Carraig Glen	59 C4
Carraig Grennane	60 E4
Carraroe Avenue	27 A1
Carrick Court	14 F1
Carrick Lawn	58 D1 [2]
Carrick Terrace	74 D2
Carrickaspinkeen	65 A3
Carrickbrack Heath	29 B2
Carrickbrack Hill	29 B2
Carrickbrack Lawn	29 B2
Carrickbrack Park	29 B2
Carrickbrack Road	29 B2
Carrickbrack Road	30 D4
Carrickbrennan Lawn	49 C4
Carrickbrennan Road	49 C4
Carrickfoyle Terrace	73 B1
Carrickhill Close	4 D4
Carrickhill Drive	15 A1
Carrickhill Heights	15 A1
Carrickhill Rise	4 D4
Carrickhill Road	15 A1
Carrickhill Road Middle	15 A1
Carrickhill Road Upper	3 C4
Carrickhill Walk	4 D4
Carrickmines	59 B4
Carrickmines Avenue	59 B4
Carrickmines Chase	59 B4
Carrickmines Dale	59 B4
Carrickmines Garth	59 B4
Carrickmines Green	63 A1
Carrickmines Little	59 A4
Carrickmines Manor	63 A1
Carrickmines Oaks	59 B4
Carrickmount Avenue	57 B1
Carrickmount Drive	57 A1
Carrig Road	11 C4
Carrigallen Drive	24 E3
Carrigallen Park	24 E3
Carrigallen Road	24 E3
Carrigeen	52 D3
Carriglea	55 B2
Carriglea Avenue (Kill O'The Grange)	59 C2
Carriglea Avenue (Tallaght)	55 B2
Carriglea Court (Kill O'The Grange)	59 C1 [14]
Carriglea Court (Tallaght)	55 B2
Carriglea Downs (Kill O'The Grange)	59 C2
Carriglea Downs (Tallaght)	55 B2
Carriglea Drive	55 B2
Carriglea Gardens	59 C1
Carriglea Grove	55 B2
Carriglea Rise	55 B2
Carriglea View	55 B2
Carriglea Walk	55 B2
Carrigmore Avenue	53 B2
Carrigmore Close (Oldbawn)	54 F3
Carrigmore Close (Saggart)	53 B2
Carrigmore Court	53 C2
Carrigmore Crescent	53 C1
Carrigmore Dale	53 B2
Carrigmore Downs	53 B1
Carrigmore Drive	54 F2
Carrigmore Elms	53 B2
Carrigmore Gardens	53 B1
Carrigmore Glen	53 B1
Carrigmore Green	53 C2
Carrigmore Grove (Oldbawn)	54 F3
Carrigmore Grove (Saggart)	53 B2
Carrigmore Lawns	53 B1
Carrigmore Manor	53 B2
Carrigmore Meadows	53 B2
Carrigmore Oak	53 B2
Carrigmore Park	54 F3
Carrigmore Place	53 B2
Carrigmore Road	54 F2
Carrigmore Terrace	53 B2
Carrigmore View	54 F3
Carrigmore Way	53 C2
Carrigwood	55 C2
Carrow Road	36 F4
Carton Avenue	18 D2
Carton Bridge	18 E3
Carton Court	17 C4
Carton Court	18 D4
Carton Demesne	18 F2
Carton Square	17 C2
Carton Square	17 C2
Carwell Court	2 E2
Carysfort Avenue	49 A4
Carysfort Downs	58 F1
Carysfort Downs	59 A1
Carysfort Drive	60 F1 [1]
Carysfort Grove	59 A1
Carysfort Hall	49 A4
Carysfort Park	49 A4
Carysfort Road	60 F1
Carysfort Woods	59 A1
Casana View	30 E2
Casement Close (off Barry Road)	24 D1 [2]
Casement Drive	24 D1
Casement Green	24 D1
Casement Grove	24 D1
Casement Park	24 D1
Casement Road	24 D1
Casement Road	24 D2
Casement Villas	59 B1
Cashel Avenue	46 E2
Cashel Road	46 D1
Casimir Avenue	46 F1
Casimir Court	46 F1 [17]
Casimir Road	46 F1
Casino Drive	3 B2
Casino Park	26 D3
Casino Road	25 C4
Cassian Court	24 D3 [2]
Castaheany	8 E4
Castilla Park	26 F4
Castle Avenue (Clondalkin)	44 E1
Castle Avenue (Clontarf)	26 E4
Castle Avenue (Swords)	2 D2
Castle Close (Clondalkin)	44 E1
Castle Close (Dalkey)	60 F1
Castle Court	58 E4
Castle Court (Booterstown)	48 F2
Castle Court (Clontarf)	26 D4
Castle Court (Dundrum)	57 C1 [4]
Castle Court (Loughlinstown)	64 E1
*Castle Court (off Cypress Lawn)	46 D4
Castle Court (Rathfarnham)	46 F4 [18]
Castle Court (Rathfarnham)	47 A4 [1]
Castle Court Apts.	3 B3 [1]
Castle Court Apts.	75 A1
Castle Cove (Dalkey)	60 F2 [32]
Castle Cove (Malahide)	3 A2
Castle Crescent	44 E1 [4]
Castle Dawson	17 B3
Castle Down Croft	2 F2
Castle Down Grove	2 F2
Castle Down Road	2 F2
Castle Drive	58 E4
Castle Drive (Clondalkin)	44 E1
Castle Drive (Swords)	2 D2
Castle Elms	26 E1
Castle Farm	64 E3
Castle Farm Wood	64 E3
Castle Gate Apartments.	75 A1
Castle Grove (Clondalkin)	44 E1
Castle Grove (Clontarf)	26 E4
Castle Grove (Swords)	2 D2
Castle Lawn	58 E4
Castle Lawns (Malahide)	2 F2
Castle Lawns (Tallaght)	45 B4
Castle Market (off Drury Street)	75 B1
Castle Oaks	3 A3 [1]
Castle Park (Clondalkin)	44 E1
Castle Park (Leixlip)	33 A1
Castle Park (Monkstown)	49 C4
Castle Park (Swords) (Swords)	2 D2
Castle Park (Tallaght)	45 B4
Castle Park Estate (Tallaght)	55 B1
*Castle Place (on Breffni Road)	60 F1
Castle Riada Avenue	34 E2
Castle Riada Crescent	34 E2
Castle Riada Drive	34 E3
Castle Riada Grove	34 E2
Castle Road (Clontarf)	26 E4
Castle Road (Lucan)	34 E2
Castle Rosse	14 F4
Castle Side	55 C1 [7]
Castle Steps (off Castle Street)	75 A1
Castle Street (Bray)	67 C2
Castle Street (Cork Hill)	75 A1
Castle Street (Dalkey)	60 F2
Castle Terrace (Malahide)	3 B2
*Castle Terrace (off Ulverton Road)	60 F1
Castle Terrace (Phibsborough Ave)	70 F1
Castle View (Carrickmines)	59 A4
Castle View (Clondalkin)	44 E1
Castle Village	31 C2
Castle Village Avenue	31 C2
Castle Village Close	31 C2
Castle Village Court	31 C2
Castle Village Crescent	31 C2
Castle Village Drive	31 C2
Castle Village Green	31 C2
Castle Village Lawns	31 C2
Castle Village Park	31 C2
Castle Village Place	31 C2
Castle Village Rise	31 C2
Castle Village Walk	31 C2
Castle Village Way	31 C2
Castle Village Woods	31 C2
Castle Villas	60 F2
Castlebridge	18 D3
Castlebrook	57 C1

STREET NAME	PAGE/GRID REFERENCE
Castlebyrne Park	49 A4
Castlecurragh Heath	9 A4
Castlecurragh Park	9 B4
Castlecurragh Vale	9 A4
Castledawson Avenue	48 F3
Castlefarm	1 C1
Castlefield Avenue	55 C1
Castlefield Court (Clonsilla)	21 C2
Castlefield Court (Firhouse)	55 C1
Castlefield Drive	55 C2
Castlefield Green	55 C2
Castlefield Grove	55 C2
Castlefield Lawn	55 C1
Castlefield Manor (Firhouse)	55 C1
Castlefield Manor (Malahide)	3 B3
Castlefield Orchard	55 C1
Castlefield Park ((Firhouse)	55 C2
Castlefield Park (Clonsilla)	21 C2
Castlefield Way	55 C2
Castlefield Woods	21 C2
Castleforbes Road	72 F3
Castleforbes Square	72 F3
Castlegate (Monkstown)	59 C1
Castlegate (Shankill)	64 D3
Castlegate Chase	33 C3
Castlegate Chase	33 C3
Castlegate Close	33 C3
Castlegate Close	33 C3
Castlegate Crescent	33 C3
Castlegate Crescent	33 C3
Castlegate Dene	33 C3
Castlegate Dene	33 C4
Castlegate Drive	33 C3
Castlegate Drive	33 C3
Castlegate Elms	33 C3
Castlegate Elms	33 C3
Castlegate Green	33 C3
Castlegate Green	33 C3
Castlegate Grove	33 C3
Castlegate Grove	33 C3
Castlegate Park	33 C3
Castlegate Park	33 C3
Castlegate Place	33 C3
Castlegate Place	33 C3
Castlegate Square	34 D3
Castlegate Walk	33 C3
Castlegate Walk	33 C3
Castlegate Way	33 C3
Castlegate Way	33 C3
Castlegrange	21 B1
Castlegrange Avenue (Clonsilla)	21 B1
Castlegrange Avenue (Swords)	2 D1
Castlegrange Close (Clondalkin)	43 B1
Castlegrange Close (Swords)	2 D1
Castlegrange Court (Clondalkin)	43 C1
Castlegrange Court (Clonsilla)	21 B1
Castlegrange Dale	21 B1
Castlegrange Drive (Clondalkin)	43 B1
Castlegrange Drive (Clonsilla)	21 B1
Castlegrange Gardens	21 B1
Castlegrange Green (Clondalkin)	43 B1
Castlegrange Green (Clonsilla)	21 B1
Castlegrange Green (Swords)	2 D1
Castlegrange Grove	21 B1
Castlegrange Heights	2 D1
Castlegrange Hill	2 D1
Castlegrange Lawn (Clondalkin)	43 C1
Castlegrange Lawn (Clonsilla)	21 B1
Castlegrange Park	21 B1
Castlegrange Road (Clondalkin)	43 C1
Castlegrange Road (Swords)	2 D1
Castlegrange Row	21 B1
Castlegrange Square (Clondalkin)	43 C1
Castlegrange Square (Clonsilla)	21 B1
Castlegrange Terrace	21 B1
Castlegrange Way	2 D1
Castleheath	3 A3
Castlekevin Road	26 D1
Castleknock	22 F3
Castleknock Avenue	22 F3
Castleknock Brook	22 F3
Castleknock Close	22 E3
Castleknock Court	22 F3 [2]
Castleknock Crescent	22 F3
Castleknock Dale	22 F3
Castleknock Downs	22 E3
Castleknock Drive	22 F3
Castleknock Elms	22 F3
Castleknock Gate	23 B4 [1]
Castleknock Glade	22 F3
Castleknock Grange	22 F3
Castleknock Green	23 A3
Castleknock Grove	22 F3
Castleknock Laurels	22 F3
Castleknock Lodge	23 A4
Castleknock Manor	23 A3 [5]
Castleknock Meadows	22 F3
Castleknock Oaks	22 F3
Castleknock Park	23 A3
Castleknock Rise	22 E3
Castleknock Road	22 F3
Castleknock Road	23 A4
Castleknock Vale	22 F3
Castleknock View	22 F3
Castleknock Walk	22 E3
Castleknock Way	22 F3
Castleknock Wood	22 F3
Castlelands	60 F1 [16]
Castlelands Grove	60 F1 [12]
Castlelyons	42 D4
Castlemoyne	14 D3
Castlepark Court	60 E2 [9]
Castlepark Road	60 E1
Castlerosse Crescent	14 F4
Castlerosse Drive	14 F4
Castlerosse View	14 F4
Castleside Drive	46 F3
Castletimon Avenue	25 C1
Castletimon Drive	25 C1
Castletimon Gardens	25 C1
Castletimon Green	25 C1
Castletimon Park	25 C1
Castletimon Road	25 C1
Castletown	32 F1
Castletown Court	32 D3
Castletown Drive	32 D3
Castletown Grove	32 D3
Castletown Lawn	32 D3
Castletymon Court	45 B4
Castletymon Gardens	45 B4
Castletymon Green	45 B4
Castleview	26 E4
Castleview Court	1 Inset
Castleview (Artane)	26 E2
Castleview (Dunboyne)	7 B3
Castleview (Dundrum)	57 C1 [7]
Castleview Avenue	1 Inset
Castleview Close	1 Inset
Castleview Crescent	1 Inset
Castleview Drive	1 Inset
Castleview Green	1 Inset
Castleview Grove	1 Inset
Castleview Heights	1 Inset
Castleview Lawns	1 Inset
Castleview Meadows	1 Inset
Castleview Park	1 Inset
Castleview Park	3 A3
Castleview Place	1 Inset
Castleview Rise	1 Inset
Castleview Row	1 Inset
Castleview Walk	1 Inset
Castleview Way	1 Inset
Castlewarden	51 A3
Castlewarden North	51 A3
Castlewood	21 C1
Castlewood Avenue	47 A1
Castlewood Close	47 A1 [24]
Castlewood Court	47 B1 [26]
Castlewood Park	47 A1
Castlewood Place	47 A1 [6]
Castlewood Terrace	47 A1 [5]
Cathal Brugha Street	71 B3
Cathedral Lane	75 A2
Cathedral Street	71 B3
Cathedral View Court	75 A2
Cathedral View Walk	75 A2
Catherine Court (off William Street North)	72 D1
Catherine Lane	70 F3
Catherine Street (Swift's Alley)	74 F1
Catherine's Well	22 F2 [3]
Cats Ladder	60 F2 [5]
Causeway Road	27 B3
Cavendish Row	71 B2
Caves Strand	3 A2
Ceanchor Road	30 D4
Ceannt Fort (off Mount Brown)	74 D1
Cecil Avenue	26 D4
Cecilia Street (off Temple Bar)	71 B4
Cedar Avenue	45 A3
Cedar Brook	35 C4
Cedar Brook Avenue	35 B3
Cedar Brook Place	35 B3
Cedar Brook Walk	35 B3
Cedar Court (Loughlinstown)	64 D1
Cedar Court (Terenure)	46 F2
Cedar Drive (Dunboyne)	7 B2
Cedar Drive (Palmerstown)	35 B2
Cedar Grove	21 C2 [2]
Cedar Hall	47 C1 [16]
Cedar House	76 D3
Cedar Lodge	23 A4
Cedar Lodge Apts	56 E2
Cedar Park (Donaghmede)	27 A1
Cedar Park (Leixlip)	19 C4
Cedar Square (Stillorgan)	48 F4 [4]
Cedar Square (Swords)	1 B3
Cedar Walk	27 B2
Cedarhurst Green	23 B3
Cedarhurst Road	23 B3
Cedarmount Road	48 E4
Cedarwood	32 D3
Cedarwood Avenue	24 F1
Cedarwood Close	24 F1
Cedarwood Green	24 F1
Cedarwood Grove	24 F1
Cedarwood Park	24 F1
Cedarwood Rise	24 F1
Cedarwood Road	24 F1
Ceder Park	1 B3
Ceder View	1 B3
Celbridge	32 D3
Celbridge Abbey	31 C4
Celbridge Road (Leixlip)	32 F2
Celbridge Road (Lucan)	33 B2
Celbridge Road (Maynooth)	18 D4
Celestine Avenue	39 A3 [42]
*Celestine Avenue (off Dermot O'Hurley Ave)	39 A3
Celtic Park Avenue	25 C2
Celtic Park Road	25 C2
Cenecle Grove	64 E1
Chalet Gardens	34 E1
Chalfont Avenue	3 B2
Chalfont Park	3 B2
Chalfont Place	3 B2
Chalfont Road	3 A2
*Chamber Court (off Chamber St)	74 F2
Chamber Street	74 F2
Chamley Gardens	2 F3
Chamley Park	2 F3
Champions Avenue	71 C3
Chancel Mews	24 D4
Chancery Hall Apts.	70 F3
Chancery Hall Apts. (Ellis Quay)	70 E4
Chancery Lane	75 A1
Chancery Place	71 A4
Chancery Street	71 A4
Chandlers Guild Apts.	74 D1
Chanel Avenue	26 E2
Chanel Grove	26 E1
Chanel Road	26 E2
*Chapel Avenue (off Bath St)	39 A3
Chapel Crescent	24 D3
Chapel Hill	34 D1
Chapel Lane (Bray)	67 B1
Chapel Lane (Parnell Street)	71 B3
Chapel Lane (Swords) (Swords)	2 D2
Chapel Road	14 D1
Chapel View Apts.	34 D1
Chapelizod	36 E2
Chapelizod Bypass	36 E2
Chapelizod Court	36 E2
Chapelizod Hill Road	36 E2
Chapelizod Road	36 F2
Chaplegate	25 A4
Chaplewood Avenue	9 C1
Chaplewood Crescent	9 C1
Chaplewood View	9 C1
Charlemont	25 C3
Charlemont Avenue	50 D4 [5]
Charlemont Court	75 B3
Charlemont Gardens	75 B3
Charlemont Mall	75 B4
Charlemont Parade	72 D1
Charlemont Place	75 C3
Charlemont Road	26 D4
Charlemont Street	75 B3
Charlemont Terrace	50 D4 [18]
Charles Lane	71 C1
Charles Sheils Houses	58 F2
Charles Street Great	71 C2
Charles Street West (off Ormond Quay Upper)	71 A4
Charleston Avenue	47 B1
Charleston Court Flats	47 B1 [9]
Charleston Road	47 B1
Charlestown Avenue	11 B4
Charlestown Court	11 B4
Charlestown Drive	11 B4
Charlestown Green	11 B4
Charlestown Mews	11 B4
Charlestown Park	11 B4
Charlestown Place	11 A4
Charlestown Way	11 B4
Charleville	47 B4
Charleville Avenue	72 D1
Charleville Close	47 A1
Charleville Mall	72 D1
Charleville Road (Phibsborough)	70 E1
Charleville Road (Rathmines)	47 A1
Charleville Square	46 E4
Charleville Terrace (on Charleville Rd)	70 E1
Charlotte Quay	76 F1
Charlotte Terrace	60 F2 [18]
Charlotte Way	75 B3
Charlton Lawn	48 D4
Charnwood (Bray)	67 C3
Charnwood (Clonsilla)	21 C2
Charnwood Avenue	21 C2
Charnwood Court	21 C2
Charnwood Dale	21 C2
Charnwood Gardens	21 C2
Charnwood Green	21 C2
Charnwood Grove	21 C2
Charnwood Heath	21 C2
Charnwood Meadows	21 C2
Charnwood Park	21 C2
Charter House	17 C3 [7]
Chatham Court (on Chatham Street)	75 B1
Chatham Lane (off Chatham Street)	75 B1
Chatham Row	75 B1
Chatham Street	75 B1
*Chaworth Terrace (Hanbury Lane)	74 F1
Cheeverstown Road	54 D1
Chelmsford Avenue	75 C4
Chelmsford Lane	47 B1 [15]
Chelmsford Road	47 B1
Chelsea Gardens	26 F4
Cheltenham Place	75 B4
Cherbury Court	48 F3
Cherbury Gardens	48 F3
Cherbury Mews	48 F3 [4]
Cherbury Park Avenue	34 D2
Cherbury Park Road	34 D2
Cherries Road	58 D2
Cherrington Close	64 E3
Cherrington Drive	64 E3
Cherrington Road	64 E3
Cherry Avenue (Carpenterstown)	22 E3
Cherry Avenue (Swords)	1 C3
Cherry Court (Loughlinstown)	64 D1 [2]
Cherry Court (Terenure)	46 F2
Cherry Drive	22 E3
Cherry Garth (Stillorgan)	48 E4
Cherry Garth (Swords)	1 C2
Cherry Grove (Crumlin)	45 C2

STREET NAME	PAGE/GRID REFERENCE
Cherry Grove (Swords)	1 B3
Cherry House	76 D3
Cherry Lawn	22 E3
Cherry Lawns	33 C2
Cherry Lodge	23 A4
Cherry Orchard Ave	36 D4
Cherry Orchard Avenue	35 C3
Cherry Orchard Court	35 C4
Cherry Orchard Crescent	35 C4
Cherry Orchard Drive	35 C4
Cherry Orchard Green	35 C4
Cherry Orchard Grove	35 C4
Cherry Orchard Parade	35 C4
Cherry Orchard Way	35 C4 [1]
Cherry Park (Carpenterstown)	22 E3
Cherry Park (Swords)	1 B3
Cherry Tree Drive	67 C3 [1]
Cherry Wood	64 D1
Cherryfield Avenue	45 C2
Cherryfield Avenue Lr	47 B1
Cherryfield Avenue Upr	47 B1
Cherryfield Close	21 C1
Cherryfield Court	21 B1
Cherryfield Drive	45 C2
Cherryfield Lawn	21 C1
Cherryfield Park	21 C1
Cherryfield Road	45 C2
Cherryfield View	21 B1
Cherryfield Walk	21 C1
Cherryfield Way	46 D4
Cherrymount Crescent	26 D3 [1]
Cherrymount Grove	26 D3 [2]
Cherrymount Park	70 F1
Cherrywood	32 D3
Cherrywood Avenue	44 D1
Cherrywood Crescent	43 C1
Cherrywood Drive	43 C1
Cherrywood Grove	44 D1
Cherrywood Lawn	43 C2
Cherrywood Park (Clondalkin)	43 C2
Cherrywood Park (Loughlinstown)	64 D1
Cherrywood Road	64 D2
Cherrywood Villas	43 C1
Cherrywood Villas	44 D1 [6]
Chester Downs	60 D1
Chester Road	47 B1
Chester Square	60 E1 [23]
Chesterfield Avenue (Castleknock)	23 B4
Chesterfield Avenue (Phoenix Park)	23 B4
Chesterfield Avenue (Phoenix Park)	36 F1
Chesterfield Close	23 B4
Chesterfield Copse	23 B4
Chesterfield Grove	23 B4
Chesterfield Park	23 B3
Chesterfield View	23 B3
Chestnut Court	25 C2 [1]
Chestnut Grove (Ballinteer)	57 B2
Chestnut Grove (Celbridge)	32 D3
Chestnut Grove (Clondalkin)	44 F3
Chestnut Grove (Dunboyne)	7 B3
Chestnut House (Swords)	1 Inset
Chestnut Park	59 A2 [5]
Chestnut Road (Clondalkin)	45 A1
Chestnut Road (Mount Merrion)	48 E3
Christchurch Hall	74 F1
Christchurch Place	75 A1
Christchurch Square	75 A1
Christchurch Square	75 A1
Church Avenue (Blanchardstown)	22 F2
Church Avenue (Drumcondra)	25 B3
Church Avenue (Glasnevin)	25 A3 [2]
Church Avenue (Irishtown)	39 A3
Church Avenue (Killiney)	60 E4
Church Avenue (Portmarnock)	14 F2 [2]
Church Avenue (Rathmines)	47 A1
Church Avenue South (Dolphin's Barn)	74 D2
Church Avenue West (Church Street)	70 F4
Church Court (Castleknock)	22 F3
Church Court (East Wall)	72 F2
Church Gardens	47 A1
Church Green	46 F1
Church Grove	55 A2
Church Lands	67 C3
Church Lane (College Green)	71 B4
Church Lane (Rathfarnham)	46 F3
Church Lane South	75 A2
Church Park	46 F1
Church Park Avenue	46 F1
Church Park Court	46 F1
Church Park Drive	46 F1
Church Park Lawn	46 F1
Church Park Way	46 F1
Church Place (off Irvine Terrace)	72 F3
Church Road (Ballybrack)	60 E4
Church Road (Bray)	67 C3
Church Road (Celbridge)	32 D4
Church Road (Dalkey)	60 F1
Church Road (East Wall)	72 F2
Church Road (Finglas)	24 D2
Church Road (Killiney)	60 D3
Church Road (Malahide)	3 B3
Church Road (Mulhuddart)	9 A4
Church Road (Rathcoole)	52 E2
Church Road (Sutton)	29 B1
Church Road (Swords) (Swords)	2 D2
*Church Row (off Irvine Terrace)	72 F3
Church Street (Finglas)	24 E2
Church Street (Four Courts)	70 F4
Church Street (Howth)	30 D1
Church Street East	72 F3
Church Street New	70 F4
Church Street Upper	70 F3
Church Terrace (Bray)	67 C2 [45]
Church Terrace (Finglas)	24 E2
Church Terrace (off Church Street)	70 F3
Church Villas	59 C4 [2]
Church Walk	24 D4
Churchfields	47 C2
Churchgate Avenue	39 C1 [1]
Churchill Mews	60 F1 [17]
Churchill Terrace	39 A4 [6]
Churchlands	58 D3 [1]
Churchtown	47 B4
Churchtown Avenue	47 B3
Churchtown Close	47 B3
Churchtown Drive	47 B3
Churchtown Road Lower	47 B3
Churchtown Road Upper	47 A4
Churchtown Road Upper	47 B4
Churchview Avenue	60 D3
Churchview Drive	60 D3
Churchview Park	60 D3
Churchview Road	60 D3
Cian Park	25 B4
Cianlea	1 B1
Cill Cais	54 F2
Cill Eanna	26 F2
Cill Manntan Park	67 C2 [9]
Cill Sarain	67 B3
City Quay	72 D4
Citywest Bridge	42 B4
Citywest Avenue	53 C1
Citywest Interchange	42 B4
Citywest Road	53 C1
Claddagh Green	35 C3
Claddagh Road	35 C3
Claddagh Terrace	68 D2 [15]
*Claddagh Terrace (On Strand Road)	67 C2
Clanawley Road	26 E3
Clanboy Road	26 E3
Clanbrassil Close	74 F4
Clanbrassil Street Lower	74 F3
Clanbrassil Street Upper	74 F3
Clanbrassil terrace	74 F2
Clancarthy Road	26 D3
Clancy Avenue	24 E1
Clancy Road	24 E1
Clandonagh Road	26 D3
Clane Road	31 B4
Clanfadda Wood	48 F3
Clanhugh Road	26 E3
Clanmahon Road	26 E3
Clanmaurice Road	26 D3
Clanmawr	64 E2
Clanmoyle Road	26 D3
Clanranald Road	26 D3
Clanree Road	26 D3
Clanwilliam Court	76 E2
Clanwilliam Place	76 E2
Clanwilliam Square	76 E1
Clanwilliam Terrace	76 E1
Clare Hall	14 D4
Clare Lane	75 C1
Clare Park Villas	25 B3 [3]
Clare Road	25 B3
Clare Street	75 C1
Claremont Avenue	25 A3 [1]
Claremont Close	24 F4
Claremont Court	39 A4 [36]
Claremont Court (Finglas)	24 F4
Claremont Court (Sandymount)	39 A4 [21]
Claremont Crescent	24 F4
Claremont Drive	24 F2
Claremont Grove	60 E3
Claremont Lawn	24 F4
Claremont Mews	29 C1
Claremont Park	39 A4
Claremont Road (Carrickmines)	59 B4
Claremont Road (Killiney)	60 E3
Claremont Road (Sandymount)	39 A4
Claremont Road (Sutton)	29 B1
Claremont Terrace	47 C4 [7]
Claremont Villas	60 E1 [4]
Claremount	64 E3
Claremount Pines	59 B4
Claremount Terrace	68 D2 [11]
Clarence Mangan Road	74 F2
Clarence Mangan Square (off John Dillon Street)	75 A1
Clarence Place Great	76 E1
Clarence St Great North	72 D2
Clarence Street	49 C4
Clarence Market (off William Street South)	75 B1
Clarendon Row (off King St South)	75 B1
Clarendon Street	75 B1
Clareville Court	24 F4 [7]
Clareville Grove	24 F4
Clareville Road	46 F1
Clarinda Manor	60 D1
Clarinda Park East	60 D1
Clarinda Park East (Dun Laoghaire)	50 D4
Clarinda Park North	50 D4
Clarinda Park West	50 D4
Clarion Quay	72 D3
Clarke Terrace	74 D2
Clarke's Bridge	72 D1
Clarkeville Terrace	35 C1 [3]
Classon's Bridge	47 B2
Claude Road	25 A4
Clayton Terrace	36 E2 [8]
Clearwater Apts.	3 C2 [2]
Clearwater Court	24 D3 [1]
Clearwater Cove	49 C4 [31]
Cleggan Avenue	35 C3
Cleggan Park	35 C3
Cleggan Road	35 C3
Clifden Drive	35 C3
Clifden Road	36 D3
Cliff Terrace	60 E1 [18]
Clifford's Lane	2 E2
Clifton Avenue	49 C4 [11]
Clifton Court Apts.	70 E4
Clifton Lane	49 C4 [10]
Clifton Park	64 E2
Clifton Terrace	49 C4 [13]
Cliftonville Road	25 A4
Clinch's Court	72 D1
Clipper Court Apts. (off Liffey Street West)	70 E4
Clipper View Apts. (off Liffey Street West)	70 E4
Clogher Road	46 E1
Cloghran	1 C4
Cloghran	13 A1
Cloghran Roundabout	1 C4
Cloister Avenue	49 A4
Cloister Close	48 F4
Cloister Court	24 D3
Cloister Gate	49 A4
Cloister Green	49 A4
Cloister Grove	49 A4
Cloister Park	49 A4
Cloister Square	49 A4
Cloister Way	49 A4
Clon Burgh	58 D3
Clonallen	46 E2 [11]
Clonard Avenue	57 C2
Clonard Close	57 C2
Clonard Court	46 E2 [8]
Clonard Drive	57 C2
Clonard Grove	57 C2
Clonard Lawn	57 C2
Clonard Park	57 C2
Clonard Road (Crumlin)	46 D1
Clonard Road (Sandyford)	57 C2
Clonasleigh	64 E2 [2]
Cloncourt Apts.	8 D3
Clondalkin	44 D1
Clonee	8 D3
Clonee Bridge	8 D3
Clonee Bypass	8 D3
Clonfert Road	46 E1
Clongriffin	14 D4
Clonkeen Court	59 B3
Clonkeen Crescent	59 B2
Clonkeen Drive	59 B2
Clonkeen Grove	59 B2
Clonkeen Lawn	59 B3 [5]
Clonkeen Road	59 B2
Clonkeen Road	59 B3
Clonlara Avenue	43 A4
Clonlara Road (Naas Road)	43 A4
Clonlara Road (Ringsend)	39 A3 [12]
Clonlea	57 C2
Clonlea Wood	57 C2 [1]
Clonliffe Avenue	72 D1
Clonliffe Gardens	25 B4
Clonliffe Road	25 B4
Clonliffe Square	25 B4 [16]
Clonmacnoise Grove	46 E1 [4]
Clonmacnoise Road	46 E1
Clonmel Road	25 A2
Clonmel Street	75 B2
Clonmellon Grove	14 D4 [3]
Clonmore Court	25 A3 [11]
Clonmore Road (Ballybough)	72 D1
Clonmore Road (Goatstown)	48 E4
Clonmore Terrace	72 D1
*Clonmore Villas (Clonmore Road)	72 D1
Clonrosse Court	26 F1
Clonrosse Drive	26 F1
Clonrosse Park	26 F1
Clonshaugh	13 B3
Clonshaugh Avenue	13 A4
Clonshaugh Close	13 B4
Clonshaugh Court	13 B4 [4]
Clonshaugh Crescent	13 A4
Clonshaugh Drive	13 B4
Clonshaugh Glen	13 B4
Clonshaugh Green	13 B4
Clonshaugh Grove	13 B4
Clonshaugh Heights	13 A4
Clonshaugh Lawns	13 B4
Clonshaugh Meadow	13 A4
Clonshaugh Park	13 B4
Clonshaugh Rise	13 B4 [2]
Clonshaugh Road	13 A3
Clonshaugh Road	13 A4
Clonshaugh Walk	13 B4
Clonsilla	21 C2
Clonsilla Close	22 E2
Clonsilla Park	22 E2
Clonsilla Road	22 E2
Clonskeagh	47 C2
Clonskeagh Drive	47 C2 [6]
Clonskeagh Road	47 C2
Clonskeagh Square	47 C2 [7]

STREET NAME	PAGE/GRID REFERENCE
Clontarf	39 C1
Clontarf Park	39 C1
Clontarf Road	26 D4
Clonturk Avenue	25 B3 [1]
Clonturk Court	25 B3 [6]
Clonturk Gardens	25 B4 [3]
Clonturk Park	25 B4
Cloonlara Crescent	24 E3
Cloonlara Drive	24 E2
Cloonlara Road	24 E3
Cloonlara Square	23 B3
Cloonmore Avenue	54 D2
Cloonmore Close	54 E2
Cloonmore Crescent	54 D2
Cloonmore Drive	54 D2
Cloonmore Gardens	54 D2
Cloonmore Green	54 D2
Cloonmore Grove	54 D2
Cloonmore Lawn	54 D2
Cloonmore Park	54 D2
Cloonmore Road	54 D2
Cloragh Road	56 E4
Clover Hill	67 A3
Clover Hill Drive	36 D3
Clover Hill Road	36 D4
Cloverhill Road	35 A4
Cloverhill Road	35 B3
Cloyne Road	46 E1 [2]
Cluain Aoibhinn	17 C4
Cluain Mhuire	60 D1
Cluain na Greine Court	64 E3 [4]
Cluain Rí	34 F2
Cluain Shee	58 D3
Club Road	45 A1
Clune Road	24 E1
Cluny Grove	60 D3
Cluny Park	60 E2
Clutterland	42 F1
Clyde Court	76 E4
Clyde House	39 A4 [43]
Clyde Lane	76 F4
Clyde Road	76 E4
Cnoc Aoibhean	33 B2
Coast Road (Baldoyle)	15 A4
Coast Road (Malahide)	3 C2
Coates Lane	17 C3 [3]
Coburg	67 B2
Coburg Place	72 D2
*Coghill's Court (off Dame Street)	71 B4
Cois Cairn	67 B1
Cois Coillte	64 D1 [3]
Cois Eala	75 A4
Cois Na hAbhann	54 F2
Cois Sleibhe	67 B4
Coke Lane	70 F4
Coke Ovens Cottages	24 F4
Colbert's Fort (off St James Walk)	74 D2
Colbert's Fort (Tallaght)	44 F4
Coldcut Road	35 B2
Coldwater Lakes	53 B2
Coldwell Street	60 D1
Colepark Avenue	36 D3
Colepark Drive	36 D3
Colepark Green	36 D3
Colepark Road	36 D3
Coleraine Street	71 A3
Colganstown	41 B2
Coliemore Road	60 F2
Coliemore Villas	60 F2 [14]
College Crescent	46 D3
College Drive	46 E3
College Fort	22 F4
College Gate	22 F3
College Green	71 B4
College Green (Maynooth)	17 C4
College Grove	22 F4
College Lane (Rathcoole)	52 F1
College Lane (Trinity College)	76 D1
College Manor	25 B4 [8]
College Mews	25 B4 [11]
College Park (Castleknock)	23 A4
College Park (Kimmage)	46 E3
College Park Avenue	57 C2
College Park Close	57 C2
College Park Court	57 C2 [2]
College Park Drive	57 C2 [3]
College Park Grove	57 C2
College Park House	75 C1
College Park Way	57 C2
College Road (Castleknock)	22 F4
College Road (Greenogue Ind Est)	42 E4
College Road (Whitechurch Road)	57 A3
College Street (Baldoyle)	15 A4 [8]
College Street (Baldoyle)	15 A4
College Street (Trinity College)	71 C4
College View (Drumcondra)	25 B3
College View (Tallaght)	55 A1 [6]
College Wood	22 F4
Collegeland	42 F4
Collier's Avenue	47 B1 [3]
Colliersland	6 F2
Collindale	25 C2 [6]
Collins Avenue	25 C2
Collins Avenue East	26 D3
Collins Avenue Extension	25 A2
Collins Avenue West	25 B2
Collins Bridge	20 F4
Collins Close	25 C3 [8]
Collins Court (Blackrock)	49 A3 [13]
Collins Court (Collins Avenue)	25 C3 [6]
Collins Drive	24 E1
Collins Green	24 E1
Collins Park	26 D3
Collins Place	24 E1
Collins Row	24 E2 [6]
Collinstown Crescent	35 A3 [3]
Collinstown Grove	35 B3
Collinstown Road	35 A3
Collinswood	25 C2
Colmanstown	51 C2
Colmanstown Lane	51 C2
Colmcille Court	2 D2 [3]
Colthurst Close	34 F2
Colthurst Crescent	34 F2
Colthurst Gardens	34 F2
Colthurst Green	34 F2
Colthurst Mews	34 F2
Colthurst Park	34 F2
Colthurst Rise	34 F2
Colthurst Road	34 F2
Colthurst Way	34 F2
Comeragh Road	36 F4
Comeran Court	74 E2
Common Little	42 D4
Commons (Hazelhatch)	41 C2
Commons (Rathcoole)	52 E1
Commons East	2 D3
Commons Little	42 D4
Commons Lower	41 A1
Commons Road (Loughlinstown)	64 E2
Commons Road (St. John's Gate)	44 D2
Commons Street	72 D3
Compass Court	23 C3
Compass Court Apts.	24 D3 [4]
Comyn Place	25 A3 [5]
Con Colbert Road	36 F3
Con Colbert Road	73 A1
Confey	20 D4
Congress Gardens	60 E1 [2]
Congress Hall	7 B3
Congress Park	7 B3 [1]
Connaught Parade	24 F4 [6]
Connaught Place	50 D4 [26]
Connaught Street	24 F4
Connawood	67 B1
Connawood Copse	67 B1
Connawood Crescent	67 B1
Connawood Drive	67 B1
Connawood Green	67 B1
Connawood Grove	67 B1
Connawood Lawn	67 B1
Connawood Walk	67 B1
Connawood Way	67 B1
Connolly Avenue (Kilmainham)	73 A2
Connolly Avenue (Malahide)	3 A4
Connolly Gardens	73 A2
Connolly's Folly	18 E4
Conor Clune Road	23 C4
Conquer Hill Avenue	39 C1
Conquer Hill Road	39 C1
Constellation Road	12 F4
Constitution Hill	71 A3
Convent Avenue (Bray)	68 D2
Convent Avenue (Marino)	25 B4
Convent Close	76 D2
Convent Court	58 E1 [4]
Convent Lane (Maynooth)	17 C3
Convent Lane (Portmarnock)	4 D4
Convent Lane (Willbrook)	46 F4
Convent Lawns	36 E3 [4]
Convent Lodge	26 F2
Convent Place	75 C3
Convent Road (Blackrock)	49 A4
Convent Road (Clondalkin)	44 E2
Convent Road (Dalkey)	60 F2
Convent Road (Dun Laoghaire)	50 D4
Convent View (Bray)	68 D2 [23]
Convent View (Oldcourt)	67 C3
Convent View Cottages (Cabra)	24 D4 [2]
Convent View Cottages (St. John's Gate)	44 D2
Convent View Crescent	24 D4 [3]
Convent Way	24 D4
Conway Court	76 E1
Conyngham Road	69 C4
Cook Street	71 A4
Cooks Road	1 A4
Cookstown	66 E3
Cookstown Court	44 F4
Cookstown Road	44 E4
Cookstown Road	44 F4
Cookstown Way	44 E4
Coolamber Court	56 D1 [1]
Coolamber Drive	52 F2
Coolamber Park	56 D1
Coolamber Road	52 F2
Coolatree Close	25 C2
Coolatree Park	25 C2
Coolatree Road	25 C2
Cooldrinagh Lane	33 B1
Cooldrinagh Terrace	33 B1
Cooldríona Court	2 D2
Cooleen Avenue	25 C1
Coolevin (Ballybrack)	60 D4
Coolevin Road	75 A2
Cooley Close	36 F4
Cooley Road	36 F4
Coolgariff Road	25 C1
Coolgreena Close	25 C2
Coolgreena Road	25 C1
Coolkill	58 D3
Coolmine	52 F3
Coolmine Boulevard	22 E2
Coolmine Close	22 D2
Coolmine Cottages	9 A4
Coolmine Court	22 E2
Coolmine Green	22 D3
Coolmine Lawn	22 D2
Coolmine Mews	22 D2 [1]
Coolmine Park	22 E2
Coolmine Road	22 E3
Coolmine Woods	22 E2
Coolnevaun	58 E1
Coolock	26 E1
Coolock Drive	26 E1
Coolock Lane (Santry)	12 F4
Coolock Village	26 E1
Coolock Village Close	26 E1 [3]
Coolrua Drive	25 C1
Coombe Court	74 F1
Coopers Way	70 F3
Coopers Yard (Smithfield)	70 F3
Coopers Yard Apts.	70 F3
Cope Bridge	20 D3
Cope Street	71 B4
Copeland Avenue	26 D4
Copeland Grove	26 D4
Copper Alley(Eustace Street)	71 A4
Copper Beech Grove	67 B2 [6]
Coppinger	49 A4
Coppinger Close	48 F4
Coppinger Glade	48 F4
Coppinger Row	75 B1
Coppinger Walk	49 A4
Coppinger Wood	48 F4
Corbally	53 C3
Corbally Avenue	53 C2
Corbally Close	53 C2
Corbally Downs	53 C2
Corbally Drive	53 C2
Corbally Glade	53 C2
Corbally Green	53 C2
Corbally Heath	53 C2
Corbally Lawn	53 C2
Corbally Park	53 C2
Corbally Rise	53 C2
Corbally Square	53 C2
Corbally Vale	53 C2
Corbally Way	53 C2
Corbawn Avenue	64 E2
Corbawn Close	64 F2
Corbawn Court	64 F2
Corbawn Dale	64 F2
Corbawn Drive	64 F2
Corbawn Glade	64 E2 [14]
Corbawn Grove	64 F2
Corbawn Lane	64 E2
Corbawn Lawn	64 E3
Corbawn Wood	64 E2
Corduff	22 F1
Corduff Avenue	22 F1
Corduff Close	22 F1
Corduff Cottages	22 E1
Corduff Crescent	22 F1
Corduff Gardens	22 F1
Corduff Green	22 F1
Corduff Grove	9 B4
Corduff Park	9 B4
Corduff Place	22 F1
Corduff Way	22 F1
Cork Hill (off Dame St)	71 A4
Cork Street	74 E2
Corkagh View	44 D2
Corke Abbey	67 C1
Corke Abbey Avenue	67 B1
Cormac Terrace	46 F2
Corn Exchange Apts.	71 C4
Corn Exchange Place	71 C4
Cornelscourt	59 B3
Cornelscourt Hill Road	59 B3
Cornelstown	6 D2
Cornerpark	42 D3
Cornmarket	74 F1
Corr Castle	29 B1
Corr Castle Apts	29 B1 [3]
Corrbridge Terrace (off Claremont Road)	29 B1 [1]
Corrib Road	46 E2
Corrig Avenue	50 D4
Corrig Close	45 B3
Corrig Hall	57 C3
Corrig Park	50 D4
Corrig Road (Dalkey)	60 F1
Corrig Road (Dun Laoghaire)	60 D1
Corrig Road (Stillorgan)	58 E2
Corrybeg	46 D4
Cosy Lodge	47 A1 [26]
Coulson Avenue	46 F2
Coultry Avenue	25 B1
Coultry Close	25 A1
Coultry Court	12 D4
Coultry Crescent	12 D4
Coultry Drive	12 D4
Coultry Gardens	12 D4
Coultry Green	12 D4
Coultry Grove	12 E4
Coultry Lawn	12 E4
Coultry Park	12 E4
Coultry Road	12 D4
Coultry Terrace	12 D4
Coultry Way	25 B1
Coundon Court	60 E4
Countess Markievicz House	72 D4
Countview Lawns	66 E2
Court House Square	17 C3 [5]
Courthill Drive	7 B2
Courthouse Square Apts.	55 A1 [13]
Courtlands	59 C3

STREET NAME	PAGE/GRID REFERENCE
Courtney Place	72 E1
Courtview	23 C3
Cow Parlour	74 E2
Cowbooter Lane	30 E2
Cowper Downs	47 A1
Cowper Drive	47 B2
Cowper Gardens	47 B2
Cowper Mews	47 A2 [4]
Cowper Road	47 B2
Cowper Street	70 D2
Cowper Village	47 A2
Cows Lane	71 A4
Crag Avenue	35 B4
Crag Crescent	35 B4
Crag Terrace	35 B4
Craigford Avenue	26 E3
Craigford Drive	26 E3
Craiglands	60 F2 [26]
Craigmore Gardens	49 A3 [5]
Crampton Avenue	76 F3
Crampton Court (off Dame St)	71 B4
Crampton Quay	71 B4
Crane Lane (off Dame Street)	71 A4
Crane Street	74 E1
Cranfield Place	39 A3
Cranford Court (Kimmage)	46 E2 [12]
Cranford Court (Stillorgan Road)	48 D2
Cranmer Lane	76 E2
Crannagh	47 C2 [9]
Crannagh Castle	46 F3 [9]
Crannagh Court	46 F3 [10]
Crannagh Grove	47 A3
Crannagh Hall	47 A3
Crannagh Park	46 F3
Crannagh Road	46 F3
Crannagh Way	47 A3 [8]
Crannogue Close	11 C4
Crannogue Road	11 C4
Crawford Avenue	25 A4
Crawford Terrace (off Kings Avenue)	72 D1
Creighton Street	72 D4
Cremona Road	36 E3
Cremore Avenue	24 F3
Cremore Crescent	24 F3
Cremore Drive	24 F3
Cremore Heights	24 F2
Cremore Lawn	24 F3
Cremore Park	25 A3
Cremore Road	24 F3
Cremore Villas	24 F3 [5]
Cremorne (Knocklyon)	56 D1
Cremorne (Terenure Road East)	46 F2
Crescent Gardens	72 E1
Crescent House	26 D4 [6]
Crescent Place	26 D4
Crescent Villas	25 A4
Crestfield Avenue	25 B2
Crestfield Close	25 B2
Crestfield Drive	25 B2
Crestfield Park	25 B2
Crestfield Road	25 B2
Crewhill	17 B1
Crinan Strand	72 D3
Crinken Glen	64 E3
Crinken Lane	64 D4
Crinstown	17 A4
Croaghpatrick Road	24 D4
Crockshane	52 E3
Crodaun Court	31 C2 [1]
Crodaun Forest Park	32 D2
Crofton Avenue	50 D4
Crofton Mansions	50 D4 [28]
Crofton Road	50 D4
Crofton Terrace	50 D4 [25]
Croftwood Crescent	35 C3
Croftwood Drive	35 C3
Croftwood Gardens	35 C3
Croftwood Green	36 D3
Croftwood Grove	35 C3
Croftwood Park	36 D3
Croke Villas	72 D1
Cromcastle Avenue	26 D1
Cromcastle Close	26 D1 [2]
Cromcastle Court	26 D1 [6]
Cromcastle Drive	26 D1
Cromcastle Green	26 D1
Cromcastle Park	26 D1
Cromcastle Road	26 D1
Cromlech Close	62 F2
Cromlech Court	11 C4
Cromlech Fields	64 E1
Cromwell's Quarters	74 D1
Cromwellsfort Road	45 C2
Crooksling	53 B4
Crosbie House	75 C4
Cross Avenue (Booterstown)	48 F3
Cross Avenue (Dun Laoghaire)	50 D4
Cross Lane	17 C3
Crosstrees Court	30 D2 [13]
Crosthwaite Park East	60 D1
Crosthwaite Park South	60 D1
Crosthwaite Park West	60 D1
Crosthwaite Terrace	50 D4 [15]
Crostick Alley (off Meath St)	74 F1
Crotty Avenue	45 C1
Crow Street (off Dame St)	71 B4
Crown Alley (Off Temple Bar)	71 B4
Croydon Gardens	25 C4
Croydon Green	25 C4
Croydon Park Avenue	25 C4
Croydon Terrace	25 C3 [4]
Cruagh Avenue	62 E1
Cruagh Close	62 E1
Cruagh Court	62 E1
Cruagh Green	62 E1
Cruagh Lane	56 E4
Cruagh Rise	62 E1
Cruagh Road	56 E4
Cruagh Wood	62 E1
Cruise Park	9 A2
Cruise Park Avenue	9 A2
Cruise Park Close	9 A2
Cruise Park Court	9 A2
Cruise Park Crescent	9 A2
Cruise Park Drive	9 A2
Cruise Park Hall	9 A2
Cruise Park Rise	9 A2
Cruise Park Square	9 A2
Cruise Park Walk	9 A2
Crumlin	46 D1
*Crumlin Park(off Crumlin Road)	46 D1
Crumlin Road	73 C4
Cuala Grove	68 D3
Cuala Road (Bray)	68 D3
Cuala Road (Cabra)	24 F4
Cuan na Mara	30 D1 [13]
Cuckoo Lane	71 A3
Cuffe Lane	75 B2
Cuffe Street	75 B2
Cuilenn Park	24 F1
Cul na Greine	54 F2
Cullen's Cottages	49 A4 [7]
Cullen's Wood House	75 C4
*Cullenswood Court (off Cullenswood Park)	47 B1
Cullenswood Gardens	47 B1
Cullenswood Park	47 B1
Cullenswood Road	47 B1 [11]
Culmore Park	35 C2 [1]
Culmore Road	35 C2
*Cumberland Place North (on North Circular Road)	70 F1
Cumberland Road	76 D3
Cumberland Street	49 C4
Cumberland Street North	71 C2
Cumberland Street South	76 D1
Cunningham Drive	60 F2
Cunningham Road	60 F2
Curlew Road	36 F4
Curracloe Drive	27 A1 [4]
Curragh Hall	9 B3
Curragh Hall Avenue	9 B3
Curragh Hall Close	9 B3
Curragh Hall Court	9 B3
Curragh Hall Crescent	9 B3
Curragh Hall Drive	9 B3
Curragh Hall Gate	9 B3
Curragh Hall Green	9 B3
Curragh Hall Grove	9 B3
Curragh Hall House	9 B3
Curragh Hall Lane	9 B3
Curragh Hall Lodge	9 B3
Curragh Hall Road	9 B3
Curragh Hall View	9 B3
Curragh Hall Way	9 B3
Curragh Hall Wood	9 B3
Curtlestown	65 B4
Curzon Street	75 A3
Cushinstown	6 F1
Cushlawn Avenue	54 F2
Cushlawn Close	54 F3
Cushlawn Dale	54 F3
Cushlawn Drive	54 F2
Cushlawn Grove	54 F2
Cushlawn Park	54 F2
Cushlawn Walk	54 F3
Cushlawn Way	54 F3
Custom Hall	71 C3
Custom House Harbour	72 D3
Custom House Quay	71 C3
Custom House Square	72 E3
Cymric Road	39 A3
Cypress Avenue	56 E2 [2]
Cypress Court	64 E1
Cypress Drive	46 D3
Cypress Garth	46 D4
Cypress Grove North	46 D3
Cypress Grove Road	46 D3
Cypress Grove South	46 D4
Cypress House	28 D1
Cypress Lawn	46 D4
Cypress Park	46 D4
Cypress Road	48 E3
Cypress Springs	20 D4 [1]

D

STREET NAME	PAGE/GRID REFERENCE
*Daisy Market (off Arran Street)	71 A4
Dakota Avenue	12 F4
Dakota Court	25 A4
Dal Riada	3 C4
Dalcassian Downs	24 F4
Dale Close	58 E1 [1]
Dale Drive	58 E1
Dale Road	58 E1
Dale View	60 E4
Dale View Park	60 E4 [2]
Dalepark Road	55 A2
Daletree Avenue	55 B2
Daletree Close	55 C3
Daletree Court	55 C3
Daletree Crescent	55 C2
Daletree Drive	55 C2
Daletree Park	55 C3
Daletree Place	55 C3
Daletree Road	55 C3
Daletree Terrace	55 C3
Daletree View	55 B3
Daleview Road	1 C1
Dalkey	60 F1
Dalkey Avenue	60 F2
Dalkey Court	60 F2 [23]
Dalkey Grove	60 F2 [6]
Dalkey Park	60 E2
Dalkey Rock	60 F2
Dalton Mews	3 B3
Dalymount	70 F1
Damastown Avenue	8 F3
Damastown Close	8 F3
Damastown Court	9 A3
Damastown Drive	8 E3
Damastown Green	8 F3
Damastown Road	8 F3
Damastown Walk	8 E3
Damastown Way	8 F3
Damastown Way	9 A3
Dame Court	75 B1
*Dame Lane	75 B3
Dame Lane	71 B4
Dame Street	71 B4
Damer Court	71 A2
Damer House	2 E2
Dane Close	11 C4
Dane Road	11 C4
Danes Court	27 A4
Danesfort	39 B1
Daneswell Road	25 A4
Danewood Castleknock	23 A3
Dangan	41 A2
Dangan Avenue	46 D2
Dangan Drive	46 D2
Dangan Park	46 D2
Daniel Street	75 A3
Danieli Drive	26 E2
Danieli Road	26 E2
Dara Court	32 D3
Dara Crescent	32 D3
Dargan Court	68 D2 [6]
Dargan Street	67 B2 [10]
Dargle Bridge	67 A4
Dargle Court	67 B2 [3]
Dargle Crescent	67 B2 [5]
Dargle Drive	57 A1
Dargle Heights	67 B2
Dargle Road (Dean's Grange)	59 A1
Dargle Road (Drumcondra)	25 A4
*Dargle Terrace (On Lower Dargle Road)	67 B2
Dargle Valley	57 A1
Dargle View	57 A1
Dargle Wood	56 D1
Darley Cottages	67 C2 [15]
Darley Street	74 F4
Darley's Terrace	74 E2
Darling Estate	23 C4
Darndale	13 C4
Dartmouth Lane	75 C4
Dartmouth Place	75 C4
Dartmouth Road	75 C4
Dartmouth Square	75 C3
Dartmouth Square East	75 C3
Dartmouth Square North	75 C3
Dartmouth Square South	75 C4
Dartmouth Square West	75 C4
Dartmouth Terrace	75 C4
Dartry Cottages	47 B2 [1]
Dartry Park	47 B2
Dartry Road	47 A2
David Park	25 A4
David Road	25 A4
Davis Place (off Thomas Davis St Sth)	74 F1
Davitt House	73 A3
Davitt Park	60 D4
Davitt Road (Bray)	67 C2
Davitt Road (Inchicore)	36 F4
Davitt Terrace	73 A3
*Dawson Court	75 B1
Dawson Court	48 F3
Dawson Court (off Stephen St Lower)	75 B1
Dawson Lane	75 C1
Dawson Street	75 C1
De Bret House	46 F4 [24]
De Burgh Road	70 D4
De Courcy Square	25 A4 [2]
De Selby	54 D2
De Selby Close	54 D2
De Selby Court	54 D2
De Selby Crescent	54 D2
De Selby Downs	54 D2
De Selby Drive	54 D2
De Selby Green	54 D2
De Selby Lane	54 D2
De Selby Lawns	54 D2
De Selby Park	53 C2
De Selby Rise	54 T4
De Selby Road	54 D2
De Velara Place	71 B1
*De Vesci Court (off Sloperton)	49 C4
De Vesci Terrace	49 C4
Dean Court	75 A1
Dean Street	75 A1
Dean Swift Green	25 A2
Dean Swift Road	25 A2
Dean Swift Square	74 F1
Deans Court	59 B1 [10]
Deans Grange	59 B2
Dean's Grange Road	59 B2
Deansrath Avenue	34 F4
Deansrath Crescent	43 C1
Deansrath Green	43 C1

STREET NAME	PAGE/GRID REFERENCE
Deansrath Grove	34 F4
Deansrath Lawn	34 F4
Deansrath Park	43 C1
Deansrath Road	43 C1
Deanstown Avenue	24 D2
Deanstown Drive	24 D2
Deanstown Green	24 D2
Deanstown Park	24 D2
Deanstown Road	24 D2
Decies Road	36 E3
Deepdales	67 B4
Deerhaven	8 F4
Deerhaven Avenue	8 F4
Deerhaven Close	8 F4
Deerhaven Crescent	8 F4
Deerhaven Green	8 F4
Deerhaven Park	8 F4
Deerhaven View	8 F4
Deerhaven Walk	8 F4
Deerpark	67 B4
Deerpark Avenue (Castleknock)	23 A4
Deerpark Avenue (Kiltipper)	54 F3
Deerpark Close (Castleknock)	23 A3
Deerpark Close (Kiltipper)	54 F3
Deerpark Downs	54 F3
Deerpark Drive (Castleknock)	23 A3
Deerpark Drive (Kiltipper)	54 F3
Deerpark Green	54 F3
Deerpark Lawn	23 B3
Deerpark Lodge	54 F3
Deerpark Place	54 F3
Deerpark Rise	54 F3
Deerpark Road (Castleknock Road)	23 A3
Deerpark Road (Kiltipper)	54 F3
Deerpark Road (Mount Merrion)	48 D4
Deerpark Square	54 F3
Deerpark Terrace	54 F3
Deerpark Walk	54 F3
Deerpark Way	54 F3
Del Val Avenue	27 C2
Del Val Court	27 C2 [2]
Delaford Avenue	55 C1
Delaford Drive	55 C1
Delaford Grove	55 C1
Delaford Lawn	55 C1
Delaford Park	55 C1
Delbrook Manor	57 C2
Delbrook Park	57 C2
Delhurst Avenue	21 B1
Delhurst Close	21 B1
Delhurst Mews	21 B1
Delhurst Terrace	21 B1
Delville Road	25 A2
Delvin Road	24 F4 [3]
Delwood Close	22 E3
Delwood Drive	22 E3
Delwood Grove	22 E3
Delwood Lawn	22 E3
Delwood Park	22 E3
Delwood Road	22 E3
Delwood Walk	22 E3
Demesne	26 E3
Denmark Street Great	71 B2
Denville Court	60 D4
Denzille Lane	76 D1
*Derby Square (off Werburgh Street)	75 A1
Dermot O'Hurley Avenue	39 A3
Derravaragh Road	46 E2
Derry Drive	46 D1
Derry Park	46 D1
Derry Road	46 D1
Derrynane Gardens	39 A3
Derrynane Parade	71 B1
Derrynane Square	71 B1
Desmond Avenue	50 D4 [3]
Desmond Cottages	60 F2 [20]
Desmond Street	75 A3
Devenish Road	46 E1
Deverell Place	71 C3
Devery's Lane	25 A4 [4]
Devitt Villas	60 E1 [8]
Devlin's Place	76 D1
Devon Close	59 B1 [11]
Devoy Road	73 B2
Dewberry Park	4 D4
Dexter Terrace	75 C4
Diamond Terrace	67 B2 [15]
Diamond Valley Apts.	67 B2
*"Digges Lane (Longford St, Little)"	75 B1
Digges Street Upper	75 B2
*Dillon Place South (off John Dillon Street)	75 A1
Dillon's Row	17 C2
Dingle Glen	63 A2
Dingle Road	24 E4
Dispensary Lane (Lucan)	34 D1 [6]
Dispensary Lane (Willbrook)	46 F4
Distillery House Apts.	36 E2 [14]
Distillery Lane	20 D4
Distillery Loft Apts.	25 B4 [15]
Distillery Road	25 B4
Diswellstown Cottages	22 E4
Diswellstown Road	22 D3
Dixon Villas	60 E1 [9]
Doctor's Lane	17 C3
Dodder Avenue	55 B2
Dodder Bank	47 B2 [10]
Dodder Court	55 B2
Dodder Crescent	55 B2
Dodder Dale	46 F4
Dodder Green	55 B2
Dodder Lawn	55 B2
Dodder Park Drive	46 F3 [3]
Dodder Park Grove	46 F3
Dodder Park Road	46 F3
Dodder Road Lower	47 A3
Dodder Terrace	39 A3 [18]
Dodder Vale	47 A3 [13]
Dodder View Cottages	76 F3
Dodsboro Cottages	33 B2
Dodsboro Road	33 C2
D'Olier Street	71 C4
Dollymount	27 A4
Dollymount Avenue	27 A4
Dollymount Grove	26 F4
Dollymount Park	27 A4
Dollymount Rise	27 A4
Dolly's Grove	5 C2
Dolmen Court	12 D4
Dolphin Avenue	74 E3
Dolphin Court	73 C3
Dolphin House	74 D3
*Dolphin Market (off Dolphin's Barn St)	74 D3
Dolphin Park	74 D3
Dolphin Road	73 C3
Dolphin's Barn	74 D3
Dolphin's Barn Street	74 D3
Dominick Lane	71 A3
Dominick Place	71 B3
Dominick Street	50 D4
Dominick Street Lower	71 A3
Dominick Street Upper	71 A2
Domville Court	12 E4 [1]
Domville Drive	46 D4
Domville Green	46 D4
Domville Grove	64 E1 [9]
Domville Road	46 D4
Donaghmede	14 F4
Donaghmede Avenue	27 B1
Donaghmede Drive	27 B1
Donaghmede Park	27 B1
Donaghmede Road	27 B1
Donaghmore	18 F3
Donard Road	36 F4
Donnellan Avenue (St Johns Terrace)	73 C1
Donnybrook	47 C1
Donnybrook Castle	47 C1 [24]
Donnybrook Close	48 D2 [2]
Donnybrook Court	47 C2
Donnybrook Green	48 D2 [3]
Donnybrook Manor	47 C1
Donnybrook Mews	47 C1
Donnybrook Road	47 C1
Donnycarney	26 D3
Donnycarney Road	26 D3
Donomore Avenue	54 E2
Donomore Crescent	54 E2
Donomore Green	54 E2
Donomore Park	54 E2
Donore Avenue	74 E2
Donore Road	74 E2
Donore Terrace	74 E2
Donovan Lane	74 F3
Doon Avenue	70 D1
Doon Court	11 C4
Doonamana Road	60 D3
Doonanore Park	60 D3
Doonsalla Drive	60 D3
Doonsalla Park	60 D3
Doreen House Apts.	24 D4 [8]
Doris Street	76 F1
Dornden Park	48 E2
Dorney Court	64 E3
Dorset Lane	71 B1
Dorset Place	71 B1
Dorset Square	71 B1
Dorset Street Lower	71 B1
Dorset Street Upper	71 A2
Double Lane	17 C3
Dowland Road	46 D1
Dowling's Court	72 D4
Downpatrick Road	73 C4
Downpatrick Road	46 E1
Dowth Avenue	24 F4
Doyles Lane	27 A4 [6]
Drapier Green	24 F2 [1]
Drapier Road	24 F2
Drayton Close	49 B4 [16]
Drimnagh	36 F4
Drimnagh Road	45 C1
Drinaghmore	58 F4
Drinagh Park	58 F4
Drinaghmore Avenue	58 F4
Drinaghmore Close	58 F4
Drinaghmore Court	58 F4
Droim na Coille Avenue	34 F2
Droim na Coille Court	34 F2
Droim na Coille Place	34 F2
Dromard Road	36 F4
Dromard Terrace	39 A4 [17]
Dromawling Road	25 C2
Drombawn Avenue	25 C2
Dromcarra Avenue	54 E2
Dromcarra Drive	54 E2
Dromcarra Green	54 D2
Dromcarra Grove	54 E2
Dromeen Avenue	25 C2
Dromheath Avenue	9 B4
Dromheath Drive	9 B4
Dromheath Gardens	9 B4
Dromheath Grove	9 B4
Dromheath Park	9 B4
Dromlee Crescent	25 C2
Dromnanane Park	25 C2 [3]
Dromnanane Road	25 C2 [2]
Dromore Road	73 A4
Druid Court	11 C4
Druid Valley	63 C1
Druid Valley	64 D1
Drumahill	58 D1
Drumalee Avenue	70 D2
Drumalee Court	70 D2
Drumalee Drive	70 D2
Drumalee Grove	70 D2
Drumalee Park	70 D2
Drumalee Road	70 D2
Drumcairn Avenue	54 E1
Drumcairn Drive	54 D1
Drumcairn Gardens	54 D1
Drumcairn Green	54 E1
Drumcairn Park	54 E1
Drumcliffe Drive	24 E4
Drumcliffe Road	24 E4
Drumcondra	25 A4
Drumcondra Park	71 C1
Drumcondra Road Lower	25 B4
Drumcondra Road Upper	25 B3
Drumderg Court	25 C4
Drumfinn Avenue	35 C2
Drumfinn Park	36 D3
Drumfinn Road	36 D2
Drumkeen Manor	60 D3
Drummartin Close	48 D4
Drummartin Crescent	58 D1 [1]
Drummartin Link Road	58 D1
Drummartin Park	58 D1
Drummartin Road	48 D4
Drummartin Terrace	48 D4
Drummond Place (off Mount Drummond Ave)	75 A4
Drumnigh	14 E3
Drumnigh Road	14 E3
Drumnigh Wood	14 E2
*Drury Hall Apts. (Stephen Street Lwr)	75 B1
Drury Street	75 B1
Drynam Avenue	2 E3
Drynam Close	2 E3
Drynam Copse	2 E3
Drynam Court	2 D2
Drynam Crescent	2 E3
Drynam Drive	2 E3
Drynam Glen	2 E3
Drynam Green	2 E3
Drynam Grove	2 E3
Drynam Hall	2 E3
Drynam Mews	2 E3
Drynam Place	2 E4
Drynam Rise	2 E4
Drynam Road	2 D2
Drynam Square	2 E3
Drynam View	2 E3
Drynam Walk	2 E3
Drynam Way	2 E3
Drysdale Close	55 A2
Dualla Court	48 E4
Dubber Cross	11 B3
Dublin Airport	12 E1
Dublin Road (Bray)	67 B1
Dublin Road (Celbridge)	32 D3
Dublin Road (Donaghmore)	18 F3
Dublin Road (Dunboyne)	7 C3
Dublin Road (Kilbarrack)	27 C2
Dublin Road (Malahide)	3 A3
Dublin Road (Maynooth)	18 D3
Dublin Road (Shankill)	64 E3
Dublin Road (Sutton)	29 A1
Dublin Road (Swords)	1 C3
Dublin Street (Baldoyle)	15 A4
Dublin Street (Swords)	15 A4
Duck Lane	70 E4
Dufferin Avenue	74 F3
Duke Lane Lower	75 C1
Duke Lane Upper	75 B1
Duke Row	72 D2
Duke Street	75 B1
Dun Aengus	54 F2
Dun an Oir	54 F2
Dun Emer Drive	57 C1
Dun Emer Park	57 C1
Dun Emer Road	57 C1
Dun Gaoithe	58 E3
Dun Laoghaire	50 D4
Dunard Avenue	69 B1
Dunard Court	69 C1
Dunard Drive	69 C1
Dunard Park	69 C1
Dunard Road	69 C1
Dunard Road	69 C1
Dunard Walk	69 C1
Dunawley Avenue	44 D1
Dunawley Drive	44 D1
Dunawley Grove	44 D1
Dunawley Way	44 D1
Dunbavin Bridge	51 A4
Dunbo Hill	30 D1 [4]
Dunbo Terrace	30 D1 [1]
Dunboy	59 A4
Dunboyne	7 B2
Dunboyne Bridge	7 C3
Dunboyne Road	18 D2
Dunbro Lane	11 C1
Dunbur Terrace	67 C2 [21]
Duncairn Avenue	67 C2
Duncairn Terrace	67 C2
Duncarraig	29 B2
Dundaniel Road	26 D2
Dundela Avenue	60 E1

STREET NAME	PAGE/GRID REFERENCE
Dundela Crescent	60 E1
Dundela Haven	60 E1 [24]
Dundela Park	60 E1
Dundrum	57 C1
Dundrum By Pass	57 C1
Dundrum Gate Apts	57 C1 [9]
Dundrum Road	47 C3
Dundrum Wood	57 B1
Dunedin Court	59 C1
Dunedin Drive	59 C1 [8]
Dunedin Park	59 C1
Dunedin Terrace	59 C1
Dungar Terrace	50 D4 [12]
Dungriffan Road	30 D2
Dungriffan Villas	30 D2 [8]
Dunleary Hill	49 C4
Dunleary Road	49 C4
Dunluce Road	26 E3
Dunmanus Court	24 E4 [4]
Dunmanus Road	24 E4
Dunmore Grove	44 F2
Dunmore Lawn	44 F3
Dunmore Park	44 F2
Dunne Street	72 D2
Dunree Park	26 F1
Dunsandle Court	23 A3
Dunsandle Grove	23 A3
Dunseverick Road	26 E4
Dunsink Avenue	24 D2
Dunsink Drive	24 D2
Dunsink Gardens	24 D2
Dunsink Green	24 D2
Dunsink Lane	23 A2
Dunsink Park	24 D2
Dunsink Road	24 D2
Dunsoghly	23 C1
Dunsoghly Avenue	23 C1
Dunsoghly Close	23 C1
Dunsoghly Court	23 C1
Dunsoghly Drive	23 C1
Dunsoghly Green	23 C1
Dunsoghly Grove	23 C1
Dunsoghly Park	23 C1
Dunstaffnage Hall Apts	58 F1 [6]
Dunville Avenue	47 B1
Durham Place	60 D1 [18]
Durham Road	39 B4
Durrow Road	46 E1
Dursey Row	22 F1
Dwyer Park	67 C1
E	
Eagle Hill	49 A3 [15]
Eagle Hill Avenue	46 F2 [4]
Eagle Park	26 D1
*Eagle Terrace (Dalkey)	60 F2
Eagle Terrace (Dundrum)	57 C1 [3]
Eagle Valley	66 E4
Eaglewood Apts	59 C2 [5]
Eaglewood House	59 C2 [7]
Eaglewood Mews	59 C2 [8]
Earl Place	71 B3
Earl Street North	71 B3
Earl Street South	74 F1
Earls Court	74 D3
Earls Court (Cabra)	69 C1
Earls Court (Terenure)	46 F2 [15]
Earlscroft	67 C4
Earlsfort	34 F3
Earlsfort Avenue	34 F3
Earlsfort Close	34 F3
Earlsfort Court	34 F2
Earlsfort Drive	34 F3
Earlsfort Gardens	34 F2
Earlsfort Green	34 F3
Earlsfort Grove	34 F3
Earlsfort Lane	34 F3
Earlsfort Lawn	34 F2
Earlsfort Meadows	34 F2
Earlsfort Park	34 F2
Earlsfort Rise	34 F3
Earlsfort Road	34 F2
Earlsfort Terrace	75 C3
Earlsfort Vale	34 F3
Earlsfort View	34 F3
Earlsfort Way	34 F3
East Pier (Dun Laoghaire)	50 E3
East Pier (Howth)	30 D1
East Road	72 F3
East Wall	39 A1
East Wall Road	72 F1
East Wall Road (Alexandra Basin)	39 A2
Eastmoreland Court	76 E3
Eastmoreland Lane	76 E3
Eastmoreland Place	76 E3
Easton Park	19 C4
Easton Road	19 B4
Eastwood	23 C2 [1]
Eaton Brae (Orwell Road)	47 A3
Eaton Brae (Shankill)	64 E2
Eaton Close	52 F2
Eaton Court (Bray)	68 D3 [1]
Eaton Court (Terenure)	46 F2 [22]
Eaton Green	52 F2
Eaton Hall	46 F2 [18]
Eaton House	52 F2 [1]
Eaton Place	49 B4
Eaton Road	46 F2
Eaton Square (Monkstown)	49 B4
Eaton Square (Terenure)	46 F2
Eaton Terrace	52 F2
Eaton Way	52 F2
Eaton Wood Avenue	64 E3
Eaton Wood Court	64 E3
Eaton Wood Green	64 E3
Eaton Wood Grove	64 E3
Eaton Wood Square	64 E2
Ebenezer Terrace	74 E2
Eblana Avenue	50 D4
Eblana Villas (Lr Grand Canal St)	76 E1
Eblana Villas (off Arbour Hill)	70 E3
Eccles Court	71 B1
Eccles Place	71 B1
Eccles Street	71 A1
Echlin Street	74 E1
Eden Avenue	57 A1
Eden Court	57 A1
Eden Crescent	57 A1
Eden Grove	57 A1
Eden Park	60 D1
Eden Park Avenue	58 D1
Eden Park Drive	48 D4
Eden Park Road	58 D1
Eden Quay	71 C4
Eden Road Lower	60 D1
Eden Road Upper	60 D1
Eden Terrace (Botanic Ave)	25 A4
Eden Terrace (Dun Laoghaire)	60 D1
Eden Villas	60 D1 [5]
Edenbrook Court	56 F1 [5]
Edenbrook Drive	46 E4
Edenbrook Park	46 E4
Edenmore	26 F2
Edenmore Avenue	26 F1
Edenmore Crescent	27 A2
Edenmore Drive	26 F2
Edenmore Gardens	26 F2
Edenmore Green	26 F2
Edenmore Grove	26 F2
Edenmore Park	26 F2
Edenvale	57 A2
Edenvale Road	47 B1
Edenwood (Goatstown)	48 D4 [1]
Edgewood (Richmond Road)	25 B4 [10]
Edgewood Lawns	22 E1
Edmondsbury Court	34 E1 [1]
Edmondstown	56 E3
Edmondstown Green	56 E2
Edmondstown Road	56 E3
Edward Court	76 D4
Edward Road	68 D3
*Edward Terrace (Off Nerano Rd)	60 F2
Edwards Court	56 E2
Edwin Court	60 E2 [5]
Effra Road	47 A1
Eglington Road	67 C2 [3]
Eglinton Court	47 C1
Eglinton Park (Donnybrook)	47 C1
Eglinton Road	47 C1
Eglinton Square	47 C1 [13]
Eglinton Terrace (Donnybrook)	47 C1
Eglinton Terrace (Dundrum)	47 C4
*Eglinton Terrace (Royal Canal Bank)	71 A2
Eglinton Wood	47 C1 [22]
Eklad Close	13 C4
Eklad Park	13 C4
El Greco Apts.	39 A4 [51]
Elbin House	39 A4 [41]
Elderberry	34 D3
Elderwood Road	35 B2
*Elford Terrace (off Donore Avenue)	74 E2
Elgin Heights	67 A4
Elgin Road	76 E3
Elgin Wood	67 B4
*Elizabeth O'Farrell Park (Lombard Street East)	72 D4
Elizabeth Street	25 B4
Elkwood	56 E1
Ellenfield Road	25 C2
Ellensborough	54 F3
Ellensborough Avenue	54 F3
Ellensborough Close	54 F3
Ellensborough Copse	54 F3
Ellensborough Court	54 F3
Ellensborough Crescent	54 F3
Ellensborough Dale	54 F3
Ellensborough Downs	54 F3
Ellensborough Grange	54 F3
Ellensborough Green	54 F3
Ellensborough Grove	54 F3
Ellensborough Lane	54 F3
Ellensborough Lawn	54 F3
Ellensborough Meadows	54 F3
Ellensborough Park	54 F3
Ellensborough Rise	54 F3
Ellensborough View	54 F3
Ellensborough Walk	54 F3
Ellensborough Way	54 F3
Ellesmere	58 F2 [4]
Ellesmere Avenue	70 D1
Ellis Court	70 E4
Ellis House Apts.	70 F4
Ellis Quay	70 E4
Ellis Street	70 E4
Elm Close	34 E3
Elm Court (Jobstown)	54 D2
Elm Court (Lucan)	34 E3
Elm Dene	34 E3
Elm Drive (Jobstown)	54 D2
Elm Drive (Lucan)	34 E3
Elm Green	34 E3
Elm Grove	49 A4
Elm Grove (Jobstown)	54 D2
Elm Grove (Lucan)	34 E3
Elm House	76 D3
Elm House Apartments	54 D2 [1]
Elm Mount Avenue	25 C2
Elm Mount Close	26 D2
Elm Mount Court	26 D3
Elm Mount Crescent	26 D2
Elm Mount Drive	26 D2
Elm Mount Grove	26 D2
Elm Mount Heights	26 D2
Elm Mount Lawn	26 D2
Elm Mount Park	26 D2
Elm Mount Rise	26 D2
Elm Mount Road	26 D2
Elm Mount View	26 D2
Elm Park (Celbridge)	32 D3
Elm Park (Nutley Lane)	48 D1
Elm Park Terrace	46 F2
Elm Road (Donnycarney)	26 D3
Elm Road (Fox & Geese)	45 A1
Elm Vale	34 E3
Elm Way (Grange Wood)	57 A2 [3]
Elm Way (Lucan)	34 E3
Elm Wood	34 E3
Elmbrook	34 E2
Elmbrook Crescent	34 E2
Elmbrook Lawn	34 E2
Elmbrook Walk	34 E2
Elmcastle Close	45 A3
Elmcastle Court	45 A3
Elmcastle Drive	45 A3
Elmcastle Green	45 A3
Elmcastle Park	45 A3
Elmcastle Walk	45 A3
Elmdale Crescent	35 C3
Elmdale Drive	35 C3
Elmdale Park	35 C3
Elmfield Avenue	14 D4
Elmfield Close	14 D4 [2]
Elmfield Court	14 D4
Elmfield Court (Clondalkin)	44 E1
Elmfield Crescent	14 E4
Elmfield Drive	14 E4
Elmfield Green	14 D4
Elmfield Grove	14 D4
Elmfield Lawn	14 E4
Elmfield Park	14 E4
Elmfield Rise	14 D4
Elmfield Vale	14 E4
Elmfield Walk	14 D4
Elmfield Way	14 D4
Elmgrove	60 D4
Elmgrove Terrace	67 C2 [22]
Elmpark Apts.	48 E2
Elmpark Avenue	47 B1
Elms	48 F3
Elmwood Avenue Lower	47 B1
Elmwood Avenue Upper	47 B1
Elmwood Close	21 B1
Elmwood Court	1 C1 [1]
Elmwood Drive	1 C1
Elmwood Park	1 C1
Elmwood Road	1 C1
Elner Court	4 D4
Elton Court (Coolock)	26 F1 [1]
Elton Court (Dalkey)	60 E1
Elton Court (Dunboyne)	7 B3
Elton Court (Leixlip)	32 F1
Elton Court (Marino)	25 C4 [17]
Elton Drive (Coolock)	27 A1
Elton Drive (Dunboyne)	7 B2
Elton Grove (Dunboyne)	7 B3
Elton Park (Coolock)	27 A1
Elton Park (Dalkey)	60 E1
Elton Walk	27 A1 [1]
Ely Close	55 B3
Ely Crescent	55 B3 [1]
Ely Drive	55 B3
Ely Green	55 B3 [3]
Ely Grove	55 B3 [2]
Ely Place	75 C2
Ely Place Upper	75 C2
Ely View	55 B3
Embassy Lawn	47 C2
Emerald Cottages	76 E3
Emerald Place	72 D3
Emerald Square	74 D2
Emerald Street	72 E3
Emerald Terrace	74 E2
Emily Lawless Court	27 C1 [2]
Emmet Court	73 A2
Emmet Crescent	73 A2
Emmet Place	70 F4
Emmet Road	73 A1
Emmet Square	48 F3
Emmet Street (Harold's Cross)	74 F4
Emmet Street (Nth Circular Rd)	71 C1
Emmet Street (Sallynoggin)	60 D1 [4]
Emor Street	75 A3
Emorville Avenue	75 A3
Empress Place	72 D2
Enaville Avenue (off Annesley Place)	72 E1
Enaville Road	72 E1
Engine Alley (off Meath St)	74 F1
English Row	32 D4
Ennafort Avenue	26 F2
Ennafort Court	26 F3
Ennafort Drive	26 F3
Ennafort Grove	26 F2
Ennafort Park	26 F3
Ennafort Road	26 F3
Ennel Avenue	26 F2
Ennel Court	64 E1 [6]
Ennel Drive	26 F2

STREET NAME	PAGE/GRID REFERENCE		STREET NAME	PAGE/GRID REFERENCE		STREET NAME	PAGE/GRID REFERENCE		STREET NAME	PAGE/GRID REFERENCE	
Ennel Park	26	F2				Ferncarrig Avenue	58	D3	Finglas West	24	D1
Ennis Grove	39	A3 [19]				Ferncarrig Court	58	D3	Finglaswood Road	24	D1
Enniskerry	66	D3	**F**			Ferncarrig Rise	58	D3	Finn Street	70	D3
Enniskerry Bridge	66	E3	Faber Grove	59	B1 [9]	Ferncourt Avenue	55	B3	Finneber Fort	24	E2
Enniskerry Demense	66	E4	Fade Street	75	B1	Ferncourt Close	55	B3	Finneber Fort Square	24	E2
Enniskerry Road (Phibsborough)	25	A4 [3]	Fagan's Lane	17	C3 [2]	Ferncourt Crescent	55	B3 [5]	Finnscourt	34	D3
Enniskerry Road (Sandyford)	58	D4	Fair Haven	3	B2 [1]	Ferncourt Drive	55	B3 [4]	Finnsgreen	34	D3
Erne Place Little	76	D1	Fairacre	2	F3	Ferncourt Green	55	B3	Finnsgrove	34	D3
Erne Place Lower	72	D4	Fairbrook Lawn	46	F4	Ferncourt Park	55	B3	Finnslawn	34	D3
Erne Place(Lansdowne Park)	76	E1	Fairfield Avenue	72	E2	Ferncourt View	55	B3	Finnspark	34	D3
Erne Street Lower	72	D4	Fairfield Court	39	A3 [47]	Ferndale (Hartstown)	21	C1	Finnstown Cloisters	34	D3
Erne Street Upper	76	D1	Fairfield House	46	F2 [24]	Ferndale (Tallaght)	55	A2	Finnstown Fairways	34	D3
Erne Terrace Front	76	D1	Fairfield Park	47	A2	Ferndale Avenue	24	F2	Finnstown Hall	34	D3
Erne Terrace Rere	76	D1	Fairfield Road	25	A4	Ferndale Glen	64	D3	Finnsvale	34	D3
Errigal Gardens	45	C1	Fairgreen	53	A2	Ferndale Hill	64	D4	Finnsview	34	D3
Errigal Road	36	F4	Fairgreen Court	67	C2 [50]	Ferndale Road (Bray)	67	A1	Finnswalk	34	D3
Errigal Road	45	C1	Fairgreen Road	67	B2 [11]	Ferndale Road (Glasnevin)	24	F2	Finnswood	34	D3
Erris Road	24	E4	Fairgreen Terrace	67	C2 [32]	Ferndale Road (Shankill)	64	D3	Finsbury Green	47	B4
Erris Square	22	F1	Fairlawn Park	24	E2	Fernhill Avenue	45	C3	Finsbury House	76	F3
Esker Drive	34	D2	Fairlawn Road	24	E2	Fernhill Park	45	C3	Finsbury Park	47	B4
Esker Glebe	34	D2	Fairlawns	60	E2 [6]	Fernhill Road	45	C2	Firgrove	60	E4 [7]
Esker Lane	34	E2	Fairview Avenue (Ringsend)	39	A3 [49]	Fernleigh	22	D3	Firhouse	55	C1
Esker Lawns	34	D1	Fairview Avenue Lower	25	C4	Fernleigh Close	22	D3	Firhouse Road	55	B2
Esker Lodge	34	E2	Fairview Avenue Upper	25	C4	Fernleigh Court	22	D3	Firhouse Road West	55	A2
Esker Lodge Avenue	34	E2	Fairview Close	25	C4	Fernleigh Crescent	22	D3	First Avenue (Belgard Heights)	44	F4
Esker Lodge Close	34	E2	Fairview Court	25	C4 [14]	Fernleigh Dale	22	D3	First Avenue (Sarsfield Road)	36	F3
Esker Lodge View	34	E2	Fairview Green	25	C4 [7]	Fernleigh Dene	22	D4	First Avenue (Seville Place)	72	E3
Esker Manor	34	E2	Fairview Lawn	64	D1	Fernleigh Drive	22	D3	Fishamble Street	71	A4
Esker Meadow	34	E2	Fairview Passage	25	C4 [10]	Fernleigh Grange	22	D4	Fisherman's Green	3	B2 [6]
Esker Meadow Close	34	E2	Fairview Strand	25	C4	Fernleigh Green	22	D3	Fishermans Wharf	39	A2 [1]
Esker Meadow Court	34	E2	Fairview Terrace	25	C4 [11]	Fernleigh Grove	22	D4	Fitzgerald Park	59	C1 [6]
Esker Meadow Green	34	E2	Fairways	46	E4	Fernleigh Heath	22	D4	Fitzgerald Street	75	A4
Esker Meadow Grove	34	E2	Fairway's Avenue	24	F2	Fernleigh Lawn	22	D3	Fitzgibbon Lane	71	C1
Esker Meadow Lawn	34	E2	Fairway's Green	24	F2	Fernleigh Park	22	D3	Fitzgibbon Street	71	C1
Esker Meadow Rise	34	E2	Fairways Grove	24	F2	Fernleigh Place	22	D3	Fitzmaurice Road (Glasnevin)	24	F2
Esker Meadow View	34	E2	Fairway's Park	24	F2	Fernleigh Vale	22	D3	Fitzmaurice Road (Rathcoole)	52	F2
Esker Park	34	E2	Fairy Castle	61	B2	Fernleigh View	22	D4	Fitzpatrick's Cottages	46	F1 [6]
Esker Pines	34	E1	Fairyhill (Oldcourt)	67	B3	Fernley Court	75	A2	Fitzroy Avenue	25	B4
Esker Road	34	D2	Fairyhill (Stillorgan)	59	A1	Ferns Road	46	E1	Fitzwilliam Court	76	D4
Esker South	34	D3	Faith Avenue	72	E1	Fernvale Drive	46	D1	Fitzwilliam Court	75	C2
Esker Villas	47	A1 [11]	Falcarragh Road	25	B2	Fernwood Avenue	54	E1	(Fitzwilliam Square)		
Esker Woods	34	E2	Falls Road	64	D2	Fernwood Close	54	E1	Fitzwilliam Court	48	E3
Esker Woods Close	34	E2	Farmhill Drive	47	C4	Fernwood Court	54	E1	(Stillorgan Road)		
Esker Woods Court	34	E2	Farmhill Park	47	C4	Fernwood Lawn	54	E1	Fitzwilliam Lane	76	D2
Esker Woods Drive	34	E2	Farmhill Road	47	C4	Fernwood Park	54	E1	Fitzwilliam Place	75	C3
Esker Woods Grove	34	E2	Farmleigh	23	A4	Fernwood Way	54	E1	Fitzwilliam Place North	70	F3
Esker Woods Rise	34	E2	Farmleigh Avenue (Castleknock)	23	A4	Ferrard Road	46	F2	(Grangegorman)		
Esker Woods View	34	E2	Farmleigh Avenue (Stillorgan)	58	F1	Ferrycarrig Avenue	13	B4	Fitzwilliam Point	39	A3 [37]
Esker Woods Walk	34	E2	Farmleigh Close (Castleknock)	23	A4	Ferrycarrig Drive	13	B4	Fitzwilliam Quay	39	A3
Esmond Avenue	25	C4	Farmleigh Close (Stillorgan)	58	F1	Ferrycarrig Green	13	B4 [3]	Fitzwilliam Quay	39	A3 [36]
Esmonde Terrace	67	B2 [18]	Farmleigh Court	23	A4	Ferrycarrig Park	13	B4	Fitzwilliam Square	75	C2
Esplanade Terrace	68	D2 [3]	Farmleigh Park (Castleknock)	23	A4	Ferrycarrig Road	13	B4	Fitzwilliam Square East	76	D2
Esposito Road	45	C1 [5]	Farmleigh Park (Stillorgan)	58	F1	Ferryman's Crossing	72	E3	Fitzwilliam Square North	76	D2
Essex Gate (off Essex Quay)	71	A4	Farmleigh View	23	A4	Fertullagh Road	24	F4 [5]	Fitzwilliam Square South	75	C2
Essex Quay	71	A4	Farmleigh Woods	23	A4	Fettercairn	44	E4	Fitzwilliam Square West	75	C2
Essex Street East	71	A4	Farney Park	39	A4	Fettercairn Road	44	E4	Fitzwilliam Street (Ringsend)	39	A3 [2]
Essex Street West	71	A4	Farnham Crescent	24	E2	Fey Yerra	58	F2 [8]	Fitzwilliam Street Lower	76	D2
(off Fishamble St)			Farnham Drive	24	E2	Fforester	34	E2	Fitzwilliam Street Upper	76	D2
Estate Avenue	48	E1	Farrenboley Cottages	47	B3	Fforester Close	34	E2	Fitzwilliam Terrace	68	D2 [21]
Estate Cottages	76	E2	Farrenboley Park	47	B3	Fforester Court	34	E2	Fleet Street	71	B4
Estate Cottages	76	E2	Farraroe	66	F3	Fforester Drive	34	F2	Fleming Road	25	A3
(Northumberland Rd)			Fassaroe	67	A2	Fforester Lawn	34	E2	Fleming's Hall Apts.	76	D3
Estate Cottages (Shelbourne Rd)	76	F3	Fassaroe Avenue	67	A3	Fforester Park	34	E2	Fleming's Place	76	D3
Estuary Court	2	D1	Fassaroe Glen	67	A2	Fforester Walk	34	E2	Flemingstown Park	47	B4
Estuary Road	2	E1	Fassaroe Lane	67	A3	Fforester Way	34	E2	Flemming House	76	D3
Estuary Road	2	F2	Father Colohan Terrace	67	C2 [11]	Fforster Crescent	34	E2	Fleurville	49	A4
Estuary Roundabout (Swords)	2	D1	Father Kit Court	46	D1 [3]	Field Avenue	45	C1 [1]	Floraville Avenue	44	E1
Estuary Row	3	B2	Father Lemass Court	36	D3	Field's Terrace	47	B1 [5]	Floraville Drive	44	E2
Estuary Walk	2	F2	Father Mathew Square	70	F3	Fieldview Cottages	49	A4 [6]	Floraville Estate	44	E1
Eugene Street	74	E2	Father Mathew Bridge	70	F4	Fiery Lane	62	D4	Floraville Lawn	44	E1
Eustace Street	71	B4	Father Scully House	71	C2	Findlater Building Apts.	30	D1 [3]	Florence Road	67	C2
Everton Avenue	70	D2	Fatima Mansions	74	D2	Findlater Place	71	B3	Florence Street	75	A3
Evora Crescent	30	D1 [12]	(off James's Walk)			Findlater Street (Dun Laoghaire)	60	E1 [7]	Florence Terrace (Bray)	67	C2 [39]
Evora Park	30	D1	Fatima Terrace	67	C2	Findlater Street	70	D3	*Florence Terrace	76	D4
Evora Terrace	30	D1 [2]	Faughart Road	46	E1 [3]	(Nth Circular Rd)			(Leeson Park Avenue)		
Ewington Lane	74	D1	Faulkner's Terrace	73	C1	Fingal Place	70	E2	Florence Villas (Bray)	67	C2 [40]
Exchange Court	71	C4	Faussagh Avenue	24	E4	Fingal Street	74	E2	Florence Villas (Sandymount)	39	A4
Exchange Street Lower	71	A4	Faussagh Road	24	F4	Finglas	24	D1	Flower Grove	60	D2
(off Wood Quay)			Fawn Lodge	23	A4	Finglas East	24	E1	Foley Street	71	C3
Exchange Street Upper	71	A4	Feltrim	3	A4	Finglas Park	24	E1	Fontenoy Street	71	A2
(off Lord Edward St)			Feltrim Hall	2	D3	Finglas Place	24	E2	Fontenoy Terrace	68	D3
Exchequer Street	75	B1	Feltrim Road	2	F4	Finglas Road	24	E2	Fonthill Abbey	56	F1 [3]
Excise Walk	72	E3	Fenian Street	76	D1	Finglas Road Old	24	F3	Fonthill Park	56	F1
Eyre Court	2	E3	Fergus Road	46	F2	Finglas Roundabout (M50 J5)	11	A4	Fonthill Road (Clondalkin)	35	A2
			Ferguson Road	25	A3	Finglas South	24	D2	Fonthill Road (Rathfarnham)	56	F1
			Fernbrook	67	B1 [6]	Finglas Square	48	D3 [2]	Fonthill Road North	35	A3

STREET NAME	PAGE/GRID REFERENCE	STREET NAME	PAGE/GRID REFERENCE	STREET NAME	PAGE/GRID REFERENCE	STREET NAME	PAGE/GRID REFERENCE
Fonthill Road South	44 D2	Foxborough Grove	34 F3	Friarsland Avenue	47 C3 [3]	Gazelle Mews	9 B2
Forbes Lane	74 E2	Foxborough Hall	34 F3 [1]	Friarsland Crescent	47 C3	Gazelle Terrace	9 B2
Forbes Street	72 E4	Foxborough Heights	34 F3	Friarsland Road	47 C3	Gazelle Walk	9 B2
Forest Avenue (Kilnamanagh)	45 A3	Foxborough Hill	34 E3	Friary Avenue	70 F3	Geoffrey Keating Road	74 F2
Forest Avenue (Swords)	1 B3	Foxborough Lane	34 F3	Friary Court	70 F3	George Reynolds Flats	39 A3 [43]
Forest Boulevard	1 B3	Foxborough Lawn	34 F3	Friary Grove	70 F3	*George Reynolds Flats (off	39 A3
Forest Close	45 A3	Foxborough Manor	34 F3	Friel Avenue	36 D4	Oliver Plunkett Ave)	
Forest Court	1 B2	Foxborough Meadows	34 E3	Fumbally Court	75 A2	George's Avenue (Blackrock)	49 A3
Forest Crescent	1 B3	Foxborough Park	34 E3	Fumbally Lane	75 A2	Georges Court	72 D4
Forest Dale	1 B2	Foxborough Place	34 E3	Furry Glen	36 D1	George's Dock	72 D3
Forest Drive (Kilnamanagh)	45 A3	Foxborough Rise	34 E3	Furry Park Court	26 E3	George's Hill	71 A3
Forest Drive (Swords)	1 B3	Foxborough Road	34 E3	Furry Park Road	26 E3	George's Lane	70 F3
Forest Green (Kilnamanagh)	45 A3	Foxborough Row	34 F3	Furze Road (Phoenix Park)	36 E1	George's Place (Blackrock)	49 A3 [6]
Forest Green (Swords)	1 B3	Foxborough Walk	34 F3	Furze Road (Sandyford)	58 E2	George's Place (Dun Laoghaire)	50 D4
Forest Grove	1 B3	Foxborough Way	34 E3			George's Place (Temple Street)	71 B1
Forest Hills (Rathcoole)	52 E2	Foxdene Avenue	34 F3	**G**		George's Quay	71 C4
Forest Hills (Swords)	1 C3	Foxdene Drive	34 F3			Georges Road	24 E1 [1]
Forest Lawn	45 A3	Foxdene Gardens	34 F3	Gables	27 A1 [6]	George's Street Great South	75 B1
Forest Park (Kilnamanagh)	45 A3	Foxdene Green	34 F3	Gaelic Street	72 E2	George's Street Lower	50 D4
Forest Park (Leixlip)	32 F1	Foxdene Grove	34 F3	Gainsborough	2 F3	George's Street Upper	50 D4
Forest Park (Swords)	1 B2	Foxdene Park	34 F3	Gainsborough Avenue	2 F3	Georgian Hamlet	15 A4
Forest Road	1 B4	Foxes Grove	64 E3	Gainsborough Close	2 F3	Georgian Village	23 A4
Forest View	1 B3	Foxe's Lane	27 B2	Gainsborough Court	2 F3	Gerald Street	76 F1
Forest Walk	1 C3	Foxfield	34 D3	Gainsborough Crescent	2 F3	Geraldine Court	17 C3 [4]
Forest Way	1 C3	Foxfield Avenue	27 B2	Gainsborough Downs	2 F3	Geraldine Street	71 A1
Forestfields Road	1 C3	Foxfield Crescent	27 B2	Gainsborough Green	2 F3	Geraldstown Woods Apts	12 D4
Forestwood Avenue	12 D4	Foxfield Drive	27 B2	Gainsborough Lawn	2 F3	Gertrude Terrace	67 B2 [25]
Forestwood Close	12 E4	Foxfield Green	27 B2	Gainsborough Park	2 F3	Gilbert Road	74 F3
Forge Court	30 D2 [15]	Foxfield Grove	27 B2	Gallaun Road	11 C4	Gilford Avenue	39 B4
Forster Way	2 D2	Foxfield Heights	27 B2	Gallery Quay	76 E1	Gilford Court	39 A4 [10]
Fort Ostman	73 C4	Foxfield Lawn	27 B2	Galloping Green	58 F1	Gilford Drive	39 A4
Fortescue Lane	75 B4	Foxfield Park	27 B2	Galloping Green	59 A1 [9]	Gilford Park	39 A4
Fortfield Avenue	46 E3	Foxfield Road	27 B2	Gallows Hill	1 C2	Gilford Pines	39 A4 [46]
Fortfield Court	46 E3 [2]	Foxfield St John	27 B2	Galmoy Road	24 F4	Gilford Place	72 D2
Fortfield Crescent	46 E3	Foxford	34 F2	Galtrim Park	67 C2	Gilford Road	39 A4
Fortfield Drive	46 E3	Foxford Court	34 F2 [2]	Galtrim Road	67 C2	Gilford Terrace	39 B4 [1]
Fortfield Gardens	47 A2	Foxhill Avenue	27 A1	Galtymore Close	36 F4	Giltspur Heights	67 B4
Fortfield Grove	46 E3	Foxhill Close	27 A1	Galtymore Drive	73 B3	Giltspur Lane	67 B4
Fortfield Park	46 E3	Foxhill Court	27 A1	Galtymore Park	36 F4	Giltspur Wood	67 B3
Fortfield Road	46 E2	Foxhill Crescent	27 A1	Galtymore Road	73 B3	Glandore Park	59 C1
Fortfield Road	46 E3	Foxhill Drive	27 A1	Gandon Close	46 F1 [9]	Glandore Road	25 C3
Fortfield Square	46 E3	Foxhill Green	14 D4	Gandon Court	34 D1 [16]	Glasanaon Court	24 E2
Fortfield Terrace	47 A2	Foxhill Grove	27 A1	Gandon Hall	71 C3	Glasanaon Park	24 E2
Forth Road	72 F2	Foxhill Lawn	27 A1	Gandon Mews	34 D1 [10]	Glasanaon Road	24 E2
Forthill Court	56 F1 [6]	Foxhill Park	27 A1	Garda Terrace (Phoenix Park)	69 C3	Glasaree Court	24 E2
Fortlawn Avenue	22 D1	Foxhill Way	27 A1	Garden Lane	74 F1	Glasaree Road	24 E2
Fortlawn Crescent	22 D1	Foxpark	34 D3	Garden Terrace	74 F4	Glasilawn Avenue	24 F2
Fortlawn Drive	22 D1	Foxrock	59 A3	Garden Terrace	74 F3	Glasilawn Road	24 F2
Fortlawn Park	22 D1	Foxrock Avenue	59 A2	(off Clanbrassil St Upper)		Glaslyn	26 D4
Fortlawns	60 E2	Foxrock Close	59 B2	Garden View	75 B4	Glasmeen Road	24 F2
Fortrose Park	46 E4	Foxrock Court	59 A2	Gardiner Lane	71 C2	Glasmore Park	1 C1
Fortunestown	53 C1	Foxrock Crescent	59 B2	Gardiner Place	71 B2	Glasnamana Place	24 F2 [2]
Fortunestown Close	53 C1	Foxrock Green	59 A2	Gardiner Row	71 B2	Glasnamana Road	24 F2
Fortunestown Crescent	53 C1	Foxrock Grove	59 B2	Gardiner St Middle	71 C2	Glasnevin	24 F1
Fortunestown Lane	53 B1	Foxrock Manor	58 F2	Gardiner Street Lower	71 C2	Glasnevin Avenue	24 E3
Fortunestown Road	54 D2	Foxrock Mount	59 A2 [4]	Gardiner Street Upper	71 B1	Glasnevin Court	24 F3
Fortunestown Way	54 D1	Foxrock Park	59 A2	Garnett Hall	7 A2	Glasnevin Downs	25 A1
Fortview Avenue	39 C1	Foxrock Wood	59 B2	Garnett Vale	7 A2	Glasnevin Drive	25 A3
Fortwilliam	48 E4	Foxwood (Lucan)	34 D3	Garnish Square	22 F1	Glasnevin Hill	25 A3
Foster Place North	72 D1	Foxwood (Swords)	2 D2	Garrison Mews	64 D1	Glasnevin North	24 F1
Foster Place South	71 B4	Foyle Road	25 C4	Garrynisk Close	44 F3	Glasnevin Oaks	24 F3 [3]
(College Green)		Frances Ball House	46 F4 [23]	Garrynisk Road	44 F3	Glasnevin Park	24 F1
Foster Terrace	72 D1	Francis Street	74 F1	Garrynure	47 B2	Glasnevin Woods	24 E3
Fosterbrook	48 E2	Frank Sherwin Bridge	70 D4	Garryowen Road	36 E3	Glasson Court	47 B3
Fosters Avenue	48 D3	Frankfort	47 B4 [10]	Gartan Avenue	25 A4	Glasthule Buildings	60 E1 [11]
Fountain Place	70 F3	Frankfort Avenue	47 A2	Gartan Court	2 E1	Glasthule Road	60 E1
Fountain Road	69 C3	Frankfort Cottages	72 D2	Gartan Drive	2 E1	Gleann na Rí	63 C1
Fountain View Apts	74 D1	Frankfort Court	46 F2 [8]	Garter Lane	53 B1	Gleann na Smol (Monkstown)	49 B4
(James's Street)		Frankfort Flats	46 F2 [9]	Garthy Wood Apts.	56 D1	Gleann na Smól (Tallaght)	54 F2
Fourth Avenue (Seville Place)	72 E3	Frankfort Mews	47 B4	Garville Avenue Upper	46 F2	Glebe (Airport)	13 B1
Fourth Avenue (Tallaght)	44 F4	Frankfort Park	47 B4	Garville Court	47 A2 [10]	Glebe (Newcastle)	41 C3
Fownes Street Lower	71 B4	Frascati Court	49 A3 [23]	Garville Drive	47 A2 [6]	Glebe (Rathcoole)	52 D3
(off Temple Bar)		Frascati Hall	49 A3 [24]	Garville Lane	47 A2	Glebe Hall	59 C1
Fownes Street Upper	71 B4	Frascati Park	49 A3	Garville Place	47 A2 [5]	Glebe View (Finglas)	24 E2 [7]
Fox and Geese	45 A1	Frascati Road	49 A3	Garville Road	47 A2	Gledswood Avenue	47 C3
Fox Hill	55 A4	Frederick Court	71 B2	Gas Yard Lane	3 B2	Gledswood Close	47 C3
Foxborough Avenue	34 E3	*Frederick House	75 C1	Gateway Avenue	25 A1	Gledswood Drive	47 C3 [5]
Foxborough Close	34 F3	(Fredrick Street South)		Gateway Court	25 A1	Gledswood Park	47 C3
Foxborough Court	34 F3	Frederick Lane North	71 B2	Gateway Crescent	25 A1	Glen Avenue	59 B3
Foxborough Crescent	34 F3 [2]	Frederick Street North	71 B2	Gateway Gardens	25 A1	Glen Close	59 B3
Foxborough Downes	34 E3	Frederick Street South	75 C1	Gateway Mews	25 A1	Glen Dale	59 B3
Foxborough Drive	34 E3	*French Mullen Flats	75 B3	Gateway Place	25 A1	Glen Drive	59 B3
Foxborough Gardens	34 F3	(Charlemont Street)		Gateway View	25 A1	Glen Druid	64 E1
Foxborough Glade	34 F3	French Park	9 B2	Gaybrook Lawns	3 A3	Glen Ellan Avenue	1 C1
Foxborough Glen	34 F3	Frenchman's Lane	71 C3	Gazelle Avenue	9 B2	Glen Ellan Close	1 C1
Foxborough Green	34 F3	Friar's Walk	44 E1 [5]	Gazelle Lane	9 B2	Glen Ellan Court	1 C1

STREET NAME	PAGE	GRID
Glen Ellan Crescent	1	C1
Glen Ellan Drive	1	C1
Glen Ellan Gardens	1	C1
Glen Ellan Green	1	C1
Glen Ellan Grove	1	C1
Glen Ellan Park	1	C1
Glen Ellan Pines	1	C1
Glen Ellan Walk	1	C1
Glen Garth	59	B3
Glen Grove	59	B3
Glen Lawn Drive	59	B3
Glen na Smol	67	C4
Glen Terrace	60	E1 [10]
Glen Walk	59	B3
Glenaan Road	25	B2
Glenabbey Road	48	E4
Glenacre	62	E4
Glenageary Avenue	60	D2
Glenageary Court	60	D2
Glenageary Hall	60	E2
Glenageary Lodge	60	D2
Glenageary Park	60	D2
Glenageary Road Lower	60	D1
Glenageary Road LR (Dun Laoghaire)	50	D4
Glenageary Road Upper	60	D1
Glenageary Woods	60	D1
Glenalbyn Road	58	F1
Glenalua Heights	60	E3
Glenalua Road	60	E3
Glenalua Terrace	60	E3
Glenamuck Cottages	63	A2
Glenamuck North	62	F1
Glenamuck Road	59	B4
Glenamuck Road	62	F2
Glenamuck Road	63	A1
Glenann	46	F4 [4]
Glenanne	46	E2
Glenard Avenue (Bray)	67	C2
Glenard Avenue (Cabra)	70	D1
Glenard Hall	47	C3 [7]
Glenarm Avenue	25	B4
Glenarriff Road	23	C3
Glenart Avenue	48	F4
Glenaulin	36	D2
Glenaulin Drive	36	D2
Glenaulin Green	35	C2 [2]
Glenaulin Park	36	D2
Glenaulin Road	35	C2
Glenavon Court	25	A3 [18]
Glenavon Park	64	D1
Glenavy Park	46	E2
Glenayle Road	26	F1
Glenayr Road	46	F2
Glenbeigh Park	69	C1
Glenbeigh Road	70	D2
Glenbourne Avenue	58	F4
Glenbourne Close	58	F4
Glenbourne Crescent	58	F4
Glenbourne Drive	58	F4
Glenbourne Green	58	F4
Glenbourne Grove	58	F4
Glenbourne Park	58	F4
Glenbourne Road	58	F4
Glenbourne View	58	F4
Glenbourne Walk	58	F4
Glenbourne Way	58	F4
Glenbower Park	47	B4 [1]
Glenbrae	64	E2
Glenbrian Hall	26	D4 [8]
Glenbrook	66	E3
Glenbrook	67	B3 [6]
Glenbrook Park	46	F4
Glenbrook Road	23	C3
Glenburgh Terrace	67	B2 [2]
Glencairn	58	E3
Glencairn Avenue	58	E3
Glencairn Chase	58	E3
Glencairn Close	58	E3
Glencairn Copse	58	E4
Glencairn Court	58	E4
Glencairn Crescent	58	E4
Glencairn Dale	58	E3
Glencairn Drive	58	E3
Glencairn Garth	58	E3 [1]
Glencairn Glade	58	E4
Glencairn Glen	58	F4
Glencairn Green	58	E3
Glencairn Grove	58	F4
Glencairn Heath	58	E3
Glencairn Heights	58	E3
Glencairn Lawn	58	E3
Glencairn Oaks	58	E4
Glencairn Park	58	E3
Glencairn Place	58	E4
Glencairn Rise	58	E3
Glencairn Road	58	E3
Glencairn Thicket	58	F3
Glencairn View	58	E3
Glencairn Walk	58	E3
Glencairn Way	58	E3
Glencar Road	69	C2
Glencarr Court	64	E1 [8]
Glencarr Lawn	64	E1
Glencarraig	29	B1
Glencarrig Court	55	B2
Glencarrig Drive	55	B2
Glencarrig Green	55	B2
Glencarthy Court Apts.	26	D3
Glencloy Road	25	B2
Glencorp Road	25	C2
Glencourt Estate	67	C3
Glencullen	61	C3
Glencullen	62	E4
Glencullen Bridge	65	B1
Glendale	20	D4
Glendale Drive	67	C3
Glendale Meadows	20	E4
Glendale Park	46	D3
Glendalough Road	25	A4 [6]
Glendenning Lane (off Wicklow Street)	75	B1
Glendhu Park	23	C3
Glendhu Road	23	C3
Glendinning Lane	75	B1
Glendoher Avenue	56	F1
Glendoher Close	56	E1
Glendoher Drive	56	F1
Glendoher Park	56	E1
Glendoher Road	56	E1
Glendoo Close	45	B3
Glendown Avenue	46	D3
Glendown Close	46	D3
Glendown Court	46	D3
Glendown Crescent	46	D3
Glendown Drive	46	D3
Glendown Green	46	D3
Glendown Grove	46	D3
Glendown Lawn	46	D3
Glendown Park	46	D3
Glendown Road	46	D3
Glendun Road	25	B2
Glenealy Downs	8	F4
Glenealy Road	74	D4
Gleneaston	19	B4
Gleneaston Avenue	19	B4
Gleneaston Close	19	B4
Gleneaston Crescent	19	B4
Gleneaston Drive	19	B4
Gleneaston Gardens	19	B4
Gleneaston Green	19	B4
Gleneaston Grove	19	B4
Gleneaston Lawns	19	B4
Gleneaston Manor	19	B4
Gleneaston Park	19	B4
Gleneaston Rise	19	B4
Gleneaston Square	19	B4
Gleneaston View	19	B4
Gleneaston Way	19	B4
Gleneaston Woods	19	B4
Glenesk Court	39	A4 [32]
Glenfarne Road	26	F1
Glenfield Avenue	35	A2
Glenfield Close	35	A2
Glenfield Drive	35	A2
Glenfield Grove	35	A2
Glenfield Park	35	A2
Glengara Close	60	D1 [15]
Glengara Park	60	D1
Glengariff Parade	71	A1
Glengarriff Crescent	71	B1
Glengarriff Parade	71	B1
Glenhill Avenue	24	E2
Glenhill Court	24	E2
Glenhill Drive	24	E2
Glenhill Grove	24	E2
Glenhill Road	24	E2
Glenhill Villas	24	E2 [2]
Glenlucan	67	B2
Glenlyon Crescent	55	C2
Glenlyon Grove	55	C2
Glenlyon Park	55	C2
Glenmalure Park	73	C2
Glenmalure Square	47	B2
*Glenmalure Villas	74	D2
Glenmaroon Park	35	C2
Glenmaroon Road	35	C2
Glenmore	8	E1
Glenmore Court	56	F2
Glenmore Park	56	F2
Glenmore Road	69	C1
Glenmurry Park	45	C3
Glenomena Grove	48	E2
Glenomena Park	48	E2
Glenpark Close	35	B1
Glenpark Drive	35	B1
Glenpark Road	35	B1
Glenshane Close	54	D1
Glenshane Crescent	54	D1
Glenshane Dale	54	D1 [5]
Glenshane Drive	54	D1
Glenshane Gardens	54	D1
Glenshane Green	54	D1
Glenshane Grove	54	D1
Glenshane Lawns	54	D1
Glenshane Park	54	D1
Glenshane Place	54	D1 [6]
Glenshesk Road	25	C2
Glenside Villas	35	C1 [2]
Glenthorn	67	B4
Glenties Drive	24	D2
Glenties Park	24	D2
Glentow Road	25	B2
Glentworth Park	27	A1 [2]
Glenvale	34	E3
Glenvar Park	48	F3
Glenvara Park	55	C2
Glenview (Enniskerry)	66	D3
Glenview (Rochestown Avenue)	60	D3
Glenview Drive	55	B1
Glenview Lawns	55	B1
Glenview Park	55	B1
Glenville Avenue	22	E2
Glenville Court	22	E3
Glenville Drive	22	E3
Glenville Garth	22	E3
Glenville Green	22	E2
Glenville Grove	22	E2
Glenville Lawn	22	E2
Glenville Road	22	E3
Glenville Terrace	47	C4 [8]
Glenville Way	22	E2
Glenwood	67	B2
Glenwood Road	26	F1
Glin Avenue	13	B4
Glin Close	13	B4 [6]
Glin Court	13	B4 [7]
Glin Crescent	13	B4
Glin Drive	13	B4
Glin Grove	13	B4
Glin Park	13	B4
Glin Road	13	B4
Glitspur Brook	67	C3
Gloucester Diamond	71	C2
Gloucester Lane (off Sean McDermott Street Lower)	71	C2
Gloucester Place	71	C2
Gloucester Place Lower	71	C2
Gloucester Place Lower	71	C2
Gloucester Place Upper	71	C2
Gloucester Street South	72	D4
Glovers Alley	75	B1
Glovers Court (off York Street)	75	B1
Goatstown	48	D4
Goatstown Avenue	47	C4
Goatstown Road	47	C4
Gobán Saor	58	E4
Godfrey Place (off Oxmanstown Road)	70	D2
Gofton Hall	24	E1 [2]
Golden Ball	62	F2
Golden Lane	75	A1
Goldenbridge Avenue	73	B2
Goldenbridge Gardens	73	A2
Goldenbridge Terrace	73	A2
Goldenbridge Walk	36	F4
Goldenbridge Walk	73	A2
Goldsmith Hall Apts.	72	D4
Goldsmith Street	71	A1
Goldsmith Terrace	67	C2 [25]
Goldstone Court Apts.	74	D4
Golf Links Road	15	A2
Gordon Avenue	59	A3
Gordon Place	75	B3
Gordon Street	76	F1
Gorsefield Court	26	F2 [1]
Gort na Mona Drive	59	B3
Gortbeg Avenue	24	E3
Gortbeg Drive	24	E3
Gortbeg Park	24	E3
Gortbeg Road	24	E3
Gortmore Avenue	24	E2
Gortmore Drive	24	E2
Gortmore Park	24	E3
Gortmore Road	24	E3
Gosworth Park	60	E1
Gowrie Park	60	D1
Grace O'Malley Drive	30	D2
Grace O'Malley Road	30	D2
Grace Park Avenue	25	B4
Grace Park Court	25	C2
Grace Park Gardens	25	B4
Grace Park Heights	25	C3
Grace Park Lawns	25	C2 [9]
Grace Park Manor	25	B3
Grace Park Meadows	25	C3
Grace Park Road	25	C3
Grace Park Terrace	25	C3
Gracefield Avenue	26	F2
Gracefield Road	26	E2
Grafton Street	75	B1
Graham Court	71	B2
Graham's Row	71	A2
Graigue Court	11	C4
Granby Lane	71	A2
Granby Place	71	B3
Granby Row	71	A2
Grand Canal Docks	76	F1
Grand Canal Place	74	E1
Grand Canal Quay	76	E1
Grand Canal Street Lower	76	E1
Grand Canal Street Upper	76	E2
Grand Canal View	73	B2
Grand Parade	75	C3
Grange (Malahide)	14	E1
Grange (Meath)	6	E4
Grange Abbey Crescent	14	E4
Grange Abbey Drive	14	E4
Grange Abbey Grove	14	E4
Grange Abbey Road	14	E4
Grange Avenue	14	F4
Grange Brook	56	F2
Grange Close (Kilbarrack)	27	C1
Grange Close (Pottery Road)	59	C3
Grange Cottages	58	F1 [3]
Grange Court	57	A1
Grange Crescent	59	B2
Grange Downs	57	A1
Grange Drive	27	C1
Grange Grove	59	B1 [2]
Grange Hall	57	B3
Grange Hall Apts.	27	A2
Grange Lodge Avenue	14	D4
Grange Lodge Court	14	D4
Grange Manor	34	D3
Grange Manor Avenue	57	A1
Grange Manor Close	57	A1
Grange Manor Drive	57	A1
Grange Manor Grove	57	A1
Grange Manor Road	57	A1
Grange Parade	27	C1
Grange Park (Baldoyle)	14	F4
Grange Park (Cornelscourt)	59	B2

STREET NAME	PAGE/GRID REFERENCE
Grange Park (Willbrook)	56 F1
Grange Park Avenue	27 A2
Grange Park Close	27 B2
Grange Park Crescent	27 B2
Grange Park Drive	27 A2
Grange Park Green	27 B2
Grange Park Grove	27 A2
Grange Park Rise	27 B1
Grange Park Road	27 A2
Grange Park View	27 B1
Grange Park Walk	27 A2
Grange Rise	14 F4
Grange Road (Baldoyle)	14 F4
Grange Road (Marley Park)	57 A2
Grange Road (Rathfarnham)	46 F4
Grange Road (The Priory)	56 F1
Grange Terrace	59 B1 [6]
Grange View Close	43 B1
Grange View Court	43 B1
Grange View Green	43 B1
Grange View Grove	43 B1
Grange View Lawn	43 B1
Grange View Park	43 B1
Grange View Road	43 B1
Grange View Walk	43 B1
Grange View Way	43 B1
Grange View Wood	43 B1
Grange Way	27 C1
Grange Wood (Ballinteer)	57 A2
Grangebrook Avenue	56 F2
Grangebrook Close	56 F2
Grangebrook Park	56 F2
Grangebrook Vale	56 F2
Grangefield	57 B3
Grangegorman Lower	70 F3
Grangegorman Upper	70 F2
Grangegorman Villas (Grangegorman Upper)	70 F2
Grangemore	14 E4
Grangemore Avenue	14 D4
Grangemore Court	14 D4
Grangemore Crescent	14 D4
Grangemore Drive	14 E4
Grangemore Grove	14 E4
Grangemore Lawn	14 E4
Grangemore Park	14 E4
Grangemore Rise	14 D4
Grangemore Road	14 D4
Grangeway	59 C1
Granite Hall	60 D1 [7]
Granite Place	76 F4
Granite Terrace	36 F3 [11]
Granitefield	59 C3
Granitefield	60 D3
Granitefield Manor	59 C3
Granitefield Mews	59 C3
Grantham Place	75 B3
Grantham Street	75 A3
Grants Avenue (Greenogue Ind Est)	42 E4
Grants Court (Greenogue Ind Est)	42 E4
Grants Cresents (Greenogue Ind Est)	42 E4
Grants Drive (Greenogue Ind Est)	42 E4
Grants Hill (Greenogue Ind Est)	42 E4
Grants Lane (Greenogue Ind Est)	42 F4
Grants Park (Greenogue Ind Est)	42 E4
Grants Place (Greenogue Ind Est)	42 E4
Grants Rise (Greenogue Ind Est)	42 E4
Grants Road (Greenogue Ind Est)	42 E4
Grant's Row	76 D1
Grants Row (Greenogue Ind Est)	42 E4
Grants View (Greenogue Ind Est)	42 E4
Grants Way (Greenogue Ind Est)	42 E4
Granville Close	60 D3
Granville Crescent	60 D3 [2]
Granville Park	59 A1
Granville Road (Cabinteely)	59 C3
Granville Road (Deans Grange)	59 A2
Grattan Bridge	71 A4
Grattan Court	31 C4
Grattan Court	76 E1
Grattan Court East	76 E1
Grattan Crescent	36 F3
Grattan Hall	14 E4
Grattan Lodge	14 E4
Grattan Parade	25 A4
Grattan Place	76 E1
Grattan Street	76 E1
Gravel Walk Church Apts. (off Hendrick Street)	70 E4
Gray Square	74 F1
Gray Street (off Meath St)	74 F1
Great Western Avenue	70 F1
Great Western Square	70 F1
Great Western Villas	70 F1
Greeg Court	71 B3
Greek Street	71 A4
Green Acre Court	56 D1
Green Court View Apts.	71 A3
Green Isle Court	44 D2 [2]
Green Lane (Celbridge)	31 A2
Green Lane (Leixlip)	19 C4
Green Lane (Rathcoole)	52 E2
Green Park (Rathgar)	47 B3
Green Park Road	67 B2
Green Road (Blackrock)	48 F3
Green Street	71 A3
Green Street East	72 F4
Green Street Little	71 A3
Greencastle Avenue	26 E1
Greencastle Crescent	26 E1
Greencastle Drive	13 B4
Greencastle Parade	26 F1
Greencastle Park	13 B4
Greencastle Road	13 B4
Greendale Avenue	27 C2
Greendale Court	27 B2 [2]
Greendale Road	27 B2
Greenfield Close	17 C4
Greenfield Crescent	48 D2
Greenfield Drive	18 D4
Greenfield Manor	48 D2 [4]
Greenfield Park (Ballycullen Road)	55 C2
Greenfield Park (Stillorgan Road)	48 D2
Greenfield Place (off Mount Drummond Ave)	75 A4
Greenfield Road (Mount Merrion)	48 E4
Greenfield Road (Sutton)	29 B1
Greenfort Avenue	35 A2
Greenfort Close	35 A2
Greenfort Crescent	35 A2
Greenfort Drive	35 A2
Greenfort Gardens	35 A2
Greenfort Lawns	35 A2
Greenfort Park	35 A2
Greenfort Walk	35 A2
Greenhills	45 B3
Greenhills Court	55 A1
Greenhills Road	45 A4
Greenisle Road	42 C3
Greenlands	58 D2
Greenlawns	13 B4 [1]
Greenlea Avenue	46 E2
Greenlea Drive	46 E2
Greenlea Grove	46 E2
Greenlea Park	46 E3
Greenlea Place	46 F2 [12]
Greenlea Road	46 E3
Greenmount Avenue	74 F4
Greenmount Court	74 F4
Greenmount Lane	74 F4
Greenmount Lawns	46 F2
Greenmount Lodge	62 F2
Greenmount Road	46 F2
Greenmount Square	74 F4
Greenoge	42 F4
Greenogue Drive	52 F2
Greenore Court	76 E1
Greenore Terrace	76 E1
Greenpark Road	33 C2
Greenridge Court	22 E1
Greentrees Drive	45 C2
Greentrees Park	45 C2
Greentrees Road	45 C2
Greenview	14 E2
Greenville Avenue	74 F3
Greenville Parade (Blackpitts)	74 F3
Greenville Place	74 F3
Greenville Road	49 B4
Greenville Terrace	74 F3
Greenwood	13 C1
Greenwood Avenue	14 D4
Greenwood Close	14 D4
Greenwood Court	14 D4
Greenwood Drive	14 D4
Greenwood Park	14 D4
Greenwood Walk	14 D4
Greenwood Way	14 D4
Grenville Lane	71 B2
Grenville Street	71 B2
Greygates	48 E3
Greygates	48 E4 [1]
Grey's Lane	30 D2
Greythorn Park	60 D1
Griannan Fidh	58 D3
Griffeen	34 E3
Griffeen Avenue	34 D3
Griffeen Glen Avenue	34 E3
Griffeen Glen Boulevard	34 E3
Griffeen Glen Chase	34 E3
Griffeen Glen Close	34 E3
Griffeen Glen Court	34 E3
Griffeen Glen Court Yard	34 E3
Griffeen Glen Crescent	34 E3
Griffeen Glen Dene	34 E3
Griffeen Glen Drive	34 E3
Griffeen Glen Green	34 E3
Griffeen Glen Grove	34 E3
Griffeen Glen Lawn	34 E3
Griffeen Glen Park	34 E3
Griffeen Glen Road	34 E3
Griffeen Glen Vale	34 E3
Griffeen Glen View	34 E3
Griffeen Glen Way	34 E3
Griffeen Glen Wood	34 D3
Griffeen Road	34 E3
Griffeen Way	34 E2
Griffin Rath Hall	18 D4
Griffin Rath Manor	18 D4
Griffin Rath Road	18 D4
Griffith Avenue	25 B3
Griffith Bridge	73 B2
Griffith Close	24 F2
Griffith Court	25 C4
Griffith Crescent	24 F2
Griffith Downs	25 B3
Griffith Drive	24 F2
Griffith Hall	25 C3
Griffith Heights	24 F2
Griffith Lawns	25 A3
Griffith Parade	24 F2
Griffith Road	24 F2
Griffith Square	74 F3
Grosvenor Avenue	68 D3 [3]
Grosvenor Court (Clontarf)	26 E4
Grosvenor Court (Templeville Road)	46 D3
Grosvenor Lane	47 A1
Grosvenor Lodge	47 A1
Grosvenor Park	47 A1 [7]
Grosvenor Place	47 A1
Grosvenor Road	47 A1
Grosvenor Square	47 A1
Grosvenor Terrace (Dalkey)	60 F2 [17]
Grosvenor Terrace (Dun Laoghaire)	49 C4 [9]
*Grosvenor Villas (Off Sorrento Rd)	60 F2
Grosvenor Villas (Rathmines)	47 A1
Grotto Avenue	48 F2
Grotto Place	48 F2
Grove Avenue (Finglas)	24 E1
Grove Avenue (Harold's Cross)	75 A4
Grove Avenue (Malahide)	3 C3
Grove Avenue (Mount Merrion)	48 F4
Grove Court	22 D1
Grove Court (Bluebell)	36 F4 [4]
Grove Court (Brackenstown Road)	1 A2 [1]
Grove Court Apts.	22 D1
Grove House Apts.	59 A3
Grove House Gardens	48 F4 [5]
Grove Lane	13 C4
Grove Lawn	3 C3
Grove Lawn (Stillorgan)	48 F4
Grove Lawns (Malahide)	3 C3
Grove Paddock	48 F4
Grove Park (Coolock)	13 C4
Grove Park (Rathmines)	75 B4
Grove Park Avenue	24 F1
Grove Park Crescent	24 F1
Grove Park Drive	24 F1
Grove Park Road	24 F1
Grove Road (Blanchardstown)	22 D2
Grove Road (Finglas)	24 E1
Grove Road (Malahide)	3 C3
Grove Road (Rathmines)	75 A4
Grove Wood (Finglas)	24 E1
Grove Wood (Foxrock)	59 A3
Grovedale	63 B2
Guild Street	72 E3
Guilford Terrace	64 E3 [1]
Gulistan Cottages	47 A1
Gulistan Place	47 A1
Gulistan Terrace	47 A1
Gunny Hill	55 C3
Gurteen Avenue	36 D3
Gurteen Park	36 D3
Gurteen Road	36 D2

H

STREET NAME	PAGE/GRID REFERENCE
Hacketsland	64 E1
Haddington Lawns	60 E2
Haddington Park	60 E2
Haddington Place	76 E2
Haddington Road	76 E2
Haddington Terrace	50 D4 [7]
Haddon Court	39 B1 [2]
Haddon Park	26 D4 [5]
Haddon Road	26 E4
Hadleigh Court	23 A3
Hadleigh Green	23 A3 [2]
Hadleigh Park	23 A3
Hagan's Court	76 D2
Haigh Terrace	50 D4
Hainault Drive	59 B3
Hainault Grove	59 B3
Hainault Lawn	59 B3
Hainault Park	59 A3
Hainault Road	59 A3
Halfpenny or Liffey Bridge	71 B4
Halliday Road	70 E3
Halliday Square	70 D3
Hallscourt	67 C2
Halston Street	71 A3
Hamilton Court (Dunboyne)	7 B3 [2]
Hamilton Court (off Strand St Little)	71 A4
Hamilton Hall	7 B3
Hamilton Street	74 E3
Hammond Lane	70 F4
Hammond Street	74 F2
Hampstead Avenue	25 A2
Hampstead Court	25 A2
Hampstead Park	25 A3
Hampton Court	76 E4
Hampton Court (Clontarf)	26 F4
Hampton Court (Tyreconnell Road)	36 F3 [16]
Hampton Crescent	48 E3
Hampton Green	69 B1
Hampton Park	48 E3
Hampton Square	69 C1
Hampton Wood	11 C4
Hampton Wood Avenue	11 B4
Hampton Wood Court	11 C4
Hampton Wood Crescent	11 B4
Hampton Wood Drive	11 C4
Hampton Wood Green	11 B4
Hampton Wood Lawn	11 C4

STREET NAME	PAGE/GRID REFERENCE	STREET NAME	PAGE/GRID REFERENCE	STREET NAME	PAGE/GRID REFERENCE	STREET NAME	PAGE/GRID REFERENCE
Hampton Wood Park	11 B4	Harty Avenue	45 C1	Hazelwood Court (Beaumont)	26 D1	Hermitage Park (Lucan)	34 F1
Hampton Wood Road	11 B4	Harty Court	45 C1 [8]	Hazelwood Court (Hartstown)	21 C1	Hermitage Place	34 F1
Hampton Wood Square	11 C4	Harty Court (off Daniel Street)	75 A2	Hazelwood Crescent (Bray)	67 B2	Hermitage Road	34 F1
Hampton Wood Way	11 C4	Harty Place	75 A2	Hazelwood Crescent	44 D2	Hermitage Valley	34 F1
Hamwood	6 F3	Harvard	48 D3	(Clondalkin)		Hermitage View	56 F1
Hanbury Court	74 F1	Hastings Street	76 F1	Hazelwood Crescent (Hartstown)	21 C1	Hermitage Way	34 F1
*Hanbury Hall (Hanbury Lane)	74 F1	Hastings Terrace	60 E1 [12]	Hazelwood Drive	26 D2	Heronford Lane	63 C2
Hanbury Lane (Lucan)	34 D1 [3]	Hatch Lane	75 C3	Hazelwood Green	21 C1	Heuston Square	73 A1
Hanbury Lane (The Coombe)	74 F1	Hatch Place	75 C3	Hazelwood Grove	26 E1	Hewardine Terrace	72 D2
*Hanbury Mews (Hanbury Lane)	74 F1	Hatch Street Lower	75 C3	Hazelwood House	75 B4	(off Killarney Street)	
Hanlon's Lane	61 B1	Hatch Street Upper	75 B3	Hazelwood Lane	44 D2	Heytesbury Court	76 E3
Hannaville Park	46 F2	Hatter's Lane	74 F4	Hazelwood Park	26 D1	Heytesbury Lane	76 E4
*Hanover Lane	71 A1	Havelock Square	76 F2	Hazelwood View	44 D2	Heytesbury Street	75 A3
Hanover Quay	72 F4	Havelock Terrace	39 A3 [17]	Hazlebury Park	8 E4	Hibernian Avenue	72 E2
Hanover Square	75 A1	Haven View	3 B2 [2]	Headford Grove	47 B4	Hibernian Terrace	36 E2 [3]
Hanover Street East	72 D4	Haverty Road	25 C4	Healthfield Road	46 F2	High Park	25 C2
Hanover Street West	74 F1	Hawkins Street	71 C4	Healy Street	71 C2	High Street (Christ Church)	75 A1
Hansfield	8 E4	Hawkridge	33 B2	(off Rutland Place North)		High Street (Tallaght)	55 A1 [2]
Hansted Close	34 D4	Hawthorn Avenue	72 E2	Heaney Avenue	35 C4	Highdownhill	51 C1
Hansted Crescent	34 D4	Hawthorn Drive	57 B1 [2]	Heany Avenue	60 F2 [19]	Highfield Avenue (Dundrum)	57 A2
Hansted Dale	34 D4	Hawthorn Lawn	22 F3	Heath Square	24 E1 [3]	Highfield Close	1 C2
Hansted Drive	34 D4	Hawthorn Lodge	22 F3	Heather Close	57 A2	Highfield Court	47 A2 [3]
Hansted Park	34 D4	Hawthorn Lodge	23 A4	Heather Drive	57 A2	Highfield Crescent	1 C2
Hansted Place	34 D4	Hawthorn Manor	59 A1 [4]	Heather Gardens	4 D4	Highfield Downs	1 C2
Hansted Road	34 D4	Hawthorn Park	1 C2	Heather Grove (Ballinteer)	57 B2	Highfield Drive	57 A2
Hansted Way	34 D4	Hawthorn Road (Bray)	67 B1	Heather Grove (Palmerston)	35 B2	Highfield Green	1 C2
Harbour Court	71 C4	Hawthorn Road (Clondalkin)	44 F1	Heather Lawn	57 A2	Highfield Grove	47 A2
Harbour Crescent	60 F1	Hawthorn Terrace	72 E2	Heather Park	57 B2	Highfield Lawn	1 C2
Harbour Master Place	72 D3	Hawthorn View	32 D2	Heather Road (Ballinteer)	57 A2	Highfield Manor	47 A2
Harbour Road (Dalkey)	60 F1	Hawthorns Road	58 D2	Heather Road (Burton Hall)	58 E2	Highfield Park (Celbridge Road)	33 A1
Harbour Road (Dun Laoghaire)	50 D4	Hayden Square	48 D3 [3]	Heather View Avenue	54 F2	Highfield Park (Churchtown)	47 B3
Harbour Road (Howth)	30 D1	Hayden's Lane	34 D3	Heather View Close	54 F2	Highfield Road	47 A2
Harbour Square	50 D4	Haydens Park	34 D3	Heather View Drive	54 F2	Highland Avenue	59 B3
Harbour Terrace	49 C4 [8]	Haydens Park Avenue	34 D3	Heather View Lawn	54 F2	Highland Grove	59 B3
Harbour View (Dún Laoghaire)	50 D4	Haydens Park Close	34 D3	Heather View Park	54 F2	Highland Lawn	59 B3
Harbour View (Howth)	30 D1 [6]	Haydens Park Dale	34 D3	Heather View Road	54 F2	Highland View	59 B3
Harcourt Green	75 B3	Haydens Park Drive	34 D3	Heather Walk	4 D4	Highridge Green	58 E1
Harcourt Hall	75 B3	Haydens Park Glade	34 D3	Heatherwood	67 B4	Highthorn Park	59 C1
Harcourt Lane	75 B3	Haydens Park Green	34 D3	Heathfield	49 B4 [17]	Highthorn Woods	59 C1 [10]
Harcourt Lodge	73 B2	Haydens Park Grove	34 D3	*Heatley Villas (on Pearse Road)	59 C2	Hill Cottages	60 E3 [1]
Harcourt Place	75 B3	Haydens Park Lawn	34 D3	Heidelberg	48 D3	Hill Court	14 F1
Harcourt Road	75 B3	Haydens Park View	34 D3	Hempenstal Terrace	39 B4 [5]	Hill Crest	3 C4
Harcourt Street	75 B2	Haydens Park Walk	34 D3	Hendrick Place	70 E4	Hill Drive	3 B3
Harcourt Terrace	75 C3	Haydens Park Way	34 D3	Hendrick Street	70 F4	Hill Street	71 B2
*Harcourt Villas	47 C3	Haymarket	70 F4	Henley Court	47 B4 [8]	Hill View	57 B1
(off Dundrum Rd/Mulvey Pk)		Haymarket House	70 F4	Henley Park	47 B4	Hillbrook Woods	22 D1
Hardebeck Avenue	45 C1	Haymarket Way	70 F4	Henley Villas	47 B4	Hillcourt	47 A2
Hardiman Road	25 A3	*Hayworth Close	21 B1	Henrietta Lane	71 A2	Hillcourt Park	60 D2
Hardwicke Arch	71 B2	Hayworth Court	21 B1	Henrietta Place	71 A3	Hillcourt Road	60 D2
(off Hardwicke St)		Hayworth Drive	21 B1	Henrietta Street	71 A3	Hillcrest (Lucan)	34 D2
Hardwicke Lane	71 B2	Hayworth Mews	21 A1	Henry Place	71 B3	Hillcrest (Malahide)	3 A2 [1]
Hardwicke Place	71 B2	Hayworth Place	21 A1	Henry Road	36 D4	Hillcrest (Rathgar)	47 A2
Hardwicke Street	71 B2	Hayworth Rise	21 A1	Henry Street	71 B3	Hillcrest (Templeogue)	46 D4 [1]
Harelawn Avenue	35 A3	Hayworth Terrace	21 A1	Herbert Avenue	48 E1	Hillcrest Avenue	33 C2
Harelawn Crescent	35 A3	Hazel Avenue	58 D1	Herbert Cottages	76 F3	Hillcrest Close	33 C2
Harelawn Drive	35 A2	Hazel Court	14 F2 [7]	Herbert Court	39 A4 [48]	Hillcrest Court	25 A3 [19]
Harelawn Green	35 A3	Hazel Grove	14 F2	Herbert Crescent	22 F2 [1]	Hillcrest Court	34 D2
Harelawn Grove	35 A2	Hazel Lawn (Blanchardstown)	22 E2	Herbert House	76 E1	Hillcrest Downs	58 D3
Harelawn Park	35 A2	Hazel Lawn (Kill O'The Grange)	59 C2 [4]	Herbert Lane	76 D2	Hillcrest Drive	33 C2
Harlech Crescent	48 D3	Hazel Park	46 E2 [2]	Herbert Park (Ballsbridge)	76 F4	Hillcrest Green	33 C2
Harlech Downs	47 C3	Hazel Road	26 D3	Herbert Park (Oldcourt)	67 B3	Hillcrest Grove	34 D2
Harlech Grove	48 D3	Hazel Villas	58 D1	Herbert Park Lane	76 F4	Hillcrest Heights	33 C2
Harlech Villas	47 C3 [4]	Hazelbrook (Kilmacud)	58 D1	Herbert Park Mews	47 C1	Hillcrest Lawns	33 C2
Harmac Court	46 F2	Hazelbrook (Malahide)	14 E1	Herbert Place	76 D2	Hillcrest Manor	46 D4 [2]
Harman Street	74 E2	Hazelbrook (Tymon North)	45 B4	(Baggot Street Lower)		Hillcrest Park (Glasnevin)	24 F2
Harmoney Court	76 E1	Hazelbrook Apts.	46 E2 [7]	*Herbert Place (off Bath St)	39 A3	Hillcrest Park (Lucan)	33 C2
Harmonstown Road	26 F2	Hazelbrook Court	46 E2	Herbert Road (Blanchardstown)	22 F2	Hillcrest Road (Lucan)	34 D2
Harmony Avenue	47 C1 [5]	Hazelbrook Drive	46 E2	Herbert Road (Oldcourt)	67 B3	Hillcrest Road (Sandyford)	58 D3
Harmony Court	47 C1 [20]	Hazelbrook Road	46 E2	Herbert Road (Sandymount)	39 A4	Hillcrest View	33 C2
Harmony Row	76 D1	Hazelbury Green	8 E4	Herbert Street	76 D2	Hillcrest Walk	33 C2
Harold Bridge Court	74 F4	Hazelbury Park	8 E4	Herbert View	67 B2 [26]	Hillcrest Way	33 C2
*Harold Crescent	60 E1	Hazelcroft Gardens	24 E2	Herberton Drive	74 D3	Hillsbrook Avenue	46 D2
(off Eden Rd Lower)		Hazelcroft Park	24 E2	Herberton Park	73 C2	Hillsbrook Crescent	46 D2
Harold Road	70 E3	Hazelcroft Road	24 E2	Herberton Road	73 C3	Hillsbrook Drive	46 D2
Harold Ville Avenue	74 D2	Hazeldene	47 C1	Hermitage Avenue	56 F1	Hillsbrook Grove	46 D2
Harold's Cross	46 F1	Hazeldine Apts.	67 C4	Hermitage Close	56 F1	Hillside	60 E2
Harold's Cross Cottages	74 F4	Hazelgrove	54 D2	Hermitage Court	57 A1	Hillside Drive	47 A3
Harold's Cross Cottages	75 A4	Hazelgrove Court	54 E2	Hermitage Crescent	34 F1	Hillside Park	56 E1
Harold's Cross Road	46 F1	Hazelhatch	41 B1	Hermitage Downs	57 A1	Hillside Terrace	30 D2 [7]
Harold's Grange Road	57 B3	Hazelhatch Road	41 C3	Hermitage Drive	56 F1	Hilltop Lawn	64 D3
Harrington Court	75 B3	Hazelwood	12 E4	Hermitage Garden	34 F1	Hilltown	1 B3
Harrington Street	75 A3	Hazelwood (Bray)	67 B2	Hermitage Green	34 F1	Hilltown Close	1 C2
Harrison Row	46 F2	Hazelwood (Shankill)	64 E2	Hermitage Grove	56 F1	Hilltown Court	1 C2
Harristown	5 A2	Hazelwood Avenue	21 C1	Hermitage Lawn	56 F1	Hilltown Crescent	1 A2
Harry Street	75 B1	Hazelwood Bank	44 D2	Hermitage Manor	34 F1	Hilltown Green	1 C2
Hartstown Road	21 C1	Hazelwood Close	44 D2	Hermitage Park (Grange Road)	56 F1	Hilltown Grove	1 C2

STREET NAME	PAGE/GRID REFERENCE
Hilltown Lawn	1 C2
Hilltown Park	1 C2
Hilltown Road	1 C2
Hilltown Way	1 C2
Hillview	52 E2
Hillview Cottages	59 C2 [1]
Hillview Court	57 B1 [6]
Hillview Drive	59 C2
Hillview Glade	57 B1 [5]
Hillview Grove	57 B1
Hillview Lawn	59 C2
Hilton Gardens	57 C2
Hoey Close	14 D4
Hoey Court	14 D4
Hoey Place	14 D4
*Hoeys Court (off Werburgh Street)	75 A1
Hogan Avenue	76 E1
Hogan House	46 F4 [25]
Hogan Place	76 D1
Hogan Square	76 E1
Holles Place	76 D1
Holles Row	76 D1
Holles Street	76 D1
Holly Avenue	58 D1
Holly Court	64 D1
Holly Park	64 E2
Holly Park Avenue	59 A1
Holly Road (Donnycarney)	26 D3
Holly Road (Fox and Geese)	44 F1
Holly Tree Square	11 C4
Holly Tree Terrace	11 C4
Hollybank Avenue Lower	47 B1
Hollybank Avenue Upper	47 B1
Hollybank Road	25 A4
Hollybrook	59 A3
Hollybrook Court	26 D4 [3]
Hollybrook Court Drive	26 D4 [2]
Hollybrook Grove	26 D4
Hollybrook Manor	26 D4
Hollybrook Mews	26 D4 [11]
Hollybrook Park (Clontarf)	26 D4
Hollybrook Park (Irishtown)	67 C4
Hollybrook Road	26 D4
Hollybrook Wood	26 D4
Hollybrooke	36 E4 [4]
Hollyrood Apts	39 A4 [47]
Hollystown	9 B1
Hollystown Park	9 B1
Hollyville Lawn	35 C1
Hollywell	11 C4
Hollywell Avenue	2 E3
Hollywell Close	2 E3
Hollywell Court	2 D3
Hollywell Gardens	2 D3
Hollywell Grove	2 E3
Hollywell Heath	2 D3
Hollywell Place	2 D3
Hollywell Rise	2 D3
Hollywell Road	2 D3
Hollywell Square	2 E3
Hollywell View	2 E3
Hollywell Walk	2 D3
Hollywell Wood	2 D3
Hollywood Drive	48 D4
Hollywood Park	48 D4
*Holme's Cottages (on Church Avenue Rathmines)	47 A1
Holmston Avenue	60 D1
Holmwood	59 B4
Holycross Avenue	25 B4 [5]
*Holycross Cottages (off Holycross Avenue)	25 B4
Holyrood Park	39 A4
Holywell	58 D1
Holywell Avenue	27 B1
Holywell Crescent	27 B1
Holywell Road	27 B1
Home Farm Park	25 B3
Home Farm Road	25 A3
Home Villas	47 C1
Homelawn Avenue	55 B1
Homelawn Drive	55 B1
Homelawn Gardens	55 B1
Homelawn Road	55 A1
Homelawn Villas	55 A1
Homelee	39 A4 [11]
Homeleigh	22 D4
Homeville	55 C1 [4]
Homeville Court	55 C1 [3]
Honey Park	60 D2 [1]
Hope Avenue	72 E1
Hope Street (off Gordon Street)	76 F1
Hopkins Square	48 D3 [1]
Horan Hall (Belgard Square)	54 F1 [5]
Horse Fair	72 E4
Horton Court	46 F2
Hospital Lane	69 B4
Hotel Yard	71 B3
Houghton Terrace	70 E3
Howard Street (off Gordon Street)	76 F1
Howth	30 D2
Howth Harbour	30 D1
Howth House Apts	30 D1 [10]
Howth Junction Cottages	27 B1 [1]
Howth Lodge Apts.	29 C1
Howth Peninsula Apts.	30 D1 [14]
Howth Road (Howth)	29 C1
Howth Road (Killester)	26 E3
Howth Road (Marino)	26 D4
Howth Road (Raheny)	26 F3
Howth Road (Raheny)	27 B2
Howth Road (Sutton)	29 B1
Howth Road Apts.	26 E3
Howth Terrace	30 D1 [5]
Howth View Park	27 B1
Huband Road	36 F4
Hudson Road	60 E1
Hughes Road East	45 C1
Hughes Road North	45 C1
Hughes Road South	45 C1
Hume Ave	36 D4
Hume Avenue	35 C4
Hume Street	75 C2
Hunters Avenue	55 C3
Hunters Court	55 C3
Hunters Crescent	55 C3
Hunters Green	55 C3
Hunters Grove	55 C3
Hunters Hall	55 C3
Hunters Hill	55 C3
Hunters Lane	55 C3
Hunters Meadow	55 C3
Hunters Parade	55 C3
Hunters Place	55 C3
Hunters Road	55 C3
Hunter's Row	26 F4 [2]
Hunters Run	8 E4
Hunters Run The Close	8 E4
Hunters Run The Drive	8 F4
Hunters Run The Glade	8 E4
Hunters Run The Grove	8 E4
Hunters Run The Park	8 E4
Hunters Run The Rise	8 F4
Hunters Run The View	8 E4
Hunters Run The Way	8 F4
Hunters Walk	55 C3
Hunters Way	55 C3
Huntstown Avenue	21 C1
Huntstown Close	8 F4
Huntstown Court	8 F4
Huntstown Drive	8 F4
Huntstown Glen	8 F4
Huntstown Green	8 F4
Huntstown Grove	8 F4
Huntstown Lawn	22 D1
Huntstown Park	8 F4
Huntstown Rise	9 A4
Huntstown Road	21 C1
Huntstown Way	8 F4
Huntstown Way	9 A4
Huntstown Wood	8 F4
Hutchinson's Strand	2 E1
Huttonread	51 C4
Huxley Court	74 E2
Huxley Crescent	74 E2
Hyacinth Street	72 E2
Hybreasal	73 B2
Hybreasal Apts.	73 B2
Hyde Park (Dalkey)	60 E1
Hyde Park (Templeogue)	46 E3
Hyde Park Avenue	48 F3
Hyde Park Gardens	48 F3
Hyde Road	60 F1
Hyde Square (Fosters Avenue)	48 D3 [4]
*Hyde Square (Kilmainham)	73 B2
Hynestown	42 D2

I

STREET NAME	PAGE/GRID REFERENCE
Idrone Avenue	56 D1
Idrone Close	56 D1
Idrone Drive	56 D1
Idrone Mews	49 A3 [11]
Idrone Park	56 D1
Idrone Terrace	49 A3
Imaal Road	70 E1
Inagh Court	64 E1
Inagh Road	36 D3
Inbhir Ide	3 A2
Inbhir Ide Close	3 A2
Inbhir Ide Drive	3 A2
Inchicore	36 F3
Inchicore Road	73 A1
Inchicore Square	36 F3 [13]
Inchicore Terrace North	36 F3 [3]
Inchicore Terrace South	36 F3
Infirmary Road	69 C3
Inglewood Close	21 C2
Inglewood Crescent	21 C2
Inglewood Drive	21 C2
Inglewood Road	21 C2
Ingram Road	74 F3
Inis Fáil	54 F2
Inis Thiar	54 F2
*Inkerman Cottages (off Amiens Street)	72 D2
Innisfallen Parade	71 B1
Innishmaan Road	25 B2
Innishmore Terrace (St Mary's Road)	46 D1
Innismore	46 D1
*Inns Court (on Winetavern Street)	75 A1
Inns Quay	70 F4
Inver Road	24 E4
Invermore Grove	27 A1 [3]
Inverness Road	25 C4
Iona Avenue	25 A4
Iona Crescent	25 A4
Iona Drive	25 A4
Iona Park	25 A4
Iona Road	25 A4
Iona Villas	25 A4
Iris Grove	48 E3
Irishtown (Bray)	67 C4
Irishtown (Ringsend)	39 A3
Irishtown Road	39 A3
Irvine Cottages	72 F3
Irvine Terrace	72 F3
Irwin Court	73 C1
Irwin Street	73 C1
Island Street	70 E4
Island View (Kilbarrack)	27 C2
Island View (Malahide)	3 C3
Island View Apts.	30 D1 [9]
Island View Court Apts.	27 C2
Island Villa	76 E1
Islandbridge	69 B4
Islandbridge Court	69 B4
Islington Avenue	50 E4
Isolda Road	39 A3
Isolde Gardens	36 E2 [6]
Isolde House Apts.	36 E2 [13]
Ivar Street	70 E3
Iveagh Buildings	75 A2
Iveagh Court	75 B3
Iveagh Gardens	73 A4
Iveagh Gardens	73 B4
Iveleary Road	25 B2
Iveragh Court	76 F3
Iveragh Road	25 B2
Ivy Cottages	75 C4
Ivy Court	25 C1 [1]
Ivy Terrace	74 E2

J

STREET NAME	PAGE/GRID REFERENCE
Jackson's Bridge	17 A3
James Connolly Park	35 A4
James Connolly Square	67 C2 [5]
James Everett Park	67 B2
James Joyce Bridge	70 E4
James Joyce Court	25 A3 [21]
James Joyce Court	27 C1 [5]
James Joyce St	71 C3
James Larkin Road	27 B2
James McCormack Gardens	29 A1 [1]
James Plunkett House	36 F3
James's Place East	76 D2
James's Street	74 D1
James's Street East	76 D2
James's Street North	72 E1
James's Terrace	3 B2
James's Terrace Upper	3 B2 [11]
James's Walk	74 D2
Jamestown	62 F1
Jamestown Avenue	36 F4
Jamestown Cottages	62 E1
Jamestown Court	36 F4
Jamestown Road	11 B4
Jamestown Road (Finglas)	24 D3
Jamestown Road (Grand Canal)	36 E4
Jamestown Road (Inchicore)	36 F4
Jamestown Road (Poppintree)	11 B4
*Jane-Ville (Off Tivoli Road)	50 D4
Jerome Connor Place	69 C3
Jervis Lane Lower	71 A4
Jervis Lane Upper	71 A3
Jervis Street	71 A3
Jobstown	54 D2
Jobstown Road	54 D2
Jobstown Village Square	54 D1 [2]
John Dillon Street	75 A1
John F Kennedy Avenue	45 A1
John F Kennedy Drive	45 A1
John F Kennedy Park	36 D4
John F Kennedy Road	36 D4
John Field Road	75 A1
John MacCormack Avenue	45 C1
John McCormack Bridge	72 F1
John Street North	70 F4
John Street North (off Ellis Quay)	70 E4
John Street South	74 F2
John Street West	74 F1
John's Court	74 E2
John's Lane East	75 A1
John's Lane West	74 F1
Johnsbridge	34 D3
Johnsbridge Avenue	34 D3
Johnsbridge Close	34 D3
Johnsbridge Green	34 D3
Johnsbridge Grove	34 D3
Johnsbridge Meadows	34 D3
Johnsbridge Park	34 D3
Johnsbridge Walk	34 D3
Johnson Place	75 B1
Johnson's Court	75 B1
Johnstown	51 C4
Johnstown Avenue	59 C3
Johnstown Court	59 C2
Johnstown Gardens	24 E2 [5]
Johnstown Grove	59 C3
Johnstown House	24 F2 [3]
Johnstown Lane	59 C3
Johnstown Park (Cornelscourt)	59 C3
Johnstown Park (Glasnevin)	24 F2
Johnstown Road (Cornelscourt)	59 C3
Johnstown Road (Rathcoole)	52 E2
Jones Terrace	68 D2 [18]
Jones's Road	71 C1
Jordanstown	42 F4
Jordanstown Avenue (Greenogue Ind Est)	42 F4
Jordanstown Drive (Greenogue Ind Est)	42 F4
Jordanstown Road (Greenogue Ind Est)	42 F4
Josephine Avenue	71 B1
Joy Street (off Gordon Street)	76 F1
Joyce Avenue	59 A3

STREET NAME	PAGE/GRID REFERENCE	STREET NAME	PAGE/GRID REFERENCE	STREET NAME	PAGE/GRID REFERENCE	STREET NAME	PAGE/GRID REFERENCE
Joyce Hall	59 B4	Kew Park Crescent	33 B1	Kill Abbey	59 B1	Kilmahuddrick Road	43 B1
Joyce Road	25 A3	Kickham Road	73 B2	Kill Avenue	59 C1	Kilmahuddrick Walk	43 B1
Joyce Way	35 C4	Kilakee Close	45 B3	Kill Lane	59 B2	Kilmahuddrick Way	43 B1
Jugback Close	1 C1	Kilakee Drive	45 B3	Kill O' the Grange	59 C1	Kilmainham	73 B1
Jugback Court	1 C1	Kilbarrack	27 C1	Killadoon Park	31 C4	Kilmainham Bank	73 A1
Jugback Crescent	1 C1	Kilbarrack Avenue	27 C2	Killakee Avenue	55 B2	Kilmainham Lane	73 C1
Jugback Green	1 Inset	Kilbarrack Gardens	27 C2	Killakee Court	55 B2	Kilmainham Orchard	73 B1
Jugback Lane	1 C1	Kilbarrack Grove	27 C2	Killakee Gardens	55 B2	Kilmalin	65 C3
K		Kilbarrack Parade	27 B1	Killakee Green	55 B2	Kilmantain Place	67 C2 [10]
Kavanagh Avenue	36 D4	Kilbarrack Road	27 B1	Killakee Grove	55 B2	Kilmartin Avenue	54 D1
Keadeen Avenue	45 B2	Kilbarrack Way	27 B1	Killakee Lawns	55 B2	Kilmartin Crescent	44 D4
Kearneystown Lower	41 A3	Kilbarron Avenue	26 D1	Killakee Park	55 B2	Kilmartin Drive	54 D1
Kearn's Place	73 B2	Kilbarron Court	26 D1 [1]	Killakee Rise	55 B2	Kilmartin Gardens	54 D1
Keatingspark	52 D2	Kilbarron Drive	26 D1	Killakee Road	56 D4	Kilmartin Green	54 D1
*Keegan's Cottages (off Merrion Rd)	48 E1	Kilbarron Park	26 D1	Killakee View	55 B2	Kilmartin Park	54 D1
Keeloges	42 D3	Kilbarron Road	26 D1	Killakee Walk	55 B2	Kilmashogue Bridge	56 F3
Keeper Road	73 C3	Kilbegnet Close	60 F2 [24]	Killakee Way	55 B2	Kilmashogue Close	45 B3
Kells Road	46 E1	Kilbogget Grove	59 C4	Killala Road	24 E4	Kilmashogue Drive	45 B3
Kelly's Avenue	50 D4	Kilbogget Villas	59 C4 [1]	Killan Court	72 F3	Kilmashogue Grove	45 B3
Kelly's Lane (Maynooth)	17 C3 [1]	Kilbride Grove	67 B3	Killan Road	72 F3	Kilmashogue Lane	56 F3
Kelly's Lane (Phibsborough)	71 A1	Kilbride Lane	67 B3	Killarney Avenue	72 D2	Kilmore	26 D1
Kelly's Row	71 B1	Kilbride Road	26 E3	Killarney Court	67 B3 [4]	Kilmore Avenue (Coolock)	26 E1
Kelly's Square	71 B1	Kilbrina	7 B2	Killarney Glen	67 B2	Kilmore Avenue (Killiney)	60 E4
Kellystown Lane	19 A3	Kilcarberry Ave	43 C2	Killarney Heights	67 B3	Kilmore Close	26 E1
Kellystown Road	57 B4	Kilcarberry Close	43 C2	Killarney Lane	67 B3	Kilmore Court	26 D1 [5]
Kelston Avenue	59 A2	Kilcarberry Court	43 C2	Killarney Parade	71 B1	Kilmore Crescent	26 E1
Kelston Drive	59 A2	Kilcarberry Lawn	43 C2	Killarney Park	67 B3	Kilmore Drive	26 E1
Kelston Hall	59 A2 [11]	Kilcarrig Avenue	44 E4	Killarney Road	67 B3	Kilmore Place Apts.	26 D1
Kelston Park	59 A2	Kilcarrig Close	54 E1	Killarney Street	72 D2	Kilmore Road	26 D1
Kelston View	59 A2	Kilcarrig Crescent	44 E4	Killarney Villas	67 C2 [48]	Kilmorony Close	27 A1
Kelvin Close	4 D4	Kilcarrig Green	44 E4	Killary Grove	27 B1	Kilnamanagh	45 A3
Kempton	23 C3	Kilclare Avenue	54 E2	Killeany	5 A4	Kilnamanagh Court	45 C1
Kempton Avenue	23 C3	Kilclare Crescent	54 E2	Killeck	1 A2	Kilnamanagh Estate	45 A3
Kempton Court	23 C3	Kilclare Drive	54 E2	Killeck Lane	1 A3	Kilnamanagh Road	45 C1
Kempton Green	23 C3	Kilclare Gardens	54 E2	Killeen	2 F3	Kilrock Road	30 E2
Kempton Grove	23 C3	Kilcloon	5 A2	Killeen Avenue	2 F3	Kilronan Court	26 D4 [7]
Kempton Heath	23 C3	Kilcloon Lawns	5 A2	Killeen Court	2 F3	Kilshane	10 E2
Kempton Lawn	23 C3	Kilcock Maynooth Leixlip ByPass	32 E1	Killeen Crescent	2 F3	Kilshane Avenue	10 D2
Kempton Park	23 C3	Kilcock Road	17 C3	Killeen Mews	3 B2	Kilshane Cross	10 F2
Kempton Rise	23 C3	Kilcock-Maynooth-Leixlip Bypass	33 A1	Killeen Park	2 F3	Kilshane Drive	10 D2
Kempton View	23 C3	Kilcolman Court	60 E2 [4]	Killeen Road (Bluebell)	36 D4	Kilshane Park	10 D2
Kempton Way	23 C3	Kilcronan Avenue	34 E4	Killeen Road (Fox and Geese)	45 A1	Kilshane Road (North Road)	10 E3
Kenah Court	60 E3	Kilcronan Close	34 E4	Killeen Road (Rathmines)	47 B1	Kilshane Road (North Road)	10 E3
Kengar Mews	46 F1 [14]	Kilcronan Court	34 E4	Killeen Terrace	3 B2	Kilshane Road (Rathoath Road)	23 C2
Kenilworth Lane	46 F1	Kilcronan Crescent	34 E4	Killegar	65 C1	Kilshane View	10 D2
Kenilworth Manor	46 F1 [11]	Kilcronan Grove	34 E4	*Killery Terrace (on Upper Dargle Road)	67 B2	Kilshane Way	10 D3
Kenilworth Park	46 F1	Kilcronan Lawns	34 E4	Killester	26 E3	Kiltalown	54 D3
Kenilworth Road	47 A1	Kilcronan View	34 E4	Killester Avenue	26 E3	Kiltalown Avenue	54 D2
Kenilworth Square	46 F1	Kilcroney Lane	67 A4	Killester Court	26 E3 [4]	Kiltalown Close	54 D2
Kenilworth Square East	47 A1	Kilcross Avenue	58 D3	Killester Park	26 E3	Kiltalown Cottages	54 T4
Kenilworth Square North	46 F1	Kilcross Close	58 D3	Killester Park	26 E3 [5]	Kiltalown Court	54 D2
Kenilworth Square South	46 F1	Kilcross Court	57 C3	Killinarden	54 E3	Kiltalown Crescent	54 D2
Kenilworth Square West	46 F1	Kilcross Crescent	57 C3	Killinarden Estate	54 E2	Kiltalown Drive	54 D2
Kenmare Parade	71 B1	Kilcross Drive	57 C3	Killinarden Heights	54 E2	Kiltalown Green	54 D2
Kennedy Court	39 A3 [31]	Kilcross Grove	57 C3	Killinarden Road	54 E3	Kiltalown Grove	54 D2
Kennedy Park	67 C3 [5]	Kilcross Lawn	58 D3	Killiney	60 E3	Kiltalown Heights	54 D2
Kennelsfort Green	35 B2	Kilcross Park	57 C3	Killiney Avenue	60 E4	Kiltalown Hill	54 D2
Kennelsfort Road Lower	35 C1	Kilcross Road	58 D3	Killiney Court	64 E1 [1]	Kiltalown Park	54 D2
Kennelsfort Road Upper	35 C2	Kilcross Square	57 C3	Killiney Gate	60 E4	Kiltalown Road	54 D2
Kennilworth Lodge	46 F1 [19]	Kilcross Way	57 C3	Killiney Grove	60 E2	Kiltalown View	54 D2
Kennington Close	45 C4	Kildare Bridge	18 D2	Killiney Heath	60 E4	Kiltalown Walk	54 D2
Kennington Crescent	45 C4	Kildare Park	46 D1	Killiney Hill Road	60 E3	Kiltalown Way	54 D2
Kennington Lawn	45 C4	Kildare Place	75 C1	Killiney Hill Road	64 E1	Kilteel Road	52 E2
Kennington Road	45 C3	Kildare Road	46 D1	Killiney Oaks	64 E1 [2]	Kilteragh Drive	59 A3
*Kent Terrace (on Barnhill Road)	60 F2	Kildare Street	75 C1	Killiney Road	60 E2	Kilteragh Pines	59 A3 [2]
Kentfield	64 E2	Kildonan Avenue	24 D1	Killiney Terrace	60 E1 [15]	Kilteragh Road	59 A3
Kerlogue Road	39 A3	Kildonan Court	24 D1	Killiney Towers	60 E2 [2]	Kilternan	62 F2
Kerrygold House	46 F1 [18]	Kildonan Drive	24 D1	Killiney View	60 E1	Kiltiernan Bridge	62 F3
Kerrymount Avenue	59 A4	Kildonan Road	24 D1	Killininny Cottages	55 B2	Kiltipper	54 F3
Kerrymount Close	59 B3 [1]	Kildress House	76 D2	Killininny Court Apts	55 B2 [2]	Kiltipper Avenue	55 A2
Kerrymount Green	59 B3	Kilfenora Drive	27 A1	Killininny Road	55 B2	Kiltipper Close	55 A2
Kerrymount Mall	59 B3	Kilfenora Road	46 E1	Kilmactalway	42 F3	Kiltipper Drive	55 A2
Kerrymount Rise	59 B3	Kilgarran	66 D3	Kilmacud	58 E1	Kiltipper Gate	54 F3
Kettles Drive	2 E4	Kilgarron Park	66 D3	Kilmacud Avenue	58 E1	Kiltipper Rise	54 F3
Kettles Lane	2 E4	Kilgobbin Grove	58 E4	Kilmacud Park	58 E1	Kiltipper Road	55 A3
Kettles Place	2 E4	Kilgobbin Heights	58 E4	Kilmacud Road Upper	58 E1	Kiltipper View	54 F3
Kevin Barry Flats (off Church Street Upper)	70 F3	Kilgobbin Lane	58 D4	Kilmahuddrick Avenue	43 B1	Kiltipper Way	54 F2
*Kevin Street Cross (on New Bride Street)	75 A2	Kilgobbin Lawn	58 E4	Kilmahuddrick Close	43 B1	Kiltuck Park	64 E4 [1]
Kevin Street Lower	75 A2	Kilgobbin Road	58 E3	Kilmahuddrick Court	43 B1	Kilvere	46 E4
Kevin Street Upper	75 A2	Kilgobbin Wood	58 E4	Kilmahuddrick Crescent	43 B1	Kilvere Park	46 D4
Kew Park	33 C1	Kilgraigue	5 B3	Kilmahuddrick Drive	43 B1	Kilwogan Manor	31 C2
Kew Park Avenue	33 B2	Kilgrastor Court	67 B3 [5]	Kilmahuddrick Green	43 B1	Kilworth Road	36 F4
		Kilkieran Court	24 E4 [1]	Kilmahuddrick Grove	43 B1	Kimmage	46 D2
		Kilkieran Road	24 E4	Kilmahuddrick Lawn	43 B1	Kimmage Court	46 E2 [3]
				Kilmahuddrick Place	43 B1	Kimmage Grove	46 E2
						Kimmage Manor Way	46 D2

STREET NAME	PAGE/GRID REFERENCE	STREET NAME	PAGE/GRID REFERENCE	STREET NAME	PAGE/GRID REFERENCE	STREET NAME	PAGE/GRID REFERENCE
Kimmage Road Lower	46 F1	Knockcullen	56 D1	Lakelands Drive	58 E1	Larkfield Close	34 F2
Kimmage Road West	46 D2	Knockcullen Drive	56 D1	Lakelands Grove	58 D1	Larkfield Court	34 F2
Kinahan Street	70 D3	Knockcullen Lawn	56 D1	Lakelands Lawn	58 D1	Larkfield Gardens	46 F1
Kincora Avenue	26 E4	Knockcullen Park	56 D1	Lakelands Park	46 E3	Larkfield Green	34 F2
Kincora Court	39 C1	Knockcullen Rise	56 D1	Lakelands Place	58 D1	Larkfield Grove (Harold's Cross)	46 F1
Kincora Drive	26 E4	Knockdara	3 C3	Lakelands Road	58 E1	Larkfield Grove (Liffey Valley)	34 F2
Kincora Grove	26 E4	Knockfield Manor	55 C1	Lakeshore Drive	2 D3	Larkfield Mews	32 D3
Kincora Park	26 E4	Knocklyon	56 D1	Lakeview Drive	2 D3	Larkfield Park	46 F1
Kincora Road	26 E4	Knocklyon Avenue	55 C1	Lally Road	36 E3	Larkfield Place	34 F2
King Edward Court	67 C2 [53]	Knocklyon Close	56 D1	Lamb Alley	74 F1	Larkfield Rise	34 F2
King Edward Lawn	67 C2	Knocklyon Court	56 D1	Lambay Close	64 E1	Larkfield Square	34 F2
King Edward Park	67 B2	Knocklyon Drive	56 D1	Lambay Court	3 C3	Larkfield View	34 F2
King Edward Road	67 B2	Knocklyon Gate Apts	55 C2 [3]	Lambay Drive	64 E1	Larkfield Way	34 F2
King Street North	70 F3	Knocklyon Green	56 D1	Lambay Road	25 A3	Larkhill Road	25 B2
King Street South	75 B1	Knocklyon Grove	56 D1	Lambourne Avenue	21 C2	Larrisa Court	46 E1 [7]
King William's Rampart	24 D2	Knocklyon Heights	55 C1	Lambourne Court	21 C2	Latchford	21 B1
Kingram Place	75 C3	Knocklyon Mews	55 C1 [2]	Lambourne Drive	21 C2	Latchford Close	21 B1
King's Avenue	72 D1	Knocklyon Park	55 C1	Lambourne Park	21 C2	Latchford Court	21 B1
King's Court	70 E2	Knocklyon Road	55 C1	Lambourne Road	21 C2	Latchford Green	21 B1
King's Hall	36 E2	Knockmaree Apartments	36 E2	Lambourne Village	26 E4 [3]	Latchford Park	21 B1
Kings Inns	71 A3	Knockmaroon Hill	36 D1	Lambourne Wood	59 C4	Latchford Row	21 B1
King's Inn's Court	71 A2	Knockmaroon Road	36 D1	Lamb's Brook	58 D3	Latchford Square	21 B1
King's Inns Street	71 A3	Knockmeenagh Lane	44 E2	Lamb's Court (off James Street)	74 D1	Latchford Terrace	21 B1
Kingsbury	17 C4	Knockmeenagh Road	44 E2	Landen Road	36 E3	Latouka Apts.	34 F1
Kingsland Parade	75 A4	Knockmitten Close	44 F1 [1]	Landore	47 A3 [9]	Latouka Apts.	34 F1 [1]
Kingsland Park Avenue	75 A3	Knockmitten Lane	45 A1	Landscape Avenue	47 A3	Lauderdale Estate	67 C3
Kingsmill Road	67 C2	Knockmitten Lane North	44 F1 [2]	Landscape Crescent	47 A4	Lauderdale Terrace	67 C3 [16]
Kingston	57 B3	Knockmore Avenue	54 E2	Landscape Gardens	47 B4	*Lauderdale Terrace	75 A2
Kingston Avenue	57 B3	Knockmore Crescent	54 E2	Landscape Park	47 A4	(on New Row South)	
Kingston Close	57 B3	Knockmore Drive	54 E2	Landscape Road	47 A3	Lauder's Lane	29 A1
Kingston Court	56 F2	Knockmore Gardens	54 E2	Landsdown Valley Place	45 C1	Laundry Lane	46 F1
Kingston Crescent	57 B3	Knockmore Green	54 E2	Landsdowne Valley	45 C1 [6]	Laurel Avenue (Ballybrack)	64 E1
Kingston Drive	57 C3	Knockmore Grove	54 E2	*Landsdowne Valley Apts	45 C1	Laurel Avenue (Dundrum)	57 B1
Kingston Green	57 B3	Knockmore Park	54 E2	(Landsdowne Valley)		Laurel Bank	59 C1
Kingston Grove	57 B3	Knock-na-Cree Grove	60 F2	Landsdowne Valley Park	36 F4 [5]	Laurel Court	22 E3
Kingston Hall	57 B3	Knock-na-Cree Park	60 F2	Lanesborough Avenue	11 B4	Laurel Drive	57 B1
Kingston Heights	57 C3	Knock-na-Cree Road	60 F2	Lanesborough Court	11 B4	Laurel Hill	60 D1 [6]
Kingston Lawn	57 B3	Knocknagow	49 B4 [23]	Lanesborough Drive	11 B4	Laurel Lodge Road	22 F3
Kingston Lodge	25 B4 [4]	Knocknarea Avenue	73 A4	Lanesborough Gardens	11 B4	Laurel Park	44 E1
Kingston Park	57 B3	Knocknarea Road	73 A4	Lanesborough Grove	11 B4	Laurel Place	46 F2
Kingston Rise	57 B3	Knocknarrow Terrace	73 C1	Lanesborough Mews	11 B4	Laurel Road	57 B1
Kingston View	57 B3	(Kilmainham Lane)		Lanesborough Park	11 B4	Laurelton (Rathbeale Road)	1 C1
Kingston Walk	57 B3	Knocknashee	47 C4	Lanesborough Road	11 B4	Laurelton (Terenure)	46 F3
Kingswood	43 C3	Knocknashee	48 D4	Lanesborough Square	11 B4	Laurence Brook	36 E2
Kingswood Avenue (Citywest)	43 C4	Knocksedan Bridge	1 A2	Lanesborough Terrace	11 B4	Laurence Court	46 F1
Kingswood Avenue	44 F3	Knocksedan Drive	1 A2	Lanesborough View	11 B4	Laurence Place East	72 E3
(Kilnamanagh)		Knocksedan Wood	1 A2	Lanesville	59 B1	Laurleen	58 F1
Kingswood Castle	45 A2	Knocksink Bridge	66 E3	Lanesville Terrace	59 B1	Lavarna Grove	46 E2
Kingswood Drive (Citywest)	43 C4	Knocksinna	59 A2	Lanewood Mews	76 E3	Lavarna Road	46 E2
Kingswood Drive (Kilnamanagh)	44 F3	Knocksinna Court	59 A2 [2]	Langrishe Place	71 C2	Laverna Avenue	22 E3
Kingswood Heights	44 F3	Knocksinna Crescent	59 A2	Lanndale Lawns	54 E1	Laverna Dale	22 E3
Kingswood Interchange	42 C3	Knocksinna Grove	59 A2 [1]	*Lansdowne Court	76 F3	Laverna Grove	22 E3
Kingswood Road	43 C4	Knocksinna Park	59 A2	Lansdowne Crescent	76 F2	Laverna Way	22 E3
Kingswood View	44 F3	Knowth Court	11 C4	Lansdowne Gardens	76 F3	Lavery Avenue	35 C4
Kinsaley	14 D1	Kyber Road	36 F2	Lansdowne Hall	39 A3 [25]	Lavista Avenue	26 E3
Kinsaley Bridge	14 D1	Kyle-Clare Road	39 A3 [13]	Lansdowne Lane	76 F2	Lawnswood Park	58 F1
Kinsaley Lane	3 A4	Kylemore Avenue	36 D3	Lansdowne Park (Ballsbridge)	76 F2	Lawrence Grove	26 D4
Kinsealy Court	2 E3	Kylemore Drive	36 D3	Lansdowne Park (Templeogue)	56 D1	Lawrence's Avenue	18 D4
Kinsealy Downs	2 E3	Kylemore Park North	36 D4	Lansdowne Road	76 F3	Lawson Spinney	3 A3
Kinsealy Lane	14 D1	Kylemore Park South	36 D4	Lansdowne Square	39 A4 [24]	Lawson Terrace	60 E1 [14]
Kinvara Avenue	24 D4	Kylemore Park West	36 D4	Lansdowne Terrace	76 F2	Le Bas Terrace	46 F1 [2]
Kinvara Drive	23 C4	Kylemore Road	36 D2	Lansdowne Village	39 A3	Le Brett Terrace	46 F3 [7]
Kinvara Grove	23 C4	Kylemore Road (Grand Canal)	36 E4	Lansdowne Villas	76 F2	Le Brocquy Avenue	36 D4
Kinvara Park	24 D4			Lansdowne Woods	39 A4 [28]	Le Fanu Drive	36 D3 [1]
Kinvara Road	23 C4	**L**		Lapwing Apts.	48 E3	Le Fanu Road	36 D3
Kippure Avenue	45 B3			Laracor Gardens	27 A1 [5]	Le Vere Terrace	74 F4
Kippure Park	24 D3	La Rochelle Apts.	74 F1	Laragh	60 E4	Lea Crescent	39 B4
Kirkfield	22 D2 [2]	La Touche Court (Ballinteer)	57 A2	Laragh Close	27 A1	Lea Road	39 B4
Kirkpatrick Avenue	22 D3	La Touche Court (Bluebell)	36 F4 [3]	Laragh Flats	25 C2 [5]	Leahy's Terrace	39 A3
Kirkpatrick Drive	22 D3	La Touche Drive	36 E4	Laragh Grove	27 A1	Lealand Avenue	43 C1
Kirkwood	39 A4	La Touche Road	36 F4	Laraghbryan East	17 B2	Lealand Close	43 C1
Kirwan Street	70 E3	La Vallee	67 A3	Laraghbryan West	17 A2	Lealand Crescent	43 C1
Kirwan Street Cottages	70 E2	La Vista Avenue	29 B2	Laraghon	34 D1	Lealand Drive	43 C1
Kitestown Road	30 E3	Labre Park	36 E4	Larch Drive	56 E2 [3]	Lealand Gardens	43 C1
Knapton Court	49 C4 [21]	Laburnum Road	47 C2	Larch Grove	21 C2	Lealand Grove	43 C1
Knapton Lawn	49 C4 [22]	Laburnum Walk	35 B2	Larch Grove	47 B1	Lealand Road	43 C1
Knapton Road	49 C4	Lad Lane	76 D2	Larch Hill	12 F4	Lealand Walk	43 C1
Knapton Terrace	49 C4 [27]	Lad Lane Apts.	76 D3	Larch House (Swords)	1 Inset	Leaunstown	59 C4
*Knapton Villas	49 C4	Lad Lane Upper	76 D3	Larchfield	7 C3	Leda Mews	76 E3
(on Knapton Road)		Lady's Lane	73 B1	Larchfield	47 C4	Ledwidge Crescent	67 B1
Knights Bridge	26 E4 [4]	Lady's Well Road	9 A4	Larchfield Park	47 C4	Lee Road	24 E3
Knights Wood	12 F4	Lagan Road	24 E3	Larchfield Road	47 C4	Leeson Close	75 C3
Knock Riada	36 D2	Lake Drive	53 C1	Larkfield	34 F2	Leeson Court	76 D4
Knockaire	56 D1	Lakelands Avenue	58 D1	Larkfield Avenue	46 F1	Leeson Lane	75 C2
Knockandinny	52 E4	Lakelands Close	58 D1	(Harold's Cross)		Leeson Mews	75 C4
Knockaulin	20 D4	Lakelands Crescent	58 E1	Larkfield Avenue (Liffey Valley)	34 F2	Leeson Park	75 C4

STREET NAME	PAGE/GRID REFERENCE
Leeson Park Avenue	76 D4
Leeson Place	75 C3
Leeson Street Lower	75 C2
Leeson Street Upper	76 D4
Leeson Village	76 D4
Leeson Walk	75 C4
Lehaunstown Road	63 C1
Leicester Avenue	47 A1
Leighlin Road	46 E1
Lein Gardens	26 F2
Lein Park	26 F2
Lein Road	26 F2
Leinster Avenue	72 E1
Leinster Cottages	17 C3 6
Leinster Court	18 D3 2
Leinster Lane	75 C1
Leinster Lawn	47 C3
Leinster Lodge Apts.	18 D3 1
Leinster Market	71 C4
Leinster Park (Harold's Cross)	46 F1
Leinster Park (Maynooth)	18 D3
Leinster Place	46 F1
Leinster Road	47 A1
Leinster Road West	46 F1
Leinster Square	47 A1 2
Leinster Street	17 C3
Leinster Street East	72 E1
Leinster Street North	24 F4
Leinster Street South	75 C1
Leinster Terrace	44 D1 2
Leitrim Place	76 E2
Leix Road	70 D1
Leixlip	33 B1
Leixlip Bridge	33 A1
Leixlip Gate	32 E1
Leixlip Park	32 F1
Leixlip Road	33 B1
Leixlip Road	33 C1
Lemon Street	75 B1
Lennox Place	75 A3
Lennox Street	75 B3
Lennox Terrace	75 B3
Lentisk Lawn	27 A1
Leo Avenue	71 B1
Leo Street	71 B1
Leonard's Court	74 F3
Leopardstown	58 F3
Leopardstown Abbey	58 F4
Leopardstown Avenue	58 F2
Leopardstown Court	58 F2 1
Leopardstown Drive	58 F2
Leopardstown Gardens	58 F2
Leopardstown Grove	58 F2
Leopardstown Heights	58 E3
Leopardstown Lawn	58 F2 2
Leopardstown Oaks	58 F2
Leopardstown Park	58 F2
Leopardstown Rise	58 E3
Leopardstown Road	58 D3
Leopardstown Road	58 F2
Leopardstown Valley	58 F4
Leslie Avenue	60 F1
Leslie's Buildings	70 F1
Leukos Road	39 A3 11
Liberty House	71 C2
Liberty Lane	75 B2
Library Road (Dún Laoghaire)	50 D4
Library Road (Shankill)	64 E2
Library Square	52 F2
Library View Villas	71 A1
Liffey Ave	34 F2
Liffey Close	34 F2
Liffey Court	34 F2
Liffey Crescent	34 F2
Liffey Dale	34 F2
Liffey Downs	34 F2
Liffey Drive	34 F2
Liffey Gardens	34 F2
Liffey Glen	34 F2
Liffey Green	34 F2
Liffey Grove	34 F2
Liffey Hall	34 F2 1
Liffey Junction	24 E4
Liffey Lawn	34 F2
Liffey Park	34 F2
Liffey Place	34 F2
Liffey Road	34 F2
Liffey Row	34 F2
Liffey Street Lower	71 B4
Liffey Street South	36 F3
Liffey Street Upper	71 B3
Liffey Street West	70 E4
Liffey Terrace	36 E2 7
Liffey Vale	34 F2
Liffey Valley Park	34 F2
Liffey View	34 F2
Liffey View Apts.	33 A1 2
Liffey Villas	34 F2
Liffey Walk	34 F2
Liffey Way	34 F2
Liffey Wood	34 F2
Lilys Way	21 A1
Lime Street	72 E4
Limekiln Avenue	45 B3
Limekiln Close	45 C3
Limekiln Drive	45 C3
Limekiln Green	45 B3
Limekiln Grove	45 C2
Limekiln Lane (Harold's Cross)	74 F4
Limekiln Lane (Kimmage)	45 C2
Limekiln Park	45 C3
Limekiln Road	45 C3
Limelawn Court	22 D2
Limelawn Glade	22 D2
Limelawn Green	22 D2
Limelawn Hill	22 D2
Limelawn Park	22 D2
Limelawn Wood	22 D2
Limes Road	58 D2
Limetree Avenue	3 C4
Limetree Avenue	4 D4
Limewood Avenue	26 F1
Limewood Park	26 F1
Limewood Road	27 A1
Lincoln Hall (Swords)	1 Inset
*Lincoln House	70 F4
Lincoln Lane	70 F4
Lincoln Place	76 D1
Linden Court	48 F4
Linden Grove	48 F4
Linden Lea Park	58 F1
Linden Square	48 F4
Lindenvale	49 A4 4
Lindisfarne Avenue	43 C1
Lindisfarne Drive	43 C1
Lindisfarne Green	43 C1
Lindisfarne Grove	43 C1
Lindisfarne Lawns	43 C1
Lindisfarne Park	34 F4
Lindisfarne Vale	43 C1
Lindisfarne Walk	43 C1
Lindsay Grove	25 A4 15
Lindsay Road	25 A4
Linenhall Parade	71 A3
Linenhall Street	71 A3
(off King Street North)	
Linenhall Terrace	71 A3
Link Road	60 E1
Link Road	49 C4
(Off Monkstown Crescent)	
Linnbhlá	12 D4
Linnetfields	21 A1
Linnetfields Avenue	8 E4
Linnetfields Close	8 E4
Linnetfields Court	21 A1
Linnetfields Drive	8 E4
Linnetfields Park	21 A1
Linnetfields Rise	8 E4
Linnetfields Square	8 E4
Linnetfields View	8 D4
Linnetfields Walk	21 A1
Lios na Sídhe	54 F2
Lioscian	1 B1
Lisalea	49 A3 22
Lisburn Street	71 A3
Liscannor Road	24 E4
Liscanor	60 F1 9
Liscarne Court	35 A3
Liscarne Dale	35 A3 2
Liscarne Gardens	35 A3
Lisle Road	46 D1
Lismeen Grove	26 E1 1
Lismore	18 E4
Lismore Road	46 E1
Lissadel Avenue	73 B4
Lissadel Court	73 A4
Lissadel Crescent	2 F2
Lissadel Drive	73 A4
Lissadel Green	73 A3
Lissadel Grove	2 F2
Lissadel Park	2 F2
Lissadel Road	73 A4
Lissadel Wood	2 F2
Lissane Apts.	22 E1
Lissen Hall	2 E1
Lissen Hall Drive	2 E1
Lissenfield	75 B4
Lissenhall Avenue	2 D1
Lissenhall Bridge	2 E1
Lissenhall Court	2 D1
Lissenhall Drive	2 D1
Lissenhall Park	2 D1
Little Britain Street	71 A3
Little Fitzwilliam Place	76 D2
Little Meadow	59 C3 1
Little Orchard	59 C3 5
Littlepace	8 E4
Littlepace Close	8 E4
Littlepace Court	8 E4
Littlepace Crescent	8 E4
Littlepace Drive	8 E4
Littlepace Gallops	8 E4
Littlepace Meadow	8 E4
Littlepace Park	8 E4
Littlepace Road	8 E4
Littlepace View	8 E4
Littlepace Walk	8 E4
Littlepace Way	8 E4
Littlepace Woods	8 E4
Littlewood	58 D4
Litton Lane	71 B4
Llewellyn Close	57 A1
Llewellyn Court	57 A1
Llewellyn Grove	57 A1
Llewellyn Lawn	57 A1
Llewellyn Park	57 A1
Llewellyn Way	57 A1
Llex House	76 D3
Lock Road	34 D3
Lockkeeper's Walk	24 D3
Loftus Hall (Belgard Square)	54 F1 9
Loftus Lane	71 A3
Loftus Square	46 F4 14
Lohunda Close	22 D2
Lohunda Court	22 D2
Lohunda Crescent	21 C2
Lohunda Dale	22 D2
Lohunda Downs	22 D2
Lohunda Drive	22 D2
Lohunda Grove	22 D2
Lohunda Park	21 C2
Lohunda Road	22 D2
Lombard Court	74 F3
Lombard Court	72 D4
Lombard Street East	72 D4
Lombard Street West	75 A3
Lomond Avenue	25 C4
Londonbridge Drive	39 A3 20
Londonbridge Road	39 A3
Long Lane	75 A2
Long Lane Close	75 A2
(off Long Lane)	
Long Meadow Apts.	69 C4
Long Mile Road	45 B1
Longdale Terrace	25 A1
Longdale Way	25 A1
Longford Lane	75 B1
Longford Place	49 C4
Longford Street Great	75 A1
Longford Street Little	75 B1
Longford Terrace	49 C4
Longlands	2 D2
Longmeadow	59 C3
Longmeadow Grove	59 C3
Long's Place	74 E1
Longwood Avenue	75 A3
Longwood Park	46 F4
Looceville Court	46 D1 7
Lorcan Avenue	25 C1
Lorcan Crescent	25 C1
Lorcan Drive	25 B1
Lorcan Green	25 C1
Lorcan Grove	25 C1
Lorcan O'Toole Court	46 D2 2
Lorcan O'Toole Park	46 D2
Lorcan Park	25 C1
Lorcan Road	25 B1
Lorcan Villas	25 C1
Lord Edward Court	75 A1
Lord Edward Street	75 A1
Lordello Road	64 D3
Lords Walk	69 B2
Loreto Abbey	47 A4
Loreto Avenue (Dalkey)	60 F1
Loreto Avenue	47 A4
(Nutgrove Avenue)	
Loreto Court	47 A4
Loreto Crescent	47 A4
Loreto Grange	67 C3
Loreto Park	47 A4
Loreto Road	74 E2
Loreto Row	47 A4
Loreto Terrace	46 F4
Loretto Avenue	67 C2 34
Loretto Terrace	67 C2 35
Loretto Villas	67 C2 54
Lorne Terrace	73 C2
(off Almeida Avenue)	
Losset Hall (Belgard Square)	54 F1 6
Lotts	71 B4
Lough Conn Avenue	36 D2
Lough Conn Drive	36 D2
Lough Conn Road	36 D2
Lough Conn Terrace	36 D2
Lough Derg Road	27 A2
Lough na Mona	19 C4
Loughlinstown	64 D1
Loughlinstown Drive	64 D1
Loughlinstown Park	64 D1
Loughlinstown Wood	64 D1
Loughmorne House	46 F2 27
Loughoreen Hills	30 D3
Loughsallagh Bridge	7 C3
Loughtown Lower	41 C1
Loughtown Upper	42 D1
Louis Lane	47 A1 23
Louisa Vally	19 C4
Lourdes House	71 C2
Lourdes Road	74 D2
Louvain	48 D3
Louvain Glade	48 D3
Love Lane	76 E2
Love Lane East	76 E2
Lower Dargle Road	67 B2
Lower Glen Road	36 D1
Lower Kilmacud Road	48 D4
(Goatstown)	
Lower Kilmacud Road	58 D1
(Stillorgan)	
Lower Lucan Road	21 C4
Lower Lucan Road	34 D1
Lower Road (Shankill)	64 E3
Lower Road (Strawberry Beds)	35 B1
Luby Road	73 B1
Lucan	34 D2
Lucan Bridge	34 D1
Lucan Bypass	34 D2
Lucan Heights	34 E1
Lucan Newlands Road	34 D2
Lucan Newlands road	35 A4
Lucan Road (Chapelizod)	36 D2
Lucan Road (Lucan)	34 D1
Lucan Road (near Qaurryvale)	35 A1
Lucan Road (Palmerston)	35 C1
Lucan-Newlands Road	34 F3
Ludford Drive	57 B1
Ludford Park	57 B1
Ludford Road	57 B2
Lugg	52 F4
Lugmore	54 D3
Lugmore Lane	53 C3
Lugnaquilla Avenue	45 B3
Luke Street	71 C4
Lullymore Terrace	74 E3

STREET NAME	PAGE/GRID REFERENCE
Lurgan Street	71 A3
Lutterell Hall	7 A2
Luttrell Park	22 D3
Luttrell Park Close	22 D3
Luttrell Park Court	22 D3
Luttrell Park Crescent	22 E3
Luttrell Park Drive	22 E3
Luttrell Park Green	22 E3
Luttrell Park Grove	22 D3
Luttrell Park Heath	22 E3 [2]
Luttrell Park Lawn	22 D3
Luttrell Park View	22 D3
Luttrellstown Avenue	22 E4
Luttrellstown Chase	22 D4
Luttrellstown Close	22 E4
Luttrellstown Court	22 D4
Luttrellstown Dale	22 D4
Luttrellstown Drive	22 D4
Luttrellstown Glade	22 D4
Luttrellstown Green	22 D4
Luttrellstown Grove	22 D4
Luttrellstown Heath	22 D4
Luttrellstown Heights	22 D4
Luttrellstown Lawn	22 D4
Luttrellstown Oaks	22 D4
Luttrellstown Park	22 D4
Luttrellstown Place	22 D4
Luttrellstown Rise	22 D3
Luttrellstown Thicket	22 D4
Luttrellstown View	22 E4
Luttrellstown Walk	22 D4
Luttrellstown Way	22 D4
Luttrellstown Wood	22 E4
Lymewood Mews	12 E4
Lynches Lane	34 E4
Lynch's Lane	36 E3 [2]
Lynch's Place	71 A1
Lyndon Gate	24 D4 [4]
Lynton Court	39 A4 [12]
Lynwood	57 C1
Lyons	41 A4
Lyons Road	41 B4
Lyreen Court	17 C3
Lyreen Park	18 D2

M

STREET NAME	PAGE/GRID REFERENCE
Ma Tuire Apts.	48 D4
Mabbot House	71 C3
Mabbot Lane	71 C3
Mabel Street	25 B4
Macken Street	76 E1
Macken Villa	76 E1
Mackies Place	75 C2
Mackintosh Park	59 C2
Macroom Avenue	13 B4
Macroom Road	13 B4
Madden Road	74 F2
*Madden's Court (off Thomas Street)	74 E2
Madden's Lane	60 E4
Madison Road	73 C2
Magdalen Terrace	39 A3 [39]
*Magdalen Terrace (off Oliver Plunket Ave)	39 A3
Magennis Place	72 D4
Magennis Square	72 D4
Magenta Crescent	25 B1
Magenta Hall	25 B1
Magenta Place	60 D1 [8]
Magna Drive	53 C2
*Maher's Terrace (on Main Street Dundrum)	47 C4
Maidens Row	36 E2 [2]
Main Street	14 D4
Main Street (Baldoyle)	15 A4
Main Street (Blackrock)	49 A3
Main Street (Blanchardstown)	22 E2
Main Street (Bray)	67 C2
Main Street (Celbridge)	32 D3
Main Street (Clondalkin)	44 E1
Main Street (Dunboyne)	7 B2
Main Street (Dundrum)	47 C4
Main Street (Finglas)	24 E2
Main Street (Howth)	30 D2
Main Street (Leixlip)	33 A1
Main Street (Lucan)	34 D1
Main Street (Malahide)	3 B2
Main Street (Maynooth)	17 C3
Main Street (Newcastle)	42 D4
Main Street (Raheny)	27 A2
Main Street (Rathcoole)	52 F2
Main Street (Rathfarnham)	46 F4
Main Street (Swords)	2 D2
Main Street (Tallaght)	55 A1
Maitland Street	67 B2
Malachi Place	72 E2
Malachi Road	70 E3
Malahide	3 B2
Malahide Demesne	3 A3
Malahide Road	13 C4
Malahide Road (Artane)	26 E2
Malahide Road (Balgriffin)	14 D3
Malahide Road (Coolock)	26 F1
Malahide Road (Marino)	26 D4
Malahide Road (Swords)	2 E2
Malahide Roundabout (Swords)	2 D2
Malborough Court	70 D2
Malborough Court	60 E2 [8]
Mallin Avenue	74 D2
Malone Gardens	76 F2
Malpas Court	75 A2
Malpas Place (off Malpas Street)	75 A2
Malpas Street (off New Street)	75 A2
Malpas Terrace	75 A2
Mander's Terrace	75 C4
Mangerton Road	36 F4
Mannix Road	25 A4
Manor Avenue	46 E3
Manor Close	57 A2
Manor Court	17 C3
Manor Crescent	21 B1
Manor Drive	14 D4
Manor Green	57 A2
Manor Grove	46 D2
Manor Hall Apts. (Mount Brown)	74 D1
Manor Heath	57 A1
Manor Mews (off Norseman Place)	70 E3
Manor Park (Ballinteer)	57 A2
Manor Park (Palmerston)	35 C2
Manor Place (Clonsilla)	21 A1
Manor Place (Stoneybatter)	70 E3
Manor Rise	57 A2
Manor Road	35 C2
Manor Square	21 A1
Manor Street	70 E3
Manor Villas	46 F1 [4]
Manorfields	21 B1
Mantua Park	2 D1
Maolbuille Road	25 A2
Mapas Avenue	60 E2
Mapas Road	60 E2
Maple Avenue (Carpenterstown)	22 E3
*Maple Avenue (off Blackthorn Drive)	58 D2
Maple Close	22 E3
Maple Drive (Carpenterstown)	22 E3
Maple Drive (Dunboyne)	7 B2
Maple Drive (Harold's Cross)	46 F2 [6]
Maple Glen	22 E3
Maple Green	22 E3
Maple Grove (Bray)	67 B2
Maple Grove (Carpenterstown)	22 E3
Maple Grove (Rathcoole)	52 F2
Maple House	76 D3
Maple Lawn	22 E3
Maple Lodge	23 A4
Maple Manor	59 C3
Maple Road	47 C2
Maples Road	58 D2
Maplewood Avenue	54 E1
Maplewood Close	54 E1
Maplewood Court	54 E1
Maplewood Drive	54 E1
Maplewood Green	54 E1
Maplewood Lawn	54 E1
Maplewood Park	54 E1
Maplewood Road	54 E1
Maplewood Way	54 E1
Maretimo Gardens East	49 A3
Maretimo Gardens West	49 A3 [4]
Maretimo Place	49 A3 [17]
Maretimo Road	49 A3 [2]
Maretimo Terrace	49 A3 [16]
Maretimo Villas	49 A3 [18]
Marewood Crescent	24 F1
Marewood Drive	11 C4
Marewood Drive	24 F1
Marewood Grove	24 F1
Margaret Place	76 F2
Marguerite Road	25 A4
Marian Court	14 F4
Marian Crescent	46 E4
Marian Drive	46 E4
Marian Grove	46 E4
Marian Park (Baldoyle)	27 C1
Marian Park (Blackrock)	59 A1
Marian Park (Templeogue)	46 E4
Marian Road	46 E4
Marianella	47 A2
Mariavilla	17 C2
Marie Villas	67 C2 [55]
Marigold Avenue	13 C4
Marigold Court	13 C4
Marigold Crescent	13 C4
Marigold Drive	13 C4
Marigold Grove	13 C4
Marigold Park	13 C4
Marina House Apts	49 C4 [32]
Marina Village	3 B2
Marine Avenue	60 E1
Marine Court (Dalkey)	60 E1
Marine Court (Dún Laoghaire)	50 D4 [17]
Marine Cove	28 D1 [4]
Marine Drive	39 A4
Marine Parade	60 E1
Marine Road	50 D4
Marine Terrace (Bray)	68 D2 [17]
Marine Terrace (Dún Laoghaire)	50 D4 [9]
Marine View	48 F3
Marine Villas	30 D1 [7]
Mariners Court	27 C2 [1]
Mariners Cove	30 E2
Mariner's Port	72 E3
Marino	25 C4
Marino Avenue	26 D4
Marino Avenue East	60 E4
Marino Avenue West	60 E4
Marino Court	25 C4 [13]
Marino Crescent	25 C4
Marino Green	25 C4
Marino Mart	25 C4 [9]
Marino Park	25 C4
Marino Park Avenue	25 C4
Marino Villa	26 D3 [3]
Marion Villas	74 E2
Mark Street	72 D4
Market House	67 C2
Market Square	70 F3
Market Square	67 C2 [49]
Market Square Apts.	71 A3
Market Street South	74 E1
Mark's Alley West	74 F1
Mark's Lane	72 D4
Marlay View	57 B2
Marlborough Court	71 C3
Marlborough Lane	47 B1 [25]
Marlborough Mews	70 D2
Marlborough Park	60 D1 [9]
Marlborough Place	71 C3
Marlborough Road (Donnybrook)	47 B1
Marlborough Road (Glenageary)	60 E1
Marlborough Road (Nth Circular Rd)	70 D2
Marlborough Street	71 C3
Marlborough Terrace	68 D2 [16]
Marley Avenue	57 A1
Marley Close	57 A1
Marley Court North	57 A1
Marley Court South	57 A1
Marley Drive	57 A1
Marley Grove	57 A1
Marley Lawn	57 A1
Marley Rise	57 A1
Marley Villas	57 A1 [1]
Marley Walk	57 A1
Marlfield	59 C3
Marlfield Close	54 F3
Marlfield Court	54 F3
Marlfield Crescent	54 F3
Marlfield Green	54 F3
Marlfield Grove	54 F3
Marlfield Lawn	54 F3
Marlfield Mall	54 F3
Marlfield Place	54 F3
Marmion Court Flats	70 F3
Marne Villas	70 F2
Marrowbone Lane	74 E2
Marrowbone Lane Close (off Marrowbone Lane)	74 E1
Marrowbone Lane Flats	74 E1
Marshal Court Apts.	74 E1
Marshal Lane (Marshalsea Lane)	74 E1
Marshalsea Court	70 E4
Marshalsea Lane	70 E4
Marsham Court	58 E1
Mart Lane	59 B3
Martello Avenue	50 D4 [14]
Martello Court	4 D4
Martello Mews	48 E1
Martello Terrace (Booterstown)	48 F3 [1]
Martello Terrace (Bray)	67 C1 [2]
Martello Terrace (Dun Laoghaire)	50 E4 [2]
Martello Terrace (Sutton)	29 B3 [2]
Martello View	39 B4 [3]
Martello Wood	39 B4 [6]
Martin Grove	24 D4
Martin Savage Park	23 C3
Martin Street	75 A3
Martin White Chalets	39 A4 [9]
Martin's Row	36 E2
*Martin's Terrace (off Hanover Street East)	72 D4
Mary Street	71 A3
Mary Street Little	71 A4
Maryfield Avenue	26 E2 [1]
Maryfield Crescent	26 E2
Maryfield Drive	26 D2
Maryland	64 E2 [5]
Mary's Abbey	71 A4
Mary's Lane	71 A4
Maryville Road	26 F3
Mask Avenue	26 E2
Mask Crescent	26 E2
Mask Drive	26 E2
Mask Green	26 E2
Mask Road	26 E2
Mather Road North	48 E3
Mather Road South	48 D3
Matt Talbot Court	71 C2
Maunsell Place	71 A2
Maxwell Court	47 A1 [18]
Maxwell Lane	47 A2
Maxwell Road	47 A1
Maxwell Street	74 E2
May Lane	70 F4
May Park	26 D3
*May Street (off Fitzroy Ave)	25 B4
Mayberry Park	45 A4
Mayberry Road	44 F4
Mayeston Boulevard	11 B3
Mayeston Close	11 B3
Mayeston Court	11 B4
Mayeston Crescent	11 B4
Mayeston Downs	11 C4
Mayeston Drive	11 B3
Mayeston Lawn	11 B3
Mayeston Rise	11 B4
Mayeston Square	11 B4
Mayeston Walk	11 C4
Mayfair	3 C2
Mayfield	47 A2
Mayfield Park	35 B4
Mayfield Road (Kilmainham)	73 C2
Mayfield Road (Terenure)	46 F2
Mayfield Terrace (Ballinteer)	57 C2
Mayfield Terrace (Bray)	67 C3 [17]
Mayne Bridge	14 F3
Maynetown	14 F3
Maynooth	18 D2

STREET NAME	PAGE/GRID REFERENCE	STREET NAME	PAGE/GRID REFERENCE	STREET NAME	PAGE/GRID REFERENCE	STREET NAME	PAGE/GRID REFERENCE
Maynooth Park	18 D4	Méile an Rí Green	34 F3	Merrion Street Lower	76 D1	*Milltown Collonade (on	47 B2
Maynooth Road (Celbridge)	31 C1	Méile an Rí Park	34 F3	Merrion Street Upper	75 C2	Milltown Road)	
Maynooth Road (Dunboyne)	7 A3	Méile an Rí Road	34 F3	Merrion View Avenue	48 D1 [1]	Milltown Drive	47 A3
Mayola Court	47 B4	Méile an Rí View	34 F3	Merrion Village	48 E1	Milltown Grove (Churchtown)	47 A3
Mayor Square	72 E3	Mellifont Avenue	50 D4	Merry Bush	39 A4 [34]	Milltown Grove (Clonskeagh)	47 B2 [6]
Mayor Street Lower	72 D3	Mellowes Avenue	24 D1	Merrycourt	8 E2	Milltown Hill	47 B2 [7]
Mayor Street Upper	72 F3	Mellowes Court	24 D2 [3]	Merton Avenue	74 F3	Milltown Park	47 B1
Mayville Terrace	60 F1 [11]	Mellowes Crescent	24 D2 [4]	Merton Drive	47 B1	Milltown Path	47 B2
Maywood Avenue	27 B2	Mellowes Park	24 D1	Merton Park	74 F3	Milltown Road	47 B2
Maywood Close	27 B2	Mellowes Road	24 D1	Merton Road	47 B2	*Milltown Terrace (Dundrum)	47 B3 [4]
Maywood Crescent	27 B3	Mellows Bridge	70 F4	Merville Avenue (Fairview)	25 C4	Millview	44 E1 [7]
Maywood Drive	27 B2	Melrose Avenue (Clondalkin)	43 C1	Merville Avenue (Stillorgan)	58 F1	Millview Close	3 A3
Maywood Grove	27 B2	Melrose Avenue (Fairview)	25 C4	Merville Road	58 F1	Millview Cottages	73 A2
Maywood Lawn	27 B3	Melrose Court	25 C4 [16]	Mespil Estate	76 D3	Millview Court	3 A2
Maywood Park	27 B2	Melrose Crescent	43 C1	Mespil Lodge	76 D3	Millview Lawns	3 A3
Maywood Road	27 B2	Melrose Green	43 C1	Mespil Road	76 D3	Millview Road	3 A3
McAuley Avenue	26 F2	Melrose Grove	43 C1	Metropolitan Apts.	73 A1	Millwood Court	27 A1
McAuley Drive	26 F2	Melrose Lawn	34 F4	Michael Collins Park	35 A4	Millwood Park	27 A1
McAuley Park	26 F2	Melrose Park (Clondalkin)	43 C1	Michael Collins Park	44 D1	Millwood Villas	27 A1
McAuley Road	26 F2	Melrose Park (Swords) (Swords)	2 E3	Middle Third	26 E3	Milton Hall	1 C2
McCabe Villas	48 E3	Melrose Park The Avenue	2 E3	Middle Third Terrace	26 E3	Milton Terrace	2 D2
McCarthy Terrace	74 D2	Melrose Park The Close	2 E3	Milesian Avenue	2 E2	Milton Terrace	67 C2 [13]
McCreadies Lane	3 A3	Melrose Park The Crescent	2 E3	Milesian Court	2 E2	Milward Terrace	68 D2 [13]
McDowell Avenue	74 D1	Melrose Park The Drive	2 E3	Milesian Grove	2 E2	Mine Hill Lane	63 B3
McGrane Court	57 C1 [5]	Melrose Park The Green	2 E3	Milesian Lawn	2 E2	Minnow Brook	46 F2
McKee Avenue	24 E1	Melrose Park The Grove	2 E3	Milestown	6 F4	*Minstrel Court	58 F2
McKee Park	69 C1	Melrose Park The Heights	2 E3	Milestown	19 C1	(Charles Sheil's Houses)	
McKee Road	24 E1	Melrose Park The Lawn	2 E3	Milford	3 A2	Misery Hill	72 E4
McKelvey Avenue	11 A4	Melrose Park The Park	2 E3	Military Road (Killiney)	60 E4	Moat Lane	1 A2
McKelvey Road	11 A4	Melrose Park The Rise	2 E3	Military Road (Kilmainham)	73 C1	Moatfield Avenue	26 F1
McMahon Street	75 A3	Melrose Park The Villa	2 E3	Military Road (Phoenix Park)	36 F2	Moatfield Park	26 F1
McMorrough Road	46 F2 [14]	Melrose Park The Walk	2 E3	Military Road (Rathmines)	75 B4	Moatfield Road	26 F1
Meade's Terrace	76 D1	Melrose Road	34 F4	Mill Bank	34 D1 [15]	Moatview Avenue	13 B4
Meadow Avenue	57 B1 [1]	Melville Close	11 B4	Mill Bridge (Swords)	2 D2	Moatview Court	13 B4
Meadow Close (Dundrum)	57 A1	Melville Court	11 B4	Mill Brook Apts.	35 C1	Moatview Drive	13 B4
Meadow Close	59 A1	Melville Cove	11 B4	Mill Court Avenue	43 C1	Moatview Gardens	13 B4
(Newtown Park Ave)		Melville Crescent	11 B4	Mill Court Drive	43 C1	Moatview Terrace	13 B4 [5]
Meadow Copse	21 C1	Melville Drive	11 B4	Mill Field (Enniskerry)	66 E3	Mobhi Court	25 A3 [16]
Meadow Court	60 D4 [2]	Melville Green	11 B4	Mill House	62 F3	Mobhi Road	25 A3
Meadow Dale	21 C1 [1]	Melville Grove	11 B4	Mill Lane (Ashtown)	23 B3 [1]	Moeran Road	45 C1
Meadow Downs	21 C1	Melville Lawn	11 B4	Mill Lane (Leixlip)	33 A1	Moira Road	70 D3
Meadow Drive	21 C1	Melville Park	11 B4	Mill Lane (Loughlinstown)	64 E2	(off Oxmanstown Road)	
Meadow Green	21 C1	Melville Rise	11 B4	Mill Lane (Newmarket)	74 F2	Moland House	71 C3
Meadow Grove	57 B1	Melville Square	11 B4	Mill Lane (Palmerstown)	35 C1	Moland Place	71 C3
Meadow Mount	57 A1	Melville Terrace	11 B4	Mill Park	44 D1	Molesworth Close	1 A2
Meadow Park	57 A1	Melville View	11 B4	Mill Road (Blanchardstown)	22 F2	Molesworth Place	75 C1
Meadow Park Avenue	47 A4	Melville Way	11 B4	Mill Road (Saggart)	53 A2	Molesworth Street	75 C1
Meadow Vale	59 B2	Melvin Road	46 F2	Mill Street (Dun Laoghaire)	50 D4 [19]	Mollison Avenue	14 D4
Meadow View (Dunboyne)	7 B2	Memorial Court	69 B4	Mill Street (The Coombe)	74 F2	Molyneux Yard	74 F1
Meadow View	57 A1	Memorial Road	71 C3	Millar's Hall	74 F2	Monalea Grove	55 C1
(Nutgrove Avenue)		(Custom House Quay)		Millar's Hall	74 F1	Monalea Park	55 C1
Meadow Villas	57 A1 [2]	Memorial Road	73 A1	Millbank	14 F2	Monalea Wood	55 C1
Meadow Way	21 C1	(Inchicore Road)		Millbourne Avenue	25 A4	Monaloe Avenue	59 C3
Meadowbank	46 F3	Mercer House	75 B2	Millbrook Avenue	27 A1	Monaloe Court	59 B3 [6]
Meadowbrook	17 C4	Mercer Street Lower	75 B1	Millbrook Court	73 C1	Monaloe Crescent	59 B3 [4]
Meadowbrook Avenue	17 C4	Mercer Street Upper	75 B2	Millbrook Drive	27 A1	Monaloe Drive	59 C3
(Maynooth)		Merchamp	26 F4	Millbrook Grove	27 A1	Monaloe Park	59 C3
Meadowbrook Avenue (Sutton)	28 D1	Merchants Arch	71 B4	Millbrook Lawns	55 A1	Monaloe Park Road	59 C3
Meadowbrook Close	17 C4	(off Temple Bar)		Millbrook Road	27 A1	Monaloe Way	59 C3
Meadowbrook Court	17 C4	Merchant's Court	70 F4	Millbrook Terrace	73 B1	Monasterboice Road	46 D1
Meadowbrook Crescent	17 C4	Merchant's Hall	70 F4	Millbrook Village	47 C1 [17]	Monastery	66 E3
Meadowbrook Drive	17 C4	(Merchants Quay)		Millennium Bridge	71 B4	Monastery Crescent	44 E1
Meadowbrook Lawn	28 D1	Merchant's House	70 F4	Millers Wood	67 B3	Monastery Drive	44 E1
Meadowbrook Lawns	17 C4	Merchant's Quay	70 F4	Millfarm	7 C2	Monastery Gate	44 F1
Meadowbrook Park	28 D1	Merchant's Road	39 A1	Millfield (Portmarnock)	14 F2	Monastery Gate Avenue	44 F1
Meadowbrook Road	17 C4	Merchant's Square	72 F3	Millgate Drive	45 C3	Monastery Gate Close	44 F1
Meadowfield	58 E4	Meretimo Villas	68 D3 [2]	Millmount Avenue	25 A4	Monastery Gate Copse	44 F1
Meadowlands	59 C1	Merlyn Drive	48 D1	Millmount Grove	47 B3	Monastery Gate Green	44 F1
Meadowlands Avenue	59 C1	Merlyn Park	48 D1	Millmount Place	25 B4	Monastery Gate Lawn	44 F1
Meadowlands Court	59 C1 [17]	Merlyn Road	48 D1	*Millmount Terrace	25 B4	Monastery Gate Villas	44 F1
Meadowlands Mews	59 C1 [18]	Merrion	48 E1	(Drumcondra)		Monastery Grove	66 E2
Meadowview Grove	33 C2	Merrion Close	76 D1	Millmount Villas	25 A4 [1]	Monastery Heath	44 E1
Meakstown Cottages	11 B3	Merrion Court	48 E1 [1]	Millrace Avenue	53 A2	Monastery Heath Avenue	44 E1
Meath Market	74 F1	Merrion Crescent	48 E2 [3]	Millrace Court	53 A2	Monastery Heath Court	44 E1
Meath Place (Bray)	67 C2	Merrion Gates	48 E1 [2]	Millrace Crescent	53 A2	Monastery Heath Green	44 E1
Meath Place (Meath Street)	74 F1	Merrion Grove	48 E3	Millrace Green	53 A2	Monastery Heath Square	44 E1
Meath Road	68 D2	Merrion Hall	48 E4	Millrace Park	53 A2	Monastery Heights	44 E1 [2]
Meath Square	74 F1	Merrion Park	48 E3	Millrace Road	23 B3	Monastery Park	44 E1
Meath Street	74 F1	Merrion Place	75 C2	Millrace Walk	53 A2	Monastery Rise	44 E1
*Meath Terrace (on Meath Place)	74 F1	Merrion Road	39 A4	Millrose Estate	36 E4 [2]	Monastery Road	44 E1
*Meathville Terrace	75 A2	Merrion Row	75 C2	Millstead	22 F2	Monastery Walk	44 E1
(on Long Lane)		Merrion Square East	76 D2	Millstream	14 F2	Monck Place	70 F1
Meenan Square	48 D3 [5]	Merrion Square North	76 D1	Millstream Road	33 C2	Monks Hill	66 E2
Meetinghouse Lane	71 A4	Merrion Square South	76 D2	Milltown (Clonskeagh)	47 C2	Monks Meadow	4 D4
Méile an Rí Crescent	34 F3	Merrion Square West	76 D1	Milltown (Peamount)	42 F2	Monksfield	44 F1
Méile an Rí Drive	34 F3	Merrion Strand	48 E1	Milltown Bridge Road	47 C2	Monksfield Court	44 F1

STREET NAME	PAGE/GRID REFERENCE
Monksfield Downs	44 F1
Monksfield Grove	44 F1
Monksfield Heights	44 F1
Monksfield Lawn	44 F1
Monksfield Meadows	44 F1
Monksfield Walk	44 F1
Monkstown	49 B4
Monkstown Avenue	59 B1
Monkstown Crescent	49 C4
Monkstown Farm	59 C1
Monkstown Gate	49 C4 [29]
Monkstown Grove	59 C1
Monkstown Road	49 B4
Monkstown Square	59 B1 [12]
Monkstown Valley	49 B4
Montague Court	75 B2
Montague Lane	75 B2
Montague Place	75 B2
Montague Street	75 B2
Monte Vella	60 F2 [9]
Montebello Terrace	68 D2 [2]
Montpelier Court	70 D3
Montpelier Drive	70 D3
Montpelier Gardens	70 D3
Montpelier Hill	70 D3
Montpelier Manor	49 B4 [2]
Montpelier Parade	49 B4
Montpelier Park	70 D3
Montpelier Place	49 B4 [1]
Montpelier Square	70 D4
Montpelier View	54 D2
Montpelier Walk	54 D2 [2]
Montrose Avenue	26 D2
Montrose Close	26 D2
Montrose Court	26 D2
Montrose Crescent	26 D1
Montrose Drive	26 D1
Montrose Grove	26 D2
Montrose Park	26 D2
Moore Lane	71 B3
Moore Street	71 B3
Moorefield	60 E4
Moore's Cottages	59 A1 [3]
Mooretown	1 B1
Mooretown Avenue	1 C1
Mooretown Grove	1 C1
Mooretown Park	1 C1
Moorfield	35 A4
Moorfield Avenue	35 A4
Moorfield Close	35 A4 [2]
Moorfield Drive	35 A4
Moorfield Green	35 A4
Moorfield Grove	35 A4
Moorfield Lawns	35 A4
Moorfield Parade	35 A4
Moorfield Walk	35 A4
Moracrete Cottages	73 C4
Moran's Cottages	47 B1 [12]
Moreen Avenue	58 D2
Moreen Close	58 D2
Moreen Lawn	58 D2 [2]
Moreen Park	58 D2
Moreen Road	58 D2
Moreen Walk	58 D2
Morehampton Lane	76 E4
Morehampton Mews	76 E4
Morehampton Road	76 E4
Morehampton Square	76 E4
Morehampton Terrace	47 C1
Morgan Place	70 F4
Morgans Place	23 A3
Moritz House	55 B2
Morning Star Avenue	70 F3
Morning Star Road	74 D2
Mornington Avenue	50 E4 [1]
Mornington Grove	26 E2
Mornington Park	26 E2
Mornington Road	47 B1
Morrogh Terrace	25 C3 [2]
Moss Street	71 C4
Mount Albany	59 A1
Mount Albion Road	57 B1
Mount Albion Road	57 B1 [3]
Mount Alton	55 C1
Mount Alton Court	56 D1
Mount Andrew	34 F2
Mount Andrew Avenue	34 F2
Mount Andrew Close	34 F1
Mount Andrew Court	34 F1
Mount Andrew Crescent	34 F1
Mount Andrew Dale	34 F2
Mount Andrew Grove	34 F1
Mount Andrew Place	34 F1
Mount Andrew Rise	34 F1
Mount Anthony Estate	47 A1 [22]
Mount Anville Lawn	48 D4
Mount Anville Park	48 D4
Mount Anville Road	48 D4
Mount Anville Wood	48 D4
Mount Argus Avenue	46 F1
Mount Argus Close	46 F1
Mount Argus Court	46 F1
Mount Argus Crescent	46 F1
Mount Argus Green	46 F1
Mount Argus Grove	46 F1
Mount Argus Park	46 F1
Mount Argus Road	46 F1
Mount Argus Square	46 F1 [15]
Mount Argus Terrace	46 F1
Mount Argus View	46 F1
Mount Argus Way	46 F1
Mount Auburn	60 E3 [2]
Mount Bellew Crescent	34 F2
Mount Bellew Green	34 F2
Mount Bellew Rise	34 E2
Mount Bellew Way	34 E2
Mount Brown	73 C1
Mount Carmel Avenue	47 C4
Mount Carmel Park	55 C1
Mount Carmel Road	47 C4
Mount Dillon Court	26 E2
Mount Drinan Avenue	2 E3
Mount Drinan Crescent	2 E3
Mount Drinan Grove	2 E3
Mount Drinan Lawn	2 E3
Mount Drinan Park	2 E3
Mount Drinan Walk	2 E3
Mount Drummond Avenue	74 F4
Mount Drummond Court	74 F4
Mount Drummond Square	75 A4
Mount Eagle Court	58 E3
Mount Eagle Drive	58 E3
Mount Eagle Green	58 E3
Mount Eagle Grove	58 E3
Mount Eagle Lawn	58 E3
Mount Eagle Park	58 E3
Mount Eagle Rise	58 D3
Mount Eagle View	58 E3
Mount Eagle Way	58 E3
Mount Eden Road	47 C1
Mount Eustace	9 B2
Mount Eustace Avenue	9 B2
Mount Eustace Close	9 A2
Mount Eustace Drive	9 B2
Mount Eustace Green	9 B2
Mount Eustace Grove	9 A2
Mount Eustace Park	9 B2
Mount Eustace Rise	9 B2
Mount Eustace Walk	9 B2
Mount Gandon	34 D1 [9]
Mount Garrett	9 B2
Mount Harold Terrace	46 F1 [1]
Mount Hybla Court	23 A4
Mount Hybla House	23 A4
Mount Merrion	48 E4
Mount Merrion Avenue	48 F3
Mount Norris Villas	68 D2 [19]
Mount Olive Grove	27 B1
Mount Olive Park	27 B1
Mount Olive Road	27 B1
Mount Prospect Avenue	26 F4
Mount Prospect Drive	26 F4
Mount Prospect Grove	26 F4
Mount Prospect House	27 A4 [4]
Mount Prospect Lawn	26 F4
Mount Prospect Park	26 F4
Mount Salus Road	60 F2
Mount Sandford	47 C1 [14]
Mount St. Annes	47 B2
Mount Street Crescent	76 E2
Mount Street Lower	76 D1
Mount Street Upper	76 D2
Mount Symon Avenue	21 C2
Mount Symon Close	21 C2
Mount Symon Crescent	21 B2
Mount Symon Dale	21 B2
Mount Symon Drive	21 C2
Mount Symon Estate	21 B2
Mount Symon Green	21 B2
Mount Symon Lawn	21 C2
Mount Symon Park	21 C2
Mount Symon Rise	21 B2
Mount Talbot	44 F1
Mount Tallant Avenue	46 F2
Mount Temple Road	70 E3
Mount Venus Road	56 D4
Mount View Road	22 D2
Mount Wood	59 C1
Mountain Park	55 A1
Mountain View	54 D2
Mountain View	64 E3
Mountain View Apts.	67 C3 [11]
Mountain View Avenue	46 F1 [3]
Mountain View Cottages (Castleknock)	22 D4
Mountain View Cottages (Ranelagh)	47 B1 [13]
Mountain View Court	71 C2
Mountain View Court (Harold's Cross)	46 F1 [16]
Mountain View Court (off Summerhill Place)	71 C2
Mountain View Drive	57 A1
Mountain View Park	47 A4
Mountain View Road (Ballybrack)	60 E4 [5]
Mountain View Road (Ranelagh)	47 B1
Mountain Villa	60 E4 [3]
Mountainview Drive	67 C4
Mountbrook	48 E3 [2]
Mountdown Avenue	45 C3
Mountdown Drive	45 C3
Mountdown Park	45 C3
Mountdown Road	45 C3
Mountfield	3 B3
Mountgorry Wood Apts.	2 E2
Mountjoy Parade	71 C1
Mountjoy Place	71 C2
Mountjoy Square	71 C2
Mountjoy Square Apts	71 C2
Mountjoy Square Apts.	71 B2
Mountjoy Square East	71 C2
Mountjoy Square North	71 C2
Mountjoy Square South	71 C2
Mountjoy Square West	71 B2
Mountjoy Street	71 A2
Mountjoy Street Middle	71 A2
Mountpleasant Avenue Lower	75 B4
Mountpleasant Avenue Upper	75 B4
Mountpleasant Parade	75 B4
Mountpleasant Place	75 C4
Mountpleasant Square	75 B4
Mountpleasant Terrace	75 B4
*Mountpleasant Terrace Upper (off Mountpleasant Place)	75 C4
*Mountpleasant Terrace Upper (Mountpleasant Villas)	75 C4
Mountpleasant Villas	75 C4
Mountpleasant Villas	67 B2 [13]
Mountsandel	59 B4
Mountshannon Road	73 C2
Mounttown Cottages	49 C4 [26]
Mounttown Park	59 C1 [3]
Mounttown Road Lower	59 C1
Mounttown Road Lower	59 C1
Mounttown Road Upper	49 C4
Mourne Road	36 F4
Mourne Road	73 A3
Moy Elta Road	72 E2
Moy Glas Avenue	34 E3
Moy Glas Chase	34 E3
Moy Glas Close	34 E3
Moy Glas Court	34 E3
Moy Glas Dale	34 E3
Moy Glas Dene	34 E3
Moy Glas Drive	34 E3
Moy Glas Glen	34 E3
Moy Glas Green	34 E3
Moy Glas Grove	34 E3
Moy Glas Lawn	34 E3
Moy Glas Park	34 E3
Moy Glas Road	34 E3
Moy Glas Vale	34 E3
Moy Glas View	34 E3
Moy Glas Way	34 E3
Moy Glas Wood	34 E3
Moyclare Avenue	28 D1
Moyclare Close	28 D1
Moyclare Drive	28 D1
Moyclare Gardens	28 D1 [6]
Moyclare Park	28 D1
Moyclare Road	28 D1
Moycullen Road	35 C3
Moygaddy	18 D1
Moyglare	17 A1
Moyglare Abbey	17 B2
Moyglare Hall	17 C2
Moyglare Meadows	17 C2
Moyglare Road	17 C2
Moyglare Village	17 C2
Moyle Crescent	44 E1
Moyle Road	24 E3
Moyne	14 F3
Moyne Court	47 B1 [22]
Moyne Park	14 F3
Moyne Road (Balgriffin)	14 E3
Moyne Road (Ranelagh)	47 B1
Moynihan Court	55 B1 [6]
Moyville	56 E2
Moyville Lawns	56 E1
Muckross Avenue	46 D2
Muckross Crescent	46 D2
Muckross Drive	46 D2 [1]
Muckross Green	46 D2
Muckross Grove	46 D2
Muckross Parade	71 B1
Muckross Park	46 D2
Muirfield Drive	36 F4 [1]
Mulally's Lane	52 F2
Mulberry Crescent	22 F4
Mulberry Drive	22 E4
Mulberry Park	22 E4
Muldowney Court	3 C3
Mulgrave Street	50 D4
Mulgrave Terrace	50 D4
Mulhuddart	9 A4
Mulhuddart Bridge	9 A4
Mulhuddart Wood	9 A4
Mullauns	42 D1
Mullen Bridge	18 D3
Mullinastill Road	64 D2
Mullingar Terrace	36 E2 [10]
Mulroy Road	24 E4
Mulvey Park	47 C3
Munster Street	24 F4
Munster Terrace	60 E1 [16]
Murphy's Lane	63 B4
Murphy's Lane	66 E1
Murphystown Road	58 E3
Murragh	14 F2
Murray's Cottages	36 F3 [4]
Murtagh Road	70 E3
Muskerry Road	36 E3
Mutton Lane	56 E4
Myra Cottages	73 A1
Myra Manor	3 A4
Myrtle Avenue	60 D1 [3]
Myrtle Grove (Bray)	67 B1 [3]
Myrtle Grove (Stillorgan)	58 F1
Myrtle Park	60 D1
Myrtle Square	14 F4
Myrtle Street	71 A2

N

STREET NAME	PAGE/GRID REFERENCE
Naas Road (Kingswood)	43 C4
Naas Road (Rathcoole)	52 F1
Naas Road (Saggart)	53 B1
Naas Road (Walkinstown)	45 A1
Nagle Court	18 D2
Nangor Crescent	44 D1 [5]
Nangor Place	43 C1 [2]
Nangor Road (Clondalkin)	44 D1

STREET NAME	PAGE/GRID REFERENCE
Nangor Road (Fox & Geese)	44 F1
Nangor Road (Grange Castle)	43 A2
Nanikin Avenue	27 A3
Nash Street	36 F3
Nashville Park	30 E2
Nashville Road	30 D2
Nassau Street	75 C1
Naul Road (Brackenstown Road)	1 A3
Naul Road (Cloghran)	1 C4
Navan Road	23 A3
Navan Road (Blanchardstown)	22 E1
Navan Road (Cabra)	24 D4
Navan Road (Clonee)	8 E3
Navan Road (Dunboyne)	7 B2
Navan Road (Mulhuddart)	8 F4
Neagh Road	46 E2
Neilstown Avenue	35 A3
Neilstown Cottages	35 A4 [3]
Neilstown Crescent	35 A3
Neilstown Drive	35 A3
Neilstown Gardens	35 A3
Neilstown Park	35 A3
Neilstown Road	35 A3
Neilstown Village Court	35 A3 [1]
Nelson Street	71 A1
Nephin Road	24 D4
Neptune Terrace	60 E1 [17]
Nerano Road	60 Inset
Nerney's Court	71 B2
Nethercross Court	2 D1
Nethercross Court	2 D1
Neville Road	47 A2
Nevinstown Lane	1 C3
New Bancroft Hall	55 A1 [11]
New Bancroft Place	55 A1 [9]
New Bancroft Square	55 A1 [12]
New Bawn Drive	55 A2
New Bawn Park	55 A2
New Bride Street	75 A2
New Bridge	32 F2
New Brighton Terrace	67 C2 [47]
New Cornelscourt	59 B3 [7]
New Grange Road	59 A1
New Grove Estate	14 E4
New Ireland Court	73 C2
New Ireland Road	73 C2
New Lucan Road	35 B1
New Nangor Road	43 C1
New Park Lodge	59 A2 [3]
New Park Road	59 A1
New Rathmore Terrace	67 B2 [23]
New Ravenswell Row	67 B2 [20]
New River Road	23 A2
New Road (Clondalkin)	44 E2
New Road (Howth)	30 E3
New Road (Inchicore)	36 F3
New Road (Swords)	2 D2 [5]
New Row	36 E2 [12]
New Row Place	75 A2
New Row South	74 F2
New Row Square	74 F2
New Street	3 B2
New Street Garden's (off New Street)	75 A2
New Street North (off Church Street)	70 F3
New Street South	75 A2
New Vale	64 E3
New Vale Cottages	64 D3
New Vale Crescent	64 E3
New Wapping Street	72 F3
Newbridge Avenue	39 A3
Newbridge Drive	39 A3
Newbrook Avenue	27 B1
Newbrook Road	27 B1
Newbury Avenue	13 A4
Newbury Drive	13 A4
Newbury Grove	13 A4
Newbury Lawns	13 B4
Newbury Park	13 A4
Newbury Terrace	13 A4 [1]
Newcastle	41 C4
Newcastle Demesne	41 B4
Newcastle Farm	41 B4
Newcastle Lyons	42 D4
Newcastle Manor	42 D4
Newcastle Road (Lucan)	34 D2
Newcastle Road (Rathcoole)	52 E1
Newcomen Avenue	72 D1
Newcomen Bridge	72 D2
Newcomen Court	72 D1
Newcourt (Bray)	68 D4
Newcourt (Swords) (Swords)	2 D1
Newcourt Avenue	68 D3
Newcourt Mews	2 D1
Newcourt Road	68 D3
Newcourt Villas	67 C3 [8]
Newgrange Road	24 F4
Newgrove Avenue	39 B4
Newhall Court	54 D2
Newington Terrace	47 A1 [27]
Newlands Avenue	44 E2
Newlands Court	26 D2 [1]
Newlands Cross	44 E2
Newlands Drive	44 E2
Newlands Manor	44 D3
Newlands Manor Court	44 D3
Newlands Manor Drive	44 D3
Newlands Manor Fairway	44 D3
Newlands Manor Green	44 D3
Newlands Manor Park	44 D3
Newlands Park	44 E2
Newlands Road (Clondalkin)	44 E2
Newlands Road (Ronanstown)	34 F3
Newman Place	18 D3
Newmarket	74 F2
Newmarket Street	74 F2
Newpark	59 A2
Newport Street	74 E1
Newtown (Dunboyne)	7 A3
Newtown (Glencullen)	62 E3
Newtown (Rathfarnham)	56 E3
Newtown (Tinnehinch)	66 E4
Newtown Avenue (Blackrock)	49 A3
Newtown Avenue (Coolock)	26 F1
Newtown Bridge	7 A2
Newtown Close	13 C4
Newtown Cottages (Coolock)	26 F1
Newtown Cottages (St. Margaret's)	11 A1
Newtown Court (Coolock)	13 C4
Newtown Court (Maynooth)	17 B4
Newtown Court (Rathgar)	47 A3 [5]
Newtown Drive	26 F1
Newtown Glendale	20 D4
Newtown Grove	17 C3
Newtown House	47 A3 [12]
Newtown Lower	51 C4
Newtown Park (Blackrock)	59 A1
Newtown Park (Coolock)	26 F1
Newtown Park (Leixlip)	20 D4
Newtown Park (Tallaght)	55 B1
Newtown Park Court	59 A1 [8]
Newtown Road (Celbridge)	32 D4
Newtown Road (Coolock)	13 C4
Newtown Road (Maynooth)	17 B4
Newtown Road (Maynooth)	17 C3
Newtown Upper	52 D4
Newtown Villas (Blackrock)	49 A3 [1]
Newtown Villas (Braemor Road)	47 A3 [4]
Newtown Way	13 C4
Newtownpark Avenue	49 A4
Newtownpark House	59 A1 [11]
Newtownsmith	50 E4
Niall Street	70 D3
Nicholas Avenue	70 F3
Nicholas Street	75 A1
Ninth Lock Road	44 D1
No2 Nth. Road Extension	39 B1
Noel Purcell Park	75 B1
Nore Road	24 E3
Norfolk Road	24 F4
Norseman Court (off Norseman Place)	70 E3
Norseman Place	70 E3
North Avenue	48 E3
North Bull Island	27 B4
North Circular Road (Phibsborough)	71 C1
North Circular Road (Phoenix Park)	70 D2
North Clarence St Flats	72 D2
North Great George's St	71 B2
North Quay Extension	39 A2
North Road (Finglas)	24 D1
North Road (Phoenix Park)	23 B4
North Road (Phoenix Park)	69 B1
North Strand Road	72 E1
North Street	2 D1
North Wall	72 E3
North Wall Quay	72 E4
Northbrook Avenue (Ranelagh)	75 C4
Northbrook Avenue Lower	72 E1
Northbrook Avenue Upper	72 E1
Northbrook Lane	75 C4
Northbrook Road	75 C4
Northbrook Terrace	72 E1
*Northbrook Villas (on Northbrook Road Ranelagh)	75 C4
Northcote Avenue	49 C4
Northcote Place	49 C4 [23]
Northcote Terrace	49 C4 [20]
Northern Close	13 B3
Northern Cross Route	11 B3
Northern Cross Route	23 A2
Northland Drive	24 F3 [2]
Northland Grove	24 F3 [1]
Northumberland Avenue	50 D4
Northumberland Park	50 D4 [11]
Northumberland Place (Dún Laoghaire)	50 D4 [10]
Northumberland Place (Grand Canal St. Upr.)	76 E2
Northumberland Road	76 E2
Northumberland Square	71 C3
Northway Estate	11 A4
Northwood	12 E4
Norton's Avenue	70 F1
Norwood	64 E1
Norwood Park	47 C1 [7]
Nottingham Street	72 E1
Novara Avenue	67 C2
Novara Mews	67 C2 [57]
Novara Park	67 C2 [7]
Novara Terrace	67 C2 [27]
Nugent Road	47 A4
Nunciature Road (Phoenix Park)	23 C4
Nun's Lane	26 E3
Nuns Walk	26 E3
Nurney Lawn	14 D4
Nutgrove Avenue	47 A4
Nutgrove Avenue	47 B4 [14]
Nutgrove Court	47 A4 [2]
Nutgrove Crescent	57 A1
Nutgrove Park (Clonskeagh)	47 C2
Nutgrove Way	57 A1
Nutley Avenue	48 D1
Nutley Lane	48 D2
Nutley Park	48 D2
Nutley Road	48 D1
Nutley Square	48 D2 [1]

O

O'Neill's Park	18 D3
Oak Apple Green	47 A2
Oak Avenue	12 F4
Oak Close	44 F1
Oak Court	12 F4
Oak Crescent	12 F4
Oak Dene	60 E3
Oak Downs	44 D2
Oak Drive (Fox & Geese)	44 F1
Oak Drive (Santry)	12 F4
Oak Glen Park	67 C4
Oak Glen View	67 C4
Oak Green	12 F4
Oak Grove	12 F4
Oak Hall	3 B3
Oak House	76 D3
Oak House (Swords)	1 Inset
Oak Lawn (Castleknock)	22 F3
Oak Lawn (Santry)	12 F4
Oak Lodge	23 A4
Oak Rise (Clondalkin)	44 D2
Oak Rise (Santry)	12 F4
Oak Road (Donnycarney)	26 D3
Oak Road (Fox & Geese)	44 F1
Oak View	12 E4
Oak Way	44 D2
Oakbury Court	39 A4 [44]
Oakcourt Avenue	35 C2
Oakcourt Close	35 C2
Oakcourt Drive	35 C2
Oakcourt Grove	35 C2
Oakcourt Lawn	35 C2
Oakcourt Park	35 C2
Oakdale Close	55 B3
Oakdale Crescent	55 B3
Oakdale Drive (Firhouse)	55 B3
Oakdale Drive (Sallynoggin)	59 C2
Oakdale Grove	55 B3
Oakdale Park	55 B3
Oakdale Road	55 B3
Oakdown Road	47 A4
Oakfield Place	75 A3
Oaklands Avenue	2 D2
Oaklands Court	39 A4 [38]
Oaklands Crescent	47 A2
Oaklands Drive (Rathgar)	47 A2
Oaklands Drive (Sandymount)	39 A4
Oaklands Park (Sandymount)	39 A4
Oaklands Park (Swords)	2 D2
Oaklands Terrace	46 F2
Oaklawn	19 C4
Oaklawn Close	19 C4
Oaklawn West	19 C4
Oakleigh	31 C4
Oakleigh Court	3 A3 [3]
Oakley Court	47 B1 [10]
Oakley Grove	49 A4
Oakley Park (Blackrock)	49 A4
Oakley Park (Clontarf)	26 F4
Oakley Park (Ranelagh)	47 B1 [23]
Oakley Road	47 B1
Oakley Square	47 B1 [20]
Oakpark Avenue	25 C1
Oakpark Close	25 C1
Oakpark Drive	25 C1
Oakpark Grove	25 C1
Oakton Court	60 E1 [4]
Oakton Drive	60 D4
Oakton Green	60 D4 [3]
Oakton Park	60 D4
Oakton Park	64 D1
Oaktree Avenue	22 E3
Oaktree Drive	22 E3
Oaktree Green	22 E3
Oaktree Grove	22 E3
Oaktree Lawn	22 E3
Oaktree Road	58 F1
Oakview Avenue	21 C1
Oakview Close	21 C1
Oakview Court	21 C1
Oakview Drive	21 C1
Oakview Grove	21 C1 [2]
Oakview Lawn	21 C1
Oakview Park	21 C1
Oakview Rise	21 C1
Oakview Walk	21 C1
Oakview Way	21 C1
Oakwood	49 C4 [7]
Oakwood Apts.	27 B3 [3]
Oakwood Avenue (Glasnevin)	24 E1
Oakwood Avenue (Swords)	1 C2
Oakwood Close	24 E1
Oakwood Grove Estate	35 A4
Oakwood Park	24 E1
Oakwood Road	24 E1
Oatfield Avenue	35 B3
Oatfield Close	35 B3
*Oatfield Crescent (off Oatfield Drive)	35 B2
Oatfield Drive	35 B3
Oatfield Grove	35 B3
Oatfield Lawn	35 B3
Oatfield Park	35 B3
Obelisk Avenue	59 A1 [12]
Obelisk Court (Malahide)	3 C2 [3]
Obelisk Court (Stillorgan)	59 A1
Obelisk Grove	59 A1
Obelisk Lane	18 E4
Obelisk Rise	59 A1
Obelisk Walk	59 A1

STREET NAME	PAGE/GRID REFERENCE	STREET NAME	PAGE/GRID REFERENCE	STREET NAME	PAGE/GRID REFERENCE	STREET NAME	PAGE/GRID REFERENCE
Oblate Drive	36 F3 [14]	Old Quay	29 B2	O'Neill's Buildings	75 A2	Ormond Place	71 A4
O'Brien Road	45 C1	Old Quay Mews	29 B2	Ongar Chase Estate	21 A1	(off Ormond Quay Upper)	
O'Brien's Place North	25 A3 [13]	Old Quay Terrace	29 B2	Ongar Green	21 A1	Ormond Quay Lower	71 B4
Observatory Court	75 B4	Old Rathmichael	64 D3	Ongar Park Estate	21 B1	Ormond Quay Upper	71 A4
Observatory Lane	47 A1 [14]	Old Rathmore Terrace	67 B2 [22]	Ongar Road	21 B2	Ormond Road	25 B4
O'Byrne Road	67 C3	Old Ravenswell Row	67 B4 [29]	Ongar Village	21 A1	Ormond Road South	47 B1
O'Byrne Villas	67 C3 [9]	Old Rectory	34 D1 [11]	Ongar-Hartstown Relief Road	21 C2	Ormond Square	71 A4
O'Carolan Road	74 F2	Old Rectory Park	47 C4	Ontario Terrace	75 B4	Ormond Street	74 F2
O'Casey Avenue	35 C4	Old Road	14 E2	Onward Close	3 C4	*Ormond Terrace	60 F2
O'Connell Avenue	71 A1	Old Street	3 B2	Onward Walk	3 C4	(off Sorrento Road)	
O'Connell Bridge	71 B4	Old Yellow Walls Road	3 A2	Ophaly Court	47 C4	Ormond View	1 B1
O'Connell Gardens	39 A3	Oldbawn	55 A2	O'Quinns Avenue	74 D1	Ormond Way	1 B1
O'Connell Street	71 B3	Oldbridge	34 E3	O'Rahilly House Flats	39 A3 [28]	O'Rourke Park	59 C2
O'Curry Avenue	74 F2	Oldbridge Close	34 E3	O'Rahilly Parade	71 B3	Orpen	58 F1
(off O'Curry Road)		Oldbridge Court	34 E3	Oranmore Road	35 C3	Orpen Close	48 F4
O'Curry Road	74 F2	Oldbridge Glen	34 E3	Oratory Mews Court	50 D4 [24]	Orpen Dale	48 F4 [2]
O'Daly Road	25 A3	Oldbridge Green	34 E3	Orby Avenue	58 E3	Orpen Green	58 F1
Odd Lamp Road	36 F1	Oldbridge Grove	34 E3	Orby Close	58 F3	Orpen Hill	58 F1
O'Devaney Gardens	70 D3	Oldbridge Park	34 E3	Orby Court	58 F3	Orpen Rise	58 F1
O'Donnell Gardens	60 D1 [1]	Oldbridge View	34 E3	Orby Lawn	58 E3	Orr's Terrace	74 F4
O'Donoghue Street	36 F3	Oldbridge Walk	34 E3	Orby Park	58 F3	Orwell Bank	47 A3 [7]
O'Donovan Road	74 F3	Oldbridge Way	34 E3	Orby View	58 E3	Orwell Court	47 A3 [3]
O'Donovan Rossa Bridge	71 A4	Oldcarton	18 F1	Orby Village	58 E3	Orwell Gardens	47 A3
O'Dwyer Road	45 C1 [4]	Oldcastle Avenue	29 B2	Orby Way	58 E3	Orwell Mews	47 A2 [8]
Offaly Bridge	18 E1	Oldcastle Drive	43 B1	Orchard Avenue (Citywest)	53 B1	Orwell Park	46 D4
Offaly Road	24 F4	Oldcastlepark	43 B1	Orchard Avenue (Clonsilla)	21 C2	Orwell Park (Rathgar)	47 A3
Offington Avenue	29 B2	Oldcastlepark Close	43 B1	Orchard Close	22 D2	Orwell Park (Templeogue)	45 C4
Offington Court	29 B2	Oldcastlepark Green	43 B1	Orchard Cottages	59 A1 [1]	Orwell Park Avenue	46 D3
Offington Drive	29 B2	Oldcastlepark Grove	43 B1	Orchard Court	22 E2	Orwell Park Close	46 D3
Offington Lawn	29 B2	Oldcastlepark Lawn	43 B1	Orchard Green	22 D2	Orwell Park Crescent	46 D3
Offington Manor Apts	29 B1 [4]	Oldcastlepark View	43 B1	Orchard Grove	22 E2	Orwell Park Dale	45 C4
Offington Park	29 B1	Oldchurch Avenue	43 C1	(Blanchardstown)		Orwell Park Drive	46 D3
Ogham	60 D3	Oldchurch Close	43 C1	Orchard Grove (Newcastle)	42 D4	Orwell Park Glade	45 C3
O'Hanlon's Lane	3 B2	Oldchurch Court	43 C1	Orchard Lane (Blackrock)	59 A1	Orwell Park Glen	46 D3
O'Hara Avenue	75 A4	Oldchurch Crescent	43 C1	Orchard Lane (Clondalkin)	44 E1	Orwell Park Green	46 D3
O'Hogan Road	36 E3 [1]	Oldchurch Drive	43 C1	Orchard Lane (Ranelagh)	75 C4	Orwell Park Grove	45 C3
O'Hogan Road	36 E3	Oldchurch Grove	43 C1	Orchard Lawns	35 C3	Orwell Park Heights	45 C4
Oisin Court	39 A4 [35]	Oldchurch Lawn	43 C1	Orchard Lodge	44 E1	Orwell Park Lawns	45 C3
Olaf Hall	58 D2 [8]	Oldchurch Park	43 C1	Orchard Road (Ballybough)	25 B4	Orwell Park Rise	45 C4
Olaf House Apts. (Ushers Quay)	70 F4	Oldchurch Way	43 C1	Orchard Road (Raheny)	27 B2	Orwell Park View	45 C4
Olaf Road	70 E3	Oldcourt	67 B3	Orchard Road South	47 B2	Orwell Park Way	46 D3
Olcovar	64 E3	Oldcourt Avenue	67 B3	Orchard Square	47 C3	Orwell Road	47 A2
Old Bawn Avenue	55 A2	(Boghall Road)		Orchard Terrace (Bray)	67 C3 [19]	Orwell Walk	47 A3
Old Bawn Bridge	55 A2	Oldcourt Avenue	55 B2	Orchard Terrace	70 F2	Orwell Woods	47 A2
Old Bawn Close	55 A2	(Bohernabreena)		(Grangegorman Upper)		*Osborne Terrace	75 C4
Old Bawn Court	55 A1 [5]	Oldcourt Close	55 B2	*Orchard View	70 F2	(Northbrook Road)	
Old Bawn Drive	55 A2	Oldcourt Cottages	55 B3	Orchardstown Avenue	46 E4	Oscar Square	74 F2
Old Bawn Park	55 A2	Oldcourt Drive	67 B3	Orchardstown Drive	46 E4	Oscar Traynor Road	26 E1
Old Bawn Road	55 A1	Oldcourt Farm	55 B2	Orchardstown Park	46 E4	Oscar Traynor Road (Kilmore)	13 A3
Old Bawn Terrace	55 A2	Oldcourt Grove	67 B4	Orchardstown Villas	56 E1	O'Shea's Cottages	59 C3 [4]
Old Bawn Way	55 A2	Oldcourt Lawn	55 B2 [1]	Orchardton	56 E1 [1]	Osprey Avenue	45 C3
Old Belgard Road	44 F4	Oldcourt Lodge	55 B2	Ordnance Survey Road	36 E1	Osprey Court	64 E3 [3]
Old Blessington Road	55 A1	Oldcourt Manor	55 B3	O'Reilly Avenue	73 C1	Osprey Drive	45 C3
Old Brazil Way	1 A2	Oldcourt Park	67 B3	O'Reilly's Cottages	74 F4	Osprey Lawn	45 C3
Old Bridge Road	46 D4	Oldcourt Road	55 B3	Oriel Street Lower	72 E2	Osprey Park	45 C3
Old Brighton Terrace	67 C2 [46]	Oldcourt Terrace	67 C3 [15]	Oriel Street Upper	72 D3	Osprey Road	45 C3
Old Cabra Road	70 D1	Oldcourt View	55 B2	Orlagh Avenue	56 D2	Ossory Road	72 E2
Old Camac Bridge	73 B1	Oldfarm	22 E3	Orlagh Close	56 D2	Ostman Place	70 E3
Old Carrickbrack Road	30 D4	Oldfield Hall	57 C3	Orlagh Court	56 D2	O'Sullivan Avenue	72 D1
Old Connaught	67 A1	Oldtower Crescent	35 A2	Orlagh Crescent	56 D2	Oswald Road	39 A3
Old Connaught Avenue	67 B1	Oldtown Avenue	25 A1	Orlagh Downs	56 D2	Otranto Place	60 E1
Old Connaught Grove	67 B2	Oldtown Cottages	31 C3	Orlagh Grange	56 D2	Otterbrook	46 F4 [16]
Old Connaught View	67 B2	Oldtown Mill	31 C3	Orlagh Green	56 D2	Oulart	1 C3
Old Corduff Road	22 E1	Oldtown Mill Road	31 C3	Orlagh Grove	56 D2	Oulton Road	26 E4
Old Cornmill Road	33 C2	Oldtown Park	25 A1 [3]	Orlagh Lawn	56 D2	Our Lady's Close	74 E2
Old County Glen	73 C4	Oldtown Road	25 A1	Orlagh Lodge	56 D2	(off Our Lady's Road)	
Old County Road	73 B4	O'Leary Road	73 B2	Orlagh Meadows	56 D2	Our Lady's Road	74 E2
Old Dublin Road (Stillorgan)	48 E4	Olivemount Grove	47 C3 [2]	Orlagh Park	56 D2	Outer Ring Road	43 B2
Old Dunleary	49 C4	Olivemount Road	47 C3	Orlagh Pines	56 D2	Outfarm Lane	22 E3
Old Estuary Mill	2 F2	Olivemount Terrace	47 C3 [6]	Orlagh Rise	56 D2	Outlands	1 B1
Old Fairgreen	7 B2	Oliver Bond House Flats	70 F4	Orlagh View	56 D2	Overend Way	57 C1
Old Fort Road	1 A2	Oliver Bond Street	70 F4	Orlagh Way	56 D2	Ovoca Road	75 A3
Old Greenfield	17 C3	Oliver Plunkett Avenue	59 C1	Orlagh Wood	56 D2	Owendoher Haven	56 E1
Old Greenfield	17 C4	(Dun Laoghaire)		Ormeau Drive	60 F1 [2]	Owendoher Lodge	56 E1
Old Hill	20 D4	Oliver Plunkett Avenue	39 A3	Ormeau Street	76 F1	Owendore Avenue	46 F4
Old Kilmainham	73 C1	(Ringsend)		Ormond Avenue	1 B1	Owendore Crescent	46 F4
Old Kilmainham Village	74 D1	Oliver Plunkett Road	59 C1	Ormond Close	1 B1	Owen's Avenue	73 C1
Old Mill Court	74 F2	Oliver Plunkett Square	59 C1 [1]	Ormond Crescent	1 B1	Owensilla	24 F1
Old Mountpleasant	75 C4	Oliver Plunkett Terrace	59 C1 [5]	Ormond Drive	1 B1	Owenstown Park	48 D3
Old Naas Road (Bluebell)	36 E4	Oliver Plunkett Villas	59 B1 [3]	Ormond Grove	1 B1	Oxford Lane	75 C4
Old Naas Road (Brownsbarn)	43 C4	Olney Crescent	46 F2	Ormond Lawn	1 B1	Oxford Road	47 B1
Old Naas Road Cottages	36 E4 [1]	Olney Grove	46 F2 [17]	Ormond Market	71 A4	Oxford Terrace	72 E2
Old Navan Road	22 F2	Omni Park	25 B1	(off Ormond Quay Upper)		(on Hawthorn Terrace)	
Old Quarry (Dalkey)	60 F2	O'Moore Road	36 E3	Ormond Place	71 A4	Oxmantown Lane	70 F4
Old Quarry (Kilshane)	10 D2	O'Neachtain Road	25 A3 [14]			Oxmantown Road	70 D2

STREET NAME	PAGE/GRID REFERENCE
P	
Pace Avenue	8 E4
Pace Crescent	8 E4
Pace Road	8 E4
Pace View	8 E4
Pacelli Avenue	27 C1
Pairc Gleann Trasna	55 A3
Páirc Mhuire	53 A2
Páirc View	53 A2
Pakenham	49 C4 28
Pakenham Bridge	21 A2
Pakenham Road	49 C4
Palace Street (off Dame Street)	71 B4
Palmer Park	56 E2
Palmer Park	56 F2
Palmers Avenue	35 B2
Palmers Close	35 B2
Palmers Copse	35 B2
Palmers Court	35 B2
Palmers Crescent	35 B2
Palmers Drive	35 B2
Palmers Glade	35 B2
Palmers Grove	35 B2
Palmers Lawn	35 B2
Palmers Park	35 B2
Palmers Road	35 B2
Palmers Walk	35 B2
Palmerston	35 C1
Palmerston Close	47 B1 21
*Palmerston Close	47 B1
(rere of Palmerston Road)	
Palmerston Court	47 A1
Palmerston Gardens	47 B2
Palmerston Grove	47 C2 5
Palmerston Lane	47 B2
Palmerston Park (Rathgar)	47 B2
Palmerston Place	71 A2
Palmerston Road	47 B1
Palmerston Villas	47 A2
Palmerstown Avenue	35 C2
Palmerstown Close	35 B2
Palmerstown Court	35 C2
Palmerstown Drive	35 C2
Palmerstown Green	35 B2
Palmerstown Heights	35 B2
Palmerstown Lawn	35 B2
Palmerstown Manor	35 B2
Palmerstown Park	35 B2
(Kennelsfort Road)	
Palmerstown Woods	35 B4
Paradise Place	71 A2
Park Avenue	1 B2
(Brackenstown Road)	
Park Avenue (Castleknock)	22 F3
Park Avenue (Deans Grange)	59 A1
Park Avenue (Sandymount)	39 B4
Park Avenue (Willbrook)	56 F1
Park Avenue West	70 D3
Park Boulevard	9 B2
Park Close (Sallynoggin)	60 D2
Park Court (Sandymount)	39 A4 16
Park Court Apts	23 A3 4
Park Crescent	69 A1
(Blackhorse Avenue)	
Park Crescent (Kimmage)	46 D2
Park Crescent House	24 D4 6
Park Drive (Cabinteely)	59 B3
Park Drive (Ranelagh)	47 B1
Park Drive Avenue	22 F3
Park Drive Close	22 F3
Park Drive Court	22 F3
Park Drive Crescent	22 F3
Park Drive Green	22 F3
Park Drive Grove	22 F3
Park Drive Lawn	22 F3
Park Lane (Chapelizod)	36 E2 1
Park Lane (Dún Laoghaire)	50 D4 21
Park Lane (Sandymount)	39 A4
Park Lawn	27 A4
Park Lodge	22 F3
Park Manor	22 E3
Park Place	69 B4
Park Road (Dun Laoghaire)	50 D4
*Park Road (off Navan Road)	23 C3
Park Road (Sallynoggin)	60 D2

STREET NAME	PAGE/GRID REFERENCE
Park Spring's	24 D4 5
Park Street	36 F3 1
*Park Street	74 F1
(off Hanover St West)	
Park Terrace (Coombe)	74 F1
Park View (Cabra)	69 C1
Park View (Castleknock)	23 B4
Park View (Clonsilla)	22 D2
Park View (Enniskerry Road)	58 D4
Park View	26 F4 1
(Mount Prospect Lawns)	
Park View (Portmarnock)	15 A1
Park View (Rathgar)	47 A3 10
Park View House	9 B2
Park View Lawns	44 D2
Park View Manor	9 B2
Park Villas (Castleknock)	23 A3
Park Villas (Stillorgan)	48 F4 3
Park West Avenue	35 C4
Park West Road	35 C4
Park West Road	36 D4
Parker Hill	47 A1 12
Parker House	14 F4
Parkgate Street	70 D4
Parkhill Avenue	44 F3
Parkhill Close	45 A3
Parkhill Court	44 F3
Parkhill Drive	44 F3
Parkhill Green	44 F3
Parkhill Heights	45 A3 1
Parkhill Lawn	44 F3
Parkhill Rise	44 F3
Parkhill Road	44 F3
Parkhill Way	45 A3
Parkhill West	44 F4
Parklands (Castleknock)	22 F3
Parklands (Maynooth)	18 D3
Parklands (Santry)	12 E4
Parklands Avenue	55 B2
Parklands Close	18 D3
Parklands Court (Maynooth)	18 D3
Parklands Court	55 B2
(Scholarstown Link Road)	
Parklands Crescent	18 D3
Parklands Drive	55 B2
Parklands Grove	18 D3
Parklands Lawns	18 D3
Parklands Lodge	18 D3
Parklands Rise	18 D3
Parklands Road	55 B2
Parklands Square	18 D3
Parklands View	55 B2
Parklands Way	18 D3
Parkmore	23 A3
Parkmore Drive	46 E2
Parknasilla Avenue	64 D2
Parknasilla Close	64 D2
Parknasilla Lane	64 D2
Parknasilla Rise	64 D2
Parknasillog	65 C2
Parkside View	24 D4 7
Parkvale (Dundrum)	57 C1
Parkvale (Sutton)	28 D1
Parkview	23 C3
Parkview (Kilnamanagh)	45 A3 2
Parkview (Swords)	1 B2
Parkview Avenue	46 F1
(Harold's Cross)	
Parkview Court	69 B1
(Blackhorse Avenue)	
Parkview Court (Harold's Cross)	46 F1 8
Parkview Place	39 A3 14
Parkview Terrace	67 B2 16
Parkwood Avenue	55 A2
Parkwood Grove	55 A2
Parkwood Lawn	55 A2
Parkwood Road	55 A2
Parliament Street	71 A4
Parnell Avenue	74 F4
Parnell Cottages	3 B3
Parnell Court	74 F4
Parnell Drive	9 A4
Parnell Green	9 A4 1
Parnell Hall	74 E4
Parnell Lane	9 A4
Parnell Place	71 B2

STREET NAME	PAGE/GRID REFERENCE
Parnell Road (Bray)	67 C2
Parnell Road (Harold's Cross)	74 E3
Parnell Square East	71 B2
Parnell Square North	71 B2
Parnell Square West	71 B2
Parnell Street (O'Connell Street)	71 B3
Parnell Street (Sallynoggin)	60 D1
Parochial Avenue	15 A4 2
Parslickstown Avenue	9 A4
Parslickstown Close	9 A4
Parslickstown Court	9 A4
Parslickstown Drive	9 A4
Parslickstown Gardens	9 A3
Parslickstown Green	9 A4
Parson Court	17 C3
Parson Lodge	17 C3
Parson Street	17 C3
Parson's Court	42 D4
Parsons Hall	17 B3
Partridge Terrace	36 F3 5
Pass If You Can	11 A1
Patrician Park	59 C1 2
Patrician Villas	48 F4
Patrick Doyle Road	47 B2
Patrick Street (Dun Laoghaire)	50 D4
Patrick Street	75 A1
(Kevin Street Upper.)	
Patrick's Row	49 A3 14
Patrickswell Court	24 D2 8
Patrickswell Place	24 D2
Paul Street	70 F3
Pavillion Gate	59 A4
Pea Field	48 F3
Peamount	42 D2
Peamount Road	42 D3
Peamount Road	42 E2
Pear Tree Field	58 F1 5
Pearse Avenue	60 D2
Pearse Brothers Park	56 F1
Pearse Close	60 D2 3
Pearse Drive	60 D2
Pearse Gardens	59 C2
Pearse Green	60 D2
Pearse Grove	76 E1
Pearse House	72 D4
Pearse Park	60 D2
Pearse Road (Bray)	67 B2 12
Pearse Road (Sallynoggin)	60 D2
Pearse Square (Bray)	67 B2
Pearse Square (Pearse Street)	76 E1
Pearse Street (Sallynoggin)	60 D2
Pearse Street (Westland Row)	71 C4
Pearse Villas	60 D2
Pebble Hill	18 D2
Pebble Hill Lodge	18 D2
Peck's Lane	23 A3
Pelletstown Avenue	23 C3
Pemberton	67 A3
Pembroke Cottages	48 F3 2
(Booterstown)	
Pembroke Cottages	47 C1 2
(Donnybrook)	
Pembroke Cottages (Dundrum)	47 C4 5
Pembroke Cottages (Ringsend)	39 A2
Pembroke Court	76 F3
Pembroke Gardens	76 E3
Pembroke Lane	76 D2
(Lr Baggot Street)	
Pembroke Lane	76 E3
(Pembroke Road)	
Pembroke Park	76 E4
Pembroke Place (Ballsbridge)	76 F4
Pembroke Place	75 C3
(Pembroke St Upr)	
Pembroke Road	76 E3
Pembroke Row	76 D2
Pembroke Street	39 A3
Pembroke Street Lower	75 C2
Pembroke Street Upper	75 C2
Pembroke Terrace	47 C4 6
Penrose Street	76 F1
Percy French Road	45 C1 3
Percy Lane	76 E2
Percy Place	76 E2
Peter Place	75 B3
Peter Row	75 A2

STREET NAME	PAGE/GRID REFERENCE
Peter Street	75 A2
Peter's Court	71 A1
Peterson's Court	72 D4
Petrie Road	74 F3
Pheasant Run	8 F4
Pheasant Run The Drive	8 F4
Pheasant Run The Green	8 F4
Pheasant Run The Grove	8 F4
Pheasant Run The Park	8 F4
Phelan Avenue	24 D3
Phibblestown Avenue	21 A1
Phibblestown House Apts.	21 B1
Phibsborough	71 A1
Phibsborough Avenue	70 F1
Phibsborough Place	71 A2
Phibsborough Road	71 A1
Philipsburgh Avenue	25 C4
Philipsburgh Terrace	25 C4
Philomena Terrace	39 A3 41
*Philomena Terrace	39 A3
(off Oliver Plunket Ave)	
Phoenix Avenue	23 A3
Phoenix Court (Arbour Hill)	70 D3
Phoenix Court (Castleknock)	23 A3
Phoenix Court	70 D2
(North Circular Road)	
Phoenix Court Apartments	69 C3
Phoenix Drive	23 A3
Phoenix Gardens	23 A3
Phoenix Manor	70 D2
Phoenix Park	69 A2
Phoenix Park Way	23 B3
Phoenix Place	23 A3
Phoenix Street	36 F3 2
Phoenix Street North	70 F4
Phoenix Street West	70 F4
Phoenix Terrace	48 F3
Phoenix View	74 D1
Phrompstown	66 F1
Pickford's Terrace	72 F3
Pig Lane	71 C2
Pigeon House Road (Ringsend)	39 A2
Pigeon House Road (Ringsend)	39 B3
Pike Bridge	18 F3
*Pile's Terrace	76 D1
(Sandwith St Upper)	
Pilot View	60 F1 14
Pim Street	74 E1
Pimlico	74 F1
Pimlico Cottages	74 E1
Pine Avenue	59 A2
Pine Copse Road	57 B1
Pine Court (Deans Grange)	59 A1
Pine Court (Portmarnock)	15 A1
Pine Grove	56 D1 2
Pine Grove Park	1 C1
Pine Grove Road	1 C1
Pine Haven	48 F3
Pine Hurst	24 E4
Pine Lawn (Deans Grange)	59 A1
Pine Lawn (Tallaght)	55 A2
Pine Road	39 A3
Pine Valley Avenue	57 B2
Pine Valley Drive	57 B3
Pine Valley Grove	57 B3
Pine Valley Park	57 B3
Pine Valley Way	57 B3
Pinebrook Avenue	26 D2
Pinebrook Close	21 C1
Pinebrook Crescent	26 D2
Pinebrook Downs	21 C1
Pinebrook Drive	26 D2
Pinebrook Glen	21 C1
Pinebrook Grove	26 E2
Pinebrook Heights	21 C1
Pinebrook Lawn	21 C1
Pinebrook Rise	26 D2
Pinebrook Road	26 D2
Pinebrook Vale	21 C1
Pinebrook View	21 C1
Pinebrook Way	21 C1
Pinecroft	62 F1
Pinetree Crescent	44 F4 1
Pinetree Grove	44 F3 1
Pineview Avenue	55 A2
Pineview Drive	55 A2

STREET NAME	PAGE/GRID REFERENCE	
Pineview Grove	55	A2
Pineview Lawn	55	A2
Pineview Park	55	A2
Pineview Rise	55	A2
Pineview Road	55	A2
Pinewood	60	D4
Pinewood Avenue	24	F1
Pinewood Close	67	C4
Pinewood Court	8	F4
Pinewood Crescent	24	F1
Pinewood Drive	24	F1
Pinewood Green	24	F1
Pinewood Grove	25	A1 [1]
Pinewood Park	56	E1
Pinewood Villas	24	F1
Pinewoods	44	D2
Pinnockhill Roundabout	1	C3
Pipe Hill	1	C2
Pleasants Lane	75	B2
Pleasants Place	75	B2
Pleasants Street	75	A2
Pluckstown	51	A2
Plums Road	58	D1
Plunket Hall	2	E2
Plunkett Avenue (Finglas)	24	D1
Plunkett Avenue (Foxrock)	59	A3
Plunkett Crescent	11	A4
Plunkett Drive	24	D1
Plunkett Green	24	D1
Plunkett Grove	24	D1
Plunkett Hall	7	A2
Plunkett Road	24	D1
Poddle Close	46	E1
Poddle Green	46	E1 [6]
Poddle Park	46	E2
Polo Road	69	A2
Poolbeg Quay	39	A3
Poolbeg Street	71	C4
Poole Street	74	F2
Poplar Row	72	E1
Poplar Row Flats	72	E1
Poppintree	11	C4
Poppintree Lane	11	C4
Poppintree Parade	11	C4
Poppintree Park Lane West	11	C4
Poppintree Terrace	11	C4
Port Tunnel (East Wall)	71	C1
Port Tunnel (Santry Entrance)	25	C1
Port View House	39	A2
Porters Avenue	22	D2
Porters Gate	21	B2
Porters Gate Avenue	21	C2
Porters Gate Close	21	B2
Porters Gate Court	21	B2
Porters Gate Drive	21	B2
Porters Gate Green	21	B2
Porters Gate Grove	21	B2
Porters Gate Heights	21	C2
Porters Gate Lawn	21	B2
Porters Gate Rise	21	C2
Porters Gate View	21	B2
Porters Gate Way	21	B2
Porters Road	22	D2
Portersfield Apts.	22	D2
Porterstown	5	A3
Porterstown Road	22	D2
Portland Close	72	D2
Portland Court	71	C1
Portland Court	71	C1
(off Portland Place)		
*Portland Lock	71	C1
Portland Lock Apts.	71	C1
Portland Place	71	B1
Portland Row	72	D2
Portland Square	71	C1
Portland Street North	71	C1
Portland Street West	74	E1
Portmahon Drive	73	C2
Portmarnock	15	A1
Portmarnock Avenue	4	D4
Portmarnock Crescent	15	A1
Portmarnock Drive	4	D4
Portmarnock Grove	4	D4
Portmarnock Park	4	D4
Portmarnock Rise	15	A1
Portmarnock Walk	4	D4
Portobello Harbour	75	B3
Portobello Harbour Apts	75	A4
Portobello Place	75	B3
Portobello Road	75	A4
Portside Court	72	E1
Pottery Road	59	C2
Pound Hill	17	C1
Pound Lane	17	C3
Pound Park	17	C3
Pound Street	33	A1
Power's Court	76	E2
Power's Square	75	A1
(off John Dillon Street)		
Prebend Street	70	F3
Premier Square	24	E2
Preston Street	72	D2
*Price's Lane (Aston Quay)	71	B4
Price's Place (Ranelagh)	75	B4
Priestfield Cottages	74	E3
Priestfield Drive	74	E3
Primrose Avenue	71	A2
Primrose Gate	32	E4
Primrose Grove	13	C4
Primrose Hill (Celbridge)	32	D4
Primrose Hill (Dún Laoghaire)	49	C4 [25]
Primrose Lane	34	D1
Primrose Street	71	A2
(off Wellington Street Upper)		
Prince Arthur Terrace	47	A1 [3]
Prince Edward Terrace Lower	49	A4 [2]
Prince Edward Terrace Upper	49	A4 [3]
Prince of Wales Terrace (Bray)	67	C2 [26]
Prince of Wales Terrace	39	A4 [7]
(Sandymount)		
Prince's Street North	71	B3
Prince's Street South	72	D4
Princeton	48	D3
Prior Hall	74	D1
Priorswood Road	13	C4
Priory Avenue	48	F4
Priory Chase	31	C4
Priory Close	31	C4
Priory Court (Celbridge)	31	C4
Priory Court (Grange Road)	57	A2 [1]
Priory Crescent	31	C4
Priory Drive (Celbridge)	31	C4
Priory Drive (Stillorgan)	48	F4
Priory East	24	D4
Priory Green	31	C4
Priory Grove (Celbridge)	31	C4
Priory Grove (Stillorgan)	48	F4
Priory Hall	14	E4
Priory Hall (Kimmage)	46	D2
Priory Hall (Stillorgan)	48	F4
Priory Lodge	31	C4
Priory North	24	D3
Priory Road	46	F1
Priory Square	31	C4
Priory View	31	C3
Priory Walk (Celbridge)	31	C4
Priory Walk (Kimmage)	46	D2
Priory Way (Celbridge)	31	C3
Priory Way (Kimmage)	46	D2
Priory West	24	D4
Proby Garden	49	A4
Proby Hall	60	E2
Proby Park	60	E2
Proby Square	49	A4
Proby's Lane	71	B3
Promenade Road	39	A1
Prospect Avenue (Finglas Road)	25	A4
Prospect Avenue	56	E2
(Stocking Lane)		
Prospect Court	25	A4 [19]
Prospect Court	56	E3
Prospect Drive	56	E2
Prospect Glen	56	E2
Prospect Grove	56	E2
Prospect Heath	56	E2
Prospect Heights	56	E2
Prospect Lane	47	C2 [1]
Prospect Lawn	59	B3
Prospect Lodge	55	C1 [6]
Prospect Meadows	56	E2
Prospect Road	25	A4
Prospect Square	25	A4 [5]
Prospect Terrace (Kilmainham)	73	B1
Prospect Terrace (Sandymount)	39	B3 [1]
Prospect View	56	E2
Prospect Way	25	A4
Protestant Row	75	B2
Proud's Lane	75	B2
Provost Row	70	E3
Prussia Street	70	E2
Pucks Castle Lane	63	C3
Purcell Lane	67	C2 [60]
(off Main Street Bray)		
Purley Park	3	C4
Purser Gardens	47	A1 [10]
Putland Road	67	C3
Putland Villas	67	C3 [14]
Pyro Villas	74	E2

Q

Quarry Cottages	26	E3 [3]
Quarry Drive	45	C2
Quarry Road (Cabra)	24	E4
Quarry Road (Ferndale Road)	64	D4
Quarryfield Court	44	E2
Quarryvale Park	35	A2
Quartiere Bloom	71	B4
Queen's Park	49	B4
Queen's Road	50	D4
Queen's Street	70	F4
Quinn's Lane	75	C2
Quinn's Road	64	E3
Quinsborough	51	A4
Quinsborough Road	67	C2

R

Radcliff Hall	39	B4 [9]
Radcliffe	29	A1 [3]
Radharc na hAbhann	55	A2
Radlett Grove	4	D4
Rafter's Avenue	73	A4
Rafter's Lane	73	A4
Rafter's Road	73	A4
Raglan Hall Apts.	76	E4
Raglan House	39	A4 [42]
Raglan Lane	76	E4
Raglan Road	76	E4
Raheen Avenue	54	E1
Raheen Close	54	E1
Raheen Court	54	E1
Raheen Crescent	54	E1
Raheen Drive (Ballyfermot)	36	D3
Raheen Drive (Tallaght)	54	E1
Raheen Green	54	E1
Raheen Park (Ballyfermot)	36	D3
Raheen Park (Bray)	68	D3
Raheen Park (Tallaght)	54	E1
Raheen Road	54	E1
Raheny	27	A2
Raheny Park	27	A3
Raheny Road	27	A1
Railpark	18	E3
Railway Avenue (Baldoyle)	28	D1
Railway Avenue (Inchicore)	36	F3
Railway Avenue (Malahide)	3	B2
Railway Close	14	F4
Railway Cottages	39	A4 [8]
Railway Court	3	B2 [3]
Railway Mews	14	F4
Railway Road	14	F4
Railway Road	60	F2 [2]
Railway Street	71	C2
Railway Terrace (off Macken St)	76	E1
Rainsford Avenue	74	E1
Rainsford Lane	60	E4 [6]
Rainsford Street	74	E1
Ralahine	60	D4
Raleigh Square	46	D1
Ralph Square	33	A1 [1]
Ramillies Road	36	E3
Ramleh Close	47	C2
Ramleh Park	47	C2
Ramor Park	22	E2
Ranelagh	75	C4
Ranelagh Avenue	75	C4
Ranelagh Road	75	C4
Raphoe Road	46	D1
Rath Geal	43	C1
Rathbeale Court	1	C1 [2]
Rathbeale Crescent	1	C1
Rathbeale Rise	1	C2
Rathbeale Road	1	C1
Rathborne Avenue	23	C3
Rathborne Close	23	C3
Rathborne Drive	23	C3
Rathborne Place	23	C3
Rathborne Way	23	C3
Rathbourne Court	23	C3 [1]
Rathclaren	67	B3 [2]
Rathcoole Interchange (N7 J4)	52	F1
Rathcoole Park	52	F2
Rathcreedan	52	D1
Rathdown Avenue	46	F3
*Rathdown Court (off	46	F2 [10]
Templeogue Road)		
Rathdown Crescent	46	F3
Rathdown Drive	46	E3
Rathdown Grove	58	D2 [9]
Rathdown Park	46	F3
Rathdown Road	70	F1
Rathdown Square	70	E2
Rathdown Terrace	58	D2 [5]
Rathdown Villas	46	F3
Rathdrum Road	74	D4
Rathfarnham	46	F3
Rathfarnham Mill	46	F4 [12]
Rathfarnham Park	46	F3
Rathfarnham Road	46	F3
Rathfarnham Wood	46	F4
Rathgar	47	A2
Rathgar Avenue	46	F2
Rathgar Court	47	A1 [28]
Rathgar Park	46	F2 [16]
Rathgar Park	47	A2 [7]
Rathgar Place	47	A1
Rathgar Road	47	A1
Rathgar Villas	46	F2 [11]
Rathingle Road	1	B3
Rathland Drive	46	E2 [4]
Rathland Road	46	E2
Rathlawns	52	E2
Rathlin Road	25	A3
Rathlyon Grove	55	C2
Rathlyon Park	55	C2
Rathmichael	63	C3
Rathmichael Dales	64	D3
Rathmichael Haven	64	D3
Rathmichael Hill	63	C2
Rathmichael Lane	63	C2
Rathmichael Manor	64	D2
Rathmichael Park	64	E2
Rathmichael Road	63	C2
Rathmichael Woods	64	E2
Rathmines	47	A1
Rathmines Avenue	47	A1
Rathmines Avenue Court	47	A1 [25]
Rathmines Close	47	A1
Rathmines Park	47	A1 [1]
Rathmines Road Lower	47	A1
Rathmines Road Upper	47	A1
Rathmintan Close	54	D2
Rathmintan Court	54	D2
Rathmintan Crescent	54	D2
Rathmintan Drive	54	D2
Rathmore	14	F2
Rathmore Avenue	9	B2
Rathmore Avenue	58	D1
Rathmore Crescent	9	B2
Rathmore Drive	9	B2
Rathmore Grove	9	B2
Rathmore Park	27	A2
Rathmore Villas	46	F2
Rathsallagh Avenue	64	E2
Rathsallagh Drive	64	E2
Rathsallagh Grove	64	E2
Rathsallagh Park	64	E2
Rathvale Avenue	26	F1
Rathvale Drive	26	F1
Rathvale Grove	26	F1
Rathvale Park	26	F1
Rathvilly Drive	24	D2
Rathvilly Park	24	D2
Ratoath Avenue	24	D2

STREET NAME	PAGE/GRID REFERENCE	STREET NAME	PAGE/GRID REFERENCE	STREET NAME	PAGE/GRID REFERENCE	STREET NAME	PAGE/GRID REFERENCE
Ratoath Drive	23 C1	Richmond Hall	25 B4 [13]	Riverdale	20 D4	Rock Bridge	32 D4
Ratoath Estate	24 D3	Richmond Hill (Monkstown)	49 C4	Riverpark Apts.	69 C4	Rock Hall	49 A3
Ratoath Road (Cabra)	24 E4	Richmond Hill (Rathmines)	75 B4	Riverpark View	9 A4 [3]	Rock Hill	49 A3
Ratoath Road (Finglas)	23 C2	Richmond House	25 B4 [12]	Riverrun Apts.	74 D1	*Rock Lane (Baggot St Lower)	76 D2
Ratoath Road (Hollystown)	9 B1	Richmond Lane	71 C1	Riversdale (Dundrum)	57 C1 [11]	Rock Lodge	60 E3
Ratra Park	23 C4	Richmond Lodge	25 B4	*Riversdale (Herbert Hill)	57 C1	Rock Road	49 A3
Ratra Road	23 C4	*Richmond Manor	75 B4	Riversdale (Palmerstown)	35 C1	Rockbrae Hall	57 C3
Ravens Court	24 D2 [5]	Richmond Mews	75 B4	Riversdale Avenue (Clondalkin)	44 E1	Rockbrook	56 E4
Ravens Rock Road	58 E2	Richmond Parade	72 D1	Riversdale Avenue (Palmerston)	35 C1	Rockfield (Dundrum)	57 C1
*Ravensdale Drive (off	46 E2	Richmond Park (Herbert Road)	67 A4	Riversdale Avenue (Terenure)	46 F3	Rockfield (Lucan)	34 D3
Ravensdale Park)		Richmond Park (Monkstown)	49 B4	Riversdale Court	35 C1	Rockfield (Maynooth)	18 D4
Ravensdale Park	46 E2	Richmond Place (Rathmines)	75 B4	Riversdale Crescent	44 E1	Rockfield Avenue (Kimmage)	46 D2
Ravensdale Road	72 F2	Richmond Place South	75 B3	Riversdale Drive	44 E1	Rockfield Avenue (Maynooth)	18 D4
Ravenswell Road	67 C2	(Sth Richmond St)		Riversdale Green	35 B4	Rockfield Close	22 D3
Ravenswood	3 A3 [2]	Richmond Road	25 B4	Riversdale Grove (Kimmage)	46 E2 [1]	Rockfield Drive (Clondalkin)	44 D2
Ravenwood Avenue	21 B1	Richmond Row	75 B3	Riversdale Grove (Palmerstown)	35 B1	Rockfield Drive (Coolmine)	22 D3
Ravenwood Crescent	21 B1	Richmond Street North	72 D1	Riversdale Park (Clondalkin)	44 E1	Rockfield Drive (Kimmage)	46 D2
Ravenwood Drive	21 B1	Richmond Street South	75 B3	Riversdale Park (Palmerstown)	35 C1	Rockfield Gardens	18 D3
Ravenwood Estate	21 B1	Richmond Terrace	68 D2 [12]	Riversdale Road	44 E1	Rockfield Green	18 D3
Ravenwood Green	21 B1	Richmond Villas	75 B3	Riversdale View	46 F4 [26]	Rockfield Lodge	18 D4
Ravenwood Lawn	21 B1	Richview	47 C2	Riverside (Clondalkin)	44 E1 [6]	Rockfield Manor	18 D4
Ravenwood Rise	21 B1	Richview Park	47 B2	Riverside (Kimmage)	46 E2 [9]	Rockfield Park (Coolmine)	22 D2
Ravenwood Road	21 B1	Richview Villas	47 C2 [11]	Riverside (Mulhuddart)	9 A4 [4]	Rockfield Park (Maynooth)	18 D4
Ravenwood View	21 B1	Riddlesford	67 C4	Riverside Avenue	13 A4	Rockfield Rise	18 D3
Raverty Villas	67 B1 [1]	Ridge Hall	64 E1	Riverside Cottages	46 E4	Rockfield Square	18 D3
Rawson Court	76 E2	Ridge Hill	64 E1	Riverside Crescent	13 A4	Rockfield Walk	18 D3
Raymond Street	74 F3	Ridgewood Avenue	1 B3	Riverside Drive (Coolock)	13 B4	Rockford Manor	59 B1
Rectory Slopes	67 B3	Ridgewood Close	1 B3	Riverside Drive (Palmerston)	35 C1	Rockford Park	59 B1
Rectory Way	67 A3	Ridgewood Court	1 B3	Riverside Drive (Rathfarnham)	47 A3	Rockford Terrace	49 B4 [14]
Red Brick Terrace	59 A1 [2]	Ridgewood Green	1 B3	Riverside Grove	13 A4	Rockfort Avenue	60 F2
Red Cow Cottages	35 C1 [4]	Ridgewood Grove	1 B3	Riverside Park	13 A4	Rockingham Avenue	19 C4
Red Cow Interchange	44 F1	Ridgewood Park	1 B3	Riverside Road	13 A4	Rockingham Green	19 C4
Red Cow Lane	70 F3	Ridgewood Place	1 B3	Riverside Walk	47 C1 [21]	Rockingham Grove	19 C4
Redberry	34 D3	Ridgewood Square	1 B3	Riverston Abbey	24 D4	Rockingham Park	19 C4
Redesdale Crescent	48 D4	Rinawade Avenue	32 E1	Riverstown Gardens	24 D3 [5]	Rockingham Terrace	2 D2
Redesdale Road	48 D4	Rinawade Close	32 E1	Rivervale	23 C3	Rocklands	60 F1 [6]
Redfern Avenue	3 C4	Rinawade Crescent	32 E1	Rivervale Apts.	67 B2 [27]	Rockmeadon Court	46 D1 [5]
Redgap	52 E3	Rinawade Downs	32 E1	*Riverview (Grand Canal Docks)	76 E1	Rockstown	30 E2
Redmond's Court	27 B1 [3]	Rinawade Glade	32 E1	Riverview (Oldbawn)	55 A2	Rockview	57 C3
Redmond's Hill	75 B2	Rinawade Green	32 E1	Riverview (Palmerstown)	35 C1	Rockville	62 F2
Redwood	9 B1	Rinawade Grove	32 E1	Riverview Apts	32 D4	Rockville Crescent	49 B4
Redwood Avenue	45 A4	Rinawade Lawns	32 E1	Riverview Court	36 E2 [11]	Rockville Drive	49 B4
Redwood Close	45 A4	Rinawade Park	32 F1	Riverwood Chase	22 D3	Rockville Drive	63 A1
Redwood Court (Churchtown)	47 A3	Rinawade Rise	32 E1	Riverwood Close	22 D3	Rockville Estate	49 A4 [9]
Redwood Court (Tallaght)	44 F4	Rinawade Vale	32 E1	Riverwood Copse	22 D3	Rockville Park	49 B4
Redwood Drive	44 F4	Rinawade View	32 E1	Riverwood Court	22 D3	Rockville Road	49 A4
Redwood Grove	48 F3	Ring Street	36 F3 [12]	Riverwood Crescent	22 D3	Rockwell Cove Apts.	49 A3 [9]
Redwood Heights	45 A4	Ring Terrace	36 F3	Riverwood Dale	22 D3	Rockwood	34 D3
Redwood Lawn	44 F4	Ringsend	39 A3	Riverwood Dene	22 D3	Rocwood	58 F2
Redwood Park	45 A4	Ringsend Park	39 A2	Riverwood Drive	22 D3	Roe Lane	70 E4
Redwood Rise	45 A4	Ringsend Road	76 F1	Riverwood Gardens	22 D3	Roebuck Avenue	48 E3
Redwood View	45 A4	Rinn na Mara	27 A4 [3]	Riverwood Glebe	22 D3	Roebuck Castle	48 D3
Redwood Walk	44 F4	Ripley Court	67 B3	Riverwood Glen	22 D3	Roebuck Crescent	47 C3 [10]
Reginald Square	74 F1	Ripley Hills	67 B3	Riverwood Green	22 D3	Roebuck Downs	47 C3
Reginald Street	74 F1	River Close	64 E1 [23]	Riverwood Grove	22 D3	Roebuck Drive	46 D2
Rehoboth Avenue	74 E3	River Court	7 B3	Riverwood Hall	22 D3	Roebuck Hill	48 D3
Rehoboth Place	74 D3	*River Court Apts.	73 A1	Riverwood Heath	22 D3	Roebuck Lawn	47 C3 [9]
Reilly's Avenue	74 D3	River Drive	24 D3	Riverwood Lawn	22 D3	Roebuck Park	47 C4
Renoir Apts.	39 A4 [50]	River Forest	20 D4	Riverwood Park	22 D3	Roebuck Road	48 D3
Reuben Avenue	74 D2	River Forest View (Leixlip)	19 C3	Riverwood Place	22 D3	Roger Casement Park	67 B2
Reuben Street	74 D2	River Forest View (Leixlip)	20 D3	Riverwood Road	22 D3	Roger's Lane	75 C2
Reuben Walk	74 D2	River Gardens	25 A3 [15]	Riverwood Terrace	22 D3	Roland Court	47 A1 [20]
*Rhodaville	75 B4	River Lane (Bray)	67 B2	Riverwood Vale	22 D3	Rollins Court	60 D1 [12]
(off Mountpleasant Ave)		River Lane (Loughlinstown)	64 E2 [1]	Riverwood View	22 D3	Rollins Villas	60 D1
Riachville	25 C2 [10]	River Lane Grove	64 E2 [13]	Riverwood Way	22 D3	Ronanstown	35 A4
Rialto Buildings	74 D2	River Lawns	31 C4	Robert Emmett Close	70 E4	Roncalli Road	27 C1
Rialto Cottages	73 C2	River Mall	2 D2	Robert Place	25 B4 [7]	Rookwood View	56 E2
Rialto Drive	73 C3	River Road (Ashtown)	23 C3	Robert Street	74 E1	Roosevelt Cottages	24 D4 [1]
Rialto Park(off Rialto Street)	74 D2	River Road (Blanchardstown)	22 F2	Robert Street (Jones's Road)	25 B4 [6]	Rooske Road	7 B3
Rialto Street	74 D2	River Road Cottages	23 A2	Robin Villas	35 C1	Ropewalk Place	39 A3 [30]
Ribh Avenue	26 F2	River Valley Avenue	1 B2	Robinhood Park	45 B1	Rory O'Connor Park	59 B1
Ribh Road	26 F2	River Valley Close	1 B2	Robinhood Road	45 A1	Rory O'More Bridge	70 E4
Richelieu Park	48 E1	River Valley Court	1 B2	Robswall	3 C3	Ros Mór View	56 D2
Richmond	59 A1	River Valley Drive	1 C2	Robswall Path	4 D3	Rosary Gardens East	50 D4 [2]
Richmond Avenue (Fairview)	25 B4	River Valley Grove	1 C3	Robswall Walk	4 D3	Rosary Gardens West	49 C4 [1]
Richmond Avenue (Monkstown)	49 C4	River Valley Heights	1 C2	Rochestown Avenue	59 C2	Rosary Road	74 D2
Richmond Avenue South	47 B2	River Valley Lawn	1 C2	Rochestown House	59 C2 [9]	Rosary Terrace (Ringsend)	39 A3
Richmond Cottages	72 D1	River Valley Park	1 C2	Rochestown House Apts.	59 C2 [6]	*Rosary Terrace	50 D4
(Summerhill)		River Valley Rise	1 C3	Rochestown Park	60 D2	(off Library Road)	
Richmond Cottages North	72 D1	River Valley Road	1 C2	Rochfort Avenue	34 F2	Rosbeg Court	27 C2
Richmond Court (Marino)	25 C4	River Valley View	1 B2	Rochfort Close	34 F2	Rosberry	34 E3
Richmond Court (Milltown)	47 B2	River Valley Way	1 B2	Rochfort Crescent	34 F3	Rosberry Avenue	34 E3
Richmond Crescent	72 D1	River View	31 C4	Rochfort Downs	34 F2	Rosberry Court	34 E3
Richmond Estate	25 C4	Riverbank (Braemor Road)	47 A3	Rochfort Green	34 F2	Rosberry Lane	34 E3
Richmond Green	49 C4 [12]	Riverbank (Dundrum)	57 C1 [10]	Rochfort Park	34 F2	Rosberry Park	34 E3
Richmond Grove	49 C4	Riverbank Hall	24 F3	Rochfort Way	34 F3	Rosberry Place	34 E3

STREET NAME	PAGE/GRID REFERENCE		STREET NAME	PAGE/GRID REFERENCE		STREET NAME	PAGE/GRID REFERENCE		STREET NAME	PAGE/GRID REFERENCE	
Rose Park	59	C1	Rossfield Park	54	D1	Russell Close	54	D2	Sampson's Lane	71	B3
Rose Vale Court	22	D1 [6]	Rossfield Way	54	D1	Russell Court	54	D2	Sanderling Apts.	48	E3
Roseacre	58	E3	Rosslyn	67	C2 [37]	*Russell Court Apts.	71	A3	Sandford Avenue (Donnybrook)	47	C1
Rosebank	55	A2	Rosslyn Court	67	C2	(Little Britain Street)			Sandford Avenue	74	E3
Rosebank Court	35	B4 [2]	Rosslyn Grove	67	C2 [4]	Russell Crescent	54	D1	(Donore Avenue)		
Rosebank Hall	35	A4 [5]	Rossmeen Park	50	E4	Russell Downs	54	D1	Sandford Close	47	B1
Rosebank Place	35	A4 [4]	(Off Sumerhill Road)			Russell Drive	54	D2	Sandford Gardens (Donnybrook)	47	C1 [10]
Rosebank View	35	B4 [1]	Rossmore Avenue (Ballyfermot)	36	D3	Russell Green	54	D2	Sandford Gardens	74	F3
Rosedale (Clonsilla)	21	B1	Rossmore Avenue (Templeogue)	45	C4	Russell Grove	54	D2	(off Donore Avenue)		
Rosedale (Dunboyne)	7	B2	Rossmore Close	46	D4	Russell House	2	E2	Sandford Gardens	74	F3
Rosedale Close	21	B1	Rossmore Crescent	46	D4	Russell Lane	54	D1	(Sandford Avenue)		
Rosedale Crescent	21	B1	Rossmore Drive (Ballyfermot)	36	D2	Russell Lawns	54	D2	Sandford Lodge	47	B1
*Rosedale Terrace	74	F3	Rossmore Drive (Templeogue)	45	C4	Russell Meadows	54	D1	Sandford Park	74	F3
Rosedale Terrace	74	F3	Rossmore Grove	45	C4	Russell Place	54	D1	(off O'Donovan Road)		
(Lower Clanbrassil St)			Rossmore Lawns	46	D4	Russell Rise	54	D1	Sandford Park	74	F3
Roseglen Avenue	27	B2	Rossmore Park	46	D4	Russell Street	71	C1	(Sandford Avenue)		
Roseglen Manor	27	B2 [3]	Rossmore Road (Ballyfermot)	36	D2	Russell View	54	D2	Sandford Road	47	B1
Roseglen Road	27	B2	Rossmore Road (Templeogue)	46	D4	Russell Walk	54	D1	Sandford Row	47	B1
Rosehaven	22	E3 [1]	Rostrevor Court	76	E1	Russell's Mews	2	E3	Sandford Terrace	47	B1
Rosehill	59	A1 [5]	Rostrevor Road	47	A3	Russell's Place	2	E3	Sandford Wood	1	C1
Roselawn	34	E1	Rostrevor Terrace	76	E1	Russell's Terrace	2	E4	Sandon Cove	26	E4
Roselawn Avenue	22	F2	(Lr Grand Canal St)			Rutland Avenue (Clogher Road)	46	E1	Sandwith Street Lower	72	D4
Roselawn Close	22	F2	Rostrevor Terrace	47	A2	Rutland Avenue (Crumlin Road)	74	D4	Sandwith Street Upper	76	D1
Roselawn Court	22	F2	(Orwell Road)			Rutland Cottages	71	C2	Sandycove Avenue East	60	E1
Roselawn Crescent	22	E2	Rothe Abbey	73	B2	Rutland Court	71	C2	Sandycove Avenue North	50	E4
Roselawn Drive	22	E2	Rowan Avenue	58	D2	Rutland Grove	46	F1	Sandycove Avenue West	60	E1
(Blanchardstown)			Rowan Close	32	D3	Rutland Place North	71	C2	Sandycove Lane East	60	E1
Roselawn Drive (Oldcourt)	67	C3	Rowan Grove	67	B2	Rutland Place West	71	B2	Sandycove Point	50	E4
Roselawn Glade	22	E2	Rowan Hall	47	C1 [15]	Rutland Street Lower	71	C2	Sandycove Road	60	E1
Roselawn Grove	22	E2	Rowan Hamilton Court	24	E4 [3]	Rutledge Terrace	74	E3	Sandyford	58	D2
Roselawn Park	67	C3 [2]	Rowan House	76	D3	Ryan's Cottages (Harold's Cross)	46	F1 [7]	Sandyford Downs	58	D3
Roselawn Road	22	F2	Rowan Park	49	B4	Ryder's Row	71	A3	Sandyford Hall	58	E3
Roselawn Road	22	F2	Rowan Park Avenue	49	B4	Rye Bridge	33	A1	Sandyford Hall Avenue	58	E3
Roselawn View	22	E2	Rowanbyrn	49	B4	Rye River Avenue	20	D4	Sandyford Hall Close	58	E4
Roselawn Walk	22	E2	Rowanbyrn	59	B1	Rye River Close	20	D4	Sandyford Hall Court	58	E3
Roselawn Way	22	F2	Rowans Road	58	D2	Rye River Court	20	D4	Sandyford Hall Crescent	58	E3
Rosemount	25	C3 [10]	Rowlagh Avenue	35	A3	Rye River Crescent	20	D4	Sandyford Hall Drive	58	E4
Rosemount (Churchtown)	47	C4	Rowlagh Crescent	35	A3	Rye River Gardens	20	D4	Sandyford Hall Green	58	E3
Rosemount (Donnycarney)	26	D3	Rowlagh Gardens	35	A3	Rye River Grove	20	D4	Sandyford Hall Grove	58	E4
Rosemount Avenue	26	E2	Rowlagh Green	35	A3	Rye River Mall	20	D4	Sandyford Hall Lawn	58	E4
Rosemount Court (Booterstown)	48	F3	Rowlagh Park	35	A3	Rye River Park	20	D4	Sandyford Hall Park	58	E3
Rosemount Court (Dundrum)	47	C4	Rowserstown Lane	73	B1	Ryecroft	67	C3	Sandyford Hall Place	58	E3
Rosemount Court (Inchicore Rd)	73	A1	Royal Canal Avenue	23	C3	Ryemont Abbey	20	D4	Sandyford Hall Rise	58	E3
Rosemount Crescent	47	C3	Royal Canal Bank	25	A4	Ryevale Lawns	20	D4	Sandyford Hall View	58	E4
(Roebuck Road)			Royal Canal Bank	71	A1	Rynville Manor	67	B4	Sandyford Hall Walk	58	E3
Rosemount Glade	47	C4	Royal Canal Terrace	70	F2				Sandyford Park	58	D3
Rosemount Hall	47	C4	Royal Hibernian Way	75	C1				Sandyford Road	57	C1
Rosemount Park	47	C4	Royal Marine Terrace	67	C2 [12]	**S**			Sandyford View	57	C3
Rosemount Park Drive	10	D4	Royal Oak	12	F4				Sandyford Village	58	D3
Rosemount Park Road	10	D4	Royal Terrace East	60	D1	Sackville Court Apts.	71	B2	Sandyhill Avenue	24	F1
Rosemount Road	70	F1	Royal Terrace Lane	60	D1 [10]	Sackville Gardens	72	D1	Sandyhill Court	11	C4
Rosemount Terrace	70	E3	Royal Terrace North	60	D1 [2]	Sackville Place	71	B3	Sandyhill Gardens	24	F1
(Arbour Hill)			Royal Terrace West	60	D1	Saddlers Avenue	9	A4	Sandyhill Terrace	11	C4
Rosemount Terrace	48	E3	Royse Road	25	A4	Saddlers Close	9	A4	Sandyhill Way	11	C4
(Booterstown)			Royston	46	D2	Saddlers Court	75	B4	Sandymount	39	A4
Rosemount Terrace (Dundrum)	47	B4 [11]	Royston Village	46	D2	Saddlers Crescent	9	A4	Sandymount Avenue	39	A4
Rosevale Court	26	F3	Royston Village	46	D2	Saddlers Drive	9	A4	Sandymount Castle	39	A4 [5]
Rosevale Mansions	26	F3	Ruby Hall	59	C2	Saddlers Glade	9	A4	Sandymount Castle Drive	39	A4 [3]
Roseville Court	67	B1 [7]	Rugby Road	47	B1	Saddlers Grove	9	A4	Sandymount Castle Park	39	B4 [2]
Roseville Terrace	47	C4 [4]	Rugby Villas	47	B1 [6]	Saddlers Lawn	9	A4	Sandymount Castle Road	39	A4 [2]
Rosewood Grove	34	F3	Rushbrook	22	E2	Sadleir Hall	7	A2	Sandymount Court	39	A3 [26]
Rosmeen Gardens	50	D4	Rushbrook Avenue	45	C3	Saggart	53	B2	Sandymount Green	39	A4 [1]
Rosmeen Park	60	D1	Rushbrook Court	45	C4	Saggart Abbey	53	C2	Sandymount Road	39	A3
Ross Cottages	3	B2 [8]	Rushbrook Crescent	45	C3	Saggart Lakes	53	B1	Sans Souci Park	48	F3
Ross Road	75	A1	Rushbrook Drive	45	C3	Saint Canice's Court	23	C1	Sans Souci wood	67	C3
Ross Street	70	D2	Rushbrook Grove	45	C3	Saint Canice's Square	24	E2	Santa Sabina Manor	29	B2
Ross View	35	C1	Rushbrook Park	45	C3	Saint Pappin's Street	12	D4	Santry	25	B1
Rossaveal Court	36	D2 [1]	Rushbrook Road	45	C3	Saintdoolaghs	14	D3	Santry Avenue	12	E4
Rossberry Terrace	34	E4	Rushbrook View	45	C3	Saintsbury Avenue	60	E4	Santry Close	12	F4
Rossecourt Avenue	34	F3	Rushbrook Way	45	C4	Salamanca	48	D4	Santry Court	12	F4
Rossecourt Green	34	F3	Rusheeney	21	B1	Salem Court	47	A1 [17]	Santry Cross	12	D4
Rossecourt Grove	34	F3	Rusheeney Avenue	21	B1	Salestown	6	D4	Santry Cross (Ballymun)	12	D4
Rossecourt Heights	34	F3	Rusheeney Close	21	B1	Sallowood View	12	E4	Santry Villas	12	E4
Rossecourt Lane	34	F3	Rusheeney Court	21	B1	Sallowood Walk	12	E4	Sarah Bridge	69	B4
Rossecourt Rise	34	F3	Rusheeney Crescent	8	F4	Sally Park	55	C1	Sarah Curran Avenue	56	F1
Rossecourt Square	34	F3	Rusheeney Green	21	C1	Sally Park Close	55	C1	Sarah Curran Road	56	F1 [1]
Rossecourt Terrace	34	F3	Rusheeney Grove	21	B1	Sallyglen Road	60	D2	Sarah Place	69	B4
Rossecourt Way	34	F3	Rusheeney Manor	21	B1	Sallymount Avenue	47	B1	Sarney	6	E2
Rossfield Avenue	54	D1	Rusheeney Park	21	B1	Sallymount Gardens	47	B1 [1]	Sarsfield Court (Inchicore)	36	F3
Rossfield Close	54	D1 [4]	Rusheeney View	21	C1	Sallymount Terrace	47	B1 [14]	Sarsfield Court (Lucan)	34	D1 [4]
Rossfield Court	54	D1 [3]	Rusheeney Way	21	B1	Sallynoggin	60	D2	Sarsfield Park	34	D1
Rossfield Crescent	54	D1	Rus-in-Urbe Terrace	60	D1 [19]	Sallynoggin Park	59	C2	Sarsfield Quay	70	E4
Rossfield Drive	54	D1	Russell Avenue	54	D1	Sallynoggin Road	59	C2	Sarsfield Road	36	F3
Rossfield Gardens	54	D1	(Fortunestown Way)			Salmon Pool Apts	69	A4	Sarsfield Street (Phibsborough)	71	A1
Rossfield Green	54	D1	Russell Avenue (Jones's Road)	71	C1	Salthill	49	C4	Sarsfield Street (Sallynoggin)	60	D1
Rossfield Grove	54	D1	Russell Avenue East	72	E2	*Salthill Place (off Crofton Road)	50	D4	Sarsfield Terrace	34	D1 [1]
						Saltzburg	48	D4			

STREET NAME	PAGE/GRID REFERENCE		STREET NAME	PAGE/GRID REFERENCE		STREET NAME	PAGE/GRID REFERENCE		STREET NAME	PAGE/GRID REFERENCE	
Sarto Lawn	27	C1	Seafort Cottages	39	A4 [18]	Seven Oaks (Whitehall)	25	B3	Sheelin Walk	64	E1 [14]
Sarto Park	27	C1	Seafort Gardens	39	A3 [10]	Seventh Lock Cottages	36	D4	Sheephill Avenue	9	C4
Sarto Rise	27	C1	Seafort Parade	48	F3	Seventh Lock Place	36	D4	Sheephill Green	9	C4
Sarto Road	27	C2	Seafort Terrace	39	A4 [19]	Seville Place	72	D2	Sheephill Park	9	C4
Saul Road	46	E1	Seafort Villas	39	A4 [20]	Seville Terrace	72	D2	Sheepmoor Avenue	22	D1
Saval Grove	60	E2	Seagrange Avenue	14	F4	Seymour Road	67	C2	Sheepmoor Close	22	D1
Saval Park Crescent	60	E2	Seagrange Drive	27	C1	Shackelton	8	F4	Sheepmoor Crescent	22	D1
Saval Park Gardens	60	E2	Seagrange Road	27	C1	Shakelton	8	F4	Sheepmoor Gardens	22	D1
Saval Park Road	60	E2	Seagrave	14	F2	Shaldon Grange	62	F2	Sheepmoor Green	22	D1
Scariff House	22	F1	Seagrave Close	11	B4	Shalimar Apts.	44	F3 [3]	Sheepmoor Grove	22	D1
Scholarstown Park	56	D2	Seagrave Court	11	B4	Shamrock Cottages	72	D2	Sheepmoor Lawn	22	D1
Scholarstown Road	56	D2	Seagrave Drive	11	B4	Shamrock Hill Mews	47	C1 [23]	Sheepmoor Way	22	D1
School Avenue	26	E2	Seagrave Terrace	11	B4	Shamrock Place	72	D2	Shelbourne Avenue	76	F3
School Street	74	E1	Seagrave Way	11	B4	Shamrock Street	71	A2	Shelbourne Lane	76NS	F3
Schoolhouse Court	25	B1	Seamount	3	C3	Shamrock Terrace	72	D2	Shelbourne Park Mews	76	F1
Schoolhouse Lane	75	C1	Seamount	48	E3	Shamrock Villas	46	F1	Shelbourne Place	76	F2
(Kildare Street)			Seamount Drive	3	C3	Shanagarry	47	B2 [9]	Shelbourne Road	76	F2
Schoolhouse Lane (Santry)	25	B1	Seamount Grove	3	C3	Shanard Avenue	25	A1	Shelbourne Village	76	F1
Schoolhouse Lane West	75	A1	Seamount Heights	3	C3	Shanard Road	25	A1	Shelerin Road	21	C2
(off High Street)			Seamount Park	3	C3	Shanboley Road	25	C1	Shellys Banks Road	39	B3
Schoolhouse Mews	25	B1 [2]	Seamount Road	3	C3	Shancastle Avenue	35	A2	Shelmalier Road	72	F2
Schools Road	67	B4	Seamount View	2	E2	Shancastle Close	35	A2	Shelmartin Avenue	25	C4
Scotchstone Bridge	2	D1	Seamus Ennis Road	24	E1	Shancastle Crescent	35	A2	Shelmartin Terrace	25	C4 [2]
Scott Park	67	C3	Sean Heuston Bridge	70	D4	Shancastle Drive	35	A2	Shelton Drive	46	D2
Scribblestown	23	C3	Sean MacDermott Street Lower	71	C4	Shancastle Lawns	35	A2	Shelton Gardens	46	D2
Scribblestown Avenue	23	C3	Sean MacDermott Street Upper	71	C3	Shancastle Park	35	A2	Shelton Grove	46	D2
Scribblestown Close	23	C3	Sean Moore Road	39	A3	Shandon Crescent	24	F4	Shelton Park	46	D2
Scribblestown Grove	23	C3	Sean O'Casey Avenue	71	C2	Shandon Drive	24	F4	Sherborne	47	A2
Scribblestown Park	24	D3	Sean O'Casey Bridge	72	D4	Shandon Gardens	24	F4	Sheridan Court	71	B2
Scribblestown Place	23	C3	Sean Tracey House	72	D2	Shandon Green	24	F4 [8]	Sheridan Place	71	B2
Scribblestown Road	23	B3	Seapark (Dollymount)	26	F4	Shandon Mill	24	F4 [9]	Sheriff Street Lower	72	D3
Scribblestown Road	24	D3	Seapark (Malahide)	3	C3	Shandon Park (Monkstown)	49	B4	Sheriff Street Upper	72	F3
Sea Road	3	A2	Seapark Drive	26	F4	Shandon Park (Phibsborough)	24	F4	Sherkin Court	25	B3
Seabank Court (Dalkey)	60	E1 [21]	Seapark Hill	3	C3	Shandon Road	24	F4	Sherkin Gardens	25	B3
Seabank Court (Malahide)	3	C2 [1]	Seapark Road	26	F4	Shangan Avenue	25	B1	Sherrard Avenue	71	B1
Seabrook Manor	14	E2	Seapoint Avenue (Baldoyle)	15	A4 [1]	Shangan Court	25	A1	*Sherrard Court	71	B1
Seabury	48	E1	Seapoint Avenue (Blackrock)	49	B3	Shangan Crescent	25	A1	(off Portland Place)		
Seabury Avenue	2	F2	Seapoint Court (Baldoyle)	15	A4 [7]	Shangan Drive	25	B1	Sherrard Street Lower	71	C1
Seabury Close	2	F2	Seapoint Court (Bray)	67	C1	Shangan Gardens	25	B1	Sherrard Street Upper	71	B1
Seabury Court	2	F2	Seapoint Road	67	C2	Shangan Green	25	B1	Sherrards Court	71	B1
Seabury Crescent	2	F2	Seapoint Terrace (Blackrock)	49	B3 [4]	Shangan Hall Apts.	25	A1 [4]	Shielmartin Drive	29	B3
Seabury Dale	2	F2	Seapoint Terrace (Bray)	67	C2 [24]	Shangan Park	25	B1	Shielmartin Park	29	B3 [1]
Seabury Downs	2	F2	Seapoint Terrace (Ringsend)	39	A3 [4]	Shangan Road	25	A1	Shielmartin Road	29	B3
Seabury Drive	3	A2	Seapoint Villas	67	C2 [20]	Shanganagh Cliffs	64	E2	Shinkeen Bridge	32	E2
Seabury Gardens	2	F2	Seascout Den	40	D1	Shanganagh Grove	64	E3	Ship Street Great	75	A1
Seabury Glen	2	F2	Seatown Park	2	D1	Shanganagh Road	64	E1	Ship Street Little	75	A1
Seabury Green	2	F2	Seatown Park The Avenue	2	D1	Shanganagh Terrace	60	E4	Shrewsbury	39	A4
Seabury Grove	2	F2	Seatown Park The Court	2	D1	Shanganagh Vale	60	D4	Shrewsbury Hall	64	E3
Seabury Heights	2	F2	Seatown Park The Crescent	2	D1	Shanganagh Wood	64	E2 [8]	Shrewsbury House	59	C4
Seabury Lane	2	F2	Seatown Park The Drive	2	D1	Shanglas Road	25	C1	Shrewsbury Lawn	59	C4
Seabury Lawns	2	F2	Seatown Park The Green	2	D1	Shanid Road	46	F2	Shrewsbury Lodge	59	C3
Seabury Meadows	2	F2	Seatown Park The Grove	2	D1	Shankill	64	E3	Shrewsbury Park	48	D1
Seabury Orchard	2	F2	Seatown Road	2	D1	Shankill View	67	C2 [38]	Shrewsbury Road	48	D1
Seabury Parade	2	F2	Seatown Roundabout (Swords)	2	D1	Shanliss Avenue	25	B1	(Ailesbury Road)		
Seabury Park	2	F2	Seatown Terrace	2	D2	Shanliss Drive	25	B1	Shrewsbury Road (Shankill)	64	E3
Seabury Place	2	F2	Seatown Villas	2	D1	Shanliss Gardens	25	A1 [2]	Shrewsbury Woods	59	C4
Seabury Road	2	F2	Seatown Walk	2	D2	Shanliss Grove	25	B1	Sibthorpe Lane	76	D4
Seabury Vale	2	F2	Seatown West	2	D1	Shanliss Park	25	B1	Sidbury Court	68	D2 [5]
Seabury View	2	F2	Seaview Avenue East	72	F2	Shanliss Road	25	A1	Sidmonton Avenue	67	C2
Seabury Walk	2	F2	Seaview Avenue North	26	D4	Shanliss Walk	25	B1	Sidmonton Court	68	D3 [5]
Seabury Wood	2	F2	Seaview Cottages	63	C4	Shanliss Way	25	B1	Sidmonton Gardens	67	C2 [36]
Seacliff Avenue	27	C1	Seaview Lawn	64	E2	Shannon Terrace	73	C1	Sidmonton Gardens	67	C2
Seacliff Drive	27	C1	Seaview Park	64	E2	Shanowen Avenue	25	A1	Sidmonton Park	68	D2
Seacliff Road	27	C1	Seaview Terrace (Donnybrook)	48	D1	Shanowen Crescent	25	B1	Sidmonton Place	67	C2 [6]
Seacourt	26	F4	Seaview Terrace	49	C4 [15]	Shanowen Drive	25	B1	Sidmonton Road	67	C2
Seacrest	67	C3	(Dun Laoghaire)			Shanowen Grove	25	A1	Sidmonton Square	67	C2 [1]
Seafield (Shankill)	64	F2	Seaview Terrace (Howth)	30	D2 [2]	Shanowen Hall	25	B2	Sigurd Road	70	E3
Seafield (Sutton)	28	D1 [2]	Seaview Wood	64	E2	Shanowen Park	25	A1	Silchester Court	60	D1
Seafield Avenue (Clontarf)	26	F4	Second Avenue (Seville Place)	72	E3	Shanowen Road	25	B1	Silchester Crescent	60	D1
Seafield Avenue (Monkstown)	49	B4	Second Avenue (Tallaght)	44	F4	Shanowen Square	25	A1	Silchester Park	60	D1
Seafield Close	48	E3	Sefton	59	C2	Shanowen Square	25	B2	Silchester Road	60	D1
Seafield Court (Loughlinstown)	64	E1	Sefton Green	59	C2	Shanrath Road	25	B1	Silchester Wood	60	D1 [16]
Seafield Court (Malahide)	3	B2	Sefton Hall	59	A2 [12]	Shantalla Avenue	25	C1	Silken Vale	17	C3
Seafield Crescent	48	E3	*Selskar Terrace	75	C4	Shantalla Drive	25	C2	Silleachain Lane	20	D4
*Seafield Downs	26	F4	(Old Mountpleasant)			Shantalla Park	25	C2	Silloge Avenue	25	A1
(off Kincora Road Clontarf)			Serpentine Avenue	39	A4	Shantalla Road	25	C1	Silloge Crescent	25	A1
Seafield Drive	48	E2	Serpentine Park	39	A4	Shanvarna Road	25	B1	Silloge Gardens	25	A1
Seafield Grove	27	A4 [1]	Serpentine Road	39	A4	Sharavogue	60	E2	Silloge Road	25	A1
Seafield Park	48	E2 [1]	Serpentine Terrace	39	A4	Shaw Court Apts.	75	B3	Silver Birches (Dunboyne)	7	B2
Seafield Road (Ballybrack)	64	E1	Seskin View Avenue	55	A2	Shaw Street	71	C4	Silver Birches (Dundrum)	47	C4
Seafield Road (Booterstown)	48	E2	Seskin View Drive	55	A2	Shaw's Lane	76	F2	Silver Birches Close	7	B2
Seafield Road (Killiney)	60	E4	Seskin View Park	55	A2	Shea's Court	70	E2	Silver Birches Crescent	7	B2
Seafield Road East	26	F4	Seskin View Road	55	A2	Sheelin Avenue	64	E1	Silver Pines	58	F2 [3]
Seafield Road West	26	E4	Setanta Place	75	C1	Sheelin Drive	64	E1	Silverberry	34	D3
Seafield Terrace	60	F2 [15]	Seven Houses	60	D1 [13]	Sheelin Grove	64	E1 [7]	Silverdale	34	D3
Seafort Avenue	39	A4	Seven Oaks (Inchicore)	36	F3	Sheelin Hill	64	E1 [13]	Silverpine	67	B3

STREET NAME	PAGE/GRID REFERENCE
Silverwood	34 D3
Silverwood Drive	46 E4
Silverwood Road	46 E4
Simmon's Place (off Thompson's Cottages)	71 C2
Simmonscourt Avenue	48 D1 [2]
Simmonscourt Castle	48 D1
Simmonscourt Road	39 A4
Simmonscourt Square	48 D1 [5]
Simmonscourt Terrace	47 C1 [18]
Simmonscourt View	48 D1 [3]
Simmonstown	41 A1
Simmonstown Manor	32 D4
Simmonstown Park	32 D4
Simons Ridge	57 C3
Simpsons Lane	39 A3 [32]
Sion Hill Avenue	46 F1
Sion Hill Court	25 C3 [5]
Sion Hill Road	25 C3
Sion Road	60 D2
Sionhill	48 F3
Sir Ivor Mall	58 F2 [7]
Sir John Rogerson's Quay	72 E4
Sitric Place (off Sitric Road)	70 E3
Sitric Road	70 E3
Skeagh	41 A3
Skelligs Court	22 F1
Skelly's Lane	26 D2
Skreen Road	24 D4
Slade	53 A3
Slade Castle Avenue	53 A2
Slade Castle Close	53 A2
Slade Castle Heights	53 A2
Slade Castle View	53 A2
Slade Road	53 A2
Slade Row	70 D3
Slademore Avenue	26 F1
Slademore Close	26 F1
Slademore Court	13 C4
Slademore Drive	26 F1
Slane Road	73 C4
Slaney Close	24 E3
Slaney Road	24 E3
Slate Cabin Lane	57 C3
Slemish Road	69 B1
Slí an Chanáil	19 C4
Slieve Rua Drive	58 D1
Slievebloom Park	45 C1
Slievebloom Road	45 C1
Slievemore Road	73 A4
Slievenamon Road	73 B3
Sloan Terrace	68 D2 [8]
*Sloan Terrace (on Meath Road)	67 C2
Sloperton	49 C4
Smithfield	70 F4
Smithfield Gate Apts.	70 F3
Smithfield Market Square Apts. (Smithfield)	70 F4
Smithfield Terrace (Smithfield)	70 F4
Smith's Cottages (Donnybrook)	47 B1 [18]
Smith's Lane	46 F1 [13]
Smith's Villas	49 C4 [3]
Smyth Gardens	49 C4 [34]
Snowdrop Walk	13 C4
Snugborough	14 E3
Snugborough Road	22 F1
Snugborough Road (Extention)	22 D2
Somerset Street	76 F1
Somerton	59 C2
Somerton Mews	59 C2
Somerton Road	22 E4
Somerville Avenue	45 C1
Somerville Court	46 D1 [8]
Somerville Drive	46 D1
Somerville Park	45 C1 [7]
Sommerville	47 C4
Sonesta	3 A2
Sophie Baret Residence	48 D4
Sorbonne	48 D4
Sorrel Dale	22 D2
Sorrel Drive	21 C2
Sorrel Heath	21 C2
Sorrel Park	21 C2
Sorrell Hall	57 C3
Sorrento Close	60 F2 [25]
Sorrento Court	60 F2 [29]
Sorrento Drive	60 F2 [12]
Sorrento Heights	60 F2 [30]
Sorrento Lawn	60 F2 [13]
Sorrento Mews	60 F2 [28]
*Sorrento Park (on Sorrento Rd)	60 F2
Sorrento Road	60 F2
Sorrento Terrace	60 Inset
South Avenue	48 E4
South Bank	2 D1
South Bank (Swords)	1 C1
South Bank Road	39 B3
South Circular Road (Dolphin's Barn)	74 D3
South Circular Road (Islandbridge)	69 B4
South Circular Road (Kilmainham)	73 C2
South Circular Road (Portobello)	74 E3
South City Market (on South Great Georges Street)	75 B1
South Dock Place	76 F1
South Dock Road	76 F1
South Dock Street	76 F1
South Esplanade	68 D2
South Great George's Street	75 B1
South Hill (Howth)	29 C3
South Hill (Milltown)	47 B2
South Hill Avenue	48 F3
South Hill Park	48 E3
South Lotts Road	76 F1
South Park (Cornelscourt)	59 B3
South Park Drive	59 B2
South Richmond View	75 B3
South Winds	60 F1 [4]
South Wood Park	48 F3
Southdene	49 B4 [18]
Southern Cross Avenue	73 A2
Southern Cross Route	57 B3
Southmede	57 C1
Southview Terrace	74 D1
Spa Road (Inchicore)	36 F3
Spa Road (Phoenix Park)	69 B2
Spafield Terrace	39 A4 [13]
Spawell Cottages	45 C4 [1]
Spawell Roundabout	46 D4
Spencer Dock	72 E3
Spencer Dock (North Wall)	72 E3
Spencer Dock (Guild Street)	72 E3
Spencer Place (off Spencer Street N)	72 E1
Spencer Row	71 C3
Spencer Street North	72 E1
Spencer Street South	75 A3
Spencer Terrace (off Cork Street)	74 E2
Spencer Villas	60 E1
Spences Terrace	74 E2
Sperrin Road	73 A4
Spiddal Park	35 C3
Spiddal Road	35 C3
Spire View	24 D4
Spire View	70 F1
Spire View Lane	47 A1
Spitalfields	74 F1
Spring Garden Lane	71 C4
Spring Garden Street	72 D1
Springbank Cottages	53 A2
Springdale Court Apts.	26 F2
Springdale Road	26 F2
Springfield (Cabra)	69 B1
Springfield (Tallaght)	54 F1
Springfield Avenue	46 E4
Springfield Close	31 C4
Springfield Crescent	46 E4
Springfield Drive	46 E4
Springfield Lane	63 A1
Springfield Park (Deans Grange)	59 A2
Springfield Park (Templeogue)	46 E4
Springfield Road	46 E3
Springhill Avenue	59 A1
Springhill Cottages	59 B1 [5]
Springhill Park (Dalkey)	60 E2
Springhill Park (Deans Grange)	59 B1
Springlawn	22 E2
Springlawn Close	22 E2
Springlawn Court	22 E2
Springlawn Drive	22 E2
Springlawn Heights	22 E2
Springlawn Park	22 E2
Springlawn Road	22 E2
Springmount Apts.	24 D2
Springvale	56 E2
Springvale Hall	57 C3
Spruce Avenue	58 D2
St Agatha Court (off William St N)	72 D2
St Agnes Park	46 D1
St Agnes Road	46 D1
*St Agnes Terrace (on St Agnes Rd)	46 D1
St Agnes Terrace (Rathfarnham)	46 F3 [2]
St Aidan's Drive	48 D4
St Aidan's Halting Site	54 D1
St Aidan's Park	25 C4 [6]
St Aidan's Park Avenue	25 C4
St Aidan's Park Road	25 C4
St Aidan's Terrace	67 C2 [23]
St Alban's Park	48 E1
St Alban's Road	74 F3
St Alphonsus Avenue	25 A4 [11]
St Alphonsus Rd	25 A4
St Andrew Street	75 B1
St Andrews	34 F2
St Andrews Drive	34 F2
St Andrews Fairway	34 F2
St Andrews Green	34 F2
St Andrew's Grove	3 B3
St Andrew's Lane (off Exchequer Street)	75 B1
St Andrews Park	1 C1
St Andrews Wood	34 F2
St Anne's Court	27 A3 [2]
St Anne's (Kimmage)	46 E2
St Anne's (Ranelagh)	75 C4
St Anne's Avenue	27 A3
St Anne's Drive	27 A3
St Anne's Park	64 E3
St Anne's Road North	25 A4
St Anne's Road South	74 E3
St Anne's Square (Blackrock)	49 A3 [7]
St Anne's Square (Portmarnock)	14 F2 [6]
St Anne's Terrace (Raheny)	27 A3
St Anne's Terrace (Ranelagh)	75 C4
St Anne's Terrace (Rathcoole)	52 E2
St Ann's Square Lower	14 F2 [5]
St Anthony's Avenue	44 E2
St Anthony's Crescent	45 C2
St Anthony's Place (off Temple Street North)	71 B2
St Anthony's Road	74 D2
St Aongus Court	45 B4
St Aongus Crescent	45 B4
St Aongus Green	45 B4
St Aongus Grove	45 B4
St Aongus Lawn	45 B4
St Aongus Park	45 B4
St Aongus Road	45 B4
St Assam's Avenue	27 A2
St Assam's Drive	27 A2
St Assam's Park	27 A2
St Assam's Road East	27 B2
St Assam's Road West	27 A2
St Attracta Road	24 F4
St Aubyn's Court	64 E1 [5]
St Audoen's Terrace (off High Street)	75 A1
St Augustine Street	70 F4
St Augustine's Park	59 A1
St Barnabas Gardens	72 E2
St Begnet's Villas	60 E1
St Benedicts Gardens	71 B1
St Brendan's Avenue	26 E2
St Brendan's Cottages	39 A3 [6]
St Brendan's Crescent	45 B2
St Brendan's Drive	26 E2
St Brendan's Park	26 F2
St Brendan's Road	25 A4 [12]
St Brendan's Terrace (Coolock)	26 E1
St Brendan's Terrace (Dun Laoghaire)	49 C4 [19]
St Brendan's Terrace (Rockbrook)	56 E4
St Bricin's Park	70 D3
St Bridget's Avenue (North Strand)	72 E1
St Bridget's Drive	45 B2
St Bridget's Flats	47 C2 [8]
St Brigid's Green	26 E2
St Brigid's Grove	26 E2
St Brigid's Avenue	14 F2 [4]
St Brigid's Church Road	58 F1
St Brigid's Cottages (Blanchardstown)	22 F2
St Brigid's Cottages (Clondalkin)	44 F2
St Brigid's Cottages (North Strand)	72 E1
St Brigid's Court	26 E3 [2]
St Brigid's Crescent	26 E2
St Brigid's Drive (Clondalkin)	44 E2
St Brigid's Drive (Killester)	26 E3 [1]
St Brigid's Lawn	26 E2
St Brigid's Park (Blanchardstown)	22 F2
St Brigid's Park (Clondalkin)	44 E2 [1]
St Brigid's Park (Cornelscourt)	59 B3
St Brigid's Road (Artane)	26 E2
St Brigid's Road (Clondalkin)	44 E2
St Brigid's Road Lower	25 A4
St Brigid's Road Upper	25 A4
St Brigid's Terrace	67 C2 [33]
St Broc's Cottages	47 C1 [1]
St Canice's Park	24 F2
St Canice's Road	25 A2
St Catherine's Avenue	74 E3
St Catherines Grove	43 C1 [3]
St Catherine's Lane West	74 F1
St Catherine's Park	60 E1
St Catherine's Road	60 E1
St Catherine's Terrace	29 A1 [2]
St Catherine's View	20 E4
St Clair's Lawn	67 B3
St Clair's Terrace	67 B3 [3]
St Clare's Avenue	74 F4
St Clement's Road	25 A4 [13]
St Colmcille's Way	55 C2
St Columbanus Avenue	47 B3
St Columbanus Place	47 B3 [1]
St Columbanus Road	47 B3
St Columbas Heights	1 C2
St Columbas Rise	1 C2
St Columba's Road	45 B2
St Columba's Road Lower	25 A4
St Columba's Road Upper	25 A4
St Columcille's Crescent	2 D2 [1]
St Columcille's Drive	2 D2
St Columcille's Terrace	67 C2 [18]
St Columcills Park	2 D2
St Conleth's Road	45 C2
St Cronan's Avenue	1 B1
St Cronan's Close	1 B2
St Cronan's Cottages	1 C2
St Cronan's Court	1 B1
St Cronan's Grove	1 C1
St Cronan's Lawn	1 B1
St Cronan's Road	67 C2 [8]
St Cronan's View	1 B2
St Cronan's Way	1 C2
St David's	26 D2
St David's Court	26 E4 [5]
St David's Park	26 D2
St David's Terrace (Blackhorse Avenue)	70 D2
St David's Terrace (Glasnevin)	25 A3 [3]
St Davids Wood	26 D2
St Declan's Road	25 C4
St Declan's Terrace	25 C4 [1]
St Domhnach's Well Street	28 D1 [3]
St Dominic's Avenue	55 A1
St Dominic's Court	55 A1 [4]
St Dominic's Road	55 A1
St Dominic's Terrace	55 A1
St Donagh's Crescent	27 B1

STREET NAME	PAGE/GRID REFERENCE
St Donagh's Park	27 B1
St Donagh's Road	27 B1
St Eithne Road	24 F4
St Elizabeth's Court	70 E1
St Enda's Drive	56 F1
St Enda's Park	56 F1
St Enda's Road	46 F2
St Finbarr's Court	24 E4 [2]
St Finbarr's Close	45 B3
St Finbarr's Road	24 E4
St Finian's Grove	34 D2
St Finian's Avenue	34 D2
St Finian's Close	34 D2
St Finian's Crescent	34 D2
St Fintan Road	24 F4
St Fintan Terrace	24 F4
St Fintan's Crescent	29 B3
St Fintan's Grove	29 B3
St Fintan's Park (Dean's Grange)	59 B1
St Fintan's Park (Sutton)	29 B2
St Fintan's Road	29 B3
St Fintan's Terrace	35 C1 [5]
St Fintan's Villas	59 B1
St Francis Square	75 A1
St Gabriel's	59 C3
St Gabriel's Court	27 A4 [2]
St Gabriel's Road	26 F4
St Gall Gardens North	47 B3 [2]
St Gall Gardens South	47 B3 [3]
St Gatien Road	56 F1 [2]
St George's Avenue (Clonliffe Road)	25 B4
St George's Avenue (Killiney)	60 E3
St George's Villas (Inchicore)	36 F3 [18]
St Gerard's Road	45 C2
St Helena's Court	24 E2 [3]
St Helena's Drive	24 E2
St Helena's Road	24 E2
St Helen's	60 E1 [22]
St Helen's Road	48 E2
St Helen's Terrace	73 A2
St Helen's Villas	48 F2 [1]
St Helen's Wood	48 E3
St Helier's Copse	48 F4 [1]
St Ignatius Avenue	71 B1
St Ignatius Road	25 A4
St Ita's Road	25 A3 [6]
St Ives	3 B2
St James Avenue (Clonliffe Road)	72 D1
*St James Place (Sandymount Road)	39 A3
St James Terrace (Sandymount)	39 A3 [23]
St James's Avenue (James's Street)	74 D1
St James's Place (Inchicore)	36 F3 [17]
St James's Road	45 B2
St James's Terrace (Dolphin's Barn)	74 D3
*St James's Walk	74 D2
St Jarlath Road	24 F4
*St John Street	74 F2
St John's Court (Donnycarney)	26 D3
St John's	48 E1
St John's Avenue (Clondalkin)	44 D2
St John's Avenue (The Coombe)	74 F2
St John's Close	44 D2
St John's Cottages	73 C1
St John's Court (Beaumont)	26 D1
St John's Court (Clondalkin)	44 D2
St John's Crescent	44 D2
St John's Drive	44 D2
St John's Gate	44 D2
St John's Green	44 D2
St John's Grove	44 D2
*St John's Lane(off Strand Road)	48 E1
St John's Lawn	44 D2
St John's Park (Dun Laoghaire)	49 C4
St John's Park East	44 D2
St Johns Park West	44 D2
St John's Road	44 D2
St John's Road East	48 E1
St John's Road West (Clondalkin)	44 D2
St John's Road West (Islandbridge)	69 C4
St John's Terrace (Mount Brown)	73 C1
St John's Wood (Clondalkin)	44 D2
St John's Wood (Clontarf)	26 E4 [2]
St John's Wood West	44 D2
St Joseph Street (off Leo Street)	71 B1
St Joseph's	23 C2
St Joseph's Avenue (Ballybough)	25 B4 [2]
St Joseph's Avenue (Drumcondra)	25 A4
St Joseph's Cottages	23 C4 [3]
St Joseph's Court	70 E2
St Joseph's Grove	47 C4 [9]
St Joseph's Mansions	72 D2
St Joseph's Parade	71 A1
St Joseph's Place (Dorset Street Lower)	71 B2
St Joseph's Place (Prussia Street)	70 E2
St Joseph's Road (Aughrim Street)	70 E2
St Joseph's Road (Walkinstown)	45 C2
St Joseph's Square	39 C1 [2]
St Joseph's Terrace (Fairview)	25 C4 [4]
St Joseph's Terrace (North Circular Road)	71 C1
St Joseph's Terrace (off Dolphin's Barn)	74 D3
*St Joseph's Terrace (off Pembroke Street)	39 A3
*St Joseph's Terrace (on Tivoli Road)	50 D4
St Joseph's Villas (Summerhill)	72 D1
St Judes Apts.	31 C3 [3]
St Kevin's Avenue (off Blackpitts)	74 F2
St Kevin's Cottages	75 A3
St Kevin's Court	47 A2
St Kevin's Gardens	47 A2
St Kevin's Parade	75 A3
St Kevin's Park (Rathgar)	47 A2
St Kevin's Park (Stillorgan)	58 D1
St Kevin's Road	75 A4
St Kevin's Square	67 C2
St Kevin's Terrace (Bray)	67 C2 [14]
*St Kevin's Terrace (New Bride Road)	75 A2
St Kevin's Villas	60 D1
St Killian's Avenue	45 B2
St Killians Crescent	67 B4
St Killian's Park	44 E1 [1]
St Laurence Grove	36 E2 [4]
St Laurence Park	48 F4
St Laurence Place (Western Way)	71 A2
St Laurence Place East (Lr Sheriff Street)	72 E3
St Laurence Road	36 E2
St Laurence Terrace (Chapelizod)	36 E2 [9]
St Laurence's Terrace (Bray)	67 C2 [17]
St Lawrence Building Apts.	30 D1 [16]
St Lawrence Glen	36 E3 [3]
St Lawrence O'Toole Avenue	14 F2 [1]
St Lawrence Quay	30 D1 [8]
St Lawrence Road (Clontarf)	26 D4
St Lawrence Road (Howth)	30 D1
St Lawrence's Court	26 D4
St Lawrence's Terrace (Howth)	30 D2 [1]
St Loman's Road	34 F2
St Luke's Avenue	74 F2
St Luke's Court	26 D1 [3]
St Luke's Crescent	47 B2 [3]
St Luke's Gate	74 F2
St Maelruans Park	55 A1 [1]
St Maignenn's Terrace	73 C1
St Malachy's Drive	45 C2
St Malachy's Road	25 A3 [7]
St Margaret's Close	60 E1 [30]
St Margaret's (Booterstown)	48 F3
St Margaret's (North Road)	11 B1
St Margaret's Avenue (Kilbarrack)	27 C2
St Margaret's Avenue (Malahide)	3 B3
St Margaret's Avenue (off Pimlico)	74 F1
*St Margaret's Avenue North (Richmond Lane)	71 C1
St Margaret's Court	11 A4 [1]
St Margaret's Halting Site	11 C4
St Margaret's Park	3 B3
St Margaret's Road (Ballymun)	12 D4
St Margaret's Road (Finglas)	11 A4
St Margaret's Road (Malahide)	3 B3
St Margaret's Road (Poppintree)	11 C4
St Margaret's Terrace	74 E2
St Mark's Avenue	35 A2
St Mark's Crescent	35 A3
St Mark's Drive	35 A3
St Mark's Gardens	35 A3
St Mark's Green	35 A3
St Mark's Grove	35 A3
St Marnock's Avenue	14 F2
St Martin's Drive	46 E2
St Martin's Park	46 E1
St Mary's Ave North (Mountjoy Street)	71 A2
St Mary's Avenue (Rathfarnham)	46 F4
St Mary's Avenue West	36 F3
St Mary's Crescent	45 C1
St Mary's Drive	45 C1
St Mary's Lane	76 E2
St Mary's Mansions	71 C2
St Mary's Park (Crumlin)	45 C1
St Mary's Park (Finglas)	23 C2
St Mary's Park (Leixlip)	20 D4
St Mary's Place (Howth)	30 D2 [4]
St Mary's Place North	71 A2
St Mary's Road (Crumlin)	46 D1
St Mary's Road (Howth)	30 D2 [3]
St Mary's Road North (East Wall)	72 E2
St Mary's Road South (Ballsbridge)	76 E3
St Mary's Street	49 C4 [5]
St Mary's Terrace (Arbour Hill)	70 E3
*St Mary's Terrace (Bath Street)	39 A3
St Mary's Terrace (Boghall Road)	67 C4 [6]
St Marys Terrace (Bray)	68 D2 [20]
St Mary's Terrace (Chapelizod)	36 E2 [5]
St Mary's Terrace (Dunboyne)	7 B2 [1]
St Mary's Terrace (Mountjoy Street)	71 A2
St Mary's Terrace (Rathfarnham)	46 F4 [5]
St Mathias Wood	60 D4
St Mel's Avenue	45 B3
St Michael's Close (off High Street)	75 A1
St Michael's Estate	73 A2
St Michael's Hill (off High Street)	75 A1
St Michael's House	47 C4
St Michael's Place	71 A2
St Michael's Road	25 A3 [8]
St Michael's Terrace (Blackpitts)	74 F2
St Michael's Terrace (Dun Laoghaire)	49 C4 [18]
St Michan's Place (off Chancery Street)	71 A4
St Michan's Street	71 A4
*St Mobhi Avenue (on St. Mobhi Road)	25 A3
St Mobhi Boithirin	25 A3
St Mobhi Drive	25 A3
St Mobhi Grove	25 A3 [10]
St Mobhi Road	25 A3
St Mochtas Avenue	22 D3
St Mochtas Chase	22 D2
St Mochtas Close	22 D3
St Mochtas Drive	22 D3
St Mochtas Green	22 D3
St Mochtas Grove	22 D3
St Mochtas Lawn	22 D2
St Mochtas Road	22 D3
St Mochtas Vale	22 D3
St Mura's Terrace	72 F2
St Nathy's House	47 B4 [5]
St Nathy's Villas	47 B4 [17]
St Nessan's Apts	30 E2 [3]
St Nessan's Close	30 D2 [9]
St Nessans Court	30 D2 [12]
St Nessan's Terrace	30 D2 [5]
St Nicholas Place	75 A1
St Oliver's Park	35 B3
St Pappin's Green	24 F2
St Pappin's Road	25 A2
St Patrick's Avenue (Clondalkin)	44 D1 [1]
St Patrick's Avenue (Dalkey)	60 F2 [1]
St Patrick's Avenue (Fairview)	72 E1
St Patrick's Avenue (Portmarnock)	14 F2
St Patrick's Close (Kevin Street Upper)	75 A2
St Patrick's Close (Kill O'The Grange)	59 C1 [9]
St Patrick's Cottages	46 F4
St Patrick's Crescent (Kill O'The Grange)	59 C1
St Patrick's Crescent (Rathcoole)	52 E2
St Patrick's Parade	25 A4
St Patrick's Park (Blanchardstown)	22 E2
St Patricks Park (Celbridge)	31 C3
St Patricks Park (Celbridge)	32 D3
St Patricks Park (Clondalkin)	44 D1
St Patrick's Park (Dunboyne)	7 B2
St Patricks Park (Stepaside)	58 E4
*St Patrick's Place (off Royal Canal Bank)	25 A4
St Patrick's Road (Clondalkin)	35 A4
St Patrick's Road (Dalkey)	60 F2 [8]
St Patrick's Road (Drumcondra)	25 A4
St Patrick's Road (Walkinstown)	45 C2
St Patrick's Square (Bray)	67 C1 [1]
St Patrick's Square (Dalkey)	60 F2 [4]
St Patrick's Terrace (Inchicore)	36 F3 [9]
St Patrick's Terrace (Kill O' the Grange)	59 C1 [7]
St Patrick's Terrace (Nth Brunswick St)	70 F3
*St Patrick's Terrace (off Fitzroy Avenue)	25 B4
*St Patrick's Terrace (Russell Street)	71 C1
St Patrick's Villas	39 A3 [3]
St Paul's Terrace	60 E1 [5]
St Peter's Avenue	70 F1
St Peter's Close	71 A1
St Peter's Crescent	45 C2
St Peter's Drive	45 C2
St Peter's Park	7 B2
St Peter's Road (Bray)	67 B1
St Peter's Road (Phibsborough)	24 F4
St Peter's Road (Walkinstown)	45 C2
St Peter's Square	71 A1
St Peter's Terrace (Bray)	67 B1 [2]
St Peter's Terrace (Dun Laoghaire)	60 E1 [6]
St Peter's Terrace (Howth)	30 D2
St Peter's Terrace (Walkinstown)	45 C2 [1]
St Philomenas	9 C4
St Philomena's Court	9 C4
St Philomena's Park	9 C3
St Philomena's Road	24 F4 [1]
St Raphaels Avenue	31 C4
St Ronan's Avenue	35 A3
St Ronan's Close	35 A3
St Ronan's Crescent	35 A3
St Ronan's Drive	35 A3
St Ronan's Gardens	35 A3
St Ronan's Green	35 A3
St Ronan's Grove	35 A3
St Ronan's Park	35 A3
St Ronan's Way	35 A3
St Stephen's Green East	75 C2
St Stephen's Green North	75 C2
St Stephen's Green South	75 B2
St Stephen's Green West	75 B2
St Sylvester Villas	3 B3
St Teresa's Gardens	74 E2
St Teresa's Place	25 A4 [9]
St Teresa's Road (Crumlin)	46 D2

STREET NAME	PAGE/GRID REFERENCE
St Teresa's Road (Glasnevin)	25 A4 [8]
St Thomas Mead	48 E3
St Thomas Road (Ardee Street)	74 F2
St Thomas's Road (Mount Merrion)	48 E3
St Ultan's Flats	75 B3
St Vincent Street North	71 A1
St Vincent Street South	75 A3
St Vincent Street West	73 A2
St Vincent's Cottages	23 C4 [2]
St Vincent's Court	25 C3 [7]
St Vincent's Park	49 A4
St Werburghs	2 E2
St Wolston's Abbey	32 D4
St. Agnes Terrace	46 D1 [4]
St. Andrews Court	34 D1 [17]
St. Anns Court	71 B2
St. Anthony Crescent	74 D2
St. Anthony's Place	71 B2
St. Audoen's House Flats	70 F4
St. Berach's Place	27 B1 [6]
St. Catheryn's Court	39 B4 [7]
St. Cronan's Cottages	1 C2
St. Cuthbert's Road	43 B1
St. James Court	39 A4 [49]
St. Jame's Wood	73 B2
St. Jame's Wood (Suir Road)	73 B2
St. James's	26 D4
St. James's Court Apts.	74 E1
St. John's Court	25 B1
St. John's Well Way	73 C1
St. Joseph's Court	70 E2
St. Joseph's Place	70 E2
St. Kevins Church Apts.	75 A3
St. Laurence Court	36 E3
*St. Laurence O'Toole Court	72 D3
*St. Mary's Court (on Church Road)	72 F2
St. Michan's House Flats	71 A4
St. Patrick's Court	74 F3
*St. Samson Court	14 D3
St. Samson Square	14 D3
St. Vincent's Court	26 D3
St. Wolstan's Abbey	32 E2
St. James Place	39 A4 [31]
Stable Lane (Harcourt Street)	75 B2
Stable Lane (Leeson St Lr)	75 C2
Stable Lane (Smithfield)	70 F4
Stackstown	61 B1
Stacummy Bridge	32 E4
Staffordstown	5 C2
Staffordstown Little	5 C1
Stamer Street	75 A3
Stanford Green	45 C1
Stanhope Street	70 F3
Stanley Street	70 F3
Stannaway Avenue	46 D1
Stannaway Court	46 D2 [3]
Stannaway Drive	46 E1
Stannaway Road	46 E1
Stapolin	14 F4
Stapolin Avenue	14 F4
Stapolin House	14 F4
Stapolin Lawns	14 F4
Station Close	35 A4
Station Road (Dunboyne)	7 B3
Station Road (Glenageary)	60 E1
Station Road (Killiney)	60 E4
Station Road (Leixlip)	19 C4
*Station Road (off Clover Hill Road)	35 A4
Station Road (Portmarnock)	14 E2
Station Road (Raheny)	27 A2
Station Road (Shankill)	64 E2 [6]
Station Road (Sutton)	29 A1
Station View Apts.	22 E3 [3]
Station Way	14 D4
Stationcourt	22 D3
Stationcourt Hall	22 D3
Stationcourt Park	22 D3
Stationcourt View	22 D3
Stationcourt Way	22 D3
Steelstown	51 C3
Steelstown Interchange (N7 J5)	51 B3
Steeple Gate	39 A3 [46]

STREET NAME	PAGE/GRID REFERENCE
Steeven's Gate Apts.	74 D1
Steeven's Lane	70 D4
Stella Avenue	25 A3
Stella Gardens	39 A3
Stella Maris Apts.	17 C4
Stepaside	58 E4
Stepaside	62 E1
Stepaside Lane	62 E1
Stepaside Park	58 E4
Stepaside Park	62 E1
Stepaside Village	58 E3
Stephen Street Lower	75 B1
Stephen Street Upper	75 B1
Stephen's Lane	76 D2
Stephen's Place	76 D2
Stephen's Road	73 B2
Sterling Square Apts.	8 D3
Stewart Hall	71 A3
Stillorgan	58 F1
Stillorgan Court	58 E1 [2]
Stillorgan Grove	48 F4
Stillorgan Heath	58 E1 [3]
Stillorgan Heath	58 E1
Stillorgan Park	48 F4
Stillorgan Park	49 A4
Stillorgan Park Avenue	58 F1
Stillorgan Road (Donnybrook)	48 D1
Stillorgan Road (Foxrock)	59 A2
Stillorgan Road (Mount Merrion)	48 E3
Stillorgan Road (Stillorgan)	58 F1
Stillorgan Wood	58 E1
Stirling Park	47 A3 [2]
Stirrup Lane (off Church Street)	70 F3
Stockhole	13 A2
Stockhole Lane	12 F1
Stocking Avenue	56 D2
Stocking Lane	56 D3
Stocking Wood	56 D3
Stocking Wood Copse	56 D3
Stocking Wood Drive	56 D3
Stocking Wood Green	56 D3
Stocking Wood Hall	56 D3
Stocking Wood Manor	56 D3
Stocking Wood Rise	56 D3
Stocking Wood Way	56 D3
Stockton Court	23 A3
Stockton Drive	23 A3
Stockton Green	23 A3
Stockton Grove	23 A3
Stockton Lawn	23 A3
Stockton Park	23 A3
Stokes Place	75 B2
Stone Mason's Green	57 A2
Stone Mews	47 A1 [8]
Stonebridge	21 B2
Stonebridge Avenue	21 B2
Stonebridge Close	64 E3 [2]
Stonebridge Drive	21 B2
Stonebridge Lane	64 D2 [1]
Stonebridge Road (Clonsilla)	21 B2
Stonebridge Road (Shankill)	64 D2
Stonemasons Green	57 A2 [5]
Stonemasons Green	57 A2
Stonemasons Way	57 A2
Stonepark Abbey	46 F4
Stonepark Court	46 F4
Stonepark Orchard	46 F4 [17]
Stoneview Place	50 D4 [13]
Stoney Park	52 F2
Stoney Road (Dundrum)	47 C4
Stoney Road (East Wall)	72 E2
Stoneybatter	70 E3
Stoneylea Terrace	67 C3 [10]
Store Street	71 C3
Stormanstown Road	25 A2
Stradbrook Close	59 B1
Stradbrook Gardens	49 B4 [8]
Stradbrook Grove	49 B4
Stradbrook Hall	49 B4 [20]
Stradbrook Hill	59 B1 [4]
Stradbrook Lawn	49 B4
Stradbrook Park	49 B4
Stradbrook Road	49 B4
Straffan Avenue	17 C4

STREET NAME	PAGE/GRID REFERENCE
Straffan Close	17 C4
Straffan Court	17 C4
Straffan Crescent	17 C4
Straffan Drive	17 C4
Straffan Green	17 C4
Straffan Grove	17 C4
Straffan Lawn	17 C4
Straffan Park	17 C4
Straffan Place	17 C4
Straffan Road	17 C4
Straffan Way	17 C4
Straffan Wood	17 C4
Straleek	41 B1
Stralem Court	21 B1
Stralem Crescent	21 B1
Stralem Grove	21 B1
Stralem Mews	21 B1
Stralem Terrace	21 B1
Strand Court	3 B2 [12]
Strand Lane	48 E1 [3]
Strand Road (Baldoyle)	15 A4
Strand Road (Ballybrack)	64 E1
Strand Road (Bray)	67 C2
Strand Road (Merrion)	48 E1
Strand Road (Portmarnock)	4 D4
Strand Road (Portmarnock)	14 F2
Strand Road (Portmarnock)	15 A1
Strand Road (Sandymount)	39 B4
Strand Road (Sutton)	29 B2
Strand Street (Malahide)	3 B2
Strand Street (Ringsend)	39 A3
Strand Street Great	71 A4
Strand Street Little	71 A4
Strand Terrace	47 B2 [2]
Strandmill Avenue	14 F2
Strandmill Park	15 A2
Strandmill Road	15 A2
Strandville Avenue (North Strand)	72 E1
Strandville Avenue East (Clontarf)	26 D4
Strandville House	26 D4 [4]
Strandville Place	72 E1
Strangford Drive	42 D4
Strangford Gardens	72 E2
Strangford Road	72 E2
Strasburg Terrace	39 A3 [21]
Stratford	47 A2 [9]
Strathmore Road	60 E4
Streamstown Lane	2 F4
Streamville Court	64 E1 [10]
Streamville Road	27 A1
Strong's Court	71 B2
Suffolk Street	75 B1
Sugarloaf Crescent	67 C3
Sugarloaf Terrace	67 C3 [21]
Suir Road	73 B2
Sullivan Street	69 C3
Summer Arch	71 C1
Summer Arch (off Summer Street North)	71 C1
Summer Place	71 C2
*Summer Row (off Summer Street North)	71 C1
Summer Street North	71 C2
Summer Street South	74 E1
Summerfield (Blanchardstown)	22 E2
Summerfield (Ringsend)	39 A3 [33]
Summerfield (Tallaght)	55 A2 [1]
Summerfield Avenue	22 E2
Summerfield Close	22 E2
Summerfield Close	60 F2 [10]
Summerfield Green	22 E2
Summerfield Lawns	22 E2
Summerfield Meadows	22 E2
Summerfield Rise	22 E2
Summerhill	71 C2
Summerhill Court	50 E4 [3]
Summerhill Parade (Dun Laoghaire)	50 D4 [6]
Summerhill Parade (Summerhill)	72 D1
Summerhill Place	71 C2
Summerhill Road (Dún Laoghaire)	50 D4
Summerhill Road (Dunboyne)	7 A2

STREET NAME	PAGE/GRID REFERENCE
Summerseat	8 D4
Summerseat Cottage	8 D4
Summerseat Court	8 D4
Summerville	39 B1
Summerville Park	47 A1
*Summerville Terrace (on Dalkey Ave)	60 F2
Sunbury Court	47 A2
Sunbury Gardens	47 A2
Suncroft Avenue	14 F2 [3]
Suncroft Drive	54 D2
Suncroft Park	54 D2
Sundale Avenue	54 D2
Sundale Close	54 D2
Sundale Crescent	54 D1
Sundale Green	54 D1
Sundale Grove	54 D2
Sundale Heights	54 D1
Sundale Lawn	54 D1
Sundale Meadows	54 D1
Sundale Parade	54 D1
Sundale Park	54 D2
Sundale Road	54 D2
Sundale Villas	54 D1
Sundale Walk	54 D1
Sundrive Park	46 E1
Sundrive Road	46 E1
Sunnybank Apts.	69 B4
Sunnybank Court	47 C4 [1]
Sunnybank Court	67 B1 [8]
Sunnyside	62 F3
Sunville Green	46 D1 [1]
Susan Terrace	74 F2
Susanville Road	25 B4
Sussex Road	76 D3
Sussex Street	50 D4 [16]
Sussex Terrace	76 D3
Sutton	29 A1
Sutton Castle Apts.	29 B3
Sutton Court	28 D1 [1]
Sutton Downs	28 D1
Sutton Grove	28 D1
Sutton Lane	63 A3
Sutton Lawns	28 D1
Sutton Park	28 D1
Sutton Road	67 B2 [9]
Sutton Villas	67 B2 [17]
Swallowbrook	8 F4
Swallowbrook Crescent	8 F4
Swallowbrook Park	8 F4
Swallowbrook View	8 F4
Swan Alley	74 F1
Swan Grove	75 C4
Swan Hall (Belgard Square)	54 F1 [10]
Swan Place	76 D4
Swan Yard (off Harry Street)	75 B1
Swanbrook	67 C4
Swan's Nest Avenue	27 B1
Swan's Nest Court	27 B1 [2]
Swan's Nest Road	27 B1
Swanville Place	47 A1 [4]
Swanward Court	74 E4
Sweeney's Terrace	74 F2
Sweetbriar Lane	58 D1
Sweetman's Avenue	49 A3 [21]
Sweetman's Avenue	49 A3
Sweetmount Avenue	47 B4
Sweetmount Drive	57 B1
Sweetmount House	47 B4 [18]
Sweetmount Park	47 B4
Sweetmount Park	57 B1
Swift Hall	59 B4
Swiftbrook (Tallaght)	54 D1
Swiftbrook Avenue	54 D1
Swiftbrook Close	54 D1
Swiftbrook Drive	54 D1
Swiftbrook Park	54 D1
Swift's Alley	74 F1
Swift's Grove	13 A3
Swift's Row (off Ormond Quay)	71 A4
Swiftwood	53 B1
Swilly Road	24 E4
Swords	2 D1
Swords Manor Avenue	1 B2
Swords Manor Court	1 B1

STREET NAME	PAGE/GRID REFERENCE
Swords Manor Crescent	1 B1
Swords Manor Drive	1 B1
Swords Manor Grove	1 B2
Swords Manor View	1 B1
Swords Manor Way	1 B1
Swords Road (Collinstown)	12 F2
Swords Road (Malahide)	3 A3
Swords Road (Santry)	12 F4
Swords Road (Santry)	25 B1
Swords Street	70 D3
Sybil Hill Avenue	26 F3
Sybil Hill Road	26 F3
Sycamore Avenue (Cabinteely)	59 B3
Sycamore Avenue (Castleknock)	22 E3
Sycamore Avenue (Tallaght)	45 A3
Sycamore Close (Cornelscourt)	59 B3
Sycamore Close (Kilnamanagh)	44 F3
Sycamore Court	59 C2 [3]
Sycamore Crescent (Cabinteely)	59 B3
Sycamore Crescent (Mount Merrion)	48 E4
Sycamore Drive (Cabinteely)	59 B3
Sycamore Drive (Castleknock)	22 E3
Sycamore Drive (Dundrum)	57 B1 [4]
Sycamore Drive (Tallaght)	45 A3
Sycamore Green (Cabinteely)	59 B3
Sycamore Grove (Cabinteely)	59 B4
Sycamore Grove (Foxrock)	59 A2 [7]
Sycamore House	76 D3
Sycamore House (Shankill)	64 E2 [11]
Sycamore House (Sutton)	28 D1
Sycamore House (Swords)	1 Inset
Sycamore Lawn (Cabinteely)	59 B3
Sycamore Lawn (Castleknock)	22 E3
Sycamore Park (Castleknock)	22 E3
Sycamore Park (Finglas)	24 E1
Sycamore Park (Tallaght)	45 A3
Sycamore Road (Dundrum)	57 B1
Sycamore Road (Finglas)	24 E1
Sycamore Road (Fox & Geese)	45 A1
Sycamore Road (Mount Merrion)	48 E4
Sycamore Street	71 B4
Sycamore View	22 E3
Sycamore Walk	59 B4
Sydenham	50 D4 [23]
Sydenham Court	39 A4 [53]
Sydenham Mews	68 D3
*Sydenham Place (on Kilmacud Rd Upr)	47 C4
Sydenham Road (Ballsbridge)	39 A4 [4]
Sydenham Road (Dundrum)	47 C4
Sydenham Villas (Bray)	68 D3 [6]
Sydenham Villas (Dundrum)	57 C1
Sydney Avenue	49 A3
Sydney Parade Avenue	48 E1
Sydney Terrace	49 A3
Sylvan Avenue	45 A3
Sylvan Close	44 F3
Sylvan Drive	44 F3
Symphony House	75 C3
Synge House	47 A3
Synge Lane	75 A3
Synge Place	75 B3
Synge Street	75 B3
Synge Way	35 C4
Synnott Place	71 B1
Synnott Row	71 B1
Synnott Row	71 B1
Synnott Terrace	49 C4 [16]
Synod Hall	75 A1

T

Taaffe's Place	72 E1
Tailors Court	75 A1
Tailor's Hall	75 A1
Talbot	2 F3
Talbot Avenue	2 F3
Talbot Court (Blanchardstown)	22 F2
Talbot Court (Malahide)	3 A2
Talbot Downs	22 F2
Talbot Hall (Swords) (Swords)	1 Inset
Talbot Lane (Killiney)	60 E3 [4]
Talbot Lane (Talbot Street)	71 C3
Talbot Lodge	48 F4

STREET NAME	PAGE/GRID REFERENCE
Talbot Memorial Bridge	71 C4
Talbot Park	2 F3
Talbot Place	71 C3
Talbot Road (Killiney)	60 E3 [3]
Talbot Road (Swords)	2 F3
Talbot Street	71 C3
Tallaght	55 A1
Tallaght Bypass	54 F1
Tallaght Bypass	55 A1
Tallaght Road	45 C4
Tallaght Road	55 B1
Tallow Hall (Belgard Square)	54 F1 [7]
Tamarisk Avenue	45 A3
Tamarisk Close	45 A3
Tamarisk Court	45 A3
Tamarisk Dale	45 A3
Tamarisk Drive	45 A3
Tamarisk Grove	45 A3
Tamarisk Heights	45 A3
Tamarisk Lawn	45 A3
Tamarisk Park	45 A3
Tamarisk View	45 A3
Tamarisk Walk	45 A3
Tamarisk Way	45 A3
Tandys Lane	33 C3
Tandys Lane	34 D3
Taney Avenue	47 C4
Taney Court	47 C4
Taney Crescent	47 C4
Taney Drive	47 C4
Taney Grove	47 C4
Taney Lawn	47 C4
Taney Manor	47 C4
Taney Park	47 C4
Taney Rise	47 C4
Taney Road	47 C4
Tangier Lane (off Grafton Street)	75 B1
Tara Crescent	55 B2 [3]
Tara Hill Crescent	46 F4
Tara Hill Grove	46 F4 [2]
Tara Hill Road	46 F4
Tara Lawn	27 A1
Tara Street	71 C4
Tassagard Greens	53 B2
Tassagart Drive	53 A2
Tay Lane	52 E2
Taylors Court	56 E1
Taylor's Hill	57 A3
Taylor's Lane (Ballyboden)	56 E1
Taylor's Lane (Pimlico)	74 E1
Temple Bar	71 B4
Temple Buildings	71 A2
Temple Cottages	71 A2
Temple Court (Arbour Hill)	70 D3
Temple Court (Blackrock)	49 A3 [25]
Temple Court (Off Hogan Place)	76 E1
Temple Court Apts.	12 E4
Temple Crescent	49 B4
Temple Gardens (Milltown)	47 B2
Temple Gardens (Santry)	12 E4
Temple Grove	32 D3
Temple Hill	49 B4
*Temple Hill (on Terenure Road West)	46 E2
Temple Lane North	71 B2
Temple Lane South	71 B4
Temple Manor (Celbridge)	31 C4
Temple Manor (Dunboyne)	7 B2
Temple Manor (Greenhills)	45 C3
Temple Manor Avenue	45 C3
Temple Manor Close	45 C3
Temple Manor Court	45 C3
Temple Manor Drive	45 C3
Temple Manor Grove	45 C3
Temple Manor Way	45 C3
Temple Park	47 B2
Temple Park Apts.	12 E4
Temple Park Avenue	49 B4
Temple Place	71 B4
Temple Place	75 C4
Temple Road (Blackrock)	49 A3
Temple Road (Rathgar)	47 B2
Temple Square	47 B2 [5]
Temple Street North	71 B2

STREET NAME	PAGE/GRID REFERENCE
Temple Street West	70 D3
Temple Terrace	60 F2 [16]
Temple Villas (Arbour Hill)	70 D3
*Temple Villas (on Palmerston Road)	47 B1
Templemore Avenue	47 A2
Templeogue	46 D4
Templeogue Lodge	46 D4
Templeogue Road	46 E3
Templeogue Wood	46 D4
Templeroan	56 D1
Templeroan Avenue	56 D1
Templeroan Close	56 E1
Templeroan Court	56 D1
Templeroan Crescent	56 D1
Templeroan Downs	56 E1
Templeroan Drive	56 D1
Templeroan Green	56 D2
Templeroan Grove	56 D1
Templeroan Lodge	56 D2
Templeroan Meadows	56 E1
Templeroan Mews	56 D1
Templeroan Park	56 D1
Templeroan View	56 D1
Templeroan Way	56 D1
Templeview Avenue	14 D4
Templeview Close	14 D4
Templeview Copse	14 D4
Templeview Court	14 D4
Templeview Crescent	14 D4
Templeview Downs	14 D4
Templeview Drive	14 D4
Templeview Green	14 D4
Templeview Grove	14 D4
Templeview Lawn	14 D4
Templeview Park	14 D4
Templeview Place	14 D4
Templeview Rise	14 D4
Templeview Row	14 D4
Templeview Square	14 D4
Templeview Vale	14 D4 [1]
Templeview View	14 D4
Templeview Walk	14 D4
Templeview Way	14 D4
Templeville Avenue	46 D3
Templeville Drive	46 D3
Templeville Park	46 E3 [1]
Templeville Road	46 D3
Tenterfields	74 E2
Terenure	46 F2
Terenure Park	46 F2
Terenure Place	46 F2 [3]
Terenure Road East	46 F2
Terenure Road North	46 F2
Terenure Road West	46 E2
Terminal Road North	39 C2
Terminal Road South	39 C2
Termon Court	11 C4 [1]
Terrace Place (off Bella St)	71 C2
Tetrarch Grove	7 C1
Texas Lane	3 A2
The Alders	49 B4 [6]
The Anchora Apts.	3 B2 [10]
The Anchorage	4 D3
The Anchorage	49 C4 [33]
The Appian Way	76 D4
The Arches	17 C3
The Avenue (Ballinteer)	57 C2
The Avenue (Ballyboden)	56 E2
The Avenue (Carrickmines)	63 A1
The Avenue (Celbridge)	32 D3
The Avenue (Dunboyne Castle)	7 B3
The Avenue (Grange Manor)	34 D3
The Avenue (Louisa Valley)	19 C4
The Avenue (Lutterell Hall)	7 B2
The Avenue (Manorfields)	21 B1
The Avenue (Mulhuddart)	9 A4
The Avenue (Plunkett Hall)	7 A2
The Avenue (St Wolston's Abbey)	32 D4
The Avenue (Tallaght)	44 F3
The Avenue (Templeogue)	46 D3
The Bawn	3 B3
The Bawn Grove	3 B3
The Beeches (Abberley)	64 E1 [22]

STREET NAME	PAGE/GRID REFERENCE
The Beeches (Donaghmede)	27 A1
The Beeches (Kilmacud)	58 D1
The Beeches (Monkstown)	49 B4 [21]
The Beeches (Willbrook)	56 F1 [8]
The Belfry (Citywest Road)	53 C2
The Belfry (Inchicore)	73 A1
The Belfry (Kilbarrack)	27 B1
The Belfry Apts.	25 C2 [11]
The Birch	57 C1 [12]
The Birches	59 A3
The Birches Apts.	23 C3 [3]
The Black Avenue	33 B1
The Blackthorn	57 C1 [14]
The Bramblings	26 E3
The Briars	35 C1
The Bridge	64 E3
The Brokerage Apts.	71 C4
The Burgage	60 F2
The Castlelands	46 F4 [11]
The Cedars (Abberley)	64 E1 [21]
The Cedars (Monkstown)	49 B4 [5]
The Chandler Apts.	23 B3 [2]
The Charter	12 D4
The Chase	58 F2
The Cherries	57 A2 [2]
The Claremont Apts.	12 D4
The Cloisters (Grace Park Road)	25 B3 [5]
The Cloisters (Mount Tallant Avenue)	46 F2
The Close (Ballinteer)	57 C2
The Close (Ballyboden)	56 E2
The Close (Beaumont)	25 C1
The Close (Celbridge)	31 C3
The Close (Dunboyne Castle)	7 A3
The Close (Grange Manor)	34 D3
The Close (Lutterell Hall)	7 B2
The Close (Manorfields)	21 B1
The Close (Mount Merrion)	48 E3
The Close (Oldtown Mill)	31 C3 [2]
The Close (Plunkett Hall)	7 A2
The Close (Tallaght)	44 F3
The Close (Tallaght)	55 A2 [2]
The Close (Temple Manor)	31 C4
The Close (Templeogue)	46 D3
The Coachworks	75 A3
The Coombe	74 F1
The Coppice (Palmerston)	35 C1
The Coppins (Celbridge)	32 D3
The Coppins (Foxrock)	59 A3
The Copse	33 B2 [1]
The Copse (Ballinteer)	57 B2 [3]
The Copse (Drumcondra)	25 B3
The Court (Ballinteer)	57 B2
The Court (Ballybrack)	60 E4
The Court (Carrickmines)	59 B4
The Court (Celbridge)	31 C3
The Court (Clontarf)	26 D4
The Court (Donnybrook)	47 C2
The Court (Dunboyne Castle)	7 B3
The Court (Glenamuck Road)	63 A1
The Court (Larch Hill)	12 F4
The Court (Lutterell Hall)	7 B2
The Court (Mulhuddart)	9 A4
The Court (Oldtown Mill)	31 C3
The Court (Plunkett Hall)	7 A2
The Court (Raheny)	27 B3 [2]
The Court (Sadleir Hall)	7 A2
The Court (Shankill)	64 E3
The Court (Sutton)	29 A1
The Court (Tallaght)	44 F3
The Court (Tallaght)	44 F4
The Court (Temple Manor)	31 C4
The Court (Templeogue)	46 D3
The Court (Whitehall)	25 C2
The Courthouse	52 F2
The Courtyard	71 B2
The Courtyard	76 D1
The Courtyard (Bray)	67 B2
The Courtyard (Celbridge)	31 C4
The Courtyard (Clonsilla)	22 D3
The Courtyard (Leopardstown)	58 E2
The Courtyard (Rathfarnham)	46 F4
The Courtyard (Templelogue)	46 E3
The Coutryard (Foxrock)	59 A2 [10]
The Cove	3 A2

STREET NAME	PAGE/GRID REFERENCE
The Covert	35 C1 [1]
The Crescent (Abbeyfarm)	31 C4
The Crescent (Ballinteer)	57 B2 [1]
The Crescent (Ballyboden)	56 E2
The Crescent (Carrickmines)	63 A1
The Crescent (Castleknock)	22 F3 [1]
The Crescent (Donnybrook)	47 C1 [4]
The Crescent (Dunboyne Castle)	7 B3
The Crescent (Grange Manor)	34 D3
The Crescent (Larch Hill)	12 F4
The Crescent (Lucan)	33 C2
The Crescent (Lutterell Hall)	7 A2
The Crescent (Malahide)	4 D3
The Crescent (Mulhuddart)	9 A4
The Crescent (off Beaumont Rd)	25 C2 [8]
The Crescent (Oldtown Mill)	31 C3
The Crescent (Plunkett Hall)	7 A2
The Crescent (Ranelagh)	47 B1
The Crescent (St Wolston's Abbey)	32 D4
The Crescent (Sutton)	29 A1
The Crescent (Swords) (Swords)	2 D2 [4]
The Crescent (Tallaght)	44 E4
The Crescent (Tallaght)	44 F3
The Crescent (Tallaght)	55 A1
The Crescent (Temple Manor)	31 C4
The Crescent (Whitehall)	25 B3
The Croft	32 D2
The Dale	7 B2
The Dale (Ballinteer)	57 B2 [4]
The Dale (Belgard)	44 F4
The Dale (Bray)	67 B2
The Dale (Carrickmines)	63 A1
The Dale (Celbridge)	31 C3
The Dale (Kilnamanagh)	44 F3
The Dale (Manorfields)	21 B1
The Deanery	31 C3 [1]
The Dell	57 A2
The Dingle	35 B2
The Distillery Building Apts.	25 B4 [17]
The Downs (Dunboyne Castle)	7 A3
The Downs (St Wolston's Abbey)	32 D4
The Drive (Abbeyfarm)	31 C4
The Drive (Ballinteer)	57 B2
The Drive (Ballyboden)	56 E1
The Drive (Dunboyne Castle)	7 B3
The Drive (Grange Manor)	34 D3
The Drive (Kilnamanagh)	44 F3
The Drive (Lutterell Hall)	7 B2
The Drive (Manorfields)	21 B1
The Drive (Mulhuddart)	9 A4
The Drive (Oldtown Mill)	31 C3
The Drive (Sadleir Hall)	7 A2
The Drive (Tallaght)	55 A1
The Drive (Temple Manor)	31 C4
The Drive (Woodbrook Glen)	67 C1
The Drive Apts.	56 E1
The Dunes	15 A1
The Elm (Rockfield)	57 C1
The Elms	64 E3
The Elms (Celbridge)	32 D2
The Elms (Dunboyne)	7 B2
The Elms (Elm Park)	48 E2
The Elms (Loughlinstown)	64 E1 [4]
The Elms Apts.	23 C3 [2]
The Fairways (Portmarnock)	14 E2
The Fairways (Woodbrook Glen)	67 C1
The Fairways Apts.	8 D3
The Falls	46 F3 [5]
The Forum	58 E2
The Fosters	48 E3
The Gables (Dundrum)	57 B1
The Gables (Foxrock)	59 A3 [3]
The Gables (Grange View Road)	43 B1
The Gables (Nutgrove)	57 A1
The Gables (Rathgar)	47 A2
The Gallan	60 D3
The Gallops	58 E3
The Gardens	63 A1
The Garth (Cookstown)	44 E4
The Garth (Kingswood Heights)	44 F3
The Gasworks	76 F1
The Gate	44 D1
The Gate Lodge	30 E3
The Glade (Ballinteer)	57 B2
The Glade (Kingswood Heights)	44 F3
The Glade (Oldtown Mill)	31 C3
The Glade (Palmerstown)	35 B2
The Glade (St Wolston's Abbey)	32 D4
The Glebe	34 E2
The Glen	58 D3
The Glen (Ballinteer)	57 B2
The Glen (Ballyboden)	56 E1
The Glen (Glenageary Road)	60 D1 [14]
The Glen (Louisa Valley)	19 C4
The Glen (Raheny)	27 B3
The Glens	63 A1
The Golf Links	3 C3
The Goulding Apts	12 D4
The Grainhouse	74 E2
*The Granary	74 E1
The Grange (Deans Grange)	59 B1
The Grange (Malahide)	3 B4
The Grange (Terenure)	46 F2
The Green (Ballinteer)	57 B2
The Green (Ballyboden)	56 E1
The Green (Beaumont)	25 C1
The Green (Carrickmines)	63 A1
The Green (Celbridge)	31 C3
The Green (Dunboyne Castle)	7 B3
The Green (Larch Hill)	12 F4
The Green (Lutterell Hall)	7 B2
The Green (Malahide)	3 B2
The Green (Manorfields)	21 B1
The Green (Moyglare Abbey)	17 B2
The Green (Mulhuddart)	9 A4
The Green (Oldtown Mill)	31 C3
The Green (Tallaght)	44 F3
The Green (Templeogue)	46 D3
The Green (Woodbrook Glen)	67 C1
The Green Road	60 Inset
The Greenlands	46 F4
The Grove (Abbeyfarm)	31 C4
The Grove (Ballinteer)	57 B2
The Grove (Dunboyne Castle)	7 A3
The Grove (Dundrum)	57 A1
The Grove (Grange Manor)	34 D3
The Grove (Louisa Valley)	19 C4
The Grove (Lutterell Hall)	7 B2
The Grove (Plunkett Hall)	7 A2
The Grove (Raheny)	27 B3 [1]
The Grove (Sadleir Hall)	7 A2
The Grove (St Wolston's Abbey)	32 D4
The Grove (Tallaght)	44 E4
The Grove (Tallaght)	44 F3
The Grove (Tallaght)	55 A1
The Grove (Whitehall)	25 B3
The Grove (Woodbrook Glen)	67 C1
The Haggard (Howth)	30 D2 [6]
The Hall	46 F2
The Hampton	12 D4
The Haven (Glasnevin)	25 A3 [17]
The Haven (Malahide)	3 B2
The Hawthorns (Abberley)	64 E1 [20]
The Heath (Tallaght)	44 F4
The Heath (Templeogue)	46 D3
The Heath (The Heath)	57 B2
The Hedgerows	59 A3
The Heights (Ballinteer)	57 B2
The Heights (Dunboyne Castle)	7 B3
The Hill	58 D3
The Hill (Ballinteer)	57 C2
The Hill (Malahide)	3 B3
The Hill (Monkstown)	49 C4
The Hill (Mulhuddart)	9 A4
The Hill (Stillorgan)	58 F1
The Hole in the Wall Rd	14 E4
The Hollows	34 D2 [3]
The Holly (Rockfield)	57 C1
The Island	36 E2
The Killigeen	52 D4
The Kilmore Apts	12 D4
The Kilns	14 F2
The Lakelands	46 F4 [8]
The Larches (Abberley)	64 E1 [16]
The Laurels	47 B4
The Laurels (Bluebell)	36 E4 [3]
The Laurels (Dollymount)	26 F4
The Laurels (Rathfarnham)	46 F4 [13]
The Laurels (Tallaght)	55 A1 [10]
The Laurels (Terenure)	46 F2
The Lawn (Ballinteer)	57 B2
The Lawn (Ballyboden)	56 E2
The Lawn (Finglas)	24 E2
The Lawn (Kinsaley)	2 E3
The Lawn (Moyglare Abbey)	17 B2
The Lawn (Oldtown Mill)	31 C3
The Lawn (Plunkett Hall)	7 A2
The Lawn (Tallaght)	44 E4
The Lawn(Woodbrook Glen)	67 C1
The Lawns (Abbeyfarm)	31 C4
The Lawns (Temple Manor)	31 C4
The Lime (Rockfield)	57 C1
The Linden	57 C1 [13]
The Links	14 F2
The Little Grove	32 D4
The Lodge (Balgriffen)	14 E3
The Lodge (Clontarf)	26 D4
The Lodge (Glenageary)	60 D1
The Lodge Apts.	23 C3 [6]
The Maieston	12 D4
The Mall (Baldoyle)	15 A4 [4]
The Mall (Leixlip)	33 A1
The Mall (Lucan)	34 D1
The Mall (Malahide)	3 B2
The Malt House	74 E2
The Maltings	67 C2
The Maltings Apts.	70 E4
The Manor (Kimmage)	46 D2 [7]
The Manor (Templelogue)	46 D4
The Maples (Bird Avenue)	47 C3
The Maples (Monkstown)	49 B4 [4]
The Mayne	8 E2
The Meadow	57 B2
The Meadows (Dunboyne)	7 B2
The Meadows (Killester)	26 F3
The Meadows (Newtownpark Ave)	59 A1
The Meadows (Oldtown Mill)	31 C3
The Meadows East	44 F4
The Meadows West	44 E4
The Mews	71 B2
The Mews (Clontarf)	26 E4
The Mews (Dollymount)	27 A4 [5]
The Mews (Killester)	26 E3
The Mews (Rathmines)	47 A1 [19]
The Mews (Templeogue)	46 E3
The Mews Apts.	23 C3 [5]
The Mill	74 E2
The Mill Pond Apts.	44 D1 [4]
The Mills	22 F2
The Moorings	75 B4
The Moorings	39 A3 [38]
The Moorings (Chapelizod)	36 E2
The Moorings (Malahide)	3 C3
The Moorings Apts.	76 E3
The New Road	23 B1
The Northumberlands	76 E2
The Nurseries (Ballybrack)	60 E4 [4]
The Nurseries (Mulhuddart)	9 B4
The Nurseries (Oldcourt)	67 B3
The Nurseries (Swords)	1 C1
The Oaks (Rockfield)	57 C1
The Oaks (Abberley)	64 E1 [17]
The Oaks (Ballinteer)	57 B2
The Oaks (Belgard)	44 E4
The Oaks (Celbridge)	32 D3
The Oaks (Churchtown)	47 B4
The Oaks (Dollymount)	27 A4
The Oaks (Hollystown)	9 C1
The Oaks (Loughlinstown)	64 D1 [1]
The Oaks (Swords)	1 B3
*The Observatory (Windmill Lane)	72 D4
The Old Forge	34 D3
The Old Presbytery	39 A3 [34]
The Orchard	14 D4
The Orchard	49 B3 [5]
The Orchard (Carpenterstown)	22 D3 [1]
The Orchard (Deans Grange)	59 A1
The Orchard (Killester)	26 E3
The Orchard (Kimmage)	46 E2
The Orchard (Lucan)	34 D1 [14]
The Orchard (Oldtown Mill)	31 C3
The Orchard (Palmerston)	35 B1
The Orchard Apts.	35 B3
The Oval	35 C2
The Paddock (Ashtown)	23 C4
The Paddock (Moyglare Abbey)	17 B2
The Paddock (Oldtown Mill)	31 C2
The Paddock's (Clontarf)	26 E4 [6]
The Paddocks (Dalkey)	60 F1 [3]
The Paddocks (Dunboyne)	7 B2
The Paddocks (Kilmainham)	73 B2
The Paddocks (Swords)	2 D2
The Palms	48 D3
The Park	58 D3
The Park (Abbeyfarm)	31 C4
The Park (Beaumont)	25 C1
The Park (Celbridge)	31 C3
The Park (Dunboyne Castle)	7 B3
The Park (Grange Manor)	34 D3
The Park (Larch Hill)	12 F4
The Park (Louisa Valley)	19 C4
The Park (Oldtown Mill)	31 C3
The Park (Plunkett Hall)	7 A2
The Park (Tallaght)	44 F3
The Park (Tallaght)	55 A2
The Park (Templeogue)	46 D3
The Park Apts.	75 B4
The Park Lands	46 F4 [7]
The Pines (Ballinteer)	57 B2
The Pines (Castleknock)	23 A3
The Pines (Killester)	26 E3
The Pines (Kilmacud)	58 D1 [3]
The Pines (Oldcourt)	67 B3
The Place (Carrickmines)	63 A1
The Place (Dunboyne Castle)	7 B3
The Plantation	76 D2
The Plaza Apts.	9 B2
The Poplars	49 B4 [1]
The Priory (Cabra)	24 D4
The Priory (Grange Road)	56 F1
The Priory (Malahide)	3 B2 [4]
The Quarry	4 D4 [2]
The Ramparts	63 C1
The Rectory	27 A2
The Rectory	58 D4
The Rise (Ballinteer)	57 B2
The Rise (Ballyboden)	56 E2
The Rise (Carrickmines)	63 A1
The Rise (Dalkey)	60 E2
The Rise (Glasnevin)	25 A2
The Rise (Malahide)	3 B3
The Rise (Manorfields)	21 B1
The Rise (Mount Merrion)	48 E4
The Rise (Newcastle)	42 D4
The Rise (Tallaght)	44 E4
The Rise (Tallaght)	44 F3
The Road (Manorfields)	21 B1
The Rookery	56 D2
The Rose	9 B2
The Rowan (Rockfield)	57 C1
The Rowans (Abberley)	64 E1 [18]
The Sand Holes	22 F4 [1]
The Scalp	63 A4
The Slopes	49 C4
The Spinnaker	4 D3
The Spruce	9 B2
The Square (Greenogue Ind Est)	42 E4
The Square (Irishtown)	39 A3 [3]
The Square (Larch Hill)	12 F4
The Square (Lucan)	34 D1 [5]
The Square (Tallaght)	54 F1
The Stables	48 E3 [1]
The Stables Apts.	23 C3 [4]
The Steeple (Moyglare Abbey)	17 B2
The Steeples	36 E3
The Stiles Road	26 E4
The Summit (Howth)	30 E3
The Sweepstakes	39 A4 [22]
The Sycamore (Rockfield)	57 C1
The Sycamores	64 E1 [3]
The Tallow Apts.	23 C3 [7]
The Terrace	63 A1
The Thatch Road	25 C2
The Thicket	59 A3
The Tower (Smithfield)	70 F4

STREET NAME	PAGE/GRID REFERENCE	STREET NAME	PAGE/GRID REFERENCE	STREET NAME	PAGE/GRID REFERENCE	STREET NAME	PAGE/GRID REFERENCE
The Turnpike	12 D4	Thorndale Park	26 D2	Torlogh Gardens	25 C4 [8]	Turnstone Apts.	48 E3
The Vale	35 C1	Thornfield Square	44 E1	Torlogh Parade	25 C3 [1]	Turret Road	35 C2
The View (Ballinteer)	57 B2	Thornhill Gardens	31 C2	Torquay Road	58 F2	Turrets Flats	47 A1 [9]
The View (Carrickmines)	63 A1 [1]	Thornhill Heights	31 C2	Torquay Wood	58 F2	Turvey Avenue	73 B1
The View (Celbridge)	31 C3	Thornhill Lane	27 A4	Tory Square	22 F1	Tuscany Downs	27 A2
The View (Dunboyne Castle)	7 A3	Thornhill Meadows	31 C2	Tourmakeady Road	25 B2 [1]	Tuscany Park	28 D1
The View (Larch Hill)	12 F4	Thornhill Road (Bray)	67 A2	Tourville Lodge	46 F3 [6]	Twin Cottages	49 A4 [5]
The View (Manorfields)	21 B1	Thornhill Road (Kilmacud)	48 E4	Tower Avenue	46 F2	Tymon Close	55 A2
The View (Oldtown Mill)	31 C3	Thornhill View	67 B1 [5]	Tower Road	36 D1	Tymon Crescent	54 F2
The View (St Wolston's Abbey)	32 D4	Thornleigh Avenue	1 Inset	Tower Road (Castleknock)	22 F4	Tymon Farm	45 C4
The View (Tallaght)	44 F3	Thornleigh Close	1 Inset	Tower Road (Clondalkin)	44 D1	Tymon Grove	55 A2
The View (Tallaght)	55 B1	Thornleigh Court	1 Inset	Tower Terrace	73 B1	Tymon Heights	55 B2
The Village (Clonsilla)	21 C3	Thornleigh Green	1 Inset	(off Kilmainham Lane)		Tymon Lane	45 B4
The Village (Drumcondra)	25 B3 [2]	Thornleigh Grove	1 Inset	Tower View Cottages	24 F4 [2]	Tymon Lawn	55 A2
The Village (Raheny)	27 B3	Thornleigh Lane	1 Inset	Townsend Street	71 C4	Tymon Lodge Apts.	45 B3
The Village Centre	34 D1 [12]	Thornleigh Park	1 Inset	Townyard House Apts.	3 B2 [9]	Tymon North	45 B4
The Village Court	34 D1 [13]	Thornleigh Place	1 Inset	Townyard Lane	3 B2	Tymon North Avenue	45 B4
The Village Gate	60 F2	Thornleigh Road	1 Inset	Traders Wharf	49 C3	Tymon North Court	45 B4 [1]
The Walk (Ballinteer)	57 B2	Thornleigh Row	1 Inset	Traders Wharf Apts.	70 F4	Tymon North Gardens	45 B4
The Walk (Carrickmines)	63 A1	Thornville Avenue	27 B1	(Ushers Quay)		Tymon North Green	45 B4
The Walk (Dunboyne Castle)	7 B3	Thornville Drive	27 B2	Trafalgar Lane	49 B4	Tymon North Grove	45 B4
The Walk (Louisa Valley)	19 C4	Thornville Park	27 C1	Trafalgar Terrace (Blackrock)	49 B3	Tymon North Lawn	45 B4
The Walk (Manorfields)	21 B1	Thornville Road	27 B1	Trafalgar Terrace (Bray)	67 C2 [31]	Tymon North Park	45 B4
The Walk (Oldtown Mill)	31 C3	Thornville Terrace	27 B2 [1]	Tramway Court (Sutton)	29 A1	Tymon North Place	45 B4 [2]
The Walk (Tallaght)	55 A1	Three Rock Close	45 B3 [1]	Tramway Court (Tallaght)	55 A1 [8]	Tymon North Road	45 B4
The Walk (Templeogue)	46 D3	Three Rock Grove	57 B3	Tranquility Grove	26 D1	Tymonville Avenue	45 B4
The Walled Gardens	32 D2	Three Rock Road	58 E2	Traverslea Close	60 D1	Tymonville Court	45 A4
The Walled Orchard	33 B1	Thundercut Alley	70 F3	Traverslea Woods	60 D1	Tymonville Crescent	45 A4
The Warren	2 F3	Tibradden Close	45 B2 [1]	Traynor Place (O'Reilly Ave)	73 C1	Tymonville Drive	45 A3
The Water Rill	2 E2	Tibradden Drive	45 B2	Treepark Avenue	45 A3	Tymonville Grove	45 B3
The Waxworks Apts.	23 C3 [8]	Tibradden Grove	45 B3	Treepark Close	45 A3	Tymonville Lawn	45 B4
The Way (Dunboyne Castle)	7 B3	Tibradden Lane	56 F4	Treepark Drive	45 A3	Tymonville Park	45 B4
The Weir	36 E2	Tibradden Road	56 F3	Treepark Road	45 A3	Tymonville Road	45 A4
The Wicklow Way	61 C4	Ticknick	63 B2	Trees Avenue	48 E4	Tynan Hall	44 F3
The Willow	9 B2	Ticknock Avenue	57 C2	Trees Road Lower	48 E4	Tynan Hall Avenue	44 F3
The Willow (Rockfield)	57 C1	Ticknock Dale	57 C3	Trees Road Upper	48 E4	Tynan Hall Grove	44 F3
The Willows	39 A4 [45]	Ticknock Drive	57 C3	Treesdale	48 F4	Tynan Hall Park	44 F3
The Willows (Abberley)	64 E1 [19]	Ticknock Grove	57 C3	Tresilian	59 A3	Tyrconnell Park	36 F3
The Willows (Celbridge)	32 D3	Ticknock Hill	57 C3	Trideat Apts.	39 A4 [33]	Tyrconnell Road	36 F3
The Willows (Glasnevin)	24 F3	Ticknock Park	57 C3	Trim Road	26 D1	Tyrconnell Street	36 F3 [6]
The Willows (Monkstown)	49 B4 [3]	Ticknock Road	57 B4	Trimelston Apts.	47 C3	Tyrconnell Villas	36 F3 [7]
The Willows (Orwell Road)	47 A3 [1]	Ticknock Way	57 C3	Trimleston Avenue	48 E2	Tyrellstown Boulevard	9 B2
The Wood	58 D3	Tiknock	61 B1	Trimleston Drive	48 E2	Tyrellstown Way	9 B2
The Wood	64 E3	Tiknock Bridge	61 B1	Trimleston Gardens	48 E2	Tyrone House	71 C3
The Wood (Carrickmines)	63 A1	Timard	17 A1	Trimleston Park	48 E2	Tyrone Place	73 A2
The Wood (Tallaght)	55 A2	Timber Mills Apts.	26 E2	Trimleston Road	48 E2	Tyrrell Place	71 C1
The Woodlands (Celbridge)	32 D3	Tinkers Hill	21 A4	Trinity Hall (Rathgar)	47 A2	*Tyrrel's Lane	39 A3
The Woodlands (Rathfarnham)	46 F4 [9]	Tinkler's Path	36 E1	Trinity Square	72 D4	(off Fitzwilliam St Ringsend)	
The Woods	25 C3 [9]	Tinnehinch	66 E4	Trinity Street	71 B4		
Theresa House	46 F4 [20]	Tinnehinch Bridge	66 E4	Trinity Terrace	72 D1	**U**	
Third Avenue (Seville Place)	72 E3	Tivoli Avenue	46 F1	Tristan House Apts.	36 E2 [15]		
Third Avenue (Tallaght)	44 F4	Tivoli Close	59 C1	Tritonville Avenue	39 A3 [8]	UCD Village Belgrove	48 D3
Thirlestane Terrace	74 F1	Tivoli Road	49 C4	Tritonville Close	39 A3 [22]	Ullardmor	60 F2 [27]
Thomas Court	74 E1	Tivoli Terrace East	50 D4	Tritonville Court	39 A4	Ulster Street	24 F4
Thomas Davis Court	27 C1 [4]	Tivoli Terrace North	49 C4	Tritonville Crescent	39 A3 [9]	Ulster Terrace (North Strand)	72 D1
Thomas Davis Street (West)	36 F3	Tivoli Terrace South	49 C4	Tritonville Mews	39 A3 [45]	Ulster Terrace	58 F1 [4]
Thomas Davis Street South	74 F1	Tobernea Terrace	49 B3 [2]	Tritonville Road	39 A3	(Stillorgan Grove)	
Thomas Lane	71 B3	Tolka Cottages	24 F3	Trosyrafon Terrace	68 D2 [1]	Ulverton Close	60 F1 [5]
Thomas Moore Court	27 C1 [3]	Tolka Estate	24 F2	Tuansgate Apts.	54 F1 [1]	Ulverton Court	60 F1 [13]
Thomas Moore Road	45 C1	Tolka Estate Road	24 F3	Tubber Lane Road	33 B2	Ulverton Road	60 F1
Thomas Street	74 E1	Tolka Quay	39 A2	Tubbermore Avenue	60 F2	*Ulysses House Apts.	71 A3
Thomas Street West	74 E1	Tolka Quay Road	39 A2	Tubbermore Road	60 F2	(Little Britain Street)	
Thomastown Crescent	60 D2 [2]	Tolka Road	25 B4	Tuckett's Lane	30 D2	University Village Apartments	17 C2
Thomastown Road	60 D3	Tolka Vale	24 E3	Tudor Court	2 F2	Upper Cliff Road	30 E2 [2]
Thomond	64 E2 [9]	Tolka Valley Road	24 D3	Tudor Lawns	58 F2	Upper Dargle Road	67 A2
Thomond Road	36 E3	Tolka Valley View	24 D2	Tudor Road	47 B1	Upper Garville Avenue	47 A2
Thompson's Cottages	71 C2	Tolka View	22 F2 [2]	Tulip Court	13 C4	Upper Glen Road	36 E1
Thor Place	70 D3	Tom Clarke House	25 B4 [1]	Tullyhall	34 D4	Upper Kilmacud Road	58 E1
Thormanby Grove	30 D2 [10]	Tom Kelly Road	75 B3	Tullyhall Avenue	34 D4	Extension	
Thormanby Lawns	30 D2	Tonduff Close	45 B3	Tullyhall Close	34 D4	Uppercross	34 F1
Thormanby Lodge	30 E2	Tonguefield Road	46 E1 [1]	Tullyhall Court	34 D4	Uppercross Court	55 A1 [7]
Thormanby Road	30 E2	Tonlegee Avenue	26 F1	Tullyhall Crescent	34 E4	Uppercross Road	73 C2
Thormanby Woods	30 E2	Tonlegee Drive	26 F1	Tullyhall Drive	34 E4	Urney Grove	60 E2 [7]
Thorn Wood	48 E3	Tonlegee Road	27 A1	Tullyhall Green	34 D4	Usher Lane	1 A2
Thornberry Apts.	8 F4	Tootenhill	52 D2	Tullyhall Park	34 D4	Usher Street	70 F4
Thorncastle Court Apts.	39 A2 [3]	Tootenhill (Rathcoole)	52 E2	Tullyhall Rise	34 E4	Ushers Court Apts.	70 F4
Thorncastle Street	39 A2	Tor an Rí Close	34 F3	Tullyhall Way	34 D4	Usher's Island	70 E4
Thorncliff	47 B2 [8]	Tor an Rí Court	34 F3	Tullyvale	63 C1	Usher's Quay	70 F4
Thorncliffe Park	47 B3	Tor an Rí Lane	34 F3	Turnapin Cottages	12 F3		
Thorndale Avenue	26 D2	Tor an Rí Parade	34 F3	Turnapin Green	12 F3	**V**	
Thorndale Court	25 C2 [4]	Tor an Rí Terrace	34 F3	Turnapin Grove	12 F3		
Thorndale Crescent	26 D2	Tor an Rí Walk	34 F3	Turnapin Lane	12 F3	Vale Terrace	67 B2 [7]
Thorndale Drive	26 D3	Torca Road	60 F2	Turnberry	28 D1	(on lower Dargle Road)	
Thorndale Grove	26 D3	Torca View	60 F2 [33]	Turnberry Square	28 D1	Vale View	67 B2 [21]
Thorndale Lawns	26 D2	Torcaill	3 C4	Turnpike Road	45 A2	Vale View Avenue	59 B3
						Vale View Close	59 B3

STREET NAME	PAGE/GRID REFERENCE
Vale View Grove	59 B3
Vale View Lawn	59 B3
Valentia House	71 B1
Valentia Parade	71 B1
Valentia Road	25 B3
Valeview Crescent	24 D2 [6]
Valeview Drive	24 D2
Valeview Gardens	24 D2 [2]
Valley Drive	63 C1
Valley Park Avenue	24 D2 [1]
Valley Park Drive	23 C2
Valley Park Road	23 C2
Valley View	1 B1
Vanessa Close	31 C3
Vanessa Lawns	31 C3
Vauxhall Avenue	74 D2
Vavasour Square	76 F2
Venetian Hall	26 E3
Ventry Drive	24 D4
Ventry Park	24 E4
Ventry Road	24 E4
Verbena Avenue (Foxrock)	59 A3
Verbena Avenue (Kilbarrack)	27 C1
Verbena Grove	27 C1
Verbena Lawn	27 C1
Verbena Park	27 C1
Verdemont	22 D2
Vergemount	47 C1 [12]
Vergemount Hall	47 C1 [9]
Vergemount Park	47 C1 [6]
Verney House	62 F3
Vernon Avenue	26 F4
Vernon Court (Clontarf)	39 C1 [3]
Vernon Court (Vernon Avenue)	26 F4
Vernon Drive	26 F3
Vernon Gardens	26 F4
Vernon Grove (Clontarf)	26 F4
Vernon Grove (Rathgar)	47 A2
Vernon Heath	26 F4
Vernon Park	26 F4
Vernon Rise	26 F3
Vernon Street	75 A2
Vernon Wood	39 C1 [4]
Veronica Terrace	39 A3 [40]
*Veronica Terrace (off Oliver Plunket Ave)	39 A3
Verschoyle Avenue	53 C2
Verschoyle Close	53 C2
Verschoyle Court	76 D2
Verschoyle Crescent	53 C2
Verschoyle Drive	53 C2
Verschoyle Glen	53 C2
Verschoyle Green	53 C2
Verschoyle Heights	53 C2
Verschoyle Mews	76 D2
Verschoyle Park	53 C2
Verschoyle Place (off Lr Mount St)	76 E2
Verschoyle Rise	53 C2
Verschoyle Vale	53 C2
Verville Court	26 E4
Vesey Mews	49 C4
Vesey Park	34 D2
Vesey Place	49 C4
Vesey Terrace	34 D1 [2]
*Vevay Arcade (on Vevay Road)	67 C3
Vevay Crescent	67 C2 [58]
Vevay Road	67 C3
Vevay Villas	67 C3 [18]
Vicar Street	74 F1
Vicars Court	8 F4
Vico Road	60 F3
*Vico Terrace (Off Vico Road)	60 F3
Victoria Avenue (Bray)	68 D2
Victoria Avenue (Donnybrook)	47 C1
Victoria Cottages	39 A3 [44]
*Victoria Cottages (off Irishtown Rd)	39 A3
Victoria Lane	25 B4 [9]
*Victoria Lane (off South Zion Road)	47 A2
Victoria Quay	70 E4
Victoria Road	46 F2
Victoria Road (Clontarf)	26 E4
Victoria Road (Dalkey)	60 F2
Victoria Road (Killiney)	60 E3
Victoria Street	75 A3
Victoria Terrace	39 B1
Victoria Terrace (Dalkey)	60 F2 [11]
Victoria Terrace (Dun Laoghaire)	50 D4 [8]
Victoria Terrace (Dundrum)	47 C4
Victoria Village (Rathgar)	46 F2 [7]
Victoria Village (Rathgar)	47 A2
Victoria Villas (Clontarf)	26 D4
Victoria Villas (Rathgar)	46 F2 [5]
Viking Place	70 E3
Viking Road	70 E3
*Villa Bank (Royal Canal Bank)	71 A1
Villa Blanchard	22 F2
Villa Building Apts.	30 D1 [15]
Villa Nova	48 F4
Villa Park Avenue	24 D4
Villa Park Drive	24 D4
Villa Park Gardens	24 D4
Villa Park Road	24 D4
Village Court Apts.	46 F4 [6]
*Village Gate Arcade (on Main Street Bray)	67 C2
Village Green (Rathfarnham)	46 F3 [4]
Village Green (Tallagh)	55 A1
Village Heights	9 A4
Village Square (Tallagh)	55 A1
Village Weir	34 D1 [7]
Villarea Park	60 E1
Villiers Road	47 A2
Vintage Court	74 E2
Violet Hill Drive	24 F3
Violet Hill Park	24 F3
Violet Hill Road	24 F3
Virginia Drive	24 D2
Virginia Hall (Belgard Square)	54 F1 [8]
Virginia Heights	54 F1
Virginia Park	24 D2
Viscount Avenue	12 F4

W

STREET NAME	PAGE/GRID REFERENCE
Wadelai Green	25 A2
Wadelai Road	25 A2
Wade's Avenue	27 A3
Wainsfort Avenue	46 D3
Wainsfort Crescent	46 D3
Wainsfort Drive	46 D2
Wainsfort Gardens	46 D3
Wainsfort Grove	46 E3
Wainsfort Manor	46 D3
Wainsfort Manor Crescent	46 D3
Wainsfort Manor Drive	46 D3
Wainsfort Manor Green	46 D3
Wainsfort Manor Grove	46 D3
Wainsfort Park	46 E3
Wainsfort Road	46 D3
Waldemar Terrace	47 B4 [12]
Walker's Cottages	75 B4
Walker's Court	75 B4
Walkinstown	45 B1
Walkinstown Avenue	45 B1
Walkinstown Close	45 B1
Walkinstown Crescent	45 B1
Walkinstown Cross	45 C2
Walkinstown Drive	45 B1
Walkinstown Green	45 B1
Walkinstown Parade	45 B1
Walkinstown Park	45 B1
Walkinstown Road	45 C1
Wallace Road	45 C1 [2]
Walnut Avenue (Clondalkin)	44 F3
Walnut Avenue (Whitehall)	25 B3
Walnut Close	44 F3
Walnut Court	25 B2
Walnut Drive	44 F3
Walnut Lawn	25 B3
Walnut Park	25 B3
Walnut Rise	25 B3
Walnut View	56 E2 [5]
Walsh Road	25 A3
Waltersland Road	58 F1
Waltham Terrace	48 F4
Walton Hall (Swords)	1 Inset
Walworth Road	75 A3
Warburton Terrace	68 D2 [7]
Ward's Hill	74 F2
Warner's Lane	75 C3
Warren Avenue	22 E3
Warren Close	22 E3
Warren Court	28 D1 [5]
Warren Crescent	22 E4
Warren Green (Carpenterstown)	22 E3
Warren Green (Sutton)	28 D1
Warren Manor	2 F3
Warren Park	22 E3
Warren Street	75 A3
Warrenhouse Road	28 D1
Warrenmount	74 F2
Warrenmount Place	74 F2
Warrenpoint	26 E4 [1]
Warrenstown	9 B4
Warrenstown Close	9 B4
Warrenstown Court	9 B4
Warrenstown Drive	9 B4
Warrenstown Garth	9 B4
Warrenstown Green	9 B4
Warrenstown Grove	9 B4
Warrenstown Lawn	9 B4
Warrenstown Place	9 B4
Warrenstown Rise	9 B4
Warrenstown Row	9 B4
Warrenstown Vale	9 B4
Warrenstown View	9 B4
Warrenstown Walk	9 B4
Warrenstown Way	9 B4
Warrington Lane	76 E2
Warrington Place	76 E2
Warwick Terrace	76 D4
Wasdale Grove	46 F2
Wasdale House	46 F3 [8]
Wasdale Park	46 F3
Washington Lane	46 E4
Washington Park	46 E4
Washington Street	74 F3
Waterfall Avenue	25 B4
Waterfall Road	26 F3
Watergate Estate	55 A1
Waterloo Avenue	72 E1
Waterloo Lane	76 D4
Waterloo Mews	76 E3
Waterloo Road	76 D4
Watermeadow Drive	54 F2
Watermeadow Park	55 A2
Watermill	27 B3
Watermill Avenue	27 A3
Watermill Close	55 A2
Watermill Drive	27 A3
Watermill Grove	55 A2
Watermill Lawn (Raheny)	27 A3 [1]
Watermill Lawn (Tallaght)	55 A2
Watermill Park	27 A3
Watermill Road	27 A3
Watermint Court	24 D3 [3]
Waterside Apts.	76 F1
Waterside Avenue	2 E2
Waterside Close	2 E2
Waterside Court	2 E2
Waterside Crescent (Portmarnock)	3 C4
Waterside Crescent (Swords)	2 E2
Waterside Drive	2 E2
Waterside Green	2 E3
Waterside Grove	2 E2
Waterside King's Hall	2 E2
Waterside Lawn	2 E2
Waterside Park	2 E2
Waterside Place	2 E3
Waterside Rise	2 E2
Waterside Road	2 E2
Waterside Walk	2 E2
Waterside Way	2 E2
Waterstown	35 C1
Waterstown Avenue	35 C1
Waterville Road	22 F1
Waterville Row	22 F1
Waterville Terrace	22 F1
Watery Lane	2 D1
Watery Lane (Clondalkin)	44 E1
Watery Lane (Swords)	1 C1
Watkins Buildings	74 F2
Watling Street	70 E4
Watson Avenue	60 D4
Watson Drive	60 D4
Watson Park	60 D4
Watson Road	60 D3
Watson's Estate	60 D3
Waverley Avenue	25 C4
Waverley Terrace (Bray)	67 C2 [28]
Waverley Terrace (Harolds Cross Road)	46 F1 [12]
Waynestown	5 C1
Wayside Cottages	62 F2
Weaver Lane	71 A1
Weaver's Close	74 F2
Weaver's Row (Clonsilla)	21 C2
Weavers Row (The Coombe)	74 E2
Weaver's Square	74 F2
Weaver's Street	74 F2
Weaver's Walk	21 C2
Webster's Cottages	49 A4 [8]
Wedgewood Estate	58 D2
Weirview	34 D1
Weirview Drive	58 F1
Weldon's Lane	15 A4
Well Road	2 D2 [2]
Wellesley Place	71 C1
Wellington Cottages	45 C3 [2]
Wellington Court (Bray)	67 C2 [56]
Wellington Court (Whitehall Road West)	46 D2 [5]
*Wellington Gardens (off Oakley Road)	47 B1
Wellington House	76 E4
Wellington Lane (Tallaght Road)	45 C3
Wellington Lane (Wellington Road)	76 E4
Wellington Lodge	39 A4 [52]
Wellington Park	46 D3
Wellington Place (Leeson Street)	76 E4
Wellington Place North	71 A2
Wellington Quay	71 B4
Wellington Road (Ballsbridge)	76 E4
Wellington Road (Phoenix Park)	69 B4
Wellington Road (Templeogue)	46 D3 [1]
Wellington Street (Dun Laoghaire)	50 D4 [1]
Wellington Street Lower	71 A2
Wellington Street Upper	71 A2
Wellmount Avenue	24 D2
Wellmount Court	24 D2
Wellmount Crescent	24 D2
Wellmount Drive	24 D2
Wellmount Green	24 D2
Wellmount Parade	24 D2
Wellmount Park	24 D2
Wellmount Road	24 D2
Wellpark Avenue	25 B3
Wellview Avenue	9 A3
Wellview Crescent	9 A3
Wellview Green	9 A3
Wellview Grove	9 A3
Wellview Park	9 A3
Wendell Avenue	4 D4
Wentworth Apartments	76 E1
Werburgh Street	75 A1
Wesbury	58 E1
Wesley Heights	57 C2
Wesley House	76 D4
Wesley Lawns	57 C2
Wesley Place	74 F3
Wesley Road	47 A2
West Park Drive	24 F2
West Pier (Dun Laoghaire)	49 C3
West Pier (Howth)	30 D1
West Road	72 E2
West Terrace	36 F3
Westbourne Avenue	43 C1
Westbourne Close	43 C1
Westbourne Court	46 F3
Westbourne Drive	43 C1
Westbourne Grove	43 C1
Westbourne Lodge	56 D1

STREET NAME	PAGE/GRID REFERENCE	STREET NAME	PAGE/GRID REFERENCE	STREET NAME	PAGE/GRID REFERENCE	STREET NAME	PAGE/GRID REFERENCE
Westbourne Rise	43 C1	Whitchurch Drive	56 F2	Whitethorn Park (Coldcut Road)	35 B3	Willow Grove	59 C1 [13]
Westbourne Road	46 F3	Whitchurch Road	56 F2	Whitethorn Rise	26 D2	(Kill O'The Grange)	
Westbourne Terrace	67 C2 [52]	White Gables	64 D2	Whitethorn Road (Artane)	26 D2	Willow House	76 D3
Westbourne View	43 C1	White Hall (Ballymount Road)	44 F3	Whitethorn Road (Milltown)	47 C2	Willow Lawn	32 E4
Westbrook	46 D2	White Oak	47 C3	Whitethorn Walk (Foxrock)	59 A2 [8]	Willow Lodge	23 A4
Westbrook Lawns	53 C2	White Oaks	67 B4	Whitethorn Walk	59 C2 [2]	Willow Mews	48 E1
Westbrook Park	33 C2	Whiteacre Close	25 B1	(Kill O'The Grange)		Willow Park (Dunboyne)	7 B2
Westbrook Road	47 B3	Whiteacre Court	25 B1	Whitethorn Way	35 B3	Willow Park (Foxrock)	59 A2 [6]
Westbury	34 D3	Whiteacre Crescent	25 B1	Whitton Road	46 F2	Willow Park (Loughlinstown)	64 D1
Westbury Avenue	34 D3	Whiteacre Place	25 B1	Whitworth Avenue	71 C1	Willow Park Avenue	24 F1
Westbury Close	34 D3	Whitebank Road	39 B3	*Whitworth Parade	25 A4	Willow Park Close	24 F1
Westbury Drive	34 D2	Whitebarn Road	47 A4	(off Saint Patrick's Road)		Willow Park Crescent	24 F1
Westbury Grove	33 C3 [1]	Whitebeam Avenue	47 C2	Whitworth Place	25 A4 [16]	Willow Park Drive	25 A1
Westbury Park	34 D3	Whitebeam Road	47 C2	Whitworth Road	25 A4	Willow Park Grove	24 F1
Westcourt	74 D1	Whitebeams Road	58 D2	Whitworth Terrace	71 C1	Willow Park Lawn	24 F1
Westend Gate	22 F3	Whitebrook Park	54 E1	(off Russell Ave)		Willow Park Road	24 F1
Westend Village	22 E2	Whitechapel Avenue	22 D2	Wicklow Lane	75 B1	Willow Place (Booterstown)	48 F3
Western Parkway	35 B2	Whitechapel Court	22 D2	(off Wicklow Street)		Willow Place (Loughlinstown)	64 D1
Western Parkway Motorway	22 E4	Whitechapel Crescent	22 D2	Wicklow Street	75 B1	Willow Rise	32 E4
Western Road	74 E3	Whitechapel Green	22 D2	Wicklow Way	65 A4	Willow Road (Dundrum)	57 B1
Western Way	71 A2	Whitechapel Grove	22 D2	Wigan Road	25 A4	Willow Road (Fox & Geese)	45 A1
Westerton Rise	57 C1 [1]	Whitechapel Lawn	22 D2	Wikeford Hall (Swords)	1 Inset	Willow Terrace	48 F2
Westfield Park	68 D3	Whitechapel Park	22 D2	Wilderwood Grove	45 C4	Willow Vale	60 D4
Westfield Road	46 F1	Whitechapel Road	22 D2	Wilfield	39 A4 [15]	Willow View	32 E4
Westfield Terrace	49 A3 [10]	Whitechurch Abbey	56 F1 [4]	Wilfield Park	39 A4	Willow Wood Close	21 C2
Westhampton Place	46 F2 [2]	Whitechurch Avenue	56 F2	Wilfield Road	39 A4	Willow Wood Downs	21 C2 [1]
Westhaven	8 F4	Whitechurch Close	56 F2	Wilford Court	67 B1	Willow Wood Green	21 C2
Westland Row	76 D1	Whitechurch Court	56 F2	Wilfrid Road	46 F1	Willow Wood Grove	21 C2
Westmanstown	42 D3	Whitechurch Crescent	56 F2	Wilfrid Terrace	46 F1 [5]	Willow Wood Lawn	21 C2
Westminster Court	59 A3 [6]	Whitechurch Drive	56 F2	Willans Avenue	21 A1	Willow Wood Park	21 C1
Westminster Lawns	58 F2	Whitechurch Green	56 F2	Willans Drive	21 A1	Willow Wood Rise	21 C1
Westminster Park	59 A2	Whitechurch Grove	56 F2	Willans Green	21 A1	Willow Wood View	21 C2
Westminster Road	59 A3	Whitechurch Hill	56 F2	Willans Rise	21 A1	Willow Wood Walk	21 C1
Westmoreland Park	47 B1 [4]	Whitechurch Lawn	56 F2	Willans Row	21 A1	Willowbank	57 C1
Westmoreland Street	71 B4	Whitechurch Park	56 F2	Willans Way	21 A1	Willowbrook Grove	31 C3
Weston Avenue	47 B4	Whitechurch Pines	56 F1	Willbrook	46 F4	Willowbrook Lawns	31 C3
Weston Avenue (Leixlip)	33 B1	Whitechurch Place	56 F2	Willbrook Downs	56 F1	Willowbrook Lodge	31 C3
Weston Close (Churchtown)	47 B4	Whitechurch Road	46 F4	Willbrook Estate	56 F1	Willowbrook Park	31 C3
Weston Close (Leixlip)	33 B1	Whitechurch Road	56 F2	Willbrook Grove	46 F4 [1]	Willowfield	39 B4
Weston Court	33 B2	Whitechurch Stream	56 F1	Willbrook House	75 C4	Willowfield Avenue	47 C4
Weston Crescent	33 B1	Whitechurch View	56 F2	Willbrook Lawn	46 F4	Willowfield Park	47 C4
Weston Drive	33 B1	Whitechurch Walk	56 F2	Willbrook Park	46 F4	Willowmount	48 F3 [3]
Weston Green	33 B1	Whitechurch Way	56 F2	Willbrook Road	46 F4	Willows Court	21 C2
Weston Grove	47 B4	Whitecliff	56 F1	Willbrook Street	46 F4	Willows Drive	21 C2
Weston Heights	33 B2	Whitefriar Garden Flats	75 A1	William Beckett House	76 D2	Willows Green	21 C2
Weston Lane (Leixlip)	33 B1	(off Whitefriar Street)		William Dargan Bridge	47 B4	Willows Road	21 C2
Weston Lawn	33 B1	Whitefriar Place	75 B1	William Pallister House	46 F4 [22]	Willsbrook Avenue	34 E2
Weston Meadow	33 B2	Whitefriar Street	75 A1	William Street North	72 D1	Willsbrook Crescent	34 F1
Weston Park (Churchtown)	47 B4	Whitehall	25 B2	William Street South	75 B1	Willsbrook Drive	34 E2
Weston Park (Leixlip)	33 B1	Whitehall Close	46 D3	William's Lane	71 B3	Willsbrook Gardens	34 E1
Weston Road	47 B4	Whitehall Gardens	46 D2	William's Park	47 A1	Willsbrook Green	34 E2
Weston Terrace	47 B4 [9]	Whitehall Mews	59 A2	Williams Place Lower	71 C1	Willsbrook Grove	34 E1
Weston Way	33 B2	Whitehall Park	46 D3	(Buckingham Street Upper)		Willsbrook Park	34 E1
Westpark (Coolock)	26 F2	Whitehall Road (Churchtown)	47 A4	William's Place South	75 A2	Willsbrook Place	34 E1
Westpark (Rathcoole)	52 F2	Whitehall Road (Kimmage)	46 D2	William's Place Upper	71 B1	Willsbrook Road	34 E2
Westpark (Tallaght)	55 A1	Whitehall Road West	46 D2	William's Place Upper	71 B1	Willsbrook View	34 E2
Westview Terrace	67 C2 [29]	Whitehall Square	45 C2	(off Portland Place)		Willsbrook Way	34 E1
Westway Close	9 C4	Whites Gate (Phoenix Park)	23 A4	Willie Bermingham Place	73 C1	Wilmont Avenue	60 E1 [1]
Westway Grove	9 C4	White's Lane North	71 A2	Willie Nolan Road	15 A4	Wilson Crescent	48 D4
Westway Lawns	22 F1	White's Road	23 A4	Willington Avenue	45 C3	Wilson Road	48 E4
Westway Park	9 C4	White's Villas	60 F1 [10]	Willington Court	45 C3	Wilson Terrace	74 F1
Westway Rise	9 C4	Whitestown	22 D1	Willington Crescent	45 C3	Wilson's Place	76 D1
Westway View	9 C4	Whitestown Avenue	22 D1	Willington Drive	45 C3	Wilton Court	76 D3
Westwood Avenue	23 C2	Whitestown Crescent	22 D1	Willington Green	45 C3	Wilton Place	76 D3
Westwood Road	23 C2	Whitestown Drive	22 D1	Willington Grove	45 C3	Wilton Terrace	76 D3
Wexford Street	75 B2	(Blanchardstown)		Willington Lawn	45 C3 [1]	Windele Road	25 A3 [12]
Wharton Terrace	74 F4	Whitestown Drive (Tallaght)	54 E2	Willington Park	45 C3	Windermere	21 B2
Whately Hall	8 F4	Whitestown Gardens	22 D1	Willow Avenue	32 E4	Windermere	39 B4 [8]
Whately Hall	8 F4	Whitestown Green	22 D1	Willow Avenue (Clondalkin)	44 D2	Windgate Rise	30 D3
Whately Place	58 E1	Whitestown Grove	22 D1	Willow Avenue (Loughlinstown)	64 D1	Windgate Road	30 D3
Wheatfield	67 C3	Whitestown Park	22 D1	Willow Bank	49 C4	Windmill Avenue(Crumlin)	46 D1
Wheatfield Grove	4 D4	Whitestown Road	54 F2	Willow Bank Drive	56 E1	Windmill Avenue(Swords)	1 C2
Wheatfield Road (Palmerstown)	35 C2	Whitestown Walk	22 D1	Willow Bank Park	56 E1	Windmill Crescent (Swords)	1 A2
Wheatfield Road (Portmarnock)	4 D4	Whitestown Way	54 F2	Willow Brook	32 E4	Windmill Crescent (Crumlin)	46 D1 [2]
Wheatfields Avenue	35 B3	Whitethorn	35 B3	Willow Court (Clondalkin)	44 D2	Windmill Lands	1 C2
Wheatfields Close	35 B3	Whitethorn Avenue	26 D2	Willow Court (Loughlinstown)	64 D1	Windmill Lane	72 D4
Wheatfields Court	35 B3	Whitethorn Close	26 D2	Willow Cove	32 E4	Windmill Lane Apts.	72 D4
Wheatfields Crescent	35 B3	Whitethorn Crescent (Artane)	26 D2	Willow Crescent	32 E4	Windmill Park	22 D3 [2]
Wheatfields Drive	35 B3	Whitethorn Crescent	35 B3	Willow Crescent	64 D1	Windmill Park	46 D1
Wheatfields Grove	35 B3	(Coldcut Road)		Willow Drive	32 E4	Windmill Rise	1 C2
Wheatfields Park	35 B3	Whitethorn Drive	35 B3	Willow Drive	44 D2	Windmill Road	46 D1
Wheaton Court	36 F3 [20]	Whitethorn Gardens	35 B3	Willow Gate	57 B1	Windmill Terrace	22 D3 [3]
Whelan House Flats	39 A3 [29]	Whitethorn Grove (Artane)	26 D2	Willow Green	32 E4	Windmillhill	51 C3
Whelan's Terrace	49 A3 [19]	Whitethorn Grove (Celbridge)	32 D3	Willow Grove (Clondalkin)	44 D2	Windrush	64 E2 [7]
Whitaker Hall	71 A2	Whitethorn Park (Artane)	26 D2	Willow Grove (Cornelscourt)	59 B3	Windsor Avenue	25 C4

139 Street Index

STREET NAME	PAGE/GRID REFERENCE	STREET NAME	PAGE/GRID REFERENCE	STREET NAME	PAGE/GRID REFERENCE	STREET NAME	PAGE/GRID REFERENCE
Windsor Court	59 B1 [1]	Woodfarm Cottages	35 C1 [6]	Woodlawn Rise	12 F4	Woodview Heights (Dunboyne)	7 B3
Windsor Drive	59 B1	Woodfarm Drive	35 C2	Woodlawn Terrace	47 B4 [2]	Woodview Heights (Lucan)	33 C2
Windsor Mews	3 B2 [5]	Woodfield	56 D2	Woodlawn View	12 F4	Woodview House	48 F3
Windsor Park	59 B1	Woodfield Cottages	36 F3 [8]	Woodlawn Villas	59 C1 [16]	Woodview Park	27 A1
Windsor Place	75 C2	Woodfield Place	36 F3 [15]	Woodlawn Walk	12 F4	(Ardara Avenue)	
Windsor Road	47 B1	Woodford	58 E2	Woodlawn Way	12 F4	Woodview Park (Castleknock)	23 A3
Windsor Terrace	50 D4	Woodford Avenue	44 F1	Woodleigh	47 A2 [2]	Woodville Avenue	34 E1
(Dun Laoghaire)		Woodford Close	44 F1	Woodley Court	58 D1 [4]	Woodville Close	34 E1
Windsor Terrace (Malahide)	3 B3	Woodford Court	46 F1 [10]	Woodley Park	58 D1	Woodville Court	26 E1
Windsor Terrace (Ranelagh)	75 A4	(Harold's Cross)		Woodley Road	60 D3	Woodville Green	34 E1
Windsor Villas	25 C4 [3]	Woodford Court (Monksfield)	44 F1	Woodpark	25 A3 [20]	Woodville Grove	34 E1
Windy Arbour	47 C3	Woodford Crescent	44 E1	Woodpark (Ballinteer)	57 B2	Woodville House	26 D1 [4]
Winetavern Street	71 A4	Woodford Downs	44 E1	Woodpark (Blanchardstown)	22 F2	Woodville Lawn	34 E1
Wingfield	62 E1	Woodford Drive	44 E1	Woods End	22 F2	Woodville Road	25 A4 [7]
Winston Ville	26 D4 [12]	Woodford Garth	44 E1	Woodscape	34 D3	Woodville Walk	34 E1
Winter Garden Apts	72 E4	Woodford Green	44 F1	Woodside (Clontarf)	26 F4	Wormwood Gate	70 F4
Winton Avenue	47 A2	Woodford Grove	44 F1	Woodside (Howth)	30 D2	(off Bridge Street Lower)	
Winton Grove	46 F2 [19]	Woodford Heights	44 F1	Woodside (Leixlip)	19 C4	Wyattville	64 D1
Winton Road	76 D4	Woodford Hill	44 F1	Woodside (Rathfarnham)	47 A3	Wyattville Close	64 D1
Wogansfield	33 A1	Woodford Lawn	44 F1	Woodside Drive	47 A3	Wyattville Hill	64 D1
Wolfe Tone Avenue	50 D4 [4]	Woodford Meadows	44 E1	Woodside Grove	47 A3	Wyattville Park	64 D1
Wolfe Tone Close	71 A3	Woodford Parade	44 E1	Woodside Hall	57 C3	Wyattville Road	64 D1
Wolfe Tone Quay	70 D4	Woodford Park	44 F1	Woodside Grove	57 C3	Wyckham Grove	57 C1
Wolfe Tone Square East	67 C3	Woodford Park Road	44 E1	Woodside Road	57 C3	Wyckham Park Road	57 B1
Wolfe Tone Square Middle	67 C3	Woodford Rise	44 F1	Woodstock Court	47 B1 [2]	Wyckham Place	57 C1
Wolfe Tone Square North	67 C3	Woodford Road	44 E1	Woodstock Gardens	47 B1 [24]	Wyckham Way	57 C1
Wolfe Tone Square South	67 C3	Woodford Terrace	44 F1	Woodstock Park	56 D1	Wynberg Park	49 B4
Wolfe Tone Square West	67 C3	Woodford View	44 F1	Woodstown	55 C2	Wyndham Park	67 C2
Wolfe Tone Street	71 A3	Woodford Villas	44 E1	Woodstown Abbey	55 C2	Wynnefield Park	47 A1 [21]
Wolseley Street	74 F3	Woodford Walk	44 F1	Woodstown Abbey	56 D2	Wynnefield Road	47 A1
Wolstan Haven Avenue	31 C3	Woodford Way	44 F1	Woodstown Avenue	55 C2	Wynnsward Drive	47 C2
Wolstan Haven Road	31 C3	Woodhaven	47 C2 [10]	Woodstown Close	55 C2	Wynnsward Park	47 C2
Wolverton Glen	60 E2	Woodhazel Close	25 A1	Woodstown Court	55 C2 [2]	Wyteleaf Grove	14 D4
Wood Avens	35 A3	Woodhazel Terrace	25 A1	Woodstown Crescent	55 C2	Wyvern Estate	60 E3
Wood Dale Close	55 B2	Woodlands (Blakestown Road)	22 D1 [2]	Woodstown Dale	55 C2		
Wood Dale Crescent	55 B2	Woodlands (Malahide)	14 F1	Woodstown Drive	55 C2		
Wood Dale Drive	55 B2	Woodlands (Maynooth)	17 B3	Woodstown Gardens	55 C2	**X**	
Wood Dale Green	55 B2	Woodlands (Rathgar)	47 A2 [1]	Woodstown Green	55 C2		
Wood Dale Green	55 C2	Woodlands Avenue	59 C3	Woodstown Heath	55 C2	Xavier Avenue	72 E1
Wood Dale Grove	55 C2	(Cornelscourt)		Woodstown Height	55 C2		
Wood Dale Oak	55 C2 [1]	Woodlands Avenue (Stillorgan)	48 E4	Woodstown Hill	55 C2	**Y**	
Wood Dale View	55 C2	Woodlands Court	15 A1	Woodstown House	46 F4 [21]		
Wood Lane	70 E4	Woodlands Drive	59 C3	Woodstown Lane	56 D2	Yale	48 D3
Wood Quay	71 A4	(Johnstown Road)		Woodstown Lawn	55 C2	Yankee Terrace	49 A4
Wood Street	75 A1	Woodlands Drive (Stillorgan)	48 E4	Woodstown Meadow	55 C2	Yarnhall Street	71 A3
Woodbank Avenue	23 C2	Woodlands Park	59 C3	Woodstown Parade	55 C2	Yeates Hall	59 B4
Woodbank Drive	23 C2	(Johnstown Road)		Woodstown Park	55 C2	Yeates Way	35 C4
Woodberry (Carpenterstown)	22 E3	Woodlands Park	48 F4	Woodstown Place	55 C2	Yeats Court	39 A4 [54]
Woodberry (Lucan)	34 D3	(Mount Merrion)		Woodstown Rise	55 C2	Yellow Meadows Ave	44 F1
Woodbine Avenue	48 E2	Woodlands Road	59 C3	Woodstown Road	55 C2	Yellow Meadows Drive	44 E1
Woodbine Close	27 A1	Woodlawn	12 F4	Woodstown Vale	55 C2	Yellow Meadows Estate	44 F1
Woodbine Drive	27 A1	Woodlawn Avenue	12 F4	Woodstown Walk	55 C2	Yellow Meadows Grove	44 E1
Woodbine House	48 E2 [4]	Woodlawn Close	12 F4	Woodstown Way	55 C3	Yellow Meadows Lawn	44 E1
Woodbine Park (Booterstown)	48 E2	Woodlawn Court	12 F4	Woodthorpe	58 E1 [5]	Yellow Meadows Park	44 E1
Woodbine Park (Raheny)	27 A1	Woodlawn Crescent	47 B4	Woodtown Way	56 D3	Yellow Meadows Vale	44 E1
Woodbine Road (Booterstown)	48 E2	(Churchtown)		Woodvale Avenue	21 C1	Yellow Road	25 C2
Woodbine Road (Raheny)	27 A1	Woodlawn Crescent	12 F4	Woodvale Crescent	21 C1	Yellow Walls	3 A2
Woodbine Terrace (Dundrum)	47 C4 [2]	(Coolock Lane)		Woodvale Drive	21 C1	Yellow Walls Road	3 A2
Woodbrook Court	22 D3	Woodlawn Drive	12 F4	Woodvale Garth	21 C1	Yellownook Avenue	59 C3
Woodbrook Crescent	22 D3	Woodlawn Green	12 F4	Woodvale Green	21 C1	Yewlands Terrace	46 F2
Woodbrook Downs	64 E4	Woodlawn Grove (Churchtown)	47 B4 [7]	Woodvale Grove	21 C1	York Avenue	47 A1
Woodbrook Glen	67 C1	Woodlawn Grove	12 F4	Woodvale Park	21 C1	York Road (Dun Laoghaire)	49 C4
Woodbrook Hall	22 D3	(Coolock Lane)		Woodvale Way	21 C1	York Road (Rathmines)	47 A1
Woodbrook Lawn	67 C3	Woodlawn Park (Churchtown)	47 B4	Woodview	64 E2 [12]	York Road (Ringsend)	39 A2
Woodbrook Park	22 D3	Woodlawn Park (Coolock Lane)	12 F4	Woodview (Celbridge)	32 D2	York Street	75 B2
(Carpenterstown)		Woodlawn Park	59 C1 [4]	Woodview (Lucan)	33 C2		
Woodbrook Park (Templelogue)	46 D4	(Dun Laoghaire)		Woodview Close	27 A1	**Z**	
Woodbrook Square	22 D3	Woodlawn Park (Tallaght)	55 C2	Woodview Cottages	46 F3 [1]		
*Woodchester House	75 A1	Woodlawn Park Avenue	55 B1	Woodview Court (Dunboyne)	7 B3	York Terrace	49 C4 [4]
Woodcliff Heights	30 E2	Woodlawn Park Drive	55 B1	Woodview Court (Stillorgan)	58 F1 [1]	Zardoz Court	76 F4
Woodfarm Avenue	35 C2	(Firhouse)		Woodview Court Apts.	33 C2	Zion Road	47 A2
		Woodlawn Park Grove	55 C2	Woodview Drive	67 C3 [4]	Zoo Road	69 B3
				Woodview Grove	22 E2	Zuma Terrace	74 F4
						(on Mount Drummond Ave)	

PAGE/GRID REF	STREET NAME
1 A2	1 Grove Court (Brackenstown Road)
1 C1	1 Elmwood Court
	2 Rathbeale Court
2 D2	1 St Columcille's Crescent
	2 Well Road
	3 Colmcille Court
	4 The Crescent (Swords)
	5 New Road (Swords)
2 F3	1 Blizzard Apts.
3 A2	1 Hillcrest (Malahide)
3 A3	1 Castle Oaks
	2 Ravenswood
	3 Oakleigh Court
3 B2	1 Fair Haven
	2 Haven View
	3 Railway Court
	4 The Priory (Malahide)
	5 Windsor Mews
	6 Fisherman's Green
	7 Broadmeadow Mews
	8 Ross Cottages
	9 Townyard House Apts.
	10 The Anchora Apts.
	11 James's Terrace Upper
	12 Strand Court
3 B3	1 Castle Court Apts.
3 C2	1 Seabank Court (Malahide)
	2 Clearwater Apts.
	3 Obelisk Court (Malahide)
4 D4	1 Alder Court
	2 The Quarry
7 B2	1 St Mary's Terrace (Dunboyne)
	2 Avondale Square
7 B3	1 Congress Park
	2 Hamilton Court (Dunboyne)
9 A4	1 Ashmount
	2 Ashfield Park (Huntstown Way)
	3 Riverpark View
	4 Riverside (Mulhuddart)
11 A4	1 St Margaret's Court
11 C4	1 Termon Court
12 E4	1 Domville Court
13 A4	1 Newbury Terrace
13 B4	1 Greenlawns
	2 Clonshaugh Rise
	3 Ferrycarrig Green
	4 Clonshaugh Court
	5 Moatview Terrace
	6 Glin Close
	7 Glin Court
14 D4	1 Templeview Vale
	2 Elmfield Close
	3 Clonmellon Grove
	4 Beechbrook Grove
14 F2	1 St Lawrence O'Toole Avenue
	2 Church Avenue (Portmarnock)
	3 Suncroft Avenue
	4 St Brigid's Avenue
	5 St Ann's Square Lower
	6 St Anne's Square (Portmarnock)
	7 Hazel Court
15 A4	1 Seapoint Avenue (Baldoyle)
	2 Parochial Avenue
	3 Back Lane (Baldoyle)
	4 The Mall (Baldoyle)
	5 Breffni Gardens

PAGE/GRID REF	STREET NAME
	6 Brookstone Lane
	7 Seapoint Court (Baldoyle)
	8 College Street (Baldoyle)
	9 Admiral Court
17 C3	1 Kelly's Lane (Maynooth)
	2 Fagan's Lane
	3 Coates Lane
	4 Geraldine Court
	5 Court House Square
	6 Leinster Cottages
	7 Charter House
18 D3	1 Leinster Lodge Apts.
	2 Leinster Court
20 D4	1 Cypress Springs
21 C1	1 Meadow Dale
	2 Oakview Grove
21 C2	1 Willow Wood Downs
	2 Cedar Grove
22 D1	1 Briarwood Park
	2 Woodlands (Blakestown Road)
	3 Briarwood Road
	4 Ashcroft Grove
	5 Ashcroft Court
	6 Rose Vale Court
	7 Blake's Court
22 D2	1 Coolmine Mews
	2 Kirkfield
22 D3	1 The Orchard (Carpenterstown)
	2 Windmill Park
	3 Windmill Terrace
22 E3	1 Rosehaven
	2 Luttrell Park Heath
	3 Station View Apts.
22 F2	1 Herbert Crescent
	2 Tolka View
	3 Catherine's Well
22 F3	1 The Crescent (Castleknock)
	2 Castleknock Court
	3 Ashleigh Court
22 F4	1 The Sand Holes
23 A3	1 Beech Park Crescent
	2 Hadleigh Green
	3 Beechpark Close
	4 Park Court Apts
	5 Castleknock Manor
23 B3	1 Mill Lane (Ashtown)
	2 The Chandler Apts.
23 B4	1 Castleknock Gate
23 C2	1 Eastwood
23 C3	1 Rathbourne Court
	2 The Elms Apts.
	3 The Birches Apts.
	4 The Stables Apts.
	5 The Mews Apts.
	6 The Lodge Apts.
	7 The Tallow Apts.
	8 The Waxworks Apts.
23 C4	1 Baggot Terrace
	2 St Vincent's Cottages
	3 St Joseph's Cottages
	4 Ashtown Lodge
24 D1	1 Cardiffsbridge Grove
	2 Casement Close (off Barry Road)
24 D2	1 Valley Park Avenue
	2 Valeview Gardens
	3 Mellowes Court
	4 Mellowes Crescent
	5 Ravens Court
	6 Valeview Crescent
	7 Church View (Finglas)
	8 Patrickswell Court

PAGE/GRID REF	STREET NAME
24 D3	1 Clearwater Court
	2 Cassian Court
	3 Watermint Court
	4 Compass Court Apts.
	5 Riverstown Gardens
24 D4	1 Roosevelt Cottages
	2 Convent View Cottages (Cabra)
	3 Convent View Crescent
	4 Lyndon Gate
	5 Park Spring's
	6 Park Crescent House
	7 Parkside View
	8 Doreen House Apts.
24 E1	1 Georges Road
	2 Gofton Hall
	3 Heath Square
24 E2	1 Ballygall Place
	2 Glenhill Villas
	3 St Helena's Court
	5 Johnstown Gardens
	6 Collins Row
	7 Glebe View (Finglas)
24 E4	1 Kilkieran Court
	2 St Finbarr's Court
	3 Rowan Hamilton Court
	4 Dunmanus Court
24 F2	1 Drapier Green
	2 Glasnamana Place
	3 Johnstown House
24 F3	1 Northland Grove
	2 Northland Drive
	3 Glasnevin Oaks
	4 Bellevue Cottages
	5 Cremore Villas
	6 Addison Hall
	7 Botanic Hall
	8 Addison Avenue
24 F4	1 St Philomena's Road
	2 Tower View Cottages
	3 Delvin Road
	4 Bengal Terrace
	5 Fertullagh Road
	6 Connaught Parade
	7 Clareville Court
	8 Shandon Green
	9 Shandon Mill
25 A1	1 Pinewood Grove
	2 Shanliss Gardens
	3 Oldtown Park
	4 Shangan Hall Apts.
25 A3	1 Claremont Avenue
	2 Church Avenue (Glasnevin)
	3 St David's Terrace (Glasnevin)
	4 Barron Place
	5 Comyn Place
	6 St Ita's Road
	7 St Malachy's Road
	8 St Michael's Road
	9 Addison Place
	10 St Mobhi Grove
	11 Clonmore Court
	12 Windele Road
	13 O'Brien's Place North
	14 O'Neachtain Road
	15 River Gardens
	16 Mobhi Court
	17 The Haven (Glasnevin)
	18 Glenavon Court
	19 Hillcrest Court
	20 Woodpark
	21 James Joyce Court
25 A4	1 Millmount Villas
	2 De Courcy Square
	3 Enniskerry Road (Phibsborough)

PAGE/GRID REF	STREET NAME
	4 Devery's Lane
	5 Prospect Square
	6 Glendalough Road
	7 Woodville Road
	8 St Teresa's Road (Glasnevin)
	9 St Teresa's Place
	10 Botanic Villas
	11 St Alphonsus Avenue
	12 St Brendan's Road
	13 St Clement's Road
	14 Botanic Park
	15 Lindsay Grove
	16 Whitworth Place
	17 Botanic Square
	18 Botanic Mews
	19 Prospect Court
25 B1	1 Ailesbury
	2 Schoolhouse Mews
25 B2	1 Tourmakeady Road
25 B3	1 Clonturk Avenue
	2 The Village (Drumcondra)
	3 Clare Park Villas
	4 Beaucourt
	5 The Cloisters (Grace Park Road)
	6 Clonturk Court
	7 All Hallows Lane
25 B4	1 Tom Clarke House
	2 St Joseph's Avenue (Ballybough)
	3 Clonturk Gardens
	4 Kingston Lodge
	5 Holycross Avenue
	6 Robert Street (Jones's Road)
	7 Robert Place
	8 College Manor
	9 Victoria Lane
	10 Edgewood (Richmond Road)
	11 College Mews
	12 Richmond House
	13 Richmond Hall
	14 Brook House
	15 Distillery Loft Apts.
	16 Clonliffe Square
	17 The Distillery Building Apts.
25 C1	1 Ivy Court
	2 Beaumont Court
	3 Beaumont Wood
25 C2	1 Chestnut Court
	2 Dromnanane Road
	3 Dromnanane Park
	4 Thorndale Court
	5 Laragh Flats
	6 Collindale
	7 Beaumont Hall
	8 The Crescent (off Beaumont Rd)
	9 Grace Park Lawns
	10 Riachville
	11 The Belfry Apts.
25 C3	1 Torlogh Parade
	2 Morrogh Terrace
	3 Calderwood Grove
	4 Croydon Terrace
	5 Sion Hill Court
	6 Collins Court (Collins Avenue)
	7 St Vincent's Court
	8 Collins Close
	9 The Woods
	10 Rosemount
25 C4	1 Annadale Avenue
	2 Shelmartin Terrace
	3 Windsor Villas

PAGE/ GRID REF — STREET NAME

4 St Joseph's Terrace (Fairview)
5 St Declan's Terrace
6 St Aidan's Park
7 Fairview Green
8 Torlogh Gardens
9 Marino Mart
10 Fairview Passage
11 Fairview Terrace
12 Caragh Court
13 Marino Court
14 Fairview Court
15 Bushfield Square
16 Melrose Court
17 Elton Court (Marino)
18 Belmount Court

26 D1
1 Kilbarron Court
2 Cromcastle Close
3 St Luke's Court
4 Woodville House
5 Kilmore Court
6 Cromcastle Court

26 D2
1 Newlands Court

26 D3
1 Cherrymount Crescent
2 Cherrymount Grove
3 Marino Villa

26 D4
1 Brighton Avenue (Clontarf)
2 Hollybrook Court Drive
3 Hollybrook Court
4 Strandville House
5 Haddon Park
6 Crescent House
7 Kilronan Court
8 Glenbrian Hall
11 Hollybrook Mews
12 Winston Ville

26 E1
1 Lismeen Grove
2 Brookville Crescent
3 Coolock Village Close

26 E2
1 Maryfield Avenue
2 Artane Cottages Lower
3 Artane Cottages Upper
4 Brookwood Abbey

26 E3
1 St Brigid's Drive (Killester)
2 St Brigid's Court
3 Quarry Cottages
4 Killester Court
5 Killester Park

26 E4
1 Warrenpoint
2 St John's Wood (Clontarf)
3 Lambourne Village
4 Knights Bridge
5 St David's Court
6 The Paddock's (Clontarf)

26 F1
1 Elton Court (Coolock)
2 Ayrefield Park

26 F2
1 Gorsefield Court

26 F4
1 Park View (Mount Prospect Lawns)
2 Hunter's Row

27 A1
1 Elton Walk
2 Glentworth Park
3 Invermore Grove
4 Curracloe Drive
5 Laracor Gardens
6 Gables

27 A3
1 Watermill Lawn (Raheny)
2 St Anne's Court

27 A4
1 Seafield Grove
2 St Gabriel's Court
3 Rinn na Mara
4 Mount Prospect House
5 The Mews (Dollymount)
6 Doyles Lane

27 B1
1 Howth Junction Cottages
2 Swan's Nest Court
3 Redmond's Court
4 Briarsfield Walk
5 Briarfield Villas

6 St. Berach's Place

27 B2
1 Thornville Terrace
2 Greendale Court
3 Roseglen Manor

27 B3
1 The Grove (Raheny)
2 The Court (Raheny)
3 Oakwood Apts.

27 C1
1 Bayside Crescent
2 Emily Lawless Court
3 Thomas Moore Court
4 Thomas Davis Court
5 James Joyce Court

27 C2
1 Mariners Court
2 Del Val Court

28 D1
1 Sutton Court
2 Seafield (Sutton)
3 St Domhnach's Well Street
4 Marine Cove
5 Warren Court
6 Moyclare Gardens

29 A1
1 James McCormack Gardens
2 St Catherine's Terrace
3 Radcliffe

29 B1
1 Corrbridge Terrace (off Claremont Road)
2 Avalon Apts.
3 Corr Castle Apts
4 Offington Manor Apts

29 B3
1 Shielmartin Park
2 Martello Terrace (Sutton)

30 D1
1 Dunbo Terrace
2 Evora Terrace
3 Findlater Building Apts.
4 Dunbo Hill
5 Howth Terrace
6 Harbour View (Howth)
7 Marine Villas
8 St Lawrence Quay
9 Island View Apts.
10 Howth House Apts
11 Abbey Terrace
12 Evora Crescent
13 Cuan na Mara
14 Howth Peninsula Apts.
15 Villa Building Apts.
16 St Lawrence Building Apts.

30 D2
1 St Lawrence's Terrace (Howth)
2 Seaview Terrace (Howth)
3 St Mary's Road (Howth)
4 St Mary's Place (Howth)
5 St Nessan's Terrace
6 The Haggard (Howth)
7 Hillside Terrace
8 Dungriffan Villas
9 St Nessan's Close
10 Thormanby Grove
12 St Nessans Court
13 Crosstrees Court
15 Forge Court
16 Campbell Court

30 E2
1 Cannon Rock View
2 Upper Cliff Road
3 St Nessan's Apts

31 C2
1 Crodaun Court

31 C3
1 The Deanery
2 The Close (Oldtown Mill)
3 St Judes Apts.

33 A1
1 Ralph Square
2 Liffey View Apts.

33 B2
1 The Copse

33 C3
1 Westbury Grove

34 D1
1 Sarsfield Terrace
2 Vesey Terrace
3 Hanbury Lane (Lucan)
4 Sarsfield Court (Lucan)
5 The Square (Lucan)
6 Dispensary Lane (Lucan)
7 Village Weir

8 Brookvale
9 Mount Gandon
10 Gandon Mews
11 Old Rectory
12 The Village Centre
13 The Village Court
14 The Orchard (Lucan)
15 Mill Bank
16 Gandon Court
17 St. Andrews Court

34 D2
1 Arthur Griffith Court
2 Adams Town Court
3 The Hollows

34 E1
1 Edmondsbury Court

34 F1
1 Latouka Apts.

34 F2
1 Liffey Hall
2 Foxford Court

34 F3
1 Foxborough Hall
2 Foxborough Crescent

35 A3
1 Neilstown Village Court
2 Liscarne Dale
3 Collinstown Crescent

35 A4
1 Ballymanagin Lane
2 Moorfield Close
3 Neilstown Cottages
4 Rosebank Place
5 Rosebank Hall

35 B4
1 Rosebank View
2 Rosebank Court

35 C1
1 The Covert
2 Glenside Villas
3 Clarkeville Terrace
4 Red Cow Cottages
5 St Fintan's Terrace
6 Woodfarm Cottages

35 C2
1 Culmore Park
2 Glenaulin Green

35 C4
1 Cherry Orchard Way

36 D2
1 Rossaveal Court

36 D3
1 Le Fanu Drive

36 E2
1 Park Lane (Chapelizod)
2 Maidens Row
3 Hibernian Terrace
4 St Laurence Grove
5 St Mary's Terrace (Chapelizod)
6 Isolde Gardens
7 Liffey Terrace
8 Clayton Terrace
9 St Laurence Terrace (Chapelizod)
10 Mullingar Terrace
11 Riverview Court
12 New Row
13 Isolde House Apts.
14 Distillery House Apts.
15 Tristan House Apts.

36 E3
1 O'Hogan Road
2 Lynch's Lane
3 St Lawrence Glen
4 Convent Lawns

36 E4
1 Old Naas Road Cottages
2 Millrose Estate
3 The Laurels (Bluebell)
4 Hollybrooke

36 F3
1 Park Street
2 Phoenix Street
3 Inchicore Terrace North
4 Murray's Cottages
5 Partridge Terrace
6 Tyrconnell Street
7 Tyrconnell Villas
8 Woodfield Cottages
9 St Patrick's Terrace (Inchicore)
10 Abercorn Terrace
11 Granite Terrace
12 Ring Street
13 Inchicore Square
14 Oblate Drive

15 Woodfield Place
16 Hampton Court (Tyrconnell Road)
17 St James's Place (Inchicore)
18 St George's Villas (Inchicore)
19 Abercorn Square
20 Wheaton Court

36 F4
1 Muirfield Drive
2 Bernard Curtis House
3 La Touche Court (Bluebell)
4 Grove Court (Bluebell)
5 Landsdowne Valley Park

39 A2
1 Fishermans Wharf
2 Alexandra Quay
3 Thorncastle Court Apts.

39 A3
1 Cambridge Street
2 Fitzwilliam Street (Ringsend)
3 St Patrick's Villas
4 Seapoint Terrace (Ringsend)
5 The Square (Irishtown)
6 St Brendan's Cottages
7 Cambridge Avenue
8 Tritonville Avenue
9 Tritonville Crescent
10 Seafort Gardens
11 Leukos Road
12 Clonlara Road (Ringsend)
13 Kyle-Clare Road
14 Parkview Place
15 Canon Mooney Gardens
16 Caroline Row
17 Havelock Terrace
18 Dodder Terrace
19 Ennis Grove
20 Londonbridge Drive
21 Strasburg Terrace
22 Tritonville Close
23 St James Terrace (Sandymount)
24 Cambridge Court
25 Lansdowne Hall
26 Sandymount Court
28 O'Rahilly House Flats
29 Whelan House Flats
30 Ropewalk Place
31 Kennedy Court
32 Simpsons Lane
33 Summerfield (Ringsend)
34 The Old Presbytery
35 Caroline Row
36 Fitzwilliam Quay
37 Fitzwilliam Point
38 The Moorings
39 Magdalen Terrace
40 Veronica Terrace
41 Philomena Terrace
42 Celestine Avenue
43 George Reynolds Flats
44 Victoria Cottages
45 Tritonville Mews
46 Steeple Gate
47 Fairfield Court
48 Baggot Rath House
49 Fairview Avenue (Ringsend)

39 A4
1 Sandymount Green
2 Sandymount Castle Road
3 Sandymount Castle Drive
4 Sydenham Road (Ballsbridge)
5 Sandymount Castle
6 Churchill Terrace
7 Prince of Wales Terrace (Sandymount)
8 Railway Cottages
9 Martin White Chalets
10 Gilford Court
11 Homelee

PAGE/GRID REF	STREET NAME
	12 Lynton Court
	13 Spafield Terrace
	14 Adair
	15 Wilfield
	16 Park Court (Sandymount)
	17 Dromard Terrace
	18 Seafort Cottages
	19 Seafort Terrace
	20 Seafort Villas
	21 Claremont Court (Sandymount)
	22 The Sweepstakes
	23 Ballsbridge Park
	24 Lansdowne Square
	25 Ballsbridge Gardens
	26 Ballsbridge Avenue
	27 Ballsbridge Wood
	28 Lansdowne Woods
	29 Cannon Mews
	30 Cannon Place
	31 St.James Place
	32 Glenesk Court
	33 Trideat Apts.
	34 Merry Bush
	35 Oisin Court
	36 Claremont Court
	37 Argyle House Apts.
	38 Oaklands Court
	39 Ballsbridge Court
	40 Anglesea House
	41 Elbin House
	42 Raglan House
	43 Clyde House
	44 Oakbury Court
	45 The Willows
	46 Gilford Pines
	47 Hollyrood Apts
	48 Herbert Court
	49 St. James Court
	50 Renoir Apts.
	51 El Greco Apts.
	52 Wellington Lodge
	53 Sydenham Court
	54 Yeats Court
	55 Avondale Mews
39 B1	1 Alverno
	2 Haddon Court
39 B3	1 Prospect Terrace (Sandymount)
39 B4	1 Gilford Terrace
	2 Sandymount Castle Park
	3 Martello View
	4 Bethany House
	5 Hempenstal Terrace
	6 Martello Wood
	7 St. Catheryn's Court
	8 Windermere
	9 Radcliff Hall
39 C1	1 Churchgate Avenue
	2 St Joseph's Square
	3 Vernon Court (Clontarf)
	4 Vernon Wood
43 C1	1 Bawnogue Cottages
	2 Nangor Place
	3 St Catherines Grove
44 D1	1 St Patrick's Avenue (Clondalkin)
	2 Leinster Terrace
	3 Beech Row (Nangor Road)
	4 The Mill Pond Apts.
	5 Nangor Crescent
	6 Cherrywood Villas
44 D2	1 Church View (Clondalkin)
	2 Green Isle Court
44 E1	1 St Killian's Park
	2 Monastery Heights
	3 Bettysford
	4 Castle Crescent
	5 Friar's Walk
	6 Riverside (Clondalkin)
	7 Millview

PAGE/GRID REF	STREET NAME
44 E2	1 St Brigid's Park (Clondalkin)
44 F1	1 Knockmitten Close
	2 Knockmitten Lane North
44 F3	1 Pinetree Grove
	2 Belgard Close
	3 Shalimar Apts.
44 F4	1 Pinetree Crescent
45 A3	1 Parkhill Heights
	2 Parkview (Kilnamanagh)
45 B2	1 Tibradden Close
	2 Ballymount Cottages
45 B3	1 Three Rock Close
45 B4	1 Tymon North Court
	2 Tymon North Place
45 C1	1 Field Avenue
	2 Wallace Road
	3 Percy French Road
	4 O'Dwyer Road
	5 Esposito Road
	6 Landsdowne Valley
	7 Somerville Park
	8 Harty Court
45 C2	1 St Peter's Terrace (Walkinstown)
45 C3	1 Willington Lawn
	2 Wellington Cottages
45 C4	1 Spawell Cottages
46 D1	1 Sunville Green
	2 Windmill Crescent (Crumlin)
	3 Father Kit Court
	4 St. Agnes Terrace
	5 Rockmeadon Court
	6 Brug Chroimlinn
	7 Looceville Court
	8 Somerville Court
46 D2	1 Muckross Drive
	2 Lorcan O'Toole Court
	3 Stannaway Court
	4 Beechfield Mews
	5 Wellington Court (Whitehall Road West)
	7 The Manor (Kimmage)
46 D3	1 Wellington Road (Templeogue)
46 D4	1 Hillcrest (Templeogue)
	2 Hillcrest Manor
46 E1	1 Tonguefield Road
	2 Cloyne Road
	3 Faughart Road
	4 Clonmacnoise Grove
	5 Bedford Court
	6 Poddle Green
	7 Larrisa Court
46 E2	1 Riversdale Grove (Kimmage)
	2 Hazel Park
	3 Kimmage Court
	4 Rathland Drive
	5 Brookfield Green
	6 Brookfield Court (Kimmage)
	7 Hazelbrook Apts.
	8 Clonard Court
	9 Riverside (Kimmage)
	10 Baroma
	11 Clonallen
	12 Cranford Court (Kimmage)
46 E3	1 Templeville Park
	2 Fortfield Court
46 E4	1 Butterfield Meadow
	2 Brookmount Court
46 F1	1 Mount Harold Terrace
	2 Le Bas Terrace
	3 Mountain View Avenue
	4 Manor Villas
	5 Wilfrid Terrace
	6 Fitzpatrick's Cottages

PAGE/GRID REF	STREET NAME
	7 Ryan's Cottages (Harold's Cross)
	8 Parkview Court (Harold's Cross)
	9 Gandon Close
	10 Woodford Court (Harold's Cross)
	11 Kenilworth Manor
	12 Waverley Terrace (Harolds Cross Road)
	13 Smith's Lane
	14 Kengar Mews
	15 Mount Argus Square
	16 Mountain View Court (Harold's Cross)
	17 Casimir Court
	18 Kerrygold House
	19 Kennilworth Lodge
46 F2	1 Ashdale Park
	2 Westhampton Place
	3 Terenure Place
	4 Eagle Hill Avenue
	5 Victoria Villas (Rathgar)
	6 Maple Drive (Harold's Cross)
	7 Victoria Village (Rathgar)
	8 Frankfort Court
	9 Frankfort Flats
	10 Rathdown Court (off Templeogue Road)
	11 Rathgar Villas
	12 Greenlea Place
	13 Brighton Green
	14 McMorrough Road
	15 Earls Court (Terenure)
	16 Rathgar Park
	17 Olney Grove
	18 Eaton Hall
	19 Winton Grove
	20 Beechlawn Manor
	21 Beechlawn Mews
	22 Eaton Court (Terenure)
	23 Carlisle Court
	24 Fairfield House
	25 Beaumont House
	27 Loughmorne House
46 F3	1 Woodview Cottages
	2 St Agnes Terrace (Rathfarnham)
	3 Dodder Park Drive
	4 Village Green (Rathfarnham)
	5 The Falls
	6 Tourville Lodge
	7 Le Brett Terrace
	8 Wasdale House
	9 Crannagh Castle
	10 Crannagh Court
46 F4	1 Willbrook Grove
	2 Tara Hill Grove
	3 Beaufort Villas
	4 Glenann
	5 St Mary's Terrace (Rathfarnham)
	6 Village Court Apts.
	7 The Park Lands
	8 The Lakelands
	9 The Woodlands (Rathfarnham)
	10 Beaufort Court
	11 The Castlelands
	12 Rathfarnham Mill
	13 The Laurels (Rathfarnham)
	14 Loftus Square
	15 Blackburn Square
	16 Otterbrook
	17 Stonepark Orchard
	18 Castle Court (Rathfarnham)
	19 A.W. Pugin House
	20 Theresa House
	21 Woodstown House

PAGE/GRID REF	STREET NAME
	22 William Pallister House
	23 Frances Ball House
	24 De Bret House
	25 Hogan House
	26 Riversdale View
47 A1	1 Rathmines Park
	2 Leinster Square
	3 Prince Arthur Terrace
	4 Swanville Place
	5 Castlewood Terrace
	6 Castlewood Place
	7 Grosvenor Park
	8 Stone Mews
	9 Turrets Flats
	10 Purser Gardens
	11 Esker Villas
	12 Parker Hill
	13 Alma Terrace
	14 Observatory Lane
	15 Belgrave Place (Rathmines)
	16 Cambridge Villas
	17 Salem Court
	18 Maxwell Court
	19 The Mews (Rathmines)
	20 Roland Court
	21 Wynnefield Park
	22 Mount Anthony Estate
	23 Louis Lane
	24 Castlewood Close
	25 Rathmines Avenue Court
	26 Cosy Lodge
	27 Newington Terrace
	28 Rathgar Court
47 A2	1 Woodlands (Rathgar)
	2 Woodleigh
	3 Highfield Court
	4 Cowper Mews
	5 Garville Place
	6 Garville Drive
	7 Rathgar Park
	8 Orwell Mews
	9 Stratford
	10 Garville Court
47 A3	1 The Willows (Orwell Road)
	2 Stirling Park
	3 Orwell Court
	4 Newtown Villas (Braemor Road)
	5 Newtown Court (Rathgar)
	7 Orwell Bank
	8 Crannagh Way
	9 Landore
	10 Park View (Rathgar)
	11 Ard Na Gréine
	12 Newtown House
	13 Dodder Vale
47 A4	1 Castle Court (Rathfarnham)
	2 Nutgrove Court
47 B1	1 Sallymount Gardens
	2 Woodstock Court
	3 Collier's Avenue
	4 Westmoreland Park
	5 Field's Terrace
	6 Rugby Villas
	7 Beechwood Park (Rathmines)
	8 Bushfield Avenue
	9 Charleston Court Flats
	10 Oakley Court
	11 Cullenswood Road
	12 Moran's Cottages
	13 Mountain View Cottages (Ranelagh)
	14 Sallymount Terrace
	15 Chelmsford Lane
	16 Belgrave Villas (Rathmines)
	17 Bushfield Place
	18 Smith's Cottages (Donnybrook)

PAGE/ GRID REF	STREET NAME
	19 Beechdale Mews
	20 Oakley Square
	21 Palmerston Close
	22 Moyne Court
	23 Oakley Park (Ranelagh)
	24 Woodstock Gardens
	25 Marlborough Lane
	26 Castlewood Court
47 B2	1 Dartry Cottages
	2 Strand Terrace
	3 St Luke's Crescent
	4 Balnagowan
	5 Temple Square
	6 Milltown Grove (Clonskeagh)
	7 Milltown Hill
	8 Thorncliff
	9 Shanagarry
	10 Dodder Bank
47 B3	1 St Columbanus Place
	2 St Gall Gardens North
	3 St Gall Gardens South
	4 Milltown Terrace (Dundrum)
47 B4	1 Glenbower Park
	2 Woodlawn Terrace
	3 Beaumont Close
	4 Briarly Court
	5 St Nathy's House
	6 Ardtona Avenue
	7 Woodlawn Grove (Churchtown)
	8 Henley Court
	9 Weston Terrace
	10 Frankfort
	11 Rosemount Terrace (Dundrum)
	12 Waldemar Terrace
	13 Airfield Drive
	14 Nutgrove Avenue
	16 Annadale
	17 St Nathy's Villas
	18 Sweetmount House
	19 Camberley Oaks
	20 Camberley Elms
47 C1	1 St Broc's Cottages
	2 Pembroke Cottages (Donnybrook)
	3 Belmont Park (Donnybrook)
	4 The Crescent (Donnybrook)
	5 Harmony Avenue
	6 Vergemount Park
	7 Norwood Park
	8 Brookvale Road (Donnybrook)
	9 Vergemount Hall
	10 Sandford Gardens (Donnybrook)
	11 Auburn Road (Donnybrook)
	12 Vergemount
	13 Eglinton Square
	14 Mount Sandford
	15 Rowan Hall
	16 Cedar Hall
	17 Millbrook Village
	18 Simmonscourt Terrace
	19 Brookfield (Donnybrook)
	20 Harmony Court
	21 Riverside Walk
	22 Eglinton Wood
	23 Shamrock Hill Mews
	24 Donnybrook Castle
	25 Argyle Square
47 C2	1 Prospect Lane
	2 Beech Hill Villas
	3 Beech Hill Crescent
	4 Beech Hill Terrace
	5 Palmerston Grove
	6 Clonskeagh Drive
	7 Clonskeagh Square

PAGE/ GRID REF	STREET NAME
	8 St Bridget's Flats
	9 Crannagh
	10 Woodhaven
	11 Richview Villas
	12 Byrne's Terrace
47 C3	1 Annaville Grove
	2 Olivemount Grove
	3 Friarsland Avenue
	4 Harlech Villas
	5 Gledswood Drive
	6 Olivemount Terrace
	7 Glenard Hall
	8 Belfield Close
	9 Roebuck Lawn
	10 Roebuck Crescent
47 C4	1 Sunnybank Court
	2 Woodbine Terrace (Dundrum)
	3 Alexandra Villas
	4 Roseville Terrace
	5 Pembroke Cottages (Dundrum)
	6 Pembroke Terrace
	7 Claremont Terrace
	8 Glenville Terrace
	9 St Joseph's Grove
48 D1	1 Merrion View Avenue
	2 Simmonscourt Avenue
	3 Simmonscourt View
	4 Ailesbury Close
	5 Simmonscourt Square
48 D2	1 Nutley Square
	2 Donnybrook Close
	3 Donnybrook Green
	4 Greenfield Manor
48 D3	1 Hopkins Square
	2 Finglas Square
	3 Hayden Square
	4 Hyde Square (Fosters Avenue)
	5 Meenan Square
48 D4	1 Edenwood (Goatstown)
	2 Sophie Baret Residence
48 E1	1 Merrion Court
	2 Merrion Gates
	3 Strand Lane
48 E2	1 Seafield Park
	2 Bellevue Court
	3 Merrion Crescent
	4 Woodbine House
48 E3	1 The Stables
	2 Mountbrook
48 E4	1 Greygates
	2 Beaufield Mews
	3 Ashurst (Mount Merrion)
48 F2	1 St Helen's Villas
48 F3	1 Martello Terrace (Booterstown)
	2 Pembroke Cottages (Booterstown)
	3 Willowmount
	4 Cherbury Mews
48 F4	1 St Helier's Copse
	2 Orpen Dale
	3 Park Villas (Stillorgan)
	4 Cedar Square (Stillorgan)
	5 Grove House Gardens
49 A3	1 Newtown Villas (Blackrock)
	2 Maretimo Road
	3 Ben Inagh Park
	4 Maretimo Gardens West
	5 Craigmore Gardens
	6 George's Place (Blackrock)
	7 St Anne's Square (Blackrock)
	8 Bath Place
	9 Rockwell Cove Apts.
	10 Westfield Terrace
	11 Idrone Mews

PAGE/ GRID REF	STREET NAME
	12 Brusna Cottages
	13 Collins Court (Blackrock)
	14 Patrick's Row
	15 Eagle Hill
	16 Maretimo Terrace
	17 Maretimo Place
	18 Maretimo Villas
	19 Whelan's Terrace
	20 Carbury Place
	21 Sweetman's Avenue
	22 Lisalea
	23 Frascati Court
	24 Frascati Hall
	25 Temple Court (Blackrock)
49 A4	1 Avondale Park (Blackrock)
	2 Prince Edward Terrace Lower
	3 Prince Edward Terrace Upper
	4 Lindenvale
	5 Twin Cottages
	6 Fieldview Cottages
	7 Cullen's Cottages
	8 Webster's Cottages
	9 Rockville Estate
	10 Avoca Hall
	11 Brookfield Grove
	12 Brookfield Court (Blackrock)
49 B3	1 Ardenza Terrace
	2 Tobernea Terrace
	3 Ardenza Park
	4 Seapoint Terrace (Blackrock)
	5 The Orchard
49 B4	1 Montpelier Place
	2 Montpelier Manor
	3 The Willows (Monkstown)
	4 The Maples (Monkstown)
	5 The Cedars (Monkstown)
	6 The Alders
	7 The Poplars
	8 Stradbrook Gardens
	9 Brighton Terrace (Monkstown)
	10 Belgrave Place (Monkstown)
	11 Belgrave Terrace (Monkstown)
	12 Brooklawn Avenue
	13 Brooklawn Wood
	14 Rockford Terrace
	15 Beaupark Downs
	16 Drayton Close
	17 Heathfield
	18 Southdene
	19 Arundel
	20 Stradbrook Hall
	21 The Beeches (Monkstown)
	22 Brighton Lane
	23 Knocknagow
49 C4	1 Rosary Gardens West
	2 Barrett Street
	3 Smith's Villas
	4 York Terrace
	5 St Mary's Street
	7 Oakwood
	8 Harbour Terrace
	9 Grosvenor Terrace (Dun Laoghaire)
	10 Clifton Lane
	11 Clifton Avenue
	12 Richmond Green
	13 Clifton Terrace
	14 Alma Place
	15 Seaview Terrace (Dun Laoghaire)
	16 Synnott Terrace
	17 Bentley Villas
	18 St Michael's Terrace (Dun Laoghaire)
	19 St Brendan's Terrace (Dun Laoghaire)

PAGE/ GRID REF	STREET NAME
	20 Northcote Terrace
	21 Knapton Court
	22 Knapton Lawn
	23 Northcote Place
	24 Cambridge Terrace (Dun Laoghaire)
	25 Primrose Hill (Dún Laoghaire)
	26 Mounttown Cottages
	27 Knapton Terrace
	28 Pakenham
	29 Monkstown Gate
	30 Alma Park
	31 Clearwater Cove
	32 Marina House Apts
	33 The Anchorage
	34 Smyth Gardens
50 D4	1 Wellington Street (Dun Laoghaire)
	2 Rosary Gardens East
	3 Desmond Avenue
	4 Wolfe Tone Avenue
	5 Charlemont Avenue
	6 Summerhill Parade (Dun Laoghaire)
	7 Haddington Terrace
	8 Victoria Terrace (Dun Laoghaire)
	9 Marine Terrace (Dún Laoghaire)
	10 Northumberland Place (Dún Laoghaire)
	11 Northumberland Park
	12 Dungar Terrace
	13 Stoneview Place
	14 Martello Avenue
	15 Crosthwaite Terrace
	16 Sussex Street
	17 Marine Court (Dún Laoghaire)
	18 Charlemont Terrace
	19 Mill Street (Dun Laoghaire)
	20 Anglesea Lane
	21 Park Lane (Dún Laoghaire)
	23 Sydenham
	24 Oratory Mews Court
	25 Crofton Terrace
	26 Connaught Place
	27 Albert Terrace (Dún Laoghaire)
	28 Crofton Mansions
50 E4	1 Mornington Avenue
	2 Martello Terrace (Dun Laoghaire)
	3 Summerhill Court
52 F2	1 Eaton House
54 D1	1 Brookfield Court (Tallaght)
	2 Jobstown Village Square
	3 Rossfield Court
	4 Rossfield Close
	5 Glenshane Dale
	6 Glenshane Place
54 D2	1 Elm House Apartments
	2 Montpelier Walk
54 F1	1 Tuansgate Apts.
	2 Abberley Square Apts.
	3 Aengus Hall (Belgard Square)
	4 Alen Hall (Belgard Square)
	5 Horan Hall (Belgard Square)
	6 Losset Hall (Belgard Square)
	7 Tallow Hall (Belgard Square)
	8 Virginia Hall (Belgard Square)

PAGE/ GRID REF		STREET NAME
		9 Loftus Hall (Belgard Square)
		10 Swan Hall (Belgard Square)
55	A1	1 St Maelruans Park
		2 High Street (Tallaght)
		3 Avonbeg Court
		4 St Dominic's Court
		5 Old Bawn Court
		6 College View (Tallaght)
		7 Uppercross Court
		8 Tramway Court (Tallaght)
		9 New Bancroft Place
		10 The Laurels (Tallaght)
		11 New Bancroft Hall
		12 New Bancroft Square
		13 Courthouse Square Apts.
55	A2	1 Summerfield (Tallaght)
		2 The Close (Tallaght)
		3 Allenton Crescent
55	B1	1 Bolbrook Drive
		3 Bolbrook Avenue
		4 Bolbrook Close
		5 Avonmore Avenue
		6 Moynihan Court
55	B2	1 Oldcourt Lawn
		2 Killininny Court Apts
		3 Tara Crescent
55	B3	1 Ely Crescent
		2 Ely Grove
		3 Ely Green
		4 Ferncourt Drive
		5 Ferncourt Crescent
		6 Beechdale Close
55	C1	1 Brookmount Lawns
		2 Knocklyon Mews
		3 Homeville Court
		4 Homeville
		5 Balrothery Cottages
		6 Prospect Lodge
		7 Castle Side
55	C2	1 Wood Dale Oak
		2 Woodstown Court
		3 Knocklyon Gate Apts
56	D1	1 Coolamber Court
		2 Pine Grove
		3 Ballyroan Court
56	E1	1 Orchardton
56	E2	1 Beechview
		2 Cypress Avenue
		3 Larch Drive
		4 Beech Walk
		5 Walnut View
56	F1	1 Sarah Curran Road
		2 St Gatien Road
		3 Fonthill Abbey
		4 Whitechurch Abbey
		5 Edenbrook Court
		6 Forthill Court
		8 The Beeches (Willbrook)
57	A1	1 Marley Villas
		2 Meadow Villas
		3 Barton Court
57	A2	1 Priory Court (Grange Road)
		2 The Cherries
		3 Elm Way (Grange Wood)
		5 Stonemasons Green
57	B1	1 Meadow Avenue
		2 Hawthorn Drive
		3 Mount Albion Road
		4 Sycamore Drive (Dundrum)
		5 Hillview Glade
		6 Hillview Court
57	B2	1 The Crescent (Ballinteer)
		2 Ballinteer Court
		3 The Copse (Ballinteer)
		4 The Dale (Ballinteer)
57	C1	1 Westerton Rise
		2 Ashgrove Terrace
		3 Eagle Terrace (Dundrum)
		4 Castle Court (Dundrum)
		5 McGrane Court
		6 Ballyolaf Manor
		7 Castleview (Dundrum)
		8 Ashgrove Court
		9 Dundrum Gate Apts
		10 Riverbank (Dundrum)
		11 Riversdale (Dundrum)
		12 The Birch
		13 The Linden
		14 The Blackthorn
57	C2	1 Clonlea Wood
		2 College Park Court
		3 College Park Drive
58	D1	1 Drummartin Crescent
		2 Carrick Lawn
		3 The Pines (Kilmacud)
		4 Woodley Court
58	D2	1 Balally Terrace
		2 Moreen Lawn
		3 Blackthorn Grove
		4 Blackthorn Court
		5 Rathdown Terrace
		6 Blackthorn Green
		7 Blackthorn Close (Sandyford)
		8 Olaf Hall
		9 Rathdown Grove
58	D3	1 Churchlands
58	E1	1 Dale Close
		2 Stillorgan Court
		3 Stillorgan Heath
		4 Convent Court
		5 Woodthorpe
58	E3	1 Glencairn Garth
58	F1	1 Woodview Court (Stillorgan)
		2 Ard Lorcain Villas
		3 Grange Cottages
		4 Ulster Terrace (Stillorgan Grove)
		5 Pear Tree Field
		6 Dunstaffnage Hall Apts
58	F2	1 Leopardstown Court
		2 Leopardstown Lawn
		3 Silver Pines
		4 Ellesmere
		5 Ballymoss Parade
		6 Arkle Square
		7 Sir Ivor Mall
		8 Fey Yerra
58	F4	1 Ballyogan Park
59	A1	1 Orchard Cottages
		2 Red Brick Terrace
		3 Moore's Cottages
		4 Hawthorn Manor
		5 Rosehill
		6 Ardagh Close
		8 Newtown Park Court
		9 Galloping Green
		10 Avila Apts
		11 Newtownpark House
		12 Obelisk Avenue
59	A2	1 Knocksinna Grove
		2 Knocksinna Court
		3 New Park Lodge
		4 Foxrock Mount
		5 Chestnut Park
		6 Willow Park (Foxrock)
		7 Sycamore Grove (Foxrock)
		8 Whitethorn Walk (Foxrock)
		9 Birch Dale (Foxrock)
		10 The Coutyard (Foxrock)
		11 Kelston Hall
		12 Sefton Hall
59	A3	1 Brighton Cottages
		2 Kilteragh Pines
		3 Avalon
		4 Brighton Lodge
		5 The Gables (Foxrock)
		6 Westminster Court
59	B1	1 Windsor Court
		2 Grange Grove
		3 Oliver Plunkett Villas
		4 Stradbrook Hill
		5 Springhill Cottages
		6 Grange Terrace
		7 Abbey Court (Monkstown)
		9 Faber Grove
		10 Deans Court
		11 Devon Close
		12 Monkstown Square
59	B3	1 Kerrymount Close
		4 Monaloe Crescent
		5 Clonkeen Lawn
		6 Monaloe Court
		7 New Cornelscourt
59	C1	1 Oliver Plunkett Square
		2 Patrician Park
		3 Mounttown Park
		4 Woodlawn Park (Dun Laoghaire)
		5 Oliver Plunkett Terrace
		6 Fitzgerald Park
		7 St Patrick's Terrace (Kill O' the Grange)
		8 Dunedin Drive
		9 St Patrick's Close (Kill O'The Grange)
		10 Highthorn Woods
		11 Aspen Park (Kill O'The Grange)
		12 Birch Dale (Kill O'The Grange)
		13 Willow Grove (Kill O'The Grange)
		14 Carriglea Court (Kill O'The Grange)
		16 Woodlawn Villas
		17 Meadowlands Court
		18 Meadowlands Mews
59	C2	1 Hillview Cottages
		2 Whitethorn Walk (Kill O'The Grange)
		3 Sycamore Court
		4 Hazel Lawn (Kill O'The Grange)
		5 Eaglewood Apts
		6 Rochestown House Apts.
		7 Eaglewood House
		8 Eaglewood Mews
		9 Rochestown House
59	C3	1 Little Meadow
		2 Cabinteely Court
		3 Cabinteely Park
		4 O'Shea's Cottages
		5 Little Orchard
59	C4	1 Kilbogget Villas
		2 Church Villas
60	D1	1 O'Donnell Gardens
		2 Royal Terrace North
		3 Myrtle Avenue
		4 Emmet Street (Sallynoggin)
		5 Eden Villas
		6 Laurel Hill
		7 Granite Hall
		8 Magenta Place
		9 Marlborough Park
		10 Royal Terrace Lane
		11 Beechwood Grove
		12 Rollins Court
		13 Seven Houses
		14 The Glen (Glenageary Road)
		15 Glengara Close
		16 Silchester Wood
		17 Carlisle Terrace (Dún Laoghaire)
		18 Durham Place
		19 Rus-in-Urbe Terrace
60	D2	1 Honey Park
		2 Thomastown Crescent
		3 Pearse Close
60	D3	1 Auburn Road (Cabinteely)
		2 Granville Crescent
60	D4	1 Annabeg
		2 Meadow Court
		3 Oakton Green
60	E1	1 Wilmont Avenue
		2 Congress Gardens
		3 Albert Park
		4 Claremont Villas
		5 St Paul's Terrace
		6 St Peter's Terrace (Dun Laoghaire)
		7 Findlater Street (Dun Laoghaire)
		8 Devitt Villas
		9 Dixon Villas
		10 Glen Terrace
		11 Glasthule Buildings
		12 Hastings Terrace
		13 Brighton Terrace (Dun Laoghaire)
		14 Lawson Terrace
		15 Killiney Terrace
		16 Munster Terrace
		17 Neptune Terrace
		18 Cliff Terrace
		19 Beaufort
		20 Ballygihen Villas
		21 Seabank Court (Dalkey)
		22 St Helen's
		23 Chester Square
		24 Dundela Haven
		25 Arkendale Woods
		26 Arkendale Court
		27 Adelaide Villas (Dun Laoghaire)
		28 Adelaide Terrace (Dun Laoghaire)
		29 Atmospheric Road
		30 St Margaret's Close
		31 Avondale Court (Dalkey)
60	E2	1 Barnhill Lawn
		2 Killiney Towers
		3 Barnhill Park
		4 Kilcolman Court
		5 Edwin Court
		6 Fairlawns
		7 Urney Grove
		8 Malborough Court
		9 Castlepark Court
60	E3	1 Hill Cottages
		2 Mount Auburn
		3 Talbot Road (Killiney)
		4 Talbot Lane (Killiney)
60	E4	1 Oakton Court
		2 Dale View Park
		3 Mountain Villa
		4 The Nurseries (Ballybrack)
		5 Mountain View Road (Ballybrack)
		6 Rainsford Lane
		7 Firgrove
60	F1	1 Carysfort Drive
		2 Ormeau Drive
		3 The Paddocks (Dalkey)
		4 South Winds
		5 Ulverton Close
		6 Rocklands
		7 Bayswater Terrace
		8 Bullock Steps
		9 Liscanor
		10 White's Villas
		11 Mayville Terrace
		12 Castlelands Grove
		13 Ulverton Court
		14 Pilot View
		15 Bailey View

PAGE/ GRID REF	STREET NAME
	16 Castlelands
	17 Churchill Mews
	18 Bartra Rock Apts.
60 F2	1 St Patrick's Avenue (Dalkey)
	2 Railway Road
	3 Anastasia Lane
	4 St Patrick's Square (Dalkey)
	5 Cats Ladder
	6 Dalkey Grove
	7 Barnhill Grove
	8 St Patrick's Road (Dalkey)
	9 Monte Vella
	10 Summerfield Close
	11 Victoria Terrace (Dalkey)
	12 Sorrento Drive
	13 Sorrento Lawn
	14 Coliemore Villas
	15 Seafield Terrace
	16 Temple Terrace
	17 Grosvenor Terrace (Dalkey)
	18 Charlotte Terrace
	19 Heany Avenue
	20 Desmond Cottages
	21 Ardbrugh Villas
	22 Burmah Close
	23 Dalkey Court
	24 Kilbegnet Close
	25 Sorrento Close
	26 Craiglands
	27 Ullardmor
	28 Sorrento Mews
	29 Sorrento Court
	30 Sorrento Heights
	31 Ardbrugh Close
	32 Castle Cove (Dalkey)
	33 Torca View
63 A1	1 The View (Carrickmines)
64 D1	1 The Oaks (Loughlinstown)
	2 Cherry Court (Loughlinstown)
	3 Cois Coillte
64 D2	1 Stonebridge Lane
64 E1	1 Killiney Court
	2 Killiney Oaks
	3 The Sycamores
	4 The Elms (Loughlinstown)
	5 St Aubyn's Court
	6 Ennel Court
	7 Sheelin Grove
	8 Glencarr Court
	9 Domville Grove
	10 Streamville Court
	12 Bayview Glade
	13 Sheelin Hill
	14 Sheelin Walk
	16 The Larches (Abberley)
	17 The Oaks (Abberley)

PAGE/ GRID REF	STREET NAME
	18 The Rowans (Abberley)
	19 The Willows (Abberley)
	20 The Hawthorns (Abberley)
	21 The Cedars (Abberley)
	22 The Beeches (Abberley)
	23 River Close
64 E2	1 River Lane (Loughlinstown)
	2 Clonasleigh
	3 Beechfield Haven
	4 Athgoe Drive
	5 Maryland
	6 Station Road (Shankill)
	7 Windrush
	8 Shanganagh Wood
	9 Thomond
	10 Beechwood House
	11 Sycamore House (Shankill)
	12 Woodview
	13 River Lane Grove
	14 Corbawn Glade
64 E3	1 Guilford Terrace
	2 Stonebridge Close
	3 Osprey Court
	4 Cluain na Greine Court
64 E4	1 Kiltuck Park
67 B1	1 Raverty Villas
	2 St Peter's Terrace (Bray)
	3 Myrtle Grove (Bray)
	4 Arbutus Grove
	5 Thornhill View
	6 Fernbrook
	7 Roseville Court
	8 Sunnybank Court
67 B2	1 Auburn Villas (Bray)
	2 Glenburgh Terrace
	3 Dargle Court
	4 Ashley Heights
	5 Dargle Crescent
	6 Copper Beech Grove
	7 Vale Terrace (on lower Dargle Road)
	9 Sutton Road
	10 Dargan Street
	11 Fairgreen Road
	12 Pearse Road (Bray)
	13 Mountpleasant Villas
	15 Diamond Terrace
	16 Parkview Terrace
	17 Sutton Villas
	18 Esmonde Terrace
	19 Old Ravenswell Row
	20 New Ravenswell Row
	21 Vale View
	22 Old Rathmore Terrace
	23 New Rathmore Terrace
	24 Gertrude Terrace
	26 Herbert View
	27 Rivervale Apts.
	29 Bruce's Terrace

PAGE/ GRID REF	STREET NAME
67 B3	1 Ballynoe Court
	2 Rathclaren
	3 St Clair's Terrace
	4 Killarney Court
	5 Kilgrastor Court
	6 Glenbrook
	8 Brickfield Lane
67 B4	1 Ballywaltrim Cottages
	2 Ballymorris
67 C1	1 St Patrick's Square (Bray)
	2 Martello Terrace (Bray)
67 C2	1 Sidmonton Square
	3 Eglington Road
	4 Rosslyn Grove
	5 James Connolly Square
	6 Sidmonton Place
	7 Novara Park
	8 St Cronan's Road
	9 Cill Manntan Park
	10 Kilmantain Place
	11 Father Colohan Terrace
	12 Royal Marine Terrace
	13 Milton Terrace
	14 St Kevin's Terrace (Bray)
	15 Darley Cottages
	16 Brabazon Cottages
	17 St Laurence's Terrace (Bray)
	18 St Columcille's Terrace
	20 Seapoint Villas
	21 Dunbur Terrace
	22 Elmgrove Terrace
	23 St Aidan's Terrace
	24 Seapoint Terrace (Bray)
	25 Goldsmith Terrace
	26 Prince of Wales Terrace (Bray)
	27 Novara Terrace
	28 Waverley Terrace (Bray)
	29 Westview Terrace
	30 Augustine Villas
	31 Trafalgar Terrace (Bray)
	32 Fairgreen Terrace
	33 St Brigid's Terrace
	34 Loretto Avenue
	35 Loretto Terrace
	36 Sidmonton Gardens
	37 Rosslyn
	38 Shankill View
	39 Florence Terrace (Bray)
	40 Florence Villas (Bray)
	41 Carlton Terrace
	42 Carlton Villas (Clontarf)
	43 Alexander Terrace (Bray)
	44 Belton Terrace
	45 Church Terrace (Bray)
	46 Old Brighton Terrace
	47 New Brighton Terrace
	48 Killarney Villas
	49 Market Square

PAGE/ GRID REF	STREET NAME
	50 Fairgreen Court
	51 Bayview (Bray)
	52 Westbourne Terrace
	53 King Edward Court
	54 Loretto Villas
	55 Marie Villas
	56 Wellington Court (Bray)
	57 Novara Mews
	58 Vevay Crescent
	59 Bull Lane (Off Main Street)
	60 Purcell Lane (off Main Street Bray)
67 C3	1 Cherry Tree Drive
	2 Roselawn Park
	4 Woodview Drive
	5 Kennedy Park
	8 Newcourt Villas
	9 O'Byrne Villas
	10 Stoneylea Terrace
	11 Mountain View Apts.
	14 Putland Villas
	15 Oldcourt Terrace
	16 Lauderdale Terrace
	17 Mayfield Terrace (Bray)
	18 Vevay Villas
	19 Orchard Terrace (Bray)
	20 Bray Head Terrace
	21 Sugarloaf Terrace
67 C4	3 Bentley Avenue
	6 St Mary's Terrace (Boghall Road)
68 D2	1 Trosyrafon Terrace
	2 Montebello Terrace
	3 Esplanade Terrace
	4 Brennans Terrace
	5 Sidbury Court
	6 Dargan Court
	7 Warburton Terrace
	8 Sloan Terrace
	9 Belgrave Villas (Bray)
	10 Belgrave Terrace (Bray)
	11 Claremount Terrace
	12 Richmond Terrace
	13 Milward Terrace
	14 Brennans Parade
	15 Claddagh Terrace
	16 Marlborough Terrace
	17 Marine Terrace (Bray)
	18 Jones Terrace
	19 Mount Norris Villas
	20 St Marys Terrace (Bray)
	21 Fitzwilliam Terrace
	23 Convent View (Bray)
68 D3	1 Eaton Court (Bray)
	2 Meretimo Villas
	3 Grosvenor Avenue
	4 Brookfield Avenue (Bray)
	5 Sidmonton Court
	6 Sydenham Villas (Bray)